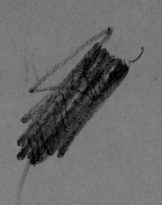

D1716405

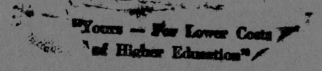

Vocational Education

SECOND EDITION

■

Vocational Education: Concepts and Operations

Calfrey C. Calhoun
UNIVERSITY OF GEORGIA

Alton V. Finch
UNIVERSITY OF MISSISSIPPI

WADSWORTH PUBLISHING COMPANY

BELMONT, CALIFORNIA

A Division of Wadsworth, Inc.

Education Editor: Marshall Aronson

Production Editor: Diane Sipes

Art Director: Patricia Dunbar

Designer: Rick Chafian

Copy Editor: Carolyn Davidson

Technical Illustrator: Evanell Towne

Cover Design: Bob Haydock

Printed in the United States of America

1 2 3 4 5 6 6 8 9 10 — 86 85 84 83 82

Library of Congress Cataloging in Publication Data

Calhoun, Calfrey C.
   Vocational education.

   First ed. published in 1976 as: Vocational and
career education.
   Includes bibliographical references and index.
   1. Vocational education. 2. Career education.
3. Vocational guidance. I. Finch, Alton V.
II. Title.
LC1044.C34 1982   370.11'3   81-3366
ISBN 0-534-00996-4   AACR2

■

Preface

This text is a revision of the first edition of *Vocational and Career Education: Concepts and Operations*. It incorporates extensive changes that have occurred in the field since 1976. These changes have made necessary a major updating and revision of the text. The fourteen original chapters have been consolidated and updated into ten chapters, an arrangement that should facilitate its coverage in the college or university time frame. Illustrative tables and figures have been updated, listings have been markedly reduced, and end-of-chapter activities have been revised.

This volume is based on the need to communicate the philosophical bases of vocational-technical education as it relates to the nature and broad goals of American education, societal needs, and personal fulfillment. It builds on the need to understand the basis for the growth of vocational education as a broad emphasis in education, and to understand the crucial role that it plays in the ultimate success of career development. Thus it integrates the foundations of vocational education, its history and philosophy, into the broader context of career education. While viewing vocational education as a component of career education, the authors have brought the two together in order to show their conceptual and operational relationships.

The text, intended for anyone with an interest in the learning or teaching of the fundamentals of vocational-technical education, is uniquely designed for undergraduate and graduate courses in principles, history, philosophy, and foundations of vocational education. It is well adapted for use in in-service teacher education classes in foundations of vocational education, vocational counseling and development, history and philosophy of vocational education, and vocational career development. Vocational educators in agribusiness education, business-office education, distributive education, home economics education, health occupations education, industrial arts education, and trade and technical education will find the book appropriate for developing student knowledge of objectives, principles, and content in these vocational fields. Researchers and consultants will find that the book provides a wealth of source material covering the history and development of vocational education, including special attention to related legislation, as well as to the organization and structure of vocational education at all levels. The relationship of vocational education to emerging programs of career development will be of interest to school counselors and to counselor teacher educators. School administrators interested in the theory, organization, and design of vocational and career development programs will find the volume to be a valuable source of information.

The authors are indebted to numerous users, including both teachers and students, who have made valuable suggestions for change. We wish to acknowledge the special assistance of Dr. Jean K. Jones, who described the organization and process of career development in use at the University of Mississippi at Oxford.

We acknowledge with deep appreciation the following publishers for permission to quote from copyrighted materials that have been cited in the text: Houghton Mifflin Company, Pitman Publishing Corporation, American Vocational Association, Inc., American Technical Society, Prentice-Hall, Inc., American Association of Colleges for Teacher Education, National Association of Secondary School Principals, Charles E. Merrill Publishing Company, Olympus Publishing Company, Association for Supervision and Curriculum Development, California State Department of Education, National Business Education Association, Arizona State Department of Education, American Association of Junior Colleges, Charles A. Jones Publishing Company, Clearing House, American Personnel and Guidance Association, College Entrance Examination Board, The Association of Childhood Education International, The Macmillan Company, McGraw-Hill Book Company, Phi Delta Kappa, Inc., and the International Reading Association.

Special appreciation is expressed to the publisher for support, cooperation, and encouragement throughout the development and revision of the manuscript, and to the publisher's reviewers: Carl W. Proehl, of the University of West Florida, and James L. Navara, of the University of North Dakota. All who have contributed to the volume have contributed to better understanding of vocational education in contemporary American life.

Calfrey C. Calhoun
Alton V. Finch

Introduction

Everyone involved in the process of educating Americans should have a working knowledge of vocational-technical education. The forces currently shaping the direction in which our society is moving require that educators as well as those outside the educational establishment be involved in the formulation and operation of effective educational programs. Because of society's current insistence that everyone leaving the public school system have some type of occupational skill appropriate to earning a living, new importance has been attached to vocational-technical education. It is thus imperative that vocational teachers and teachers of academic courses at all levels—elementary, middle school, high school, community college, and college, as well as supervisors, administrators, and other education officials at the local, state, and national levels—develop a working relationship with vocational-technical education. The purpose of this text is to articulate the foundations of vocational education and to give educators a sharper perspective of their role in it.

In Chapter 1, Personal-Societal Needs and Vocational-Technical Education, the student is introduced to the effects of societal and personal needs on educational programs designed to train workers for the labor market. Labor forecasts from the Bureau of Labor Statistics and other sources are interpreted to reflect current and emerging labor needs. The effects of change in the employment picture are examined in relation to educational opportunities and requirements. The effects on vocational education of new technology, mobility, the changing status of women, and human organizational behavior are also discussed.

Chapter 2, Historical Perspective of Vocational-Technical Education, presents the impact of federal legislation on the development of vocational-technical education in the United States. For the purposes of analysis, the legislation is divided into three developmental stages: (1) legislation enacted before 1900, (2) legislation enacted between 1900 and 1960, and (3) legislation enacted since 1960.

In Chapter 3, Factors Influencing the Development of Vocational-Technical Education, emphasis is placed on philosophic, economic, and sociological developments. The philosophical factors that are discussed focus on the question: What knowledge and/or skills are of most value to teach? The economic factors center on the effects of labor-market needs on vocational education. Sociological factors are examined with relation to the effects of social class and industrialization on preparation for vocations.

Chapter 4, Theory and Design of Career Education, focuses on a discussion of the history, theory, and structure of career education and its potential value as an influence pervading the curriculum at all levels. Different approaches to the organization and structure of career education are presented, including federal and state models. Objectives and principles of career education are cited.

The process of carrying out career education is examined in Chapter 5, Implementing Career Education. Developmental aspects of career awareness, career exploration, and career preparation are illustrated through elementary school, middle school, secondary and higher education programs. The concept of infusion, the process of career guidance, criticisms of career education, and the federal role in career education are also treated.

Chapter 6, Organization of Vocational-Technical Education, describes the structure of federal, state, and local programs of vocational education. The role of the Division of Vocational and Adult Education in the U.S. Department of Education, state boards for vocational education, and the state division of vocational education, as well as local organization of vocational programs, are treated. The use of advisory committees, the preparation of local and state plans for vocational education, and state and local tax support are also presented.

Chapter 7, Vocational-Technical Education Programs, introduces differing philosophical concepts of curriculum development, models for curriculum design, and curricular needs assessment as a planning technique, and it describes curriculums in the vocational education family.

Chapter 8, Research and Development in Vocational-Technical Education, focuses on the status and needs of research in the field; the types of research being conducted; competencies needed by vocational teachers; research centers responsible for conducting, coordinating, and disseminating vocational research; research in the U.S. Department of Education and in the National Institute of Education; and procedures for developing research proposals.

Particular attention is given in Chapter 9, Public Relations for Vocational-Technical Education, to the development of positive relationships with internal and external school publics. Principles, techniques, and media affecting school public relations are examined as they apply to the implementation of strong and viable vocational programs. Public relations is viewed as a two-way process, a cooperative effort for mutual understanding and effective teamwork between the school and the community. Emphasis is placed on the development of a continuous program of interpretation, involvement, and cooperation as the school seeks to serve the individual and vocational needs of its various programs and publics.

Chapter 10, Evaluation in Vocational-Technical Education, applies recognized principles and processes to the measurement and evaluation of outcomes of instruction in vocational education. Systems for evaluating individual progress in the classroom and for measuring the overall effectiveness of vocational courses and programs are presented. Evaluation as a basis for improving instructional decisions is stressed.

Contents

CHAPTER ONE

■

Personal-Societal Needs and Vocational-Technical Education

INTRODUCTION

Vocational education faces a unique challenge in the years ahead—a challenge rooted in the social and economic welfare of people. In the contemporary social scene with its large city problems, the ghettos, school dropouts, and a variety of disadvantaged groups, the need for vocational education stands out clearly (1).

Vocational education has always been shaped by the changing needs of people. Historically, vocational training was necessary to sustain the family unit. Later the concept of socially useful work as a means of improving oneself, in a moral sense, became a well-documented part of the Judaeo-Christian culture. As nations developed, trained workers became important to the realization of national goals and thus vocational education received national endorsement and financial support.

Vocational education as we know it in the United States grew out of a social need for an educated workforce. As a function and responsibility of our educational system, vocational education has been responsive and adaptable to societal change. Although its overall dimensions include social, educational, and labor force considerations, its basic concern is for the people who provide the goods and services required by society. Ultimately it must provide both productive and self-satisfying job settings through which institutions and individuals can realize their goals.

What Vocational Education Means

Throughout this text, *vocational education* and *occupational education* will be used as equivalent terms, and both include technical education. In 1976 the United States Congress defined vocational education as "organized educational programs which are directly related to the preparation of individuals for paid or unpaid employment, or for additional preparation for a career requiring other than a baccalaureate or advanced degree."(2). Clearly this definition gives a very broad and inclusive meaning to vocational education. Yet it expresses the concept established by the Federal Vocational Education Acts, and it defines a scope of responsibility that vocational leaders accept. Such fields as agricultural education, business and office education, distributive education, trade and industrial education, health occupations education, and home economics education are specialized programs of vocational education.

Vocational education also includes the vocational guidance and counseling that precede or parallel the preparation for employment or reemployment. Federal legislation incorporates such guidance services into vocational education and provides funds for its support. When vocational education is viewed broadly, it includes all of the above areas and services.

The terms *vocational education* and *occupational education* carry different meanings in some parts of the United States. In some states, for example, occupational education programs are legally defined as "work-study" programs for slow learners, whereas vocational education programs are defined as federally reimbursed job training programs.

Social Environment of Jobs*

Social scientists from a variety of disciplines and public leaders at all levels have begun to focus more attention on the motivational and orientation factors involved in occupational preparation, placement, and adjustment. Such interest has been a result of the growing recognition that our society is experiencing difficulty in adjusting the labor supply to changing individual and occupational requirements. In many cases, individuals desire a type of employment in demand by society, but they cannot obtain the necessary training. At the same time, persons who want lower-skilled jobs find fewer of them available as the processes of industrialization and mechanization and the use of cybernetics diminish the need for such work.

Occupational education includes two related needs: the needs of society to fill required positions so that the economic system will operate efficiently, and

---

*The term *job* is used to apply to a regular remunerative position, as opposed to a piece of work or a task. *Occupation* refers broadly to the principal business for which one is prepared. Thus an individual may hold a job inside or outside his area of specialization.

the needs of individuals to find personally satisfying positions in the occupational structure.

A basic requirement of society is that positions necessary to its continued existence be filled by capable individuals. In addition there is a widely shared premise that we should always use human talent and skills to their limits.

To the individual, an occupation is an important source of social identity. A person's occupation has direct significance for self-fulfillment and social prestige. It consumes a major portion of one's daily life and largely determines other personal facets of one's life—kinds of association with others, income security, life style, and even the life chances of one's family.

A particularly vital area of concern to vocational education is personal fulfillment. If someone aims at a particular occupation but does not attain it, he or she will likely feel some degree of deprivation. In our society many children are led to believe that their achievements are limited only by their desires and efforts. This belief tends to produce relatively high goals that are not necessarily compatible with existing opportunities or even with individual capabilities. Individuals who do not realize their career goals can allow this deprivation to affect their evaluation of society and their relationship to it. Meeting the *internalized occupational needs* of individuals is a prime objective of vocational education.

The process whereby individuals are trained and placed in the occupational structure of our society is complex. Factors that normally interact to determine the final outcome include the characteristics of the individual, the individual's network of social relations, the structure of society and its dynamic properties, and the individual's perception of the interrelationship of these factors.

Individual Rights vs. Societal Needs

This text focuses on both the occupational needs of individuals and the labor requirements of society. One's selection of a particular kind of work has important implications both for the individual and for the total society. Every society must somehow ensure that people do what has to be done to maintain a healthy environment. It must distribute its human and natural resources, both in quantity and in quality, so that societal goals will be satisfied.

As Goldhammer and Taylor (3) point out, our nation's position of leadership demands a strong economic base, which in turn requires new skills and increased levels of efficiency and productivity if we are to survive in world competition. In these rigorous times of accountability and management by objectives, it is easy to forget that the individual is paramount in our free society. The problem is one of balancing the requirements of society against the essential freedom of its individuals.

VOCATIONS AND PERSONAL NEEDS

To understand the role of the occupation in a person's life, we must first understand the individual and his or her needs. The old concept of economic security has proved inadequate to explain why people work as they do. One of the primary aims of most working people is economic security, that is, having a job available on a continuous basis so that income will not be interrupted. But if individuals worked just to make a living, as soon as food and shelter had been ensured, work would stop. On the contrary, it seems that as soon as one need is satisfied, another one takes its place. Studies of morale and job satisfaction in industry have shown conclusively that much more is involved in and expected of a job than a paycheck.

Theories of Basic Individual Needs

Many authors have discussed the needs or drives that seem related to work in various ways. Cleeton (4) lists food, bodily well-being, activity, sharing of thoughts and feelings, dominance over people and elements, self-determination, achievement, approbation, and ideation. Vernon (5) found that drives that influence university women in selecting an occupation are social conformity, altruism, activity, independence, power, superiority, social admiration, pleasure, and ease. Hendrick (6) postulates a work principle that states that people seek and find primary pleasure in the efficient use of mind, hands, and tools to control or alter the environment.

Fraser (7) classifies human needs into three general categories. First, material needs are those basic to body maintenance, including food, clothing, and shelter. Second, companion needs are associated with living and interacting with other people and encompass factors such as urbanization and job specialization. Third, ego needs include those factors that differentiate individuals from each other. This category emphasizes the worth and importance of the individual.

How do such needs affect individuals in their occupations? There is little agreement among psychologists on the structure of a basic personality theory. The work of Maslow, as it relates to occupational behavior (8), views the individual as an integrated whole, motivated by fundamental goals or needs, some of which are largely unconscious. Of particular importance for the psychology of occupations is Maslow's arrangement of needs into the following categories:

1. physiological needs
2. safety needs
3. need for belongingness and love
4. need for importance, respect, self-esteem, independence
5. need for information

6. need for understanding

7. need for beauty

8. need for self-actualization

The needs listed above are arranged in the order in which individuals strive to satisfy them. A person will first be concerned with the need for food and drink. When this need is satisfied, one can think of shelter and safety, then of companionship, and so on. The most direct way to develop a life at a higher need level is through adequate gratification of the lower needs. Maslow does not make a special point of individual differences in the strength of the basic needs, but these differences surely exist and are of considerable importance. It is obvious that the higher needs, such as a need for information or beauty, are much stronger in some individuals than in others, and the strength of these needs is of direct importance for occupational choice. Such differences can occur quite apart from the degree of satisfaction of other needs.

Relationship of Basic Needs to Occupations

The application of Maslow's theory to occupational psychology is fairly obvious. In our society there is no single situation so potentially capable of satisfying basic needs at all levels as a person's occupation. With respect to the physiological needs, the usual means for satisfying hunger and thirst is through money from the job, money that can be exchanged for food and drink.

The same is true for the safety needs. This principle applies not only to the possibility of securing housing and medical care, which cut down the incidence and severity of disease, but also to safety in a long-range sense. This principle assures that these provisions will be available to a person not only during the working period but afterward in the form of pensions, savings, and so on. It has been demonstrated repeatedly that many persons will choose a job that promises security over one that pays more but cannot be counted on to last.

The need to be a member of a group, to give and receive love, is also one that can be satisfied in part by the occupation. To work with a congenial group, to be an intrinsic part of the functioning of the group, to be needed and welcomed by it, are important aspects of a satisfactory job. One of the unconscious values inherent in a job may be the opportunity it provides for the individual to win approval—of his or her immediate superior, of groups of people, or of other particularly significant persons (9).

Satisfaction of the need for esteem from self and others may be a big part of the occupation. In the first place, entering an occupation is generally seen, in our culture, as a symbol of adulthood, an indication that a young person has reached a stage of some independence and freedom. Having a job carries a measure of esteem. What importance it has is seen most clearly in the devastating effect being out of work has on some individuals.

The need for self-actualization may be met by individuals through any one of several occupations, but the strength of this need may well be the key factor in differentiating those who put enormous yet easy and pleasant effort into their work from those who do not. This factor of happy effort and personal involvement in the work is probably the single most important factor in work success. At least, in many occupations it appears that those who have attained high status have put great effort into their work. Studies of eminent persons have noted that more effort than ability is needed for great achievement. Witty and Lehman (10), for example, have pointed out that works of genius have emanated from individuals of moderate capacity who were driven to accomplish. In a sense, unused capacities might just as well not be present.

Persons in the lower socioeconomic levels show security needs more frequently than do people in higher socioeconomic positions, as indicated by Maslow and others. This may be true because people in higher socioeconomic levels have already satisfied this need, whereas those in lower socioeconomic levels have not. With the security need satisfied, other and higher needs take its place, and so we find people in the upper occupational strata showing desires for self-expression, esteem, leadership, and interesting experiences more often than we find such manifestations among the lower occupational groups.

When considered in relation to the needs of groups, the basic needs of individuals take on additional meaning. How do we explain the basic behavior of individuals within the employment setting? Let us examine briefly the theories of McGregor and Herzberg, each of whom has conducted extensive research into the motivation of individuals in relation to their jobs.

Human Behavior in Organizations

Douglas McGregor (11) classifies the philosophies dealing with individuals into two broad divisions, *Theory X* and *Theory Y*. These theories are basic to an understanding of the two most prevalent approaches to studying human behavior in organizations. The characteristics of each approach are outlined in Table 1.1.

The early view of behavior, Theory X, is based on limited experience and little or no scientific study. Theory Y outlines some critical features of human behavior and motivation that spring from controlled experiments by highly trained researchers. It points out that people have wants or needs that are never completely fulfilled.

A third theory, called *Theory Z*, combines behavioral and nonbehavioral aspects of organization theory. Theory Z claims that effective management must take into account the interactions of a variety of factors related to the individual and the organization.

This theory is often called the systems approach to organization theory in which these six factors interact: (1) organization size, (2) degree of

Table 1.1   Traditional and Current Behavioral Theories

Theory X, the traditional view	Theory Y, the current view
The average person dislikes work inherently.	The average person does not inherently dislike work but, depending on conditions, may find work to be satisfying or punishing.
The average person will avoid work if possible.	
Most people must be coerced, controlled, or threatened with punishment to get them to work toward the achievement of organizational goals.	Most people will exercise self-direction and self-control to achieve organizational objectives under certain conditions.
	The average person will seek to attain his or her firm's objectives under certain conditions.
The average person prefers to be directed, to avoid responsibility.	Under proper conditions the average person will seek responsibility.
The average person has relatively little ambition and wants security above all.	The capacity to use imagination and originality is widely found in the population, but most people do not use all their mental potential.

interaction, (3) personality of members, (4) congruence of goals, (5) level of decision making, and (6) state of the system. By analyzing the impact of each of these factors upon an organization, one can better understand how to determine the most appropriate organizational structure and process for a given situation (12).

Herzberg (13) and others who have researched the area of job motivation have argued that one must be aware of those factors that serve as motivators to the worker and those that do not. Some factors do lead to superior job satisfaction and performance. Thus, says Herzberg, possibilities for growth, responsibility, achievement, advancement, and recognition are motivators. But there are other factors—termed *hygiene, maintenance,* or *dissatisfiers*—whose absence leads to dissatisfaction but whose presence does not motivate but merely prevents dissatisfaction. Good working conditions are not motivators; they can only reduce job dissatisfaction. For positive motivation one must turn to the motivators, such as growth and achievement possibilities. Herzberg's theory of job enrichment has gained wide acceptance in management circles because it has tended to develop among employees a feeling of greater responsibility for their work.

Although there are many similarities in their needs, individuals do vary in the intensity of those needs and in their means of satisfying them. As indicated by Fraser (14):

The need to earn a living, to feel that one is liked and accepted in the various groupings to which one belongs, and to achieve a certain significance as an individual, these are the basic elements in everyone's motivation. Where the differences appear is in the methods of satisfaction, for in the modern pluralistic society there are all sorts of activities for which one can be paid, all sorts of different groupings each with its own way of life, and all sorts of activities which will make one important in one or other of these groupings. Each individual will have his own pattern of satisfaction, or his own range of activities which give him a financial, companionship or status dividend. These will be personal and peculiar to the individual and may never accord exactly with that of another individual.

Concepts Related to Work and Individual Occupations

The preceding relationships between people and their work may be character-ized by several basic concepts.

1 We live in a work-oriented society

In our society, work and work-related activities consume the major part of an individual's waking hours. The average man expects to work approximately 40 years. The average woman will work outside her home for 40 years if she is single, 30 years if she marries but has no children, or between 15 and 25 years if she marries and has children (15). Despite the pressures for a shorter work week and earlier retirement, there is much evidence to suggest that the personal and social values of continuing employment tend to outweigh the disadvantages. Work is a major source of identity for the individual, especially those of the middle class or those who accept middle-class values.

2 Work provides situations for satisfying individual needs

People work for many reasons other than money. Ginzberg and others (16) have identified three different types of satisfaction from work. The first, and most obvious, are the *extrinsic satisfactions*, or tangible rewards of work. These include salaries and bonuses. Second are the *intrinsic satisfactions*, derived from two sources: (a) the pleasure that comes from engaging in work activity, and (b) the sense of accomplishment that is experienced from meeting social standards of success and personal realization of abilities through achievement. The third type of satisfaction includes *extrinsic satisfactions* associated with physical and psychological conditions of a person's work. These include clean, comfortable working conditions, fringe benefits, and congenial co-workers.

To the typical person in a middle-class occupation, working means having a purpose, gaining a sense of accomplishment, and expressing oneself. Not working, it seems, would leave one aimless and without opportunity to con-tribute to society. It must be remembered, however, that all workers are not middle class and so may not share such an orientation to work.

Work serves other noneconomic functions. In a national sample of 401 employed men, Morse and Weiss (17) found that work is not simply a means of earning a livelihood. Most of these men indicated that even if there were no economic necessity involved, they would continue to work. It is through the producing role that most individuals tie into society; work is an essential element in helping to maintain their sense of well-being.

3 Work is directly related to an individual's social life

An occupation is central to one's sense of dignity, opportunity, and social life. The consequence of not being able to work or of being denied the opportunity to work at the level of one's competence is not merely a matter of monetary loss; equally important is the consequent loss of social status. The individual's status in the community, based on the esteem in which he or she is held, will depend largely on the type of work that is done and how well it is performed. It is quite evident that one's choice of friends and leisure time activities, and even of one's residence, is conditioned to some degree by one's work and one's relationship with co-workers.

A person's occupation in American society today is his or her single most significant status-conferring role. Whether it be high or low, a job status allows the individual to form a stable self-concept and to establish a position in the community.

VOCATIONS AND SOCIETAL NEEDS

Vocational education through the years has been responsive to the needs of society. Historically the apprenticeship system for training workers was sufficient to meet the demands of emerging industry. But when geographic and occupational mobility of workers accelerated, and improved technology required a higher degree of trained skills, society turned to the schools to supply its need for trained workers.

Effects of Technology

Throughout history the continuous processes of technological change have influenced human culture by affecting the nature of people's efforts to earn a living. Until quite recently, however, the pace of technological change was slow, and there was much overlap from one generation to another in social, cultural, and economic patterns. Particularly in relation to occupations, the changes were not fast enough to disrupt seriously the character of most workers' performance. A useful occupation learned in youth could be counted on to produce a livelihood as long as a person was likely to work.

Today, however, the accelerating pace of technological change is able to produce complete changes in the nature of an occupation within a few years.

Although automation is usually associated with this process, it is but one aspect of a broader movement consisting of many interacting and powerful technologies. Technological advances cause present jobs to disappear and also result in the emergence of previously unknown occupations. Often the persons who performed the old jobs are not capable of undertaking the new ones because they require further education and retraining.

Occupations created by new technology seem to have several characteristics that differ from occupations that tend to be phased out: 1. They usually involve fewer manual skills and more cognitive understandings. 2. They often call for skills of a higher order and for the use of more technical knowledge. 3. Their performance usually requires a more complete, functional general education than the jobs they replaced. 4. In many cases the worker needs more maturity to fill the job successfully. As a result of these characteristics of newer occupations, a worker's versatility may be more valuable than a high degree of specialization.

Modern technology is creating an increasing number of occupations that provide services rather than goods. Sometimes these occupations call for combinations of traditional skills. In the area of agri-business, for example, occupations related to the sale and servicing of agricultural machinery demand a combination of skills. In addition, these new occupations often demand different kinds of skills, which may be described as interpersonal or social, in addition to technical knowledge. The retail clerk, for example, must be knowledgeable about the merchandise and must relate effectively to the customer in an interpersonal sense.

Although technology eliminates some unskilled and low-skilled occupations, it also tends to upgrade skill and training requirements in the more highly specialized jobs. It is beginning to affect middle-management and higher levels of the occupational structure so that retraining is becoming a continuing aspect of employment. Technology has had profound effects on agricultural occupations where increases in the average size of farms, rapid mechanization, and improved fertilizers, feeds, and pesticides have led to much increased output with sharply decreased employment.

Nevertheless, the effect of technology on occupations is quite variable. It should not be assumed that all older occupations have become obsolete or that they should be excluded from vocational education programs. The rate of change in different occupations varies widely, although in all occupations the rate of change tends to increase. It is not expected that this trend will be reversed.

Vocational educators need to be well informed about the progress and current developments in technological change, so that they may respond wisely and so that programs that are planned and operated will remain continually relevant. They should not be surprised if changes that presently seem remote occur much sooner than expected, so flexibility and the ability to anticipate need will be essential. If the program of public vocational education cannot exhibit this flexibility, other public and private agencies will be created, often on an ad hoc basis, to meet the need.

Implications of Technology

A career, in the sense of a stable pursuit of a single occupation throughout the work life of the individual, is becoming increasingly unattainable in our industralized society for a large portion of the workforce, and serial careers are becoming a reality. Thus an individual may expect to hold several different occupations during a lifetime. Also, with the passing of craftsmanship in industry and with the changes resulting from more advanced technology, an increased percentage of the working population is no longer able to follow occupations that offer the kind of identity historically available in work.

Because the portion of the day that must be devoted to the business of earning a living is decreasing, the search for a meaningful use of leisure time is becoming more intense. It is an open question whether leisure activities can supply the individual with a needed source of identity and meaning. In many instances the individual will choose to spend some of this time in continuing education and retraining for vocational or avocational purposes.

The practices and policies of vocational education have always been determined by the existing state of technology and its attendant social and economic realities. Before the rate of technological change had reached its present level, these practices did not often require reexamination or revision. The assumptions on which they were based remained valid for long periods of time. Because of social changes induced by technology, however, this is no longer true. Some of the practices and policies of the past are no longer appropriate, whereas others are still useful or need only minor modification. Still other policies may continue to be viable for the foreseeable future. Vocational educators must learn to reexamine their positions continually and to respect traditions only so long as they are compatible with the real needs of people.

In the past there has been a tendency for most pre-employment vocational education to be planned as terminal education. Provision has always been made for the periodic updating of workers through extension forms of vocational education, but this updating has usually meant only intermittent training for those engaged in stable, lifetime occupations. It is now clear that no form of education, vocational or nonvocational, can become terminal; education must be planned as open-ended and continuous. It must provide workers with complete retraining for new jobs, as well as for continuity in present jobs. A major responsibility of vocational education will be to develop a readiness and capacity for a lifetime of learning and relearning.

Need for extended scope

Vocational education has traditionally emphasized preparation for the highly skilled and technical occupations in agriculture, the skilled trades, office and distributive occupations, and home economics. This emphasis has meant that its services have largely been directed toward those who could qualify for such occupations. But current technological change requires that vocational education extend its services to all possible categories of occupational life, excluding the professions that are served by the professional schools. This extended scope will include education for persons at various social and economic levels regardless of age or sex. In short, vocational education will need to offer preparation for any form of work for which workers are needed and for which individuals can possibly be helped to qualify.

Occupational change and career choice

Vocational educators will need to be informed continually about broad occupational changes and their implications. This means more than discovering what new tools, materials, or processes are coming into use in particular trades or jobs. It involves current knowledge of major social and economic trends and of the social, political, and economic forces that shape the occupational life of the nation. To keep abreast of such trends requires more than periodic studies or surveys of local conditions; it will be necessary to tap many sources of information, including agencies of government, business, industry, and education. In addition there will be a greater need for vocational counseling to assist those who are making career choices. The vocational educator and the trained counselor will need to work hand-in-hand, with each respecting the role of the other.

 The importance of general education

Technological advances raise the basic educational requirements for most jobs. As a result the skills acquired through general education—reading, writing, speaking, and calculating—are becoming an even more essential foundation for work. Their importance is being felt in at least three ways. First, more and more jobs require a higher level of general education as a prerequisite for learning their specialized aspects. Second, the skills and understandings developed by general education—especially those of a verbal, scientific, and mathematical nature—turn out to be the actual, on-the-job skills of more and more occupations (the paramedical occupations are an example). Third, a substantial amount of general education is needed to provide the future worker with the intellectual tools needed for continued learning, in fact, for a lifetime of learning a living.

There are important training implications to this demand for workers with skills related both to technical content and to general education. As technology accelerates, there is a greater need for the development of skills composed of both intellectual and manipulative components. More jobs will take on the characteristics of technical occupations, but many of these jobs will not be related to the physical sciences. Instead, they will reflect the growing shift to occupations oriented toward the social and personal services, such as law enforcement and health care. Ultimately, most of this training will take place in programs that include part or all of the thirteenth and fourteenth years of school.

The results of technology

In planning for new programs of vocational education or for the improvement of existing programs, management and labor must understand the influence of swift technological change. The kinds of work for which individuals prepare will continue to undergo changes, both in nature and in content. For many workers, continuity in work life will be interrupted, requiring fresh preparation for new tasks. No education can be considered terminal. Generally, jobs will tend to disappear in inverse order to the amount of education and skills they require; those jobs that make the fewest educational demands will always be the most vulnerable. The relative need for manual and craft-type skills will likely decrease, even as the overall need for skilled workers increases. The new skills for the new jobs will tend to be of a different order. Technical knowledge and conceptual skills will become major ingredients of many occupations, while technical knowledge combined with social skills will be required by many others. For most workers a more complete general education will be a necessary foundation for further training. Career choice will become more complex and will call for more assistance from professionally trained people who keep up to date on the changing occupational opportunities and requirements. Career decision making will tend to be prolonged and, together with an extended period of general education, will somewhat advance the age at which serious vocational preparation will be begun. Future career programs must achieve greater flexibility to satisfy more diverse needs; the opportunity to contract for services that are not normally available in the standard school setting should increase this flexibility.

Effects of Mobility

Mobility is a characteristic of American society. A person moves from one coast to the other to accept a better position. Education helps the children of artisans and laborers to climb social and economic ladders. Our whole population shows substantial mobility, and most mobile of all are members of the specialized professions. Movement from one region to another, from one type of work to another, serves the wishes and ambitions of the individual as well as the good of society.

From the standpoint of analyzing the labor market, it is useful to think of several kinds of mobility. Mobility may be classified as moving from one place to another, from one function to another (such as from teaching to business management), from one type of employer to another, or from one specialty to another. All of these types of mobility are interrelated, and they are all related to education and ability.

Occupational mobility

By being mobile, people are able to take advantage of new and better job opportunities. This is the first advantage of mobility: the greater opportunity it provides individuals to move into the work they find most interesting or rewarding. If people could not move from one job to another, they would be stuck for life in the kind of work or in the company they had chosen—or that had chosen them—at the beginning of their career (18).

According to Taylor (19), participants in the American labor force change jobs, on the average, every three to five years. Most upward occupational mobility occurs between the ages of 25 and 45. By age 50, most workers have reached the high point on the occupational ladder, and during the last 15 to 20 years of the work cycle, little occupational mobility occurs.

Occupational mobility is good for the individual and for society. Society benefits when workers are interested in their jobs and have the freedom to move to new areas, new positions, and new kinds of work. In fact, labor mobility is one of our most effective means of keeping the supply of talent in reasonable balance with the work society wants done.

Of course, there are means other than job mobility to keep supply and demand in balance. When labor is in short supply, people come out of the labor reserve, for they are attracted by the salaries or by the kinds of work available.

Geographic mobility

At present, each year approximately 20 percent of all Americans one year of age or over change residence, and about 6.5 percent migrate across county or state lines.

Geographic mobility is most pronounced in specific segments of society, for the following reasons. First, disadvantaged workers, both rural and urban, move in hopes of bettering themselves. Second, professional and technical workers move for occupational reasons and as a means of upward social mobility. Third, many thousands of military families move periodically both within the United States and to other countries. Fourth, skilled workers, such as construction workers, move seasonally to follow demands for their services. Finally, thousands of college students attend school both in- and out-of-state and are significant participants in the increased mobility that is characteristic of our country (20).

A special aspect of mobility in recent years is the surge into the suburbs and both into and out of the inner cities. This movement is not only a shift of living locale for a considerable portion of the population, but it also involves a definite change in ethnic composition (21).

Mobility and education

The level of education completed by a worker affects both the type of job for which he or she can qualify and the amount of mobility necessary for continued growth and advancement (22). The occupational categories that are currently expanding require more education than those that are not. Because of the average increase in the educational level of United States workers, the typical labor force entrant now has at least a high school education, and the workers who do not graduate from high school tend to be screened out of better jobs. These educational patterns lead to mobility patterns as the undereducated often *must* move after a long and fruitless search for work locally, and the educated move *voluntarily* as an outgrowth of the expanding market for their services. People are either pushed into leaving an area by adverse conditions or they are pulled into an area by favorable conditions.

One should not assume, however, that because the labor market is composed of more highly trained workers, occupational mobility is essentially vertical rather than lateral. Just the opposite is true. It is difficult for individuals to begin on the bottom rung of a career ladder and with some additional training work their way to the top. In fact, there is a limited amount of vertical mobility with much lateral mobility. For example, people who are trained as electronic technicians may move laterally in and out of a variety of jobs that require similar training. But seldom does an electronic technician move vertically to the position of engineer or research scientist. The same is true of paramedical technicians, who seldom become physicians. Certification and state licensing requirements contribute to this limited vertical mobility.

Challenge of Retirement

Modern society, with its higher standards of living, its public health controls, and its advances in medical treatment, has succeeded in establishing a higher life expectancy for its workers. In the past most individuals spent about one-third of their lives preparing to enter the labor force, another third in the labor force, and a final third in retirement. In the future it is likely that increasing numbers of workers will remain on their jobs longer. This appraisal is based on the economic necessity for continued income to offset the effects of inflation, the increasing life expectancy of men and women, and an increasing recognition of the role that productive employment plays in the well-being of the individual. Moreover, on January 1, 1979, the mandatory retirement age was changed by federal law to age 70.

The retired individual is expected to "settle down" to the one remaining work-environment reinforcer (often one with reinforcement value reduced to an almost imperceptible level)—a continuing retirement check. Concurrently, there seem to be many individuals who see retirement as their reward for years of hard work, who prepare for it as an ultimate goal, and who want to retire as soon as the system will permit.

In either case, whether the worker is required to retire or whether he or she wishes to retire, it is likely that relatively few individuals have truly planned a satisfying retirement. Many of them have probably viewed retirement only in a rather abstract way as an expected, and desirable, state of affairs. For example, a view that is frequently encountered is that the life style of retired people is characterized by increased recreational activity. Now that they have the time, they can golf, camp, boat, dance, play chess, paint, and the like. They are able to do these things because they are now "free to do them," whether or not they have ever learned to do or to prefer them. It is often assumed that when people retire they will not only be able to but also want to change their life styles to include more recreational activities. A related attitude is that retired people should be encouraged to relax and do nothing. Naturally, such an abrupt change can have unsettling effects on many individuals.

Society's retirement problem is not simply one of the increase in numbers of older persons; it is a problem that requires planning and individualizing of retirement. It is a problem that might focus less on expected changes in mature people and more on what these people bring to retirement (23). The opportunity for continuing education for vocational, avocational, or aesthetic purposes can make the lives of older people more productive and satisfying to themselves and to society. One of the encouraging signs on the educational horizon is that an increasing number of universities are developing programs in gerontology, the study of problems of the aged.

Changing Status of Women in the Labor Force

Women are entering the paid workforce at steadily increasing rates. As of June 1978, half of all women 16 years of age and older (42 million) were in the labor force; these women represent 41 percent of the total workforce, a figure that is projected to reach 50 percent by 1985 (24).

Increasing entry into the paid workforce is characteristic of all groups in our society, regardless of racial-ethnic group membership, age (57 percent of all women in every age group between 18 and 54 are employed outside their homes), marital status (47 percent of the nation's marriages have two breadwinners), or maternal status (47 percent of all women with children under 18 are in the paid workforce; mothers of children under 6 are entering at a rate faster than any other group) (25). A number of developments have served to bring women as workers to new prominence, including (a) the relaxation of restrictions against entry into occupations traditionally viewed as masculine strongholds; (b) vast changes in the occupational structure that have seen the displacement of many unskilled jobs requiring sheer physical labor by others demanding general education and special skills; (c) the spread of part-time employment and the equalization of job opportunities for single and married women; (d) changing attitudes toward family roles; and (e) the establishment of day care centers.

Part of the change in the role of women stems from current patterns of family size and spacing of children. More women are completing their childbearing in the early years of marriage. This fact, when coupled with a tendency to marry at an earlier age, has produced a dramatic change in the career patterns of married women. For increasing thousands of young women, the choice is no longer between career and family but toward alternatives that combine marriage and family responsibilities with very real, if interrupted, commitments to career opportunities outside the home (26). Also linked to women's increased participation is the divorce rate; that is, more women must work to support themselves and their families.

An extraordinary increase in women's labor force activity characterized the 1970s. Nearly 12 million more women were employed in 1979 than in 1970. Women 25 to 34 years old accounted for nearly half of the increase. Sixty-four percent of the women in this age group were working or looking for work in 1980. Women tend to be concentrated in a limited number of occupations, most of them lower paying than the occupations in which males predominate. Approximately 70 percent of all women working for pay are employed in clerical, service, and professional-technical occupations. A substantial number of women have made inroads into professional-technical jobs with higher status, such as doctors, lawyers, and accountants (27).

At the beginning of the 1980s, working women were in the same earnings position as men were at the outset of the 1970s. Women working full time averaged $6 for every $10 earned by men. Although earning parity with men was nearly achieved in some newer fields such as computer science, most women were still at the lower end of the pay scale. Unemployment rates generally remain higher for men than for women, with the gap widening when business is buoyant and narrowing during sluggish periods, such as the first half of 1980 (28).

Federal antidiscrimination laws and statutes have, more recently, resulted in the redesignation of job titles previously restricted to male or female workers. For example, the job title "foreman" has been changed to "blue-collar supervisor" in the standardized job nomenclature. Another evidence of the equalization of job opportunities for women has been the increased recruitment by business and industry of qualified females for executive-level positions.

Federal laws have acted to some extent to mitigate the effects of age and sex discrimination in employment. In 1963, the Equal Pay Act, an amendment to the Fair Labor Standards Act, provided that no employer may discriminate solely on the basis of sex in determining the wage rates of men and women who are doing equal work under similar conditions. In the following year, a national policy of fair employment practices was set forth in the Civil Rights Act. Title VII, Equal Employment Opportunity, provides that in hiring and training practices, employers, employment agencies, and unions may not discriminate on the basis of race, color, religion, national origin, or sex. The Age Discrimination in Employment Act of 1967 prohibits age discrimination by employers, employment agencies, and labor unions against individuals between the ages of 40 and 65. The purpose of this act is to promote the employment of older persons based on their ability rather than on their age, to prohibit arbitrary age discrimination in employment, and to help employers and workers find ways of meeting problems arising from the impact of age on employment. Title IX of the Vocational Education Amendments of 1972 prohibits discrimination on the basis of sex in federally funded vocational programs.

EMPLOYMENT TRENDS

Employment patterns have shifted considerably over the years and are expected to continue to do so. During the 1970s eight of every ten jobs did not require a college degree, a fact that emphasizes the importance of vocational-technical education. The following section provides an overview of employment prospects for the principal occupational groups as they are expected to occur between 1978 and 1990, as projected by the Bureau of Labor Statistics of the U.S. Department of Labor (29).

Replacement and Growth Needs

Although growth is a key indicator of future job outlook, as indicated in the following section, more jobs will be created between 1978 and 1990 from death, retirement, and other labor-force separations than from employment growth, as indicated in Figure 1.1. Generally, employees in occupations requiring the least training or experience—such as many operative, clerical, service, and sales occupations—have a higher replacement rate than other occupations. These workers can quit and later easily find a similar job. Because of job transfers, deaths, retirements, and other labor-force separations, employment opportunities exist in occupations where employment is expected to decline or to increase slowly.

Growth Within Industries

The majority of our nation's workers are employed by those sectors of the economy that provide services—trade, government, finance, public utilities, personal and business services. According to the U.S. Department of Labor, by 1990 approximately 78.4 million workers will be needed in the service-producing industries. This number represents an increase of 30 percent over the 1978 level. Such growth is a reflection of changes in personal and societal needs and organization. For example, the shift from a rural to an urban society has resulted in a demand for more city services such as garbage pickup and street maintenance, police and fire protection, public health departments, and better schools and educational personnel. Rising personal incomes and living standards have brought accompanying demands for improved urban and sub-

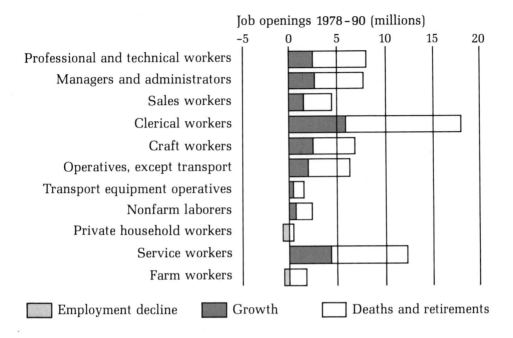

Job openings 1978–90 (millions)

Outlook Handbook, 1980–81 ed., Bulletin 2075, U.S. Dept. of Labor, p. 22.

urban services. And the increase in population has resulted in the necessity for more services.

While the growth rate is expected to be faster in the service-producing area than in goods-producing industries, the growth pattern will vary within both sectors as reflected in Figure 1.2.

Service-Producing Industries

Although trade is the largest division within the service-producing industries (24.8 million workers projected by 1990), the largest increase in growth between 1978 and 1990 will be in service industries and finance, according to the U.S. Department of Labor. Manpower requirements in health care, business services, maintenance, advertising, and commercial cleaning are the primary forces behind the projected growth rate of 53 percent, nearly twice that of service-producing industries as a group.

Finance, insurance, and real estate are also experiencing more growth than are services as a whole. Employment in these categories by 1990 is expected to have increased 34 percent over the 1978 level.

Government and transportation employment is expected to increase at a

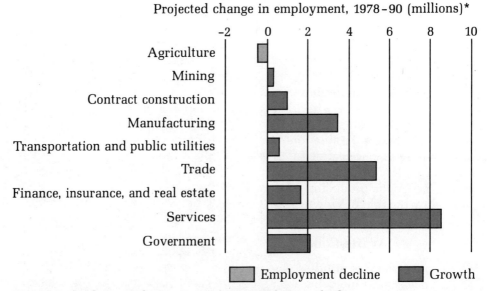

Projected change in employment, 1978–90 (millions)*

*Wage and salary workers, except for agriculture, which
includes self-employed and unpaid family workers.

Figure 1.2 Tomorrow's jobs. Through the 1980s, employment
growth will vary widely by industry. Source: *Occupational Outlook
Handbook,* 1980–81 ed., Bulletin 2075, U.S. Dept. of Labor, p. 19.

rate less than that for services as a whole between 1978 and 1990, 13 percent
and 18 percent respectively.

Goods-Producing Industries

Employment in the goods-producing industries has changed very little since
1960. Between 1978 and 1990, the projected increase is 13 percent (32.5 million) as compared to 30 percent for service-producing industries.

Since the late 1940s the goods-producing industries have accounted for
less than half the nation's workforce. This employment pattern can be attributed primarily to automation and technology and improved work skills of the
labor force, all of which have resulted in increased productivity without increased employment. Concurrently, a rising standard of living and a demand
by our society for more services have contributed to the increase in numbers of
service workers.

While manufacturing accounts for approximately three-fourths of the
goods-producing workers (23.6 million by 1990), its projected 16 percent rate
of growth is less than mining and contract construction. The need for addi-

tional energy has resulted in an abrupt increase in mining employment, especially in oil and gas exploration as well as coal. Once declining in employment, mining is expected to grow 28 percent between 1978 and 1990. Contract construction also appears to be experiencing a resurgent growth. Employment is expected to increase by 17 percent between 1978 and 1990 (30).

Employment in agriculture (3.3 million in 1978) is expected to decrease by approximately 12 percent from 1978 to 1990. Rapid mechanization and better fertilizers, feeds, pesticides, and hybrids have created large increases in output with fewer workers. Production is expected to continue to rise without reversing the employment decline in agriculture.

These widely different employment patterns and changes will continue among the goods-producing industries. Inflation and a tight money market could slow the rate of growth even more in all goods-producing industries.

White-Collar vs. Blue-Collar Employment

White-collar workers are those in professional, technical, clerical, sales, and management jobs. Blue-collar workers are those in craft, operative, and laborer jobs. Service workers and farm workers constitute separate groups. Approximately half of the labor force is white-collar workers, with about 34 million blue-collar workers, representing approximately one-third of the labor force. The number of service workers has risen rapidly, while the blue-collar workforce has grown only slowly and the number of farm workers has declined.

As American industry continues to become larger, more complex, and more mechanized, its occupational structure reflects these changes. Perhaps most significant has been the trend to fewer blue-collar and more white-collar workers. Since 1956 the number of white-collar workers has exceeded the number of blue-collar workers. Because the demand of our society for more services is likely to continue, we can expect a continuation of the rapid growth of the white-collar occupations through the 1980s.

Blue-collar workers can expect a slower than average growth; service workers will experience a faster than average growth. Farm workers can anticipate a further decline in employment, although widespread food shortages may stimulate this sector. Again, the effects of technology and automation will tend to stabilize employment in blue-collar occupations.

Outlook and Education

Employers are seeking people with higher levels of education because many occupations are more complex and require greater skill. High school education has become standard for American workers. However, many occupations are becoming increasingly complex and technical, requiring specific occupational training above the secondary level, such as that obtained in postsecondary vocational-technical schools and in community colleges.

Potential workers who do not receive good preparation for work will find competition for jobs more difficult in the years ahead. On the other hand, people who have acquired skills or good basic education will have a better chance for interesting work, good wages, and steady employment.

The intrinsic value of vocational education lies in its relationship to the social and economic development of the nation (31): "Vocational education is a social process concerned primarily with people and their part in doing the work society needs done; it is concerned with preparing people for work and with improving the work potential of the labor force." We have learned, also, that simply providing a person with job skills is not enough (32): "We must accept the belief that it is a responsibility of education to help young people find a meaningful role in society in which they can make interesting contributions and accept increasing responsibilities."

SUMMARY

Vocational education is concerned with preparing people for work and with improving the training potential of the labor force. It covers any form of education, training, or retraining designed to prepare people to enter or to continue in employment in a recognized occupation.

Vocational preparation must always be viewed against the backdrop of the needs of society and of the individual. While meeting the demands of the economy, the abilities of individuals must be used to the fullest. Individuals establish social identity and status through the occupational role. Meeting the internalized job needs of individuals is a crucial objective of vocational and career education.

Studies of human needs and job satisfaction among employees have given us insights into the psychology of occupational adjustment. Fraser classified these as material needs, companion needs, and ego needs. Maslow arranged individual needs into a hierarchy, ranging from the purely physiological needs to the need for self-actualization. He saw the occupation as a potential means of giving satisfaction to one's basic needs at all levels. McGregor developed a theory that contrasted a traditional and a current view of worker behavior. Herzberg identified "satisfiers" and "dissatisfiers" in the job environment and developed a theory that maximizes the need for job enrichment.

Vocational education has been affected by social problems such as automation, mobility, retirement, and the changing status of women. A changing technology emphasizes the need for an expanded scope of vocational education choices. The portion of the day devoted to earning a living is decreasing, and an individual may expect to experience several careers in a lifetime. Vocational curricula should facilitate occupational mobility as a means of keeping our supply of human resources in reasonable balance with society's requirements. The problem of retirement focuses on the need for planning and proper individualization to meet one's objectives. The equalization of job opportunities for women and changing attitudes toward family roles have resulted in career patterns for approximately one-half of all women.

Employment prospects maximize opportunities in the service-oriented industries as contrasted with the goods-producing sector of the economy. Occupational forecasts project a continuation of the rapid growth of white-collar occupations. Replacement needs are particularly significant in occupations that have a large proportion of part-time workers or women. For example the category of clerical workers—second largest among the occupational groups in size—ranks first in replacement and growth needs.

Employers are seeking people who have higher levels of education because jobs are more complex and require greater skill. In the long run, employment growth will be fastest in those occupations requiring the most education and training. For example, professional occupations will show the fastest growth throughout the 1980s and beyond. These facts contain significant implications for all phases of public education.

ACTIVITIES

For review

1. What is the definition of vocational education?
2. What are some of the basic or personal needs that motivate people? How do these needs affect one's choice of a vocation?
3. Contrast Theory X, Theory Y, and Theory Z as basic philosophies of worker behavior.
4. What is the essence of Herzberg's theory of job satisfaction?
5. Discuss the effects of automation and changing life styles on occupations.
6. What implications do the effects of automation and changing life styles hold for vocational education?
7. What are the beneficial effects of mobility on individuals and society? How does the level of one's education affect his or her mobility?
8. Explain why the increase in labor force needs has shifted from blue-collar to white-collar workers.
9. Why would an occupation with a large percentage of growth not necessarily be a better career choice than one with a smaller percentage of growth?
10. Discuss the effects of technology on (a) goods-producing industries, (b) service-oriented industries, (c) blue-collar workers, (d) white-collar workers.
11. Discuss the relationship between education and unemployment.

For discussion

1. Why is it becoming increasingly difficult for individuals to find their identity through an occupation?
2. Defend or refute a mandatory retirement age for workers in business, industry, and education.
3. What role should labor trends and forecasts play in vocational education curricula at the secondary and postsecondary levels?

For exploration

1. Research the meaning of the Protestant work ethic. Then debate the following: "Resolved, that every able adult should experience some type of prolonged paid employment."
2. Identify three to five specific societal concerns in your community. How does each affect vocational education?
3. Review a research study in the area of job satisfaction and prepare a summary report for the class.
4. Select a job title and review it in the current *Occupational Outlook Handbook* and in an older edition. What changes, if any, are there in description of duties, educational requirements, and demand? How has technology influenced the job?
5. Prepare a report on federal legislation that has affected the role of women in the labor force.

REFERENCES

1. Advisory Council on Vocational Education, *Vocational Education: The Bridge Between Man and His Work*, U.S. Department of Health, Education and Welfare, Office of Education (Washington D.C.: Government Printing Office, 1968), p. v.

2. U.S. Congress, House of Representatives, *Education Amendments of 1976*, Public Law 94-482 (Washington, D.C.: Government Printing Office, 1976).

3. Keith Goldhammer and Robert E. Taylor, *Career Education—Perspective and Promise* (Columbus: Charles E. Merrill Publishing Company, 1972), p. 4.

4. G. A. Cleeton, *Making Work Human* (Yellow Springs, Ohio: Antioch Press, 1949).

5. M. D. Vernon, "The Drives Which Determine Choice of a Career," *British Journal of Educational Psychology*, Vol. 8, 1938, pp. 1–15.

6. I. Hendrick, "Work and the Pleasure Principle," *Psychoanalytic Quarterly*, Vol. 12, 1943, pp. 311–29.

7. John M. Fraser, *Psychology: General-Industrial-Social,* 3rd ed. (London: Pitman Publishing Company, 1971), pp. 72–73. (Reproduced by permission.)

8. Abraham H. Maslow, *Motivation and Personality* (Boston: Harper & Row, 1954).

9. Henry Borow, ed., *Man in a World of Work* (Boston: Houghton Mifflin Company, 1964), p. xv.

10. P. A. Witty and H. C. Lehman, "Drive—A Neglected Trait in the Study of the Gifted," *Psychological Review,* Vol. 34, 1926, pp. 364–76.

11. Douglas McGregor, *The Human Side of Enterprise* (New York: McGraw-Hill Book Company, Inc., 1960), pp. 33–57.

12. John J. W. Neuner, B. Lewis Keeling, and Norman F. Kallous, *Administrative Office Management* (Cincinnati: South-western Publishing Company, 1972), p. 11.

13. Fred Herzberg, *Work and the Nature of Man* (Cleveland: World Publishing Company, 1966).

14. Fraser, *Psychology: General-Industrial-Social,* p. 83. (Reproduced by permission.)

15. Resource Center on Sex Roles in Education, National Foundation for the Improvement of Education, "Reducing Sex Stereotypes and Achieving Sex Equity in Career Education," unpublished resources compiled for the Office of Career Education Project Directors Meeting, Washington, D.C., October 24–25, 1978. (Reproduced with permission from mimeographed document), p. 45.

16. E. Ginzberg et al., *Occupational Choice* (New York: Columbia University Press, 1951), p. 217.

17. Nancy Morse and Robert Weiss, "Function and Meaning of Work and the Job," in *Vocational Behavior: Readings in Theory and Research,* Donald G. Zytowski, ed. (New York: Holt, Rinehart and Winston, 1968), pp. 7–16.

18. Dael Wolfle, *The Uses of Talent* (Princeton, N.J.: Princeton University Press, 1968), p. 80.

19. Lee Taylor, *Occupational Sociology* (New York: Oxford University Press, 1968), p. 80.

20. Alvin Toffler, *Future Shock* (New York: Bantam Books, Inc., 1971), p. 83.

21. Carrol H. Miller, "Historical and Recent Perspectives on Work and Vocational Guidance," in *Career Guidance for a New Age,* Henry Borow, ed. (Boston: Houghton Mifflin Company, 1973), pp. 23–24.

22. Kingsley Davis, "Urbanization—Changing Patterns of Living," in *The Changing American Population,* Hoke S. Simpson, ed. (New York: Institute of Life Insurance, 1962), p. 19.

23. Lloyd H. Lofquist and Rene V. Davis, *Adjustment to Work—A Psychologi-*

cal View of Man's Problems in a Work-Oriented Society (New York: Appleton-Century-Crofts, 1969), p. 80.

24. Resource Center on Sex Roles in Education, "Reducing Sex Stereotypes and Achieving Sex Equity in Career Education," p. 45.

25. Resource Center on Sex Roles in Education, National Foundation for the Improvement of Education, "Reducing Sex Stereotypes and Achieving Sex Equity in Career Education," unpublished resources compiled for the Office of Career Education Project Directors Meeting, Washington, D.C., October 24–25, 1978. (Reproduced with permission from mimeographed document, p. 47.)

26. Donald H. Blocker, "Social Change and the Future of Vocational Guidance," in *Career Guidance for a New Age*, Henry Borow, ed. (Boston: Houghton Mifflin Company, 1973), p. 52.

27. U.S. Department of Labor, *Perspectives on Working Women: A Databook*, Bulletin 2080, Bureau of Labor Statistics (Washington: U.S. Government Printing Office, 1980), pp. 1, 48.

28. Ibid.

29. U.S. Department of Labor, Bureau of Labor Statistics, Bulletin 2075, *Occupational Outlook Handbook* (Washington, D.C.: Government Printing Office, 1980–81 ed.), p. 20.

30. Ibid, p. 20.

31. Melvin L. Barlow, "Changing Goals," in *Vocational Education: Today and Tomorrow*, Gerald G. Somers and J. Kenneth Little, eds. (Madison: University of Wisconsin, Center for Studies in Vocational and Technical Education, 1971), p. 11.

32. Grant Venn, *Man, Education and Manpower* (Washington, D.C.: American Association of School Administrators, 1970), p. 16.

■

CHAPTER TWO

Historical Perspective of Vocational-Technical Education

INTRODUCTION

Many factors have influenced the development of education in our nation, not the least of which is the heritage of America's early settlers. Despite their widely divergent backgrounds, these early immigrants were strongly united on two beliefs. First, they believed in the worth of the individual and placed the dignity of the individual above the dignity of the masses. The belief "that government is best that governs least" has permeated the character of our government. The same is true with respect to government's role toward education. For many years the responsibility was left to local communities, states, and private groups to provide for the education of citizens. Even in the later decades of the twentieth century, local communities continue to strive to maintain control of their schools.

The second strong belief shared by the early settlers was the notion that individuals should be free to earn their livelihoods in whatever way proved most profitable. This belief formed the backbone of the free enterprise system, with profit as the primary motivating force. An important notion of this system was that the role of government in such areas as business, religion, the home, and education should be limited. But as the population increased and with it the complexity of life, government became more and more powerful in its efforts to protect the freedom of individuals. The quest for profit and the necessity for competition in business and industry had limited the extent to which these institutions could cope with problems of the poor. As a result the national government assumed more and more responsibility for regulating the lives of the nation's citizens in the attempt to provide equal opportunity for all.

As the nation changed from a predominantly agrarian to a highly industrialized economy, vast social, educational, religious, and cultural changes were taking place. All of these changes were reflected in the national legislation relating to education. For this reason, it seems appropriate for us to look at the historical development of the role of the federal government vis-á-vis the education of its citizens.

The social, religious, and business institutions that might have dealt successfully with many of the nation's problems neglected to do so. In effect, the failure of these institutions to deal successfully with these problems forced the federal government to fill the vacuum. As Commager (1) vividly illustrates:

> [F]or a century and a half almost every major reform in our political and
> social system has come about through the agency of the national
> government and over the opposition of powerful vested interests, states,
> and local communities. . . . It is the national government that freed the
> slaves . . . gave blacks the vote, guaranteed them political and civil
> rights . . . gave the suffrage to women . . . extended the suffrage to those
> over 18 . . . imposed a one-man, one-vote rule on reluctant states . . .
> provided labor with a Bill of Rights, wiped out child labor, regulated hours
> and set minimum wages . . . launched the campaign to conserve the
> national resources . . . provided Social Security . . . brought about
> medicaid and medicare . . . imposed "due process of law" on local police
> authorities . . . set standards for education at all levels.

Commager also points out that the national government has been able to take all of these actions because the problems involved are national, not local, in scope. When the people felt the need for national direction and unity with respect to educational problems, they turned to the national government for leadership.

Federal legislation in the field of education can be classified as falling into three developmental stages. The first stage, comprising those legislative enactments prior to 1900, may be called a period of little or no federal legislative involvement. The second stage, 1900-1960, was a period of rapid economic and industrial development and can be characterized as a period of conflict in the beliefs of the American people—conflict between the belief that the government that governs least is best and the belief that it is necessary for the national government to ensure the best kind of education for all individuals. The belief was developing during this period that it is the responsibility of the national government to see that people are trained to operate the complex machinery necessary to provide the material and service needs of the nation's people. As a result a number of education acts were passed by the national government, legislation that was characterized by an increasing yet still limited role of the national government in the field of education.

The third developmental stage began in 1960 when the federal government appeared to be entering fully into the educational processes in partnership with the states, local governments, and private institutions. For the first time the federal government seemed to be intentionally influencing, regulating, and controlling in an attempt to ensure that individuals acquire the knowledge, skills, and attitudes needed to develop and maintain careers.

In the pages that follow we shall examine in turn the legislation of each of these stages.

LEGISLATION PRIOR TO 1900

In limiting the powers of the federal government to those specifically provided in the United States Constitution, the Tenth Amendment—in effect since 1791—assured that each state would have the responsibility for educating its citizens. Even so, the federal government realized that the security and welfare of the nation as a whole lay in the ability of an educated citizenry to govern itself. It tried to make some provision for the education of citizens so that they would be competent to govern themselves.

Land Ordinance of 1785 and Northwest Ordinance of 1787

The federal government's first participation in education came indirectly in the form of laws governing the settlement of new territories in the West. In the Ordinance of 1785, Congress required that certain Western lands be divided into six-mile-square townships, which were then to be subdivided into thirty-six sections, with the sixteenth section set aside for the support of education (2). In the Northwest Ordinance of 1787, Congress specified (3): "Religion, morality, and knowledge being necessary to good government and the happiness of mankind, schools and the means of education shall be forever encouraged." By the time that Ohio, the first state in these new Western territories, was admitted to the Union, the practice of setting aside the sixteenth section of each township to support education was firmly established. Without entering directly into the education of the various states, the federal government through these two acts expressed an interest in the education of the nation's citizens.

Morrill Acts and the Hatch Act

During the nation's first century of growth, its industrial and agricultural development depended primarily on the practical, trial-and-error methods of those people carrying on these activities and on their intellectual capacity to be more often right than wrong. Because the purpose of higher education was primarily to prepare men to enter the ministry and law, the pressing needs of the country to apply scientific procedures to the use and development of its natural resources for industry and agriculture were generally ignored, except for attempts on a very small scale in some states. The purposes of grade-school education were primarily to teach reading, writing, arithmetic, and religion and to prepare pupils to enter college to study for the ministry or law.

In the first half of the nineteenth century a few institutions were established that gave indirect opportunities for students to prepare for other, more practical occupations, but these institutions were slow in developing and could not meet the expanding needs of the nation. As it became more evident with the passage of time that the nation's natural resources were being used at a rapid rate and that the need was pressing to prepare individuals for industrial and agricultural careers, the government acted. The Morrill Act of 1862 was the first legislation passed by the national government to support vocational education (4). Proposed by Congressman Justin Smith Morrill of Vermont, the act granted 30,000 acres of land to each state for each senator and representative it had in Congress. Income from the sale of such lands by the states would be used to create and maintain agricultural and mechanical arts colleges. With the passage of this act, the federal government made it possible for many private citizens who could not otherwise do so to prepare themselves for practical careers in agriculture and industry while at the same time acquiring the cultural and intellectual attributes associated with a general education. Institutions of higher education receiving support under the Morrill Act of 1862 came to be known as land-grant colleges because their financial support for vocational programs came primarily from the sale of land provided in the act. This legislation is referred to by Commager (5) as "the most important piece of legislation on behalf of education ever passed."

Additional financial support for the land-grant colleges was later provided through the Second Morrill Act of 1890. The work of these institutions in preparing individuals for careers in agriculture and industry was further supported by the passage of the Hatch Act in 1887. This act provided funds to establish agricultural experiment stations. Such stations worked closely with land-grant institutions to provide help to farmers and to upgrade the nation's agricultural methods.

The Morrill Acts of 1862 and 1890 and the Hatch Act of 1887 advanced the cause of agricultural and industrial education and research in the several states. New agricultural and mechanical arts colleges were established, and some established colleges expanded their curricula to include more practical studies in agriculture and industry. In addition those acts set a precedent for future involvement of the federal government in education. Through various amendments and additions these acts continue their influence.

LEGISLATION BETWEEN 1900 AND 1960

The federal government was much more reluctant to interfere with the rights of states and local communities to provide education at the elementary and secondary levels than it was at the college level. Prior to 1900 the Ordinances of 1785 and 1787 were the only federal acts that affected education at the elementary and secondary levels. However, to show its interest in the education of American citizens in general, the federal government established the United States Office of Education in 1867. The Office of Education was established essentially as a collecting and disseminating agency for educational information. Although its role in education has been greatly expanded, it continues to provide a means of evaluating the effectiveness of educational activities. Although several other attempts were made to pass legislation affecting vocational education below the college level prior to 1900, it was not until the second decade of the twentieth century that such legislation was enacted. The principle of states' rights was too firmly established; the states and local communities were afraid that federal legislation would mean federal control. It was felt that federal control would mean the loss to the states and local communities of the right to determine who should go to school and what should be taught.

By 1900 the nation was beginning to feel that the multiplicity of educational standards, objectives, and beliefs that resulted from relative federal inaction was having serious effects on the welfare of the nation. Under academically oriented curricula, the nation's schools were not meeting the needs of many school-age individuals. Drop outs were excessive. Industry was finding it costly to train its workers. The ability of industry to mass-produce goods was effecting a decline in the classic apprenticeship system as the primary method of developing highly skilled artisans. By assigning workers to perform only one small part of a job, industry could increase production with fewer skilled workers. Under these conditions, the nation was creating a highly uneducated, highly unmotivated class of citizens who, as they reached adulthood, became more and more a burden to the nation rather than productive, contributing citizens.

The nation's leaders began to see the need for a better educated citizenry to cope with the myriad of twentieth-century problems related to population, industrialization, urbanization, automation, and the need for more skilled workers. The clamor began for public educational institutions to perform this training. Noting the lack of attention to these problems on the part of states, local governments, and private institutions, Congress enacted a series of acts that vastly expanded the concept of federal assistance. We shall discuss the more important of these acts as they relate to vocational education.

Smith-Hughes Act

The first federal enactment designed to ease the nation's dilemma was Public Law 64-347, known as the Smith-Hughes Act of 1917 (6). The act was sponsored by Senator Hoke Smith and Representative Dudley Hughes, both from Georgia. Passage of this law followed several years of concerted efforts by professional agricultural and industrial organizations, by congressmen and senators from several states introducing numerous bills and resolutions, and by study commissions to evaluate the state of the art in vocational education. The Commission on Industrial and Technical Education (Douglas Commission of Massachusetts) and the National Society for the Promotion of Industrial Education were highly influential in providing leadership and guidelines for development (7). The Smith-Hughes Act provided funds for three areas of vocational education at the secondary level—agriculture, trade and industry, and home economics. Funds were also provided for the training of teachers in these fields, and provisions were made for the study of the need for commercial education.

To pay salaries of teachers, supervisors, or directors of agricultural subjects, the act appropriated $500,000 for 1918. This amount increased each year until 1926, when $3,000,000 was appropriated. This amount was made permanent for each year thereafter. These funds were allotted to each state on the basis of the proportion of the state's rural population to the total rural population of the nation.

Identical amounts were provided to pay salaries of teachers, supervisors, or directors of trade, home economics, and industrial subjects. These funds were allotted to the various states on the basis of the proportion of the state's urban population to the total urban population of the nation.

To pay for the preparation of teachers, supervisors, and directors of agricultural subjects and teachers of trade and industrial and home economics subjects, the act appropriated $500,000 for 1918. This amount was increased each year until 1921, when $1,000,000 was appropriated. This amount was made permanent for each year thereafter. These funds were allotted to each state on the basis of the proportion of the state's population to total population of the nation.

Note that funds were appropriated in the Smith-Hughes Act to carry out the provisions in the act. These funds were to be perpetual in nature. In most subsequent federal-aid-to-vocational-education legislation the funding has not been appropriated but rather has been authorized to be appropriated. Appropriations for funding have thus required separate legislative acts, and most often the appropriations to carry out the provisions do not equal the authorizations made in the acts.

The Smith-Hughes Act provided controls over the use and administration of these funds. To share in the funds, each state had to designate or to create a state board with power to administer the funds in cooperation with the federal board that was also created by the act. The act designated that the Federal Board of Vocational Education would be composed of the secretaries of agriculture, commerce, and labor; the United States commissioner of education; and three citizens to be appointed by the president and approved by the Senate. One of these persons was to represent manufacturing and commercial interests, one agriculture, and one labor. Their duties were to make studies pertaining to the establishment of vocational schools and to instruction in agriculture, trades and industries, commerce and commercial pursuits, and home economics.

The Smith-Hughes Act also required each state board to prepare plans showing how it expected to use its allotment of funds, the kinds of schools and equipment in use, courses of study, methods of instruction, qualifications of teachers, qualifications of agricultural supervisors and directors, plans for training teachers, and plans for supervising agricultural education. Further, each state was required to submit an annual report of the work done, showing receipts and expenditures. The act provided that funds allotted for salaries of teachers and for training teachers must be matched by the state.

Education for trade, home economics, and industrial education must be provided in schools or classes under public supervision or control. The purpose of such education was to fit students for employment. The education had to be of less than college level for persons over 14 years of age. It provided for cooperative programs for those students not employed and provided that one-third of the funds to pay salaries must be applied to the salaries of teachers of part-time students already employed. The act further provided that the Federal Board of Vocational Education make an annual report to Congress on the administration of the act.

This pioneering piece of legislation stimulated vocational education in two ways: (a) by granting federal funds to the states so that they might encourage local programs, and (b) by setting goals and standards. It was unique in a number of important respects. First, it provided funds for vocational education but earmarked them for specific purposes. Prior educational efforts had allowed wide latitude in state use of funds. Second, it included a $7.2 million permanent appropriation so that vocational educators did not have to appeal to Congress each year for funds. Third, it placed the federal government squarely on record as favoring a more active role in the extension of vocational education.

This example of the federal government's concern for the preparation of the nation's young people for productive adulthood established another precedent for future generations to follow. Although the provisions were narrow and specific, they were forward-reaching and considered appropriate in 1917.

George-Reed Act

The George-Reed Act of 1929 (Public Law 70-702) authorized funds for home economics education and agricultural education (8). The act authorized appropriations to supplement funds provided under the Smith-Hughes Act. These appropriations were to be divided equally between home economics and agriculture, for a five-year period. The authorizations ranged from $500,000 for 1930 to $2,500,000 for 1934.

The authorization did not extend beyond fiscal year 1934. The way of allotting funds under the George-Reed Act was different from the way funds were awarded under the Smith-Hughes Act. Agricultural education funds were allotted on the basis of farm population rather than rural population; home economics education funds were allotted on the basis of rural population rather than urban population.

George-Ellzey Act

The George-Ellzey Act of 1934 (Public Law 73-245) replaced the expiring George-Reed Act (9). It authorized funds as provided in the George-Reed Act through fiscal years 1935, 1936, and 1937, except for an annual authorization of $3 million. Whereas funds authorized by the George-Reed Act were to be divided equally between home economics and agriculture, funds authorized by the George-Ellzey Act were to be divided equally among agriculture, trade and industry, and home economics education. Funds for agriculture and home economics were allotted on the same basis as in the George-Reed Act. Funds for trade and industrial education were allotted on the basis of the proportion of the state's nonfarm population to the total United States nonfarm population, rather than on the basis of the proportion of the state's urban population to the total United States urban population, as provided in the Smith-Hughes Act. The funds in this act were authorized in addition to the continuing funds appropriated in the Smith-Hughes Act.

George-Deen Act

The George-Deen Act of 1936 (Public Law 74-673) replaced the expiring George-Ellzey Act with a continuing authorization, beginning with the 1938 fiscal year (10). For the first time, distributive education was authorized as an appropriation. An authorization of annual appropriations was made to be divided equally among agricultural education, home economics, and trade and industry. Funds were allotted as in the George-Ellzey Act. Funds for distributive education were allotted to each state on the basis of the proportion of the state's population to the total United States population and territories. This is the first act in which federal funds for vocational education were provided for the education of people in territories held by the United States. Authorization was also made for teacher training (above that provided in the Smith-Hughes Act). Through this act the role of the federal government in vocational education was increased substantially.

George-Barden Act

The George-Barden Act of 1946 (Public Law 79-586) expanded the role of the federal government in vocational education even more than did the George-Deen Act (11). One of the major factors contributing to this legislation was the need to provide a means for thousands of returning World War II veterans to acquire employable skills in a rapidly expanding economy. The George-Barden Act amended the George-Deen Act to include additional authorized appropriations annually for agriculture, home economics, trade and industry, and distributive education. From a beginning appropriation in 1917 under the Smith-Hughes Act of $1.5 million for salaries and training of vocational teachers, supervisors, and directors, the federal government had expanded its annual appropriations to over $28 million.

Greater flexibility was provided as to the use of funds. States could use funds for salaries and expenses of state directors of vocational education and vocational counselors, for work experience programs, for youth group activities, and for equipment and supplies. Significant amendments were made to the George-Barden Act in 1956. Practical nursing was added to the federally supported vocational program with an annual authorization of funds. Area vocational programs were provided an annual authorization to 1962.

These legislative acts illustrate an intermediate stage of legislation as the federal government moved toward a total commitment to assisting the states in the development of vocational education. Data in Table 2.1 show the methods of allotting these funds.

Table 2.1   Methods of Allotment of Federal Funds to States*

Acts	Agriculture	Trade industry	Home economics	Distributive education
Smith-Hughes Act	rural	urban	urban	——
George-Reed Act	farm	urban	rural	——
George-Ellzey Act	farm	nonfarm	rural	——
George-Deen Act	farm	nonfarm	rural	total
George-Barden Act	farm	nonfarm	rural	total

*Allotments were made to states according to the ratio a state's population (rural, urban, farm, nonfarm, or total) held to the nation's population (in the same categories). Allotments for teacher training funds under the Smith-Hughes and George-Deen Acts were determined according to the ratio of the state's total population to the national population.

Other Legislation

During the period of rapid industrial, technological, and economic growth and development following World War II, the federal government assumed more and more responsibility and authority toward all aspects of society. In addition to the vocational education acts that have been reviewed here, many other acts were passed between 1900 and 1960 that were aimed primarily toward general education but that had some effect on vocational education. Some of these acts should be briefly reviewed.

The Fess-Kenyon Act was passed in 1920. Known as the Industrial Rehabilitation Act, it provided federal aid for the vocational rehabilitation of industry-disabled persons. This act was preceded by legislation in 1918 that had provided for the rehabilitation of disabled World War I veterans. Although the legislation covered only four years, it was the beginning of a series of supplemental acts. The first appropriation, for the fiscal year ending June 30, 1921, for $.75 million, had grown to an annual appropriation of $3.5 million in 1939. The provisions for administration of the Vocational Rehabilitation Acts and for the participation in them by states (and eventually territories when allotments were made to them) were similar to the provisions for vocational education under Smith-Hughes and subsequent acts. Subsequent amendments included the LaFollette-Barden Act of 1943, which provided for the rehabilitation of war-disabled civilians. The Vocational Rehabilitation Amendments of 1954 authorized new funds and new ways of allotting these funds. By 1957, authorization was made for an annual appropriation of $65 million for vocational rehabilitation.

Another legislative act that affected the direction and development of vocational education was the Servicemen's Readjustment Act of 1944. Known as the GI Bill of Rights, the purpose of this act was to assist World War II veterans to readjust to civilian life. The act subsidized the cost of education and included subsistence for thousands of veterans. Few requirements were placed on the veterans; they simply were to select the kind of training and/or education they wanted, apply for admission to a recognized training program, and maintain the academic standards necessary to continue in the program. The veteran was allowed time for participation in accordance with the time he or she had been in service. Subsequent legislation passed along these benefits to veterans of the Korean War and the Vietnam War.

The National Defense Education Act of 1958 was passed following the Soviet Union's placement of Sputnik I, the first human-made earth satellite, into space, in 1957. The nation felt that this breakthrough indicated that the United States was behind in the sciences, and Congress acted quickly to correct the situation. Vocational education benefited in that the act provided for the training of highly skilled defense technicians in vocational education programs not of college level, and it provided for counseling and guidance programs to identify and encourage able students.

Other federal activities between 1900 and 1960 that have assisted the development of vocational education in the United States include the National Youth Administration, founded in 1935 to provide job training and part-time work for unemployed youths; the Civilian Conservation Corps, founded in 1933 to help unemployed young men obtain work; and the National Science Foundation, created to support research and education primarily in the mathematical, physical, engineering, biological, and medical sciences.

LEGISLATION SINCE 1960

The 1960s were years characterized by turmoil—the Vietnam War, internal social and religious strife, and the frustrating pace of life in a highly complex society. Out of this turmoil grew a social consciousness regarding society's problems. There was a growing consensus that the federal government should act to solve problems of unemployment, of the rising cost of living, of the rights of minority groups, and of the desperate need for qualified skilled workers in business and industry. Whereas the nation was beginning to feel the pinch of having too few trained technicians, it was also beginning to see that it had oversold the necessity of a college education. Despite the steadily increasing involvement of the federal government and the states in more and more expensive programs for vocational education, the problems of unemployment and underemployment continued to grow. There was a deepening concern that the nation's educational system was not meeting the needs of the people. The dominant learning activities in the nation's public schools continued to center around preparation for a college education. With the thrust of educational efforts continuing in this direction, the nation's drop-out problems multiplied; welfare problems mounted as people developed the attitude that "the government will care for me." Growing numbers of people who had no skills, no self-respect, and no values plagued the nation's inner cities and countryside.

One of the first efforts in the 1960s to correct these ills through vocational education was the Manpower Development and Training Act of 1962. This act was designed to train unemployed workers for available jobs and to retrain underemployed workers for jobs with greater responsibilities. A new thrust toward correcting the country's problems was the provision requiring the secretary of labor to make studies of the needs, uses, and development of the nation's workforce.

By the early 1960s the country was ready for massive assaults by the federal government on the problems of unemployment and underemployment. The nation was demanding a reorientation of education to provide for vocational education as well as for college preparation. A panel of consultants on vocational education was appointed at the request of President John F. Kennedy in 1961 to review and reevaluate federal legislation for the purpose of improving vocational education. Much of what was recommended by this panel became a part of the Vocational Education Act of 1963 (12).

Vocational Education Act of 1963

The Vocational Education Act of 1963 (Public Law 88-210) represented the beginning of the federal government's total commitment to vocational education (13). It was the purpose of this act to maintain, extend, and improve existing vocational education programs; to develop new vocational programs; and to provide part-time employment necessary for youths to continue their vocational training on a full-time basis. This legislation was designed to provide all persons with ready access to vocational training or retraining in areas for which they were suited and for which there would be employment opportunities.

The nature of the federal government's commitment to vocational education is exemplified by the fact that authorized appropriations in the Vocational Education Act of 1963 were more than double the authorizations of the George-Barden Act of 1946 and more than eight times the appropriations made under the Smith-Hughes Act in 1926.

Fifty years after the first appropriations of $1.5 million for vocational education under the Smith-Hughes Act, the federal government authorized appropriations that were nearly 150 times greater. Ninety percent of the authorized funds were to be allotted to the states on the basis of formulas designed to consider the number of persons in various age groups needing vocational education and the per capita income in each state. The formula that was used required that 50 percent of the allotted funds be used for the 15–19 age group, 20 percent for the 20–25 age group, 15 percent for the 25–65 age group, and 5 percent for all groups regardless of age. The act defined vocational education as (14):

> *vocational or technical training or retraining which is given in schools or classes (including field or laboratory work incidental thereto) under public supervision and control or under contract with a State board or local educational agency, and is conducted as part of a program designed to fit individuals for gainful employment as semiskilled or skilled workers or technicians in recognized occupations (including any program designed to fit individuals for gainful employment in business and office occupations, and any program designed to fit individuals for gainful employment which may be assisted by Federal funds under the Vocational Education Act of 1946 and supplementary vocational education acts, but excluding any program to fit individuals for employment in occupations which the Commissioner determines, and specifies in regulations, to be generally considered professional or as requiring a baccalaureate or higher degree). Such term includes vocational guidance and counseling in connection with such training, instruction related to the occupation for which the student is being trained or necessary for him to benefit from such training, the training of persons engaged as, or preparing to become vocational education teachers, teacher-trainees, supervisors, and directors for such training, travel of students and vocational education personnel, and the acquisition and maintenance and repair of instructional supplies, teaching aids and equipment, but does not include the construction or initial equipment of buildings or the acquisition or rental of land.*

The act required that an advisory committee on vocational education be established in the United States Office of Education. The responsibility of this committee was to advise the commissioner of education on the preparation of general regulations, on policy matters relating to administration of the act, and on procedures governing approval of state plans. The act also amended the

George-Barden Act and the Smith-Hughes Act to allow more flexibility in the use of funds. For example, funds allotted for agricultural education might be used for vocational education in any occupation involving knowledge and skills in agricultural subjects. It did not require that such occupation involve work on the farm or in the farm home, and such education could be provided without supervised or directed practice on the farm. This flexibility reflected new trends in agri-business activities. By defining programs designed to fit individuals for gainful employment in business and office occupations programs as vocational education, the act gave direct federal support for the first time to business and office education. The act also made permanent allotments to states for extension of practical nurse training.

The Vocational Education Act of 1963 spelled out in detail the provisions for approving work-study programs for persons aged 15 to 20. Funds were to be allotted on the basis of the proportion of each state's population in this group as compared to the total population of this age group in the United States.

The 1963 act was in many ways a landmark piece of federal vocational legislation. It retained the federal-state relationship established by the Smith-Hughes Act and added a requirement that a state must submit a state plan in order to qualify for financial grants. In many other ways, however, this act departed from the approach of the Smith-Hughes Act. The law authorized federal grants, construction of area vocational schools, research and experimentation, and work-study programs in residential vocational schools. It also amended the Smith-Hughes, George-Barden, and National Defense Education Acts, and allowed states to transfer funds among categories and between the various acts.

In the Vocational Education Act of 1963, Congress recognized that it was no longer wise or possible to specify legislatively the particular occupations to be included in the vocational education acts. This recognition represented a departure from all previous vocational legislation. The law thus permitted funds to be used to prepare persons for any recognized occupation, excluding only those occupations considered to be professional or requiring a bachelor's or higher degree. It approved courses at the secondary and postsecondary levels and specifically included courses in community or junior colleges, area vocational schools, and comprehensive high schools. It permitted the use of grant funds for the construction of buildings and the purchase of equipment, when matched with state or local funds. It required states and localities to develop cooperative arrangements with the public employment agency in deciding the occupations for which training was to be given and in providing vocational guidance and counseling.

The 1963 act centered on people in need of vocational education rather than on areas of occupational life. It stated that among those to be served were persons attending high school, persons who had completed high school, persons already at work, and persons with academic, socioeconomic, or other handicaps that prevented their succeeding in regular programs of vocational education. Funds were also provided for teacher education, curriculum development, and program evaluation. A most important provision of the law was the allocation of significant sums of money for research and for pilot programs aimed at improving the scope and quality of vocational education services. The act required that state and local programs be subjected to periodic evaluations for relevance and quality and that a national evaluation of the program be conducted by a special ad hoc commission at five-year intervals. Another section of the law, which was of special interest to local educators, was the provision of funds to compensate students for part-time work activity when students required some income to enroll or remain in an approved vocational program.

The authorization for fiscal year 1964 was set at $60 million; it increased each year to a maximum of $225 million for fiscal 1967 and thereafter. Of these sums, 90 percent were for extension and development programs and were distributed to the states by a formula based on population ratios and per capita income. The remaining 10 percent of the annual appropriation was to be used for research and for experimental and pilot programs.

Funds appropriated for fiscal year 1964 and thereafter were to be matched on a dollar-for-dollar basis by state and local funds. One-third of the individual state's annual allotment prior to 1968, and 25 percent thereafter, was used for youth who had left school and/or for the construction of area schools. Special consideration in making grants was given to areas having substantial numbers of school drop outs and unemployed persons.

The act also provided that no department, agency, officer, or employee of the United States should exercise any direction, supervision, or control over the curriculum, program of instruction, administration, or personnel of any educational institution or school system.

Vocational Education Amendments of 1968

The 1968 amendments to the Vocational Education Act of 1963 (Public Law 90-576) firmly entrenched the federal government's commitment to vocational education (15). In effect, this act virtually canceled all previous vocational education legislation except for the Smith-Hughes Act, which was retained for sentimental reasons as the first legislation passed by the federal government for secondary vocational education. Passage of the 1968 amendments appeared to illustrate a degree of national frustration, as the nation sought frantically for solutions to its growing ills. Despite all the monies channeled into activities designed to alleviate unemployment and underemployment, those problems continued to grow. New solutions would center around a reorientation of educational objectives, with equal emphasis placed on the preparation for work as well as on the preparation for higher education. It was felt that solutions should center on changing people's attitudes about work, helping people to see, to feel, and to think dignity in work, not just dignity in the professions. This act authorized the appropriation of millions of additional dollars for vocational education in the attempt to find solutions to the nation's problems.

The Vocational Education Amendments are divided into three titles: Title I, Amendments to the Vocational Education Act of 1963; Title II, Vocational Education Leadership and Professional Development Amendment of the Higher Education Act of 1965; and Title III, Miscellaneous Provisions. The act is summarized here so that the extent to which the federal government assumed responsibility for promoting vocational preparedness might be examined.

Title I is divided into nine parts—Part A, General Provisions; Part B, State Vocational Education Programs; Part C, Research and Training in Vocational Education; Part D, Exemplary Programs and Projects; Part E, Residential Vocational Education; Part F, Consumer and Homemaking Education; Part G, Cooperative Vocational Education Programs; Part H, Work-Study Programs for Vocational Education Students; and Part I, Curriculum Development in Vocational and Technical Education.

The amendments provided that the National Advisory Council be increased from 12 to 21 members to be appointed by the president for three-year terms. The council became a permanent part of the federal government's control over the use of the funds to serve the nation's needs. Several reports have been issued by the National Advisory Council on Vocational Education. These reports have dealt individually with (a) the national attitude toward vocational education as a system designed for someone else's child; (b) the approach of federal funding to reduce the flow of untrained persons into the pool of unemployment; (c) employment as an integral part of education; (d) the problems involved in local support, state plans, the lack of federal initiative, and the need for effective national planning for vocational education; (e) those forces that appeared to prevent the adoption of some of the recommendations of the first four reports; (f) counseling and guidance and what must be done to provide sound counseling systems; (g) vocational student organizations and their role in vocational and career education; and (h) a national policy on career education. Reports of the National Advisory Council have significantly influenced vocational education legislation.

The amendments of 1968 require much more detailed state plans and thus lead to considerably more control over local programs. For example, the plan must be prepared in consultation with the state advisory council. It must be based on several criteria: periodic evaluations of programs, services, and activities in terms of workforce needs and job opportunities; determination of needs of population groups by geographical locations; and ability of local communities to pay for education. Public hearings must be held to consider the state plan.

Under Part D of Title I, Exemplary Programs and Projects, provision is made to reduce the high level of youth unemployment—particularly those youth with academic, socioeconomic, or other handicaps—by providing occupational orientation and guidance. The purpose of this provision is to stimulate new ways to create a bridge between school and earning a living. Section 143 (a) (2) (A) emphasizes the need to establish, operate, and evaluate exemplary programs designed to familiarize elementary and secondary school students with a broad range of occupations and the special skills that they require. The need to upgrade people in economically depressed areas and in areas of high unemployment in terms of their abilities to be intelligent consumers is emphasized in Part F, Consumer and Homemaking Education.

The 1968 amendments made provision for the complexity of curriculum development caused by the diversity of occupational objectives, by variations due to geography, by differences in educational levels and types of programs, and by the wide range of occupations—agriculture, food processing and preparation, trade and industry, distribution and marketing, technical, public service, health services, business and office occupations. It was the purpose of Part I, Curriculum Development in Vocational and Technical Education, to assist states in developing curricula for new and changing positions and to coordinate improvements in and dissemination of existing curriculum materials.

Title II, Vocational Education Leadership and Professional Development Amendment of the Higher Education Act of 1965, provided a way for experienced vocational educators to spend full time in advanced study for a period not to exceed three years. It provided opportunities to update occupational competencies of vocational education teachers through exchanges of personnel between vocational education programs and commercial, industrial, or other private or public employment and to provide programs of in-service teacher education and short-term institutes for vocational education personnel.

Title III dealt primarily with amendments to the Elementary and Secondary Education Act of 1965, the amendments of 1967, and the Adult Education Act of 1966. It required that the commissioner of education study the feasibility of consolidating all education programs funded by the federal government.

The amendments were, essentially, a rewrite of the 1963 act. The major purpose of the 1968 amendments was to provide ready access for all citizens to suitable training or retraining. Under the provisions of the act funds were authorized on a dollar-for-dollar matching basis to the states to maintain, extend, and improve vocational education.

In addition to providing for continuing general programs and research, the act authorized several short-term programs requiring little or no matching funds from the states: exemplary programs, cooperative training programs, demonstration residential school, dormitory loans, curriculum development, professional development, and disadvantaged programs required no matching funds; work-study programs, 80-20 matching plan (80 percent federal, 20 percent state/local); state grants for residential schools, 90-10 matching plan; and homemaking, 50-50 matching plan.

Education Amendments of 1976

The Education Amendments of 1976 (Public Law 94-482) are divided into five titles (16). Title I, Higher Education, amends the Higher Education Act of 1965; Title II, Vocational Education, amends the Vocational Education Act of 1963; Title III, Extension and Revisions of Other Education Programs, amends and/or extends a number of related federal assistance programs, including the National Defense Education Act of 1958, guidance and counseling, and career education and career development legislation; Title IV, General Education Provisions, deals with administrative provisions, including the National Institute of Education structure and activities; and Title V, Technical and Miscellaneous Provisions, deals with additional administrative provisions, studies of vocational education required of the commissioner of education and the National Institute of Education, and other miscellaneous provisions.

The amendments were the result of the federal government's desire to redirect the education of Americans in an attempt to correct the nation's ills and to change attitudes regarding the roles of men and women in our society. The solutions as described in the act required millions of additional dollars above previous legislation for federal assistance to education and closer supervision of states by federal agencies to regulate the use of funds to carry out the provisions of the act.

One of the major purposes of the Education Amendments of 1976 was to extend and revise the Vocational Education Act of 1963. Federal grants were authorized to states to assist in the following: (a) extending, improving, and maintaining existing programs of vocational education; (b) developing new programs of vocational education; (c) overcoming sex discrimination and sex stereotyping; and (d) providing part-time employment to youths who need earnings to continue their vocational training on a full-time basis.

The act specifically was aimed at eliminating sex discrimination and sex stereotyping. It was intended to provide vocational education for persons in high school; for persons who had completed or discontinued their formal education, preparing to enter the labor market; for persons who had already entered the labor market but need to upgrade their skills or learn new ones; and for persons in postsecondary schools. It was aimed at providing these persons with ready access to vocational training or retraining of high quality that is realistic in the light of actual or anticipated opportunities for gainful employment, and that is suited to their needs, interests, and abilities to benefit from such training.

The amendments specifically empowered state boards or agencies appointed to supervise and administer programs: (1) to create awareness of programs and activities in vocational education designed to reduce sex stereotyping; (2) to gather, analyze, and disseminate data on the status of men and women, students, and employees in vocational education; (3) to correct any problems in sex discrimination and stereotyping; (4) to ensure that the interests and needs of women are addressed; (5) to review all programs for sex bias; (6) to monitor laws prohibiting sex discrimination in hiring, firing, and promotion procedures; (7) to review and submit recommendations to overcome sex stereotyping and sex bias, to assist in improving vocational education opportunities for women; and (8) to provide information relevant to sex discrimination and sex stereotyping to appropriate agencies.

The act made specific recommendations for the makeup, duties, and organizational structure of state and local advisory councils to monitor vocational programs. Programs shall relate to activities conducted under the Comprehensive Employment and Training Act of 1973 to ensure a coordinated approach to meeting vocational education and training needs. The act established that priority should be given to applicants located in economically depressed areas and in areas with high rates of unemployment and to applicants proposing programs new to the area and designed to meet new and emerging workforce needs and job opportunities. The act required that each state submit a five-year plan for vocational education every fifth year, beginning in 1977. Persons representing all agencies involved in vocational education must participate in formulating the plan. These agencies are specifically designated. The act also required each state to submit an annual program plan and accountability report for each year of the five-year plan.

Certain national priority programs are established by the amendments: vocational education for handicapped persons, for disadvantaged persons (other than the handicapped), for persons of limited English-speaking ability, for persons who have completed or left high school and who are enrolled in organized programs of study for which credit is given toward an associate or other degree not leading to a baccalaureate or higher degree, and for persons who have already entered the labor market or who are unemployed.

Other new directions given attention in the amendments are (1) energy education; (2) preparation of women for jobs traditionally limited to men; (3) day care services for children of students; (4) persons who had solely been homemakers but who now, because of dissolution of marriage, must seek employment; (5) single heads of households who lack adequate job skills; (6) homemakers and part-time workers who wish to secure full-time jobs; (7) women who are now in jobs traditionally considered jobs for females and who wish to seek employment in job areas not traditionally considered appropriate for females; and (8) men who are now in jobs traditionally considered jobs for males and who wish to seek employment in job areas not traditionally considered appropriate for males.

The amendments permit states to make grants to postsecondary educational institutions to carry out energy education programs for the training of miners, supervisors, technicians (particularly safety personnel), and environmentalists in the field of coal mining and coal mining technology, including acquisition of equipment. Grants may also be made to postsecondary institutions to train individuals to install solar energy equipment.

The amendments continue funding for exemplary and innovative programs, including (1) those in urban centers with high concentrations of economically disadvantaged individuals, unskilled workers, and unemployed workers; (2) training opportunities for persons in sparsely populated rural areas and for individuals migrating from farms to urban areas; (3) programs for individuals with limited English-speaking ability; (4) cooperative arrangements between public education and manpower agencies, designed to correlate vocational education opportunities with current and projected needs in the labor market; and (5) programs designed to broaden occupational aspirations and opportunities of youth, with special emphasis given to youth with academic, socioeconomic, or other handicaps. Included will be programs and projects to familiarize elementary and secondary school students with the broad range of occupations for which special skills are required, with the prerequisites for careers in such occupations, and with programs and projects to facilitate the participation of employers and labor organizations in postsecondary vocational education.

The amendments also deal with vocational guidance and counseling. Provision was made to bring individuals with experience in business and industry, the professions, and other occupational pursuits into schools as counselors or advisors for students and to bring students into work establishments of business and industry, the professions, and other occupational pursuits for the purpose of acquainting students with the nature of the work. Provision was also made for guidance counselors to gain experience in business and industry, the professions, and other occupational pursuits, so that they can better carry out their guidance and counseling duties.

The continuing need for consumer and homemaking education is reemphasized in the amendments, with particular consideration to the changing roles of men and women as workers and homemakers.

The amendments provide for the development of a national vocational education data reporting and accounting system, to be coordinated as much as possible with the occupational information data system. The National Advisory Council on Vocational Education, first established under the Vocational Education Act of 1963, was continued by the amendments with some changes to reflect new emphases and national priorities as described in the amendments.

The amendments specified that one of the most acute problems in the United States is the millions of citizens, both children and adults, whose efforts to profit from vocational education are severely restricted by their limited English-speaking ability because they come from environments where the primary language is other than English. The act identified a shortage of qualified personnel to teach such individuals and a lack of appropriate curriculum materials to use in teaching them. The amendments made provisions for dealing with these problems in vocational education.

The amendments also extended federal assistance for such programs as career education and the National Institute of Education (NIE). Many of the changes regarding the implementation of career education and the responsibilities and duties of the NIE reflect new national priorities, such as overcoming sex discrimination and sex stereotyping; improving the lot of socially, economically, or educationally disadvantaged persons; improving the lot of individuals with limited English-speaking abilities; and improving student achievement in the basic educational skills, including reading and mathematics. The amendments authorized the director of the NIE to make grants to and enter into contracts with regional educational laboratories and research and development centers established by institutions of higher education or by interstate agencies to conduct postsecondary educational research and development. The amendments also required the director of the NIE to establish a Panel for the Review of Laboratory and Center Operations. Also established within the NIE was a Federal Council on Educational Research and Development. The major purpose of this council was to coordinate programs and activities of the NIE and related programs and activities of other federal agencies.

Other Legislation

During the 1960s the federal government became totally committed to the development of "our nation's most priceless resource"—education. Other acts that were not directly aimed at vocational education nevertheless contributed financially and in other ways to vocational efforts. Many vocational programs directly benefited from such legislation as the Elementary and Secondary Education Act of 1965 and its subsequent amendments (17). The purposes of this act were to bring better education to millions of educationally disadvantaged youth; to put the best educational equipment, ideas, and innovations within reach of all students; to advance the technology of teaching and the training of teachers; and to provide incentive to those who wished to learn. In addition the act recognized the relationship between low achievers and poverty; the correspondence between quality teachers and instructional resources and effective teaching and learning; and the gap between current educational research and existing practices.

Other federal programs passed in the 1960s that supported education include the following:

Section 12 of the National Foundation on the Arts and the Humanities Act of 1965

Economic Opportunity Act of 1964

Educational Television Facilities Program of 1962

Higher Education Facilities Act of 1963

Higher Education Act of 1965, Education Professions Development Act

The Education Amendments of 1972 (Public Law 92-318) amended the Higher Education Act of 1965, the Vocational Education Act of 1963, the General Education Provisions Act, the Elementary and Secondary Education Act of 1965, and other acts, in addition to making other provisions. One of the provisions of the 1972 amendments, Section 1056 (b) (1) (D) of Title X, calls for the (18):

development of a long-range strategy for infusing occupational education (including general orientation, counseling and guidance, and placement either in a job or in postsecondary occupational programs) into elementary and secondary schools on an equal footing with traditional academic education, to the end that every child who leaves secondary school is prepared either to enter productive employment or to undertake additional education at the postsecondary level, but without being forced prematurely to make an irrevocable commitment to a particular educational or occupational choice . . .

The amendments define postsecondary occupational education as (19):

education, training, or retraining (and including guidance, counseling, and placement services) for persons 16 years of age or older who have graduated from or left elementary or secondary school, conducted by an institution legally authorized to provide postsecondary education within a State, which is designed to prepare individuals for gainful employment as semi-skilled or skilled workers or technicians or subprofessionals in recognized occupations (including new and emerging occupations), or to prepare individuals for enrollment in advanced technical education programs, but excluding any program to prepare individuals for employment in occupations which the Commissioner determines, and specifies by regulations, to be generally considered professional or which requires a baccalaureate or advanced degree.

In addition the amendments provided for the establishment of a Bureau of Occupational and Adult Education in the United States Office of Education. Title II incorporated industrial arts education into the definition of vocational education where it contributed to the purposes of vocational education. It also included volunteer firefighters. The provisions of vocational education were extended through the year 1975. Consumer education, the lack of it and the need for it, received further attention in the amendments of 1972. The act encouraged and supported development of new, improved curricula to prepare consumers for participation in the marketplace. It created the position of director of consumer education in the Office of Education. The amendments also dealt with assignment and transportation of students to school and with sex discrimination.

The Education Amendments of 1974 (Public Law 93-380) provided firm support to career education (20). In this act Congress expressed the need for every person completing secondary school to be prepared for gainful or maximum employment according to ability. Congress also provided that each state and local educational agency should carry out a program in career education. The importance Congress attached to career education was further emphasized in the act with the establishment of the Office of Career Education in the United States Office of Education. In addition, the National Advisory Council on Career Education was established to advise the commissioner of education on matters relating to the development, implementation, and evaluation of vocational education throughout the United States and to determine the need for future legislation.

Public Law 93-203, the Comprehensive Employment and Training Act of 1973 (21), and Public Law 95-924, the Comprehensive Employment and Training Act Amendments of 1978 (22), are both becoming increasingly important to vocational education. The purpose of both of these acts is to provide job training and employment opportunities for economically disadvantaged, unemployed, and underemployed persons. Both were enacted to ensure that training and other services lead to maximum employment opportunities and to enhance self-sufficiency through a flexible and decentralized system of federal, state, and local programs. The amendments provide for maximum feasible coordination of plans, programs, and activities with economic development, community development, and related activities, such as vocational education, vocational rehabilitation, public assistance, self-employment training, and social service programs. Although the act is administered by the Department of Labor, it establishes, just as other recent legislation does, means to ensure coordination and cooperation among the agencies concerned.

The Education for All Handicapped Children Act of 1975 (Public Law 94-142) contains significant and far-reaching provisions regarding the role of vocational education in serving the handicapped (23). It is the purpose of this act (1) to ensure that all handicapped children have available a free, appropriate public education emphasizing special education and related services designed to meet their unique needs, and (2) to assist states and local agencies in providing for the education of all handicapped children. It requires that handicapped learners be educated with nonhandicapped students to the maximum extent appropriate (mainstreaming). Special classes and special schools are to be used only when the nature or severity of the handicap requires supplementary services and aids that cannot be effectively provided through regular classes. Individualized instructional programs must be written for each handicapped student, and vocational teachers, counselors, and coordinators of handicapped students are required to participate in the writing of the programs.

SUMMARY

This chapter has focused on the influence of federal legislation on the development of vocational-technical education. For purposes of study, the legislation was arbitrarily divided into three stages: (a) legislation passed prior to 1900, (b) legislation passed between 1900 and 1960, and (c) legislation passed since 1960.

Five major acts passed during the decades before 1900 that affected the development of federal legislation are presented in this chapter. The Land Ordinance of 1785 and the Northwest Ordinance of 1787 established the federal government's interest in the education of United States citizens. The Land Ordinance of 1785 required that newly developing territories set aside land for the support of education, and the Northwest Ordinance of 1787 encouraged the establishment of schools and the means of education. The Morrill Acts of 1862 and 1890 provided support to establish and maintain agricultural and mechanical arts colleges. The Hatch Act of 1887 provided funds for the establishment of agricultural experiment stations. These acts reflected the need for a more scientific approach to the development of agriculture and industry.

The period between 1900 and 1960 was characterized by rapid development of the technology necessary to support an expanding industry, and by social, civil, and economic strife. During this period two world wars took place, a major depression occurred, and the civil rights movement was started. Public educational institutions were more concerned with the intellectual development of individuals than they were with preparing individuals for work. During this period there was an increasing need for skilled workers, and the nation looked primarily to the federal government to provide a means for training skilled workers. The Smith-Hughes Act of 1917 was the first of a series of acts designed with this purpose in mind. The act provided support for vocational education at the secondary level. It included support for agriculture, trade and industry, and home economics. Other acts passed during this period and supporting vocational education included the George-Reed Act of 1929, George-Ellzey Act of 1934, George-Deen Act of 1936, George-Barden Act of 1946, Fess-Kenyon Act of 1920, LaFollette-Barden Act of 1943, Servicemen's Readjustment Act of 1944, and the National Defense Education Act of 1958. All of these acts were directed toward improving the education of individuals through vocational education, increasing the availability of skilled workers, and thereby attacking some of the social, civic, and economic ailments of the nation.

The third stage, the period since 1960, has been characterized by a total commitment of the federal government to vocational education—in partnership with the states, local governments, and private institutions, yet intentionally influencing, regulating, and controlling education. The federal government has been attempting, in its legislation, to ensure that all individuals acquire the knowledge, skills, and attitudes needed to develop and to maintain careers. The legislation that has grown out of this total commitment includes the Manpower Development and Training Act of 1962, Vocational Education Act of 1963, Vocational Education Amendments of 1968, Elementary and Secondary Education Act of 1965, the Education Amendments of 1972, the Comprehensive Employment and Training Act of 1973, the Education Act of 1974, the Education for All Handicapped Children Act of 1975, the Career Education Incentive Act (1977), the Education Amendments of 1976, and the Comprehensive Employment and Training Act Amendments of 1978. The Vocational Education Act of 1963 brought most of the legislation passed prior to that time, except for the Smith-Hughes Act, into its provisions. With the legislation passed since 1960, the federal government has made a dedicated attempt to redirect the public education processes so that career development and preparation of individuals for work becomes as much a part of the goals, objectives, and activities of education as are intellectual development and the preparation of individuals for college.

The following list of selected federal educational legislation, each of which contained support for vocational services, provides a capsule view of the history of federal legislation.

Year	Program
1787	Northwest Ordinance—authorized land grants for the establishment of educational institutions.
1862	First Morrill Act—authorized public land grants to the states for the establishment and maintenance of agricultural and mechanical colleges.
1890	Second Morrill Act—provided for money grants for support of instruction in the agricultural and mechanical colleges.
1917	Smith-Hughes Act—provided for grants to states for support of vocational education.
1918	Vocational Rehabilitation Act—authorized funds for rehabilitation of World War I veterans.
1920	Smith-Bankhead Act—authorized grants to states for vocational rehabilitation programs.
1935	Bankhead-Jones Act—made grants to states for agricultural experiment stations.
1943	Vocational Rehabilitation Act—provided assistance to disabled veterans.
1944	Servicemen's Readjustment Act—provided assistance for the education of veterans.
1946	George-Barden Act—expanded federal support for vocational education.
1954	Cooperative Research Act—authorized cooperative arrangements with universities, colleges, and state education agencies for educational research.
1957	Practical Nurse Training Act—provided grants to states for practical nurse training.
1958	National Defense Education Act—provided assistance to state and local school systems for strengthening instruction in science, mathematics, foreign languages, and other critical subjects; improvement of state statistical services; guidance, counseling, and testing services and training institutes; higher education student loans and fellowships; ex-

Year	Program

perimentation and dissemination of information on more effective use of television, motion picture, and related media for educational purposes; and vocational education for technical occupations, such as data processing, necessary to the national defense.

Public Law 89-926—federal assistance for training teachers of the handicapped, was authorized.

1961 Area Redevelopment Act—included provisions for training or retraining persons in redevelopment areas.

1962 Manpower Development and Training Act—provided training in new and improved skills for the unemployed and underemployed.

1963 Vocational Education Act of 1963—increased federal support of vocational education, including support of residential vocational schools, vocational work-study programs, and research, training, and demonstrations in vocational education.

Health Professions Educational Assistance Act—provided funds to expand teaching facilities and for loans to students in the health professions.

Higher Education Facilities Act—authorized grants and loans for classrooms and laboratories in public community colleges and technical institutes as well as for undergraduate and graduate facilities in other institutions of higher education.

1964 Economic Opportunity Act—authorized grants for college work-study programs for students of low-income families; established a Job Corps program and authorized support for work-training programs to provide education and vocational training and work experience for unemployed youth; provided training and work experience opportunities in welfare programs; authorized support of education and training activities and of community action programs including Head Start, Follow Through, Upward Bound; authorized the establishment of the Volunteers in Service to America (VISTA).

1965 Elementary and Secondary Education Act—authorized grants for elementary and secondary school programs for children of low-income families; school library resources, textbooks, and other instructional materials for school children; supplementary educational centers and services; strengthening state education agencies; and educational research and development training.

Health Professions Educational Assistance Amendments—authorized scholarships to aid needy students in the health professions and grants to improve the quality of teaching in schools of medicine, dentistry, osteopathy, optometry, and podiatry.

Year	Program
	Higher Education Act—provided grants for university community service programs, college library assistance, library training and research, strengthening developing institutions, and educational opportunity; insured student loans; teacher training programs; and undergraduate instructional equipment. Established a National Teacher Corps and provided for graduate teacher training fellowships.
	Medical Library Assistance Act—provided assistance for construction and improvement of health sciences libraries.
	National Vocational Student Loan Insurance Act—encouraged state and nonprofit private institutions and organizations to establish adequate loan insurance programs to assist students to attend postsecondary business, trade, technical, and other vocational schools.
1966	International Education Act—provided grants to institutions of higher education for the establishment, strengthening, and operation of centers for research and training in international studies and the international aspects of professional and other fields of study.
	Adult Education Act—authorized grants to states for the encouragement and expansion of educational programs for adults, including training of teachers of adults and demonstrations in adult education (previously part of Economic Opportunity Act of 1964).
1967	Education Professions Development Act—amended the Higher Education Act of 1965 for the purpose of improving the quality of teaching and to help meet critical shortages of adequately trained educational personnel by authorizing support for the development of information on needs for educational personnel, training and retraining opportunities responsive to changing labor needs; attracting persons who can stimulate creativity in the arts and other skills to undertake short-term and long-term assignments in education; and helping to make educator training more responsive to the needs of schools and colleges.
1968	Vocational Education Amendments—changed the basic formula for allotting funds; provided for a National Advisory Council on Vocational Education, expansion of vocational education services to meet the needs of the disadvantaged, and the collection and dissemination of information on programs administered by the commissioner of education.
1971	Comprehensive Health Manpower Training Act—increased and expanded provisions for nurse training facilities.
1972	Education Amendments—established a National Institute of Education; general aid for institutions of higher education; federal matching grants for state student incentive grants; a National Commission on Financing Postsecondary Education; State Advisory Councils on Community Col-

Year	Program

leges; a Bureau of Occupational and Adult Education; state grants for the design, establishment, and conduct of postsecondary occupational education; and a bureau-level Office of Indian Education.

1973 Comprehensive Employment and Training Act—consolidated previous labor and public service programs; authorized funds for employment counseling, supportive services, classroom training, training on the job, work experience, and public service employment; incorporated essential principles of revenue sharing, giving state and local governments more control over use of funds and determination of programs.

1974 Education Amendments—established the National Center for Educational Statistics; continued research activities under the Education for the Handicapped Act.

1975 Education for All Handicapped Children Act—provided free, appropriate public education to the handicapped; provided funds to integrate handicapped children into regular schools and classes to the maximum extent possible.

1976 Education Amendments—extended and revised the Vocational Education Act of 1963 and the Vocational Education Amendments of 1963. Permits more latitude to states in the use of funds by consolidating programs into the basic grant. There are four exceptions: special programs for the disadvantaged, consumer and homemaking education, bilingual vocational training, and emergency assistance for remodeling and renovating vocational education facilities.

1977 Career Education Incentive Act—assisted states and local education agencies and institutions of postsecondary education in making preparation for work a major goal of all who teach and all who learn.

1978 Comprehensive Employment and Training Amendments of 1978— provided for continuation of the Comprehensive Employment and Training Act of 1973 and the Manpower Development and Training Act of 1962. Ensured coordination and cooperation among all federal, state, and local private and public agencies involved in the vocational education and training of workers.

ACTIVITIES

For review

1. Identify two strong beliefs of early settlers of the United States that affected the role of government in education.
2. Why were states and local communities afraid of legislation by the federal government?

3. What belief is considered to be the backbone of the free enterprise system?

4. Why did Commager think it necessary for the federal government to become involved with educational problems?

5. Name legislative ordinances and acts prior to 1900 that proved significant to vocational education.

6. Why was the United States Office of Education established? the Department of Education?

7. What was the first major legislation appropriating money for vocational education for secondary schools?

8. Who made up the Federal Board of Vocational Education as designated by the Smith-Hughes Act?

9. What type of vocational education was provided by the (a) Smith-Hughes Act, (b) George-Reed Act, and (c) George-Ellzey Act?

10. Under what act was distributive education first appropriated?

11. On what basis were funds for distributive education allotted to each state?

12. What was the common name of the Servicemen's Readjustment Act of 1944?

13. State the purpose of the Manpower Development and Training Act of 1962.

14. When did the federal government make a total commitment to vocational education?

15. State the purpose of the Vocational Education Act of 1963.

16. What was the responsibility of the Advisory Committee on Vocational Education established in the United States Office of Education?

17. What is the purpose of the Comprehensive Employment and Training Act?

18. Define mainstreaming.

For discussion

1. Contrast the social and economic conditions of people during the three developmental stages of federal legislation for vocational education as discussed in this chapter: (a) prior to 1900, (b) 1900–1960, and (c) 1960–present. Include specific legislation enacted during each period.

2. The idea is presented in this chapter that individuals who are governing and being governed are greater than the government itself. Would we have the same type of vocational education in the United States today if our system of government were such that the government was considered more important than the worth and dignity of the individual citizen?

3. Contrast the provisions of the George-Reed Act with the provisions of the Smith-Hughes Act.

4. Relate the following statement to the Manpower Development and Training

Act of 1962: The climate was right to reorient people toward the dignity of work.

5. What are the similarities between the Vocational Education Act of 1963 and the 1968 amendments? How are they different?

6. Discuss occupational education as provided by the Education Amendments of 1972.

For exploration

1. Investigate sixteenth-section land as provided in the Land Ordinance of 1785:
   (a) Does it exist in your county or parish?
   (b) Is income derived from it? If so, how is it obtained and used?
   (c) If no sixteenth-section land exists, how was it disposed of?

2. Determine through interviews with education officials and legislators and through published research the methods used to allocate funds for vocational education on the local, state, and national levels.

3. Prepare brief biographical sketches of the following people, including milestones in their lives that led them to support vocational education:
   (a) Hoke Smith
   (b) Dudley Hughes
   (c) Carl Perkins
   (d) Henry Steele Commager
   (e) Justin Smith Morrill

4. Compare the responsibilities of the Advisory Committee on Vocational Education in the U.S. Office of Education as authorized by the Vocational Education Act of 1963 to the responsibility of a local advisory committee for vocational education.

5. Read and evaluate one article on federal legislation pertaining to vocational education.

6. Debate the following topics:
   (a) Resolved, that vocational education is designed only for the economically, socially, and culturally deprived.
   (b) Resolved, that the Smith-Hughes Act is the most significant federal legislation passed affecting the development of vocational education.

7. Consult with educational, manpower, government, and/or labor officials to determine the types and sources of federal funds to finance vocational education programs in your locality. Identify specific acts under which funds are being received.

8. Research state and federal activities for the five years preceding the passage of the Smith-Hughes Act.

9. Investigate the most recent federal legislation not discussed in this chapter

that has become law. How is it similar to the legislation discussed? How is it different? How does it affect vocational education in your community? In your state? Invite a knowledgeable official to discuss this legislation with your class.

10. Investigate the work of the Douglas Commission, appointed in 1905 to examine manual training programs in Massachusetts. What influence did the commission have on vocational education in the United States?

REFERENCES

1. Henry Steel Commager, "Only the National Government . . .," *Today's Education,* Vol. 62, No. 6, Sept.-Oct. 1973, pp. 47-48.

2. John C. Fitzpatrick, ed., *Journals of the Continental Congress, 1774-1789,* Vol. 28 (Washington, D.C.: Government Printing Office, 1933), pp. 375-86.

3. Francis N. Thorpe, ed., *The Federal and State Constitutions, Colonial Charters, and Other Organic Laws,* Vol. 2 (Washington, D.C.: Government Printing Office, 1909), p. 961.

4. George P. Sanger, ed., *The Statutes at Large, Treaties, and Proclamations of the United States of America,* December 5, 1859, to March 3, 1863, Vol. 12 (Boston: Little, Brown & Company, 1863), pp. 503-5.

5. Henry Steele Commager, ed., *Documents of American History,* 4th ed., Vol. I (New York: Appleton-Century-Crofts, Inc., 1948), p. 412.

6. Public Law 64-347, *The Statutes at Large . . . ,* December 1915 to March 1917, Vol. 39, Part I (Washington, D.C.: Government Printing Office, 1917), pp. 929-36.

7. John A. McCarthy, *Vocational Education: America's Greatest Resource* (Chicago: American Technical Society, 1950), pp. 15-39.

8. Public Law 70-702, *The Statutes at Large . . . ,* December 1927 to March 1929, Vol. 45, Part I (Washington, D.C.: Government Printing Office, 1929), p. 1151.

9. Public Law 73-245, *The Statutes at Large . . . ,* March 1933 to June 1934, Vol. 48, Part I (Washington, D.C.: Government Printing Office, 1934), pp. 792-93.

10. Public Law 74-673, *The Statutes at Large . . . ,* January 1935 to June 1936, Vol. 49, Part I (Washington, D.C.: Government Printing Office, 1936), pp. 1488-90.

11. "Vocational Education Act of 1946," Public Law 79-586, *United States Statutes at Large,* 1946, Vol. 60, Part I (Washington, D.C.: Government Printing Office, 1947), pp. 775-78.

12. Panel of Consultants on Vocational Education, *Education for a Changing World of Work* (Washington, D.C.: Government Printing Office, 1963).

13. "Vocational Education Act of 1963," Public Law 88-210, *United States Statutes at Large,* 1963, Vol. 77 (Washington, D.C.: Government Printing Office, 1964), pp. 403-19.

14. Ibid., p. 408.

15. "Vocational Education Amendments of 1968," Public Law 90-576, *United States Statutes at Large,* 1968, Vol. 82 (Washington, D.C.: Government Printing Office, 1969), pp. 1064-98.

16. "Education Amendments of 1976," Public Law 94-482, *United States Statutes at Large,* 1976, Vol. 90 (Washington, D.C.: Government Printing Office, 1977).

17. "Elementary and Secondary Education Act of 1965," Public Law 89-10, *United States Statutes at Large,* 1965, Vol. 79 (Washington, D.C.: Government Printing Office, 1966), pp. 27-58.

18. "Education Amendments of 1972," Public Law 92-318, *United States Statutes at Large,* 1972, Vol. 86 (Washington, D.C.: Government Printing Office, 1973), p. 319.

19. Ibid., p. 322.

20. "Education Amendments of 1974," Public Law 93-380, *United States Statutes at Large,* 1974, Vol. 88 (Washington, D.C.: Government Printing Office, 1975).

21. "Comprehensive Employment and Training Act of 1973," Public Law 93-203, *United States Statutes at Large,* 1973, Vol. 87 (Washington, D.C.: Government Printing Office, 1974).

22. "Comprehensive Employment and Training Act Amendments of 1978," Public Law 95-924, *United States Statutes at Large,* 1978, Vol. 92 (Washington, D.C.: Government Printing Office, 1979).

23. "Education for All Handicapped Children Act of 1975," Public Law 94-142, *United States Statutes at Large,* 1975, Vol. 89 (Washington, D.C.: Government Printing Office, 1976).

CHAPTER THREE

■

Factors Influencing the Development of Vocational-Technical Education

INTRODUCTION

In this chapter we shall look at the philosophical construct for vocational education. This chapter focuses on the effects of three foundational factors on the evolving philosophy of vocational education: (1) philosophical factors—what knowledge and/or skill is of most value to teach? (2) economic factors—how do labor-market needs affect career development? and (3) sociological factors—what are the effects of social class and industrialization on preparation for vocations?

PHILOSOPHICAL FACTORS

Vocational educators recognize that two questions are fundamental to the development of a sound vocational program: what should be taught, and how should it be taught? Answers to these questions involve the establishment of priorities. Over the years some fundamental assumptions and principles have evolved that tend to unify and direct vocational education planning. Our beliefs about the individual and his or her role in a democratic society and about the role of education in the transmission of socially approved standards are the source of these fundamental principles.

With the development of a democratic philosophy of education in the United States, universal schooling became part of the national ideology.

Maximizing each individual's chances for lifelong learning and attainment of the "good life" became the ultimate goal of our educational system. Because it was necessary for most Americans to work in order to eat, the vocational objective became an important link in the educational chain.

Naturally, there is disagreement as to what the goals of vocational education should be. But current beliefs and practices are rather firmly rooted in the historical development of the field. The Morrill Act of 1862 placed the national government and the states in support of publicly financed education designed to train youth in two kinds of occupations that predominated at that time— agriculture and industry. Consequently, the development of vocational education was, from that point, tied closely to specific federal legislation. The philosophy and objectives of vocational education leaders were reflected in the provisions of controlling legislation.

Many of those who led the fight for the introduction of vocational education into the school curriculum did so because of a strong philosophical commitment to equality of educational opportunity. They believed that the high school of that time was concerned only with the needs of youths who were preparing for college. Because education beyond high school was pursued by only a very small minority of college-age young people, the college-preparation emphasis was held to be undemocratic and unfair to the great majority of young people, most of whom never finished high school.

Changing School Population

At the time when the famous representative committees of the National Education Association (NEA) began their work around 1893, there were only about 700,000 students in the high schools. The purposes of American secondary schools were narrow and incoherent until the committees of the NEA began to study the broad goals of the secondary school in our country. For example, the Committee of Ten in 1893 gave direction to schools and helped standardize the curriculum of the high schools. The Committee on College Relations in 1897 helped standardize college entrance requirements. The Commission on the Purposes of Secondary Education proposed the Seven Cardinal Principles of Education in 1918. The work of these and later committees clarified the goals and problems of secondary education and established the principle that the schools' purpose was preparation for life rather than for further education.

At the end of the nineteenth century, the secondary school population was still relatively homogenous, coming from about the same family backgrounds and preparing to enter occupations favored by the higher echelons of society. In contrast, the high schools of today harbor young people with widely varying aptitudes and abilities. More students are staying in school for longer periods of time. Many students, however, leave school before graduating, while many who remain participate much more passively than actively in their education. They may be potentially good citizens, but their interests lie outside, not inside, the school. It is unrealistic to believe that these young people can be attracted by the kind of exercises in abstract thinking that characterize much of the high school curriculum.

In an attempt to ensure that school curricula and courses are more relevant, some state and local education agencies are identifying minimum competencies to be demonstrated by all students prior to graduation. These competencies are usually related to the life roles of an individual, such as consumer, producer, and citizen. The increasing number of comprehensive high schools is indicative of the need to provide educational opportunities to students with wide ranges of abilities, achievements, and goals.

Socialization of Education

Whether we like it or not the American high school is not merely a scholastic institution; it is also a social institution. From the beginning, sociological and humanistic reasons have been used to justify the need for vocational education. There may also be a socioeconomic component, for it can be argued that those who are trained for a job, and so become wage earners, will more likely turn out to be contributing citizens who will be assets to society. By performing its primary function of preparation for useful employment, vocational education is likely to contribute indirectly to many other social benefits.

It is characteristic of the socialization of the high school that the only committee report of the NEA that had an effect similar to that of the Committee of Ten, namely the report of the *Cardinal Principles of Secondary Education* in 1918, defines the goal of education in a democracy in the following terms (1):

> The purpose of democracy is so to organize society that each member may develop his personality primarily through activities designed for the well-being of his fellow members and of society as a whole. . . .
>
> Consequently, education in a democracy, both within and without the school, should develop in each individual the knowledge, interests, ideals, habits, and powers whereby he will find his place and use that place to shape both himself and society toward ever nobler ends.

That was obviously a commendable goal. But a comparison of the emphasis on subject matter in the work of the Committee of Ten with the main ideas of the report on cardinal principles reveals a change from subject-centeredness, however diluted, to a social concept of education. The committee's seven cardinal principles of secondary education identified the goals for survival and social adjustment that would provide the common core of study for all: health, command of the fundamental processes, worthy home membership, vocation, citizenship, worthy use of leisure, and ethical character. To understand the change, it is worthwhile to remember that the report on the cardinal principles was written at the end of World War I, a war that had had a calamitous effect on the stability of education. A period of intense analysis and reformation of American education was underway.

Influence of Pragmatism

In the first quarter of the twentieth century, there occurred not only an enormous shift in school population but also a profound philosophical rethinking of the nature of education. Men such as William James and John Dewey were propounding a new philosophy—known as pragmatism, instrumentalism, or experimentalism—which, for many teachers, was quickly replacing the German-influenced idealism and the religious interpretation of education. Historically, pragmatism entered a vacuum that had already been opened by the disintegration of transcendentalism. The new philosophy offered the prospect of a more valid or "scientific" method, which the new "Science of Education," as well as the other "social sciences"—still uncertain of themselves—were most anxious to acquire. Pragmatism emphasized the concrete over the more abstract problems of life; it showed the significance of social institutions and the evolutionary character of societies and their ideologies. In fostering "progressive" education, it also gave the professionally interested teacher new hope that through the introduction of these experimental methods there might be an increasing chance to develop student initiative, rather than merely to convey year after year the same subject matter, irrespective of the interests of the students.

The pragmatic revolt, which was climaxed by James (2), Bode (3), Dewey (4), and Kilpatrick (5), had an enormous effect on American education. Within less than 100 years American education changed profoundly, partially because of the influence of these thinkers, who believed that education, like science, ought to be emancipated from traditionalism and based on scientific methodology and scientific assumptions. The educator should turn to the problem-solving method, which involved a felt need, analysis of the problem, experimentation with various solutions, tentative theories, verification, and the forming of a conclusion that could be concretely applied. Like the scientists, educators should be hypothetical in their approach to life, and they should be more concerned with methodology than with ultimate standards.

John Dewey was a strong proponent of vocational education. Traditional liberal education had created a snobbish spirit; it had led to a worship of the classics and had created a disdain for manual activity. Vocational education would bridge the gulf between knowledge and action and would develop a more cooperative spirit through learning by doing. The distinction between the fine arts and the industrial arts was to be minimized. *Talk* about art was regarded as being inferior to *experience* in art. Dewey contended that traditional liberal education did not provide the skills and attitudes necessary for living in an age of science.

Vocational vs. General Education

Early spokespersons for vocational education defined the general education offerings of the high schools and colleges as liberal education. They considered these liberal studies to be education for an aristocratic elite, a type of education that was contrary to the spirit of American democracy. Vocational education was needed, they felt, as a form of practical education for the masses to counterbalance the emphasis on liberal education for the elite. This distrust of liberal education by vocational educators has never been fully overcome, and attitudes ranging from suspicion to near hostility toward liberal education can still be found among some vocational educators.

Educational and social thinking has become increasingly opposed to the whole concept of separating vocational and general education. Just as educational separatism on racial grounds has become unacceptable, so any form of educational segregation based on the occupational future of young people is rejected. Such segregation leads to undesirable status distinctions between individuals because of their occupational choices, and to false superiority-inferiority attitudes toward equally essential aspects of education. The report of the 1967 Advisory Council on Vocational Education concluded that vocational education is not a separate discipline within education; rather, it is a basic objective of all education and must be a basic element of each person's education (6).

Principles of Vocational Education

The movement toward a planned system of vocational education was a gradual process. In the late 1800s and early 1900s the growing industrialization of the nation demanded more trained workers. Because vocational education was so closely related to the economic development of the nation, the need for national planning became imperative.

Public discussion and interest in the educational needs of the labor force were stimulated by the report of the Douglas Commission, which recommended a system of vocational education for the state of Massachusetts. In 1906 the National Society for the Promotion of Industrial Education brought its study of occupational needs to public attention. Subsequently this organization and its successor, the National Society for Vocational Education, served as a sounding board for early discussions related to the rationale and emerging principles of vocational education. Charles A. Prosser, executive secretary of the National Society for Vocational Education, played a major role in laying the groundwork for favorable public opinion and extensive federal support of vocational education. During the 1940s he generated a series of theories that attempted to reconcile vocational education practices to the modern psychology of learning.

Barlow (7) identifies the following as principles growing out of the foundation years that had culminated in the passage of the Smith-Hughes Act of 1917. He feels that these principles have not changed even though their implementation has brought about new approaches.

1 Vocational education is a national concern

Labor, education, business, industry, agriculture, and the public supported the economic need for a national framework of vocational education.

2 Vocational education provides for the common defense and promotes the general welfare

The effectiveness of vocational education in improving the economic welfare of individuals and families, and in providing the base of skills for defense of the nation, has been consistently demonstrated during periods of war and peace.

3 Vocational preparation of youth and adults is a public school responsibility

The democratization of public education brought with it a favorable consensus on the need for vocational education in the public school system.

4 Vocational education requires a sound basic education

The technological age has consistently placed a premium on a sound basic education for *all* students. The design of vocational education has always reinforced this assumption.

5 Vocational education is planned and conducted in close cooperation with business and industry

The concept of an advisory committee as a means of keeping programs attuned to the needs of business and industry illustrates the cooperative dimension of program planning.

6 Vocational education provides the skills and knowledge valuable in the labor market

Program content is based upon analysis of the needs of the labor market. Placement and followup studies test the degree to which the product of the program (the student) adjusts and makes progress in the job.

7 Vocational education provides continuing education for youth and adults

The outreach of vocational education through the trade extension and other adult vocational programs has contributed significantly to the "industrial intelligence'' of the labor force. The problem of retraining and lifelong learning is a foundation element in the structure of vocational education.

Barlow's principles, which describe the rationale on which vocational education was based in its foundational years, may be compared with these principles of present-day vocational education (8):

1 Vocational education is the right of everyone who desires and can profit by it, and it is the responsibility of the schools to provide for it within the curriculum

> *This principle precludes program limitations as they now exist in many instances, and establishes the need for a broader and more inclusive vocational program based upon individual needs and work opportunities. Such planning establishes the base for the schools to become responsible for the student in transition to the next level of education or to work.*

2 Vocational education is a continuous process from early childhood throughout life

> *The process can be roughly divided into four phases which prescribe themselves to general levels of education. The types of programs which are appropriate and can be planned for each level are (a) informational and orientational, (b) orientational and exploratory, (c) exploratory and preparational, and (d) upgrading and retraining.*

3 Vocational education, like general education, is a responsibility of the total school and cannot be limited to a single discipline or department

4 Vocational education programs can be developed which serve as nonblocking career ladders, and they can be planned to be consonant with the goals of both general and vocational functions of education

self improvement

Such statements of principle act as basic rules both for evaluating present programs and for guiding future actions.

Assumptions of Vocational Education

Underlying the principles of vocational education are a number of widely accepted assumptions that provide consistency and direction to overall efforts in the field. They have a democratic orientation toward the fundamental worth of the individual and toward the responsibility of society to help people develop their capabilities to the fullest extent possible.

Thompson (9) identifies the following basic assumptions:

1. *Vocational education can develop a marketable man by developing his ability to perform skills that extend his utility as a tool of production.*

2. *Vocational education is the means of acquiring the basic skills essential for equal competition in the marketplace.*

3. *There need not be a dualism between vocational and general education.*

4. *Vocational education is economic education as it is geared to the needs of the job market and thus contributes to national economic strength.*

5. *Vocational education is education for production to serve the ends of the economic system and is said to have social utility.*

6. *Vocational education at the secondary level is concerned with preparation of the individual for initial entry employment.*

7. *Vocational education should be oriented to the manpower needs of the community.*

8. *Vocational education should be evaluated on the basis of economic efficiency. Vocational education is economically efficient when (a) it prepares students for specific jobs in the community on the basis of manpower needs, (b) it insures an adequate labor supply for an occupational area, and (c) the student gets the job for which he was trained.*

It is evident to those engaged in vocational education that a body of philosophical assumptions and principles has evolved that gives direction to the field. Such assumptions and principles are rooted in the changing needs of students and of industry, and they contain elements of theory and practice that have frequently been incorporated into law.

Philosophical Effects of Federal Legislation

Unlike most other educational fields, vocational education is so closely interwoven with federal legislation that it is not surprising that the latter reflects the principles and practices of the former. Vocational education after the Smith-Hughes Act was oriented toward preparing students for specific occupations. Similarly, the vocational objectives of the 1960s and 1970s illustrate changes of a social, economic, and political nature as reflected in the Vocational Education Act of 1963, the Vocational Education Amendments of 1968, and the Education Amendments of the 1970s.

■ ■

The 1963 act and subsequent amendments declared
that vocational education cannot be limited to the
skills necessary for a particular occupation.

Mangum (10) points out that this change had deeper significance than was at first apparent:

> By implication, the test of appropriateness of training was no longer to be, "Was the skill in high and growing demand?" but "Did the individual get the job of his choice and prosper in it?" Not that training for obsolete skills was contemplated. The difference was a matter of emphasis, with training for successful employment the primary goal and meeting skill requirements a means to that end.

■ ■

The 1963 act and the subsequent amendments further changed the objectives and principles of vocational education by redefining the field.

■ ■

The new emphasis was on training not only for certain traditional occupations but also for "new and emerging ones," and not just on skills training but on remedial or related academic and technical instruction as well as on preparation for enrollment in advanced technical education.

■ ■

Special attention was to be paid to the needs of the disadvantaged and handicapped, for whom special techniques and supportive services would be necessary to enable them to achieve satisfactory employment.

■ ■

The 1963 act defined the objective of vocational education as the development of the individual rather than the filling of specific needs of the labor market.

■ ■

The acts of the 1960s specified that education should no longer be compartmentalized into general, academic, and vocational components.

■ ■

The acts of the 1970s prohibited sex discrimination and sex stereotyping in vocational education programs and continued the emphasis on persons with special needs.

Vocational Education Method

There have been frequent suggestions that vocational education, with its strong emphasis on the "doing" types of activities, could offer an alternative path to learning for those with a low aptitude for verbal learning. The value of vocational education as a teaching-learning method may be greater for some students than its substantive value as skill training. There is evidence that occupational education can often remotivate the student who has lost interest in school. When combined with well-coordinated work experiences in actual employment—experiences that are carefully coordinated with in-school studies—the general education outcomes for the student can often be excellent (11).

ECONOMIC FACTORS

At this point let us explore two major aspects of the economics of vocational education: vocational education as a contributor to society's economic mainstream, and the economics of vocational education itself.

Labor is a basic component of our economic system. About two-thirds of the national income goes to those who work for wages and salaries. Wages—including fees, commissions, and salaries—represent prices paid for labor that is expended in the production of economic goods and services. Real wages—the amount of goods and services that money wages will purchase—must be earned before they can be paid. Marginal productivity limits the amount that can be paid to workers, but it does not always determine the amount that employers actually pay.

The Role of Labor

One explanation that has been advanced to explain wages and wage rates is the theory of demand and supply. The demand for labor means the amount of labor of a certain kind that will be used in production at various wage rates. The demand for labor is derived from the demand for what labor produces. The supply of labor is derived from the amount of labor that will be offered for use in production at different wage rates. Like demand, the supply of labor is always specific. Labor is perishable; it cannot be separated from the person; its supply does not change quickly; and it is not highly mobile. Standards of living affect the supply of labor, and certain laws for the control of wages and the regulation of labor may also affect its supply. We may say that wages and wage rates depend on the demand for and supply of labor. At the same time, certain other factors usually affect wage rates, such as custom, public authority, monopoly, and bargaining by employers and employees.

Economic Bases of Vocational Education

Historically, the development and availability of vocational education, as a source of labor supply, has paralleled economic growth. Under the heavy labor demands at the end of the eighteenth century, the nation faced a serious shortage of skilled labor. The country had come to depend on European immigrants, who had brought with them a background in skilled trades. But now the immigrant stream was diminishing, and the nation lacked an adequate apprenticeship system for training workers. Trained laborers were needed to operate the rapidly growing number of farms and factories.

Faced with a labor shortage, industry and agriculture, the two largest segments of the economy, called for programs of vocational training in the public high schools. The idea that vocational education should be designed to supply the labor needs of particular segments of the economy became embedded in the law with the passage of the Smith-Hughes Act, and it persisted in vocational legislation until 1963. In the early 1960s it became obvious that vocational education, if it hoped to meet the nation's needs, must be redesigned to serve people of all employable age groups and categories rather than particular segments of the economy. As Leighbody states (12):

> The Vocational Education Act of 1963 did not reject the goal of meeting the nation's economic needs, but it turned the emphasis of the program toward meeting the needs of people. . . . This would, of course, satisfy the need for trained workers, but the change in emphasis is nevertheless significant. It reoriented vocational education to more sociological and humanitarian goals.

Technological Factors

As technology has advanced, it has left in its wake a high average unemployment among unskilled workers. The view that automation, in the long run, creates more jobs than it displaces has been widespread, but it is being challenged today. The immediate effects of technological unemployment fall heaviest on those least able to withstand its effects—the untrained and undereducated, especially the 16- to 20-year-old group.

Until recently economists generally believed that to solve our unemployment problems we must attain a sufficient increase in the rate of our national economic growth. The consensus now, however, seems to be that in simple terms of increased production and consumption, the kind of growth rate that we need cannot be fully attained. In the future the rate of economic growth will increasingly depend on the rate of technological development—which, in turn, will depend on the availability of technically trained personnel. The shortage of fuel and other natural resources may also be a major impediment to technological progress.

Federal legislation of the past quarter-century has done much to alleviate the problem. There is a feeling among many, however, that merely improving education will not eliminate or even substantially reduce unemployment, that to gain ground we must accelerate the pace at which we improve education. Thus education becomes the intermediary between technology on the one hand and labor on the other.

Vocational Education and the General Welfare

Freedom of occupational choice is both an American ideal and a national concern. Federal legislation has sought to facilitate occupational choice by providing funds to the states for the development of vocational education programs. The justifications for such funding are based on the right of each individual to a total education, the responsibility of society (through the public schools) to provide such instruction, and the effect of vocational education on the economic strength of the nation. A central tenet of vocational education has often been expressed by the phrase, "to fit for useful employment." Useful employment leads to economic improvement, which leads to a better standard of living for the individual, and this gain, in turn, becomes a gain for society. Vocational education, therefore, has been thought of as a wise business investment both for the individual and for the nation.

As shown in Figure 3.1, average yearly income rises with the number of years of school completed. College graduates in 1975 earned on the average one-third more than high school graduates, whereas persons with five years or more of college earned one-fifth more than those with four years of college.

Although college graduates do earn more, on the average, than high school graduates, there are numerous well-paying occupations that do not require a college degree. In fact, earnings in many occupations not requiring college degrees have increased faster than earnings in occupations that do require a degree. The number of persons in the labor market with college degrees has increased from 7.9 percent in 1952 to 16.5 percent in 1976 and is expected to reach 20 percent by 1985. This increase, along with economic conditions of the 1970s, has resulted in a larger percentage of college graduates in positions such as clerical, sales, and service than in the past.

There appears to be no lack of demand for graduates of postsecondary vocational-technical programs. Many of the occupations that have grown most rapidly have required vocational, apprenticeship, or junior college education. These occupations include science and health technicians and office employees, especially those working in computer-related areas. Over the past ten years, enrollments in public vocational schools have tripled and the demand for these graduates is expected to continue strong through the mid-1980s.

The nature and amount of formal education offered through the public school system reflects the social and economic demands of the times, as is

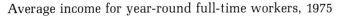

Average income for year-round full-time workers, 1975

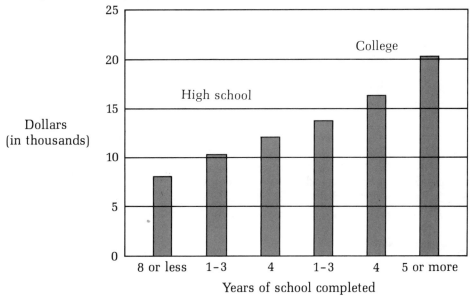

Figure 3.1   Average income by level of schooling. Source: *Occupational Outlook Handbook,* 1978–79 ed., Bulletin 1955, U.S. Department of Labor, p. 26.

evident in the philosophical changes in education over three distinctly different periods in our history.

1. Agrarian period

In its early years America was predominantly an agricultural nation. Education served two primary functions: facilitation of the basic literacy assumed necessary for meaningful participation in the democratic process, and "acculturation of the masses of immigrants of many languages and backgrounds who flooded into the new melting pot" (13). It was a fact of American society in those days that adult roles in the economy were accessible with a minimum of formal education. In addition, the growing economy had ample uses for those without formal educational preparation.

2. Industrial period

From an agricultural society emerged a complex industrialized economy, which reached its peak during World War II. "With half a world to feed and arm and with the cream of its own labor force committed to military combat, the United States economy was forced in the early 1940s to multiply its output almost overnight'' (14). A large part of the required labor force was inexperienced and, as Evans, Mangum, and Pragan (15) state,

> school shops and laboratories were re-equipped, instructors were recruited, and 24-hour-a-day vocational instruction began, oriented to skills in national as well as local demand. Before the war's end, the public schools had trained 7.5 million people for industrial contributions to the war.

Employers were now able to choose well-prepared persons who had been trained under programs such as the GI Bill. In addition, a technology was designed to use these already trained persons rather than their poorly trained competitors. During the industrial era, vocational education was guided by the Smith-Hughes Act and its prevailing philosophy of training in specific occupational categories to meet the needs of the labor market.

Technological period

Although vocational education made major progress during the industrial years, the impact of automation and technological advance pointed up two central failures of prevailing philosophy: its lack of sensitivity to changes in the labor market and its lack of sensitivity to the needs of various segments of the population. By concentrating on the job requirements of industry and restricting its efforts to secondary school–age students, the Smith-Hughes Act failed to give priority to the vocational needs of all groups in the community and to the demands of a fast-changing society (16). The rapid rate at which technological changes are occurring creates a need for vocational education programs that are flexible enough to adapt to an ever-changing economy.

Leighbody (17) summarizes the characteristics of our economy that have implications for vocational education programs:

1. *More goods are produced for more consumers, but with a smaller portion of the work force required to produce them. However, those who are thus employed must be better educated and must possess more sophisticated skills and knowledge than their predecessors.*

2. *More food and fiber is produced and more people are better fed and clothed by fewer and fewer farmers . . . but those who remain and those who will be needed in the future require much greater knowledge of scientific agriculture, coupled with business skills and training.*

3. *Nearly all jobs call for a higher level of education for entry than they formerly did, and a longer period of general education prior to occupational specialization. Today a high school education is hardly sufficient for a decent job, and a very large number of people are continuing their education beyond it.*

4. *The need for manual skills in most jobs is decreasing, while cognitive, social, and interpersonal skills are more and more in demand.*

5. *Already more people are employed in providing services for other people than in producing goods and food for them. Two-thirds of the work force is now engaged in what may be broadly classified as service occupations. This is a remarkable reversal of the distribution of occupations from the time when the first programs of vocational education were established.*

6. *In addition to the shift in the distribution of jobs, as technology advances it creates wholly new jobs and categories of jobs, and these too tend to demand better educated and better trained workers.*

ECONOMICS OF VOCATIONAL EDUCATION

In this section we shall look at the economic aspects of vocational education itself, including the matching feature of vocational legislation and the efforts toward accountability.

Matching Feature of Vocational Funds

Federal funds for vocational education have been distributed among the states on the basis of formulas determined by population and per capita income. Matching provisions of earlier laws required that the states put up an equal amount of state dollars for federal dollars allocated.

This matching feature of vocational education funds has in the past prevented many states from receiving their share of federal assistance. Because the matching of federal funds was accomplished primarily by local expenditures, local school districts with a low financial base were particularly hard hit. In practice, the wealthier school district received proportionately more and the poorer school district received less than its fair share of funds. The Vocational Education Amendments of 1968 established the limit of the matching requirement by specifying that no local district shall be denied access to federal vocational funds because of lack of matching funds.

Reimbursement on Excess-Cost Principle

Local schools and states are obligated to provide general education for all students and an equivalent expenditure for those enrolled in vocational education programs. Many states have established uniform rates of 50 percent vocational reimbursement to local schools for selected items, the largest of which is teachers' salaries. Another practice is that reimbursement should be based only on the *difference in costs* between providing general education or college preparatory, and vocational or occupationally oriented education. In this way, the federal government reimburses the local school district for the extra cost required to provide vocational programs.

Consistent with the above principle is the assumption of reimbursement, or support based on services rendered. As Tomlinson (18) observes,

> *Major changes in the amount of money accruing to a local school district will result when these principles are applied. The numbers of students served, amount of services rendered, quality of service and cost of services rendered will be used as a guide for support rather than the teacher's salary, regardless of quality, need, or number of students enrolled.*

The Principle of Accountability

The needs of education always seem to outweigh the available resources. Educational costs at all levels are escalating, and in most states a larger and larger portion of the total budget is earmarked for educational purposes annually. As the tax burden has increased, the public has increasingly looked for evidence that resources have been well spent and that quality and efficiency have been realized in accomplishing educational goals.

Measures of accountability have been difficult to apply to vocational programs because of the lack of valid data on which to base an evaluation. Even the National Advisory Council on Vocational Education has been hampered in its investigations by a lack of concrete information regarding economic effectiveness. However, improved systems of educational planning and computerized recordkeeping and evaluation now make it possible to identify cost and achievement relationships.

In the Education Amendments of 1976 Congress mandated information-gathering and evaluation based on valid samples to determine the extent to which the purposes of vocational programs are achieved. This includes the extent to which graduates and those who leave school (a) find employment in occupations related to their training, and (b) are considered by their employers well trained and prepared for the job.

It is not unreasonable to expect that in the relatively near future each vocational education department will be expected to specify its course objectives in measurable achievement terms. These objectives will then have to be justified in terms of the allocated resources and the actual results achieved. In this way, performance standards and cost effectiveness will become a basic component of vocational education.

SOCIOLOGICAL FACTORS

As society has changed, so has the nature of work. As Barlow (19) aptly phrases it:

A century ago the primary ingredients needed by people who wanted to enter the labor force were a willingness to work, a strong back, and a modicum of education. But with the passage of time, society has changed. We have moved from the farm into the factory, we have become better fed, and the result of our productive labor has produced an affluence among people in general which is without precedence in any other society.

Vocational Education and Social Welfare

An examination of federal legislation reveals that Congress has recognized the social values of vocational education, with programs open to all regardless of sex, race, creed, or national origin. The Vocational Education Amendments of 1976 stipulate that persons of all ages in all communities will have ready access to vocational training or retraining that is suited to their needs, interests, and ability to benefit from such training. Much of the emphasis of federal law in the educational arena has been toward the equating of social and economic opportunities.

The vocational education movement has from its beginning reflected concern over social and economic conditions. There has always been an element of philanthropy in the thinking of those who have been interested in vocational education, a feeling that the general uplifting of the masses through training for work was an attainable goal. This idea is still reflected in the large variety of federally funded job training programs that are directed toward improving the lot of disadvantaged members of society.

Congress has recognized the relationship of education and work in such pieces of legislation as the Manpower Development and Training Act of 1962, which provided training and retraining for the unemployed; the Area Redevelopment Act, which provided training or retraining for unemployed and underemployed persons in specified redevelopment areas; the Economic Opportunity Act, a multi-level program to aid the impoverished through such activities as work experience, community action, and the Neighborhood Youth Corps; the Comprehensive Education and Training Act of 1973, which consolidated previous manpower legislation; and the Youth Employment and Demonstration Project Act of 1977, aimed at problems associated with youth employment, unemployment, and underemployment, with special emphasis on the needs of economically disadvantaged youth.

The social and economic values of vocational education have been elaborated by Shoemaker (20), who points out the expanding role of education for work:

Most jobs today and in the future will require formal training, and preparation for initial job entry is a basic responsibility of public education.

We must choose between increased welfare or an expanded program of preparing for work. At the same time, we see that job preparation and remedial education programs for adults are too expensive to serve as a continuing solution to current social and economic problems. Instead, a complete re-evaluation and reformation of our public educational system represents the only hope to solving our economic and social problems. An expanded and improved system of vocational education and guidance must be a major part of the change in our educational system.

Educational innovation requires increased categorical financial aid for specific programs as well as general aid for overall development. This aid must come from federal, state and local sources.

The education and supportive services needed for our modern society will require a broad student base and broad tax base.

The purpose of education is to perpetuate and improve the society in which it exists. Our technological society requires that everyone receive the opportunity to earn an adequate living. It further requires that young people be prepared for the dual responsibilities of home management and wage earning.

To survive, public education must accept greater responsibility. Services must be expanded and improved. Education must be prepared to account for both successes and failures.

Social Forces Affecting Vocational Education

During the past two decades, vocational education received widespread attention and critical scrutiny. A number of forces have influenced its direction and growth.

1 The national program of vocational education has been studied by citizens' commissions

In 1961 President John F. Kennedy charged the Panel of Consultants on Vocational Education with the responsibility for considering the then-current vocational education legislation in relation to changing social conditions. Its report, *Education for a Changing World of Work*, was to serve as a basis for modernizing and improving job training, and it set the stage for the passage of the Vocational Education Act of 1963.

The National Advisory Council on Vocational Education, appointed in 1967 by President Lyndon B. Johnson in accordance with requirements of the 1963 act, produced a report, *The Bridge Between Man and His Work*, which resulted in substantial changes in the law in the form of the Vocational Education Amendments Act of 1968. Under this act, a continuing National Advisory Council on Vocational Education was created. The National Advisory Council on Vocational Education, as well as each state advisory council, is charged with the regular review of vocational education as a basis for systematic updating.

2 Job training is viewed by many as a partial solution to current social problems

Many persons look to vocational education for at least a partial solution to the social problems related to America's unemployment. The 1969 report, as well as subsequent reports, of the National Advisory Council on Vocational Education placed great faith in the capacity of vocational education to "solve the major social problems of our time." *identifying the needs of the local community*

3 Cooperative planning through advisory committees reflects the interests and priorities of employers, schools, and communities

The cooperative planning involved in developing vocational programs—ranging from the identification of needs through the discussion of alternative systems to the attainment of consensus required to put a program into operation—is basically a social process that reflects the principle of freedom of choice. Advisory committees, an innovation in vocational education, assist school boards in planning programs of vocational education at the local, state, and national levels. These committees, which largely reflect the interests and priorities of employers, schools, and communities, make their decision based on the changing social, economic, and political conditions as they perceive them. The 1976 Education Amendments ensure more effective state planning through broader representation (from ten specific groups) on state boards and advisory councils. Local advisory councils were added in this act to broaden the local planning base.

4 Automation has broadened the scope of vocational education

The recommendations of the Panel of Consultants on Vocational Education, which resulted in the Vocational Education Act of 1963, were made during a period when the effects of automation were causing large-scale unemployment. As a result the panel recommended a broadening of the scope of vocational education. To make training available to more people, new and emerging occupations were recognized. The Vocational Education Amendments of 1968 went even further in that they specified that all occupations were to be included in the realm of vocational education except those classified as professional and requiring a baccalaureate or higher degree. It has been estimated that this definition of vocational education covered 90 percent of the nation's occupations. The Education Amendments include preparation of individuals for unpaid as well as paid employment.

Concept of Social Class

The American college was originally thought of as the training ground for society's leaders, whereas the high school came to be considered as the school that offered terminal education for the masses. If in the high schools vocational education were to become the alternative to college preparatory studies, two kinds of education—one for leaders and one for workers—would become a reality. Many thoughtful educators sensed a danger in this approach, the danger of an educational dualism based on social class, which, if widely accepted, might strengthen social stratification. The possibility that a caste system might be created in American society through a dualistic educational process was debated during the discussions that led to the passage of the Smith-Hughes Act, and some clearly viewed vocational education as the appropriate form of education for the lower classes. The first report of the National Advisory Council on Vocational Education stated that the majority of Americans felt that vocational education was designed for somebody else's children. It further accused the nation of intellectual snobbery where vocational education was concerned. "Clearly, in the minds of some," Leighbody (21) states, "the goal of vocational education is to meet the needs of those who are less fortunate economically, socially, and intellectually."

Problem of Occupational Status

In most cultures, less social prestige is accorded to those who perform society's more routine tasks than to those who do the intellectual work. But from the beginning of the American experience, there has been a strong tradition of egalitarianism, which has helped sustain the ideal of the classless society. Yet every thoughtful American knows that a hierarchy of social class exists in this country and that it is closely related to occupations. What has been accomplished in the United States is a degree of economic and social mobility, which is greater than that to be found in almost any other country. Nevertheless, every occupation possesses a varying degree of prestige not entirely related to the financial rewards it carries.

At levels above the underprivileged, social stratification in the United States is less sharp and more fluid than in almost any other Western country, but nevertheless it exists. Studies (22) indicate that there is general consensus among Americans as to the prestige value of various kinds of occupations and that four factors seem to enter equally into the public's prestige ranking: (a) the economic returns of the occupation, (b) its social contribution, (c) the amount of education and training it requires, and (d) the extent to which it deals with intellectual matters. It is clear, too, that one of the factors—the amount of education and training needed—exerts an influence on each of the other factors. It would be a mistake, however, to assume that the benefits of additional education and training are automatic, because these, in turn, are affected by factors such as economic conditions, demand and supply of labor, and the effects of government regulation.

Other criteria of occupational status include the degree of responsibility required by the work; types of symbols, tools, and materials used by the worker; degree of authority given to workers; degree of intrinsic interest in the work; and degree of initiative required in the work.

SUMMARY

The philosophy of vocational education has been affected by philosophical, economic, and sociological factors. It is grounded in our democratic belief in the optimal development of each citizen in accordance with his or her interests and needs. Objectives, principles, and practices in the field have closely reflected the social and economic changes in our nation's history as well as the pragmatic educational philosophy of John Dewey, with its strong emphasis on experience-centered learning. The assumptions of vocational education, as expressed by its leaders and echoed in the Federal Vocational Education Acts, have increasingly reflected the belief that vocational education should be a basic element in every individual's education. There is also widespread consensus that it should be offered by all public school systems on a continuing basis, that it is inseparable from sound general education, and that it should serve the humanistic needs of all students as well as the demand of a technological society. There is an increasing recognition of the value of vocational education as a teaching-learning method for general education.

The availability of vocational education, as a source of labor supply, affects the economic welfare of the nation. Vocational education is sensitive to the needs of a fast-changing society, and the effects of automation have accentuated the importance of the field as an intermediary between technology and labor. There is continuing evidence of the economic value of education to individuals as reflected in increased lifetime earnings for higher levels of education and training. Current demands are being made by taxpayers for accountability for achievement in line with the costs of education. Vocational education programs and courses are being examined as a basis for the establishment of priorities and specification of measurable objectives essential to the demonstration of cost effectiveness.

Much of the emphasis of federal vocational education acts has been toward equating social and economic opportunities for all Americans. Our democratic society endorses, as a basic right of the individual, freedom in the selection of an occupation. Job training has been viewed as a partial solution to social problems of the day on the grounds that more vocational education would promote national economic security and reduce social unrest. There is still some problem with the concept of vocational education as an appropriate form of education for the lower social classes only. Despite the American ideal of a classless society, a hierarchy of social class exists that is clearly related to occupations. It is known that occupations possess varying degrees of prestige or status related to such factors as their economic returns, amount of education required, social contribution, and intellectual content. Social stratification in the United States is more fluid than in other Western countries, with the amount of education and training a strong influence on the social mobility of the individual.

ACTIVITIES

For review

1. Explain the major philosophical differences underlying the Smith-Hughes Act and the Vocational Education Acts of the 1960s and 1970s.
2. Compare the educational needs of our citizens during the agricultural, industrial, and technological periods. Relate these needs to vocational education.
3. What were the basic shortcomings of the Smith-Hughes Act? How were these corrected in the 1963 act, the 1968 amendments, and the 1976 amendments?
4. What influence does a person's occupation have on his or her social status?
5. What is the philosophy underlying the distribution of vocational education funds as defined in the Vocational Education Amendments of 1968 and 1976? What philosophy is implied by the "matching" characteristics of such legislation?

For discussion

1. Some educators and legislators have viewed vocational education as a solution to the social ills of the times. Others have expressed doubts as to the extent to which job training can alleviate the plight of the disadvantaged. Select one point of view and defend it.
2. How has our changing school population influenced the philosophy of vocational education?
3. How might vocational education minimize the problem of social stratification?
4. Why is it important for a teacher, a department, and a school to have a philosophy of education?
5. How is vocational education related to social mobility?
6. What type of vocational education is automatically included in principles of

taxation that apply to the support of *general* education? What type of vocational education requires additional justification if it is to be tax supported?

For exploration

1. Select one course that you have taught or that you plan to teach, and develop a statement of philosophy for it.

2. Interview two vocational educators and two nonvocational educators regarding their philosophy of vocational education. How are they alike? How are they different?

REFERENCES

1. *Cardinal Principles of Secondary Education*, A Report of the Commission on the Reorganization of Secondary Education, appointed by the National Education Association, Bulletin 1918, Vol. 35 (Washington, D.C.: Department of the Interior, Bureau of Education, 1918).

2. William James, *Pragmatism: A New Name for Some Old Ways of Thinking* (New York: Longmans, Green and Company, 1907).

3. Boyd H. Bode, *How We Learn* (Boston: D. C. Heath and Company, 1940).

4. John Dewey, *Democracy and Education* (New York: The Macmillan Company, 1928).

5. William H. Kilpatrick, *Philosophy of Education from the Experimentalist Outlook*, Forty-First Yearbook of the National Society for the Study of Education (Chicago: The University of Chicago Press, 1942).

6. Gerald B. Leighbody, *Vocational Education in America's Schools: Major Issues of the 1970s* (Chicago: American Technical Society, 1972), pp. 29-30.

7. Melvin L. Barlow, "Foundations of Vocational Education," in *American Vocational Journal*, Vol. 42, No. 3, March 1967, pp. 17-19. (Reproduced by permission.)

8. *Vocational Education—The Bridge Between Man and His Work*, General Report of the Advisory Council on Vocational Education (Washington, D.C.: U.S. Department of Health, Education and Welfare, Nov. 1968), p. 192.

9. John F. Thompson, *Foundations of Vocational Education* (Englewood Cliffs, N.J.: Prentice-Hall, Inc., 1973), pp. 91-102. (Reproduced by permission.)

10. Garth L. Mangum, "Curriculum Response to Occupational Trends," in *Vocational Education: Today and Tomorrow*, Gerald G. Somers and J. Kenneth Little, eds. (Madison: University of Wisconsin, Center for Studies in Vocational and Technical Education, 1971), p. 36.

11. Leighbody, *Vocational Education in America's Schools*, pp. 73-74.

12. Ibid., p. 7. (Reproduced by permission.)

13. Rupert N. Evans, Garth L. Mangum, and Otto Pragan, *Education for Employment* (Ann Arbor: University of Michigan, Institute of Labor and Industrial Relations; Wayne State University; and National Manpower Policy Task Force, 1969), p. 3.

14. Ibid., p. 4.

15. Ibid., pp. 5-6.

16. Arthur G. Wirth, *Education in the Technological Society* (Scranton, Pa.: International Textbook Company, 1971), p. 166.

17. Leighbody, *Vocational Education in America's Schools*, pp. 58-59. (Reproduced by permission.)

18. Robert M. Tomlinson, "Implications and Reflections: The Vocational Education Amendments of 1968," in *Contemporary Concepts in Vocational Education*, Gordon F. Law, ed. (Washington, D.C.: American Vocational Association, 1971), p. 31.

19. Melvin L. Barlow, "Changing Goals," in *Vocational Education: Today and Tomorrow*, Gerald G. Somers and J. Kenneth Little, eds. (Madison: University of Wisconsin, Center for Studies in Vocational and Technical Education, 1971), p. 11. (Reproduced by permission.)

20. Byrl R. Shoemaker, "People, Jobs and Society: Toward Relevance in Education," in *Contemporary Concepts in Vocational Education*, Gordon F. Law, ed. (Washington, D.C.: American Vocational Association, 1971), pp. 20-21. (Reproduced by permission.)

21. Leighbody, *Vocational Education in America's Schools*, p. 9. (Reproduced by permission.)

22. Ibid., pp. 124-25.

■

Theory and Design of
Career Education

INTRODUCTION: THE CONCEPT OF
CAREER EDUCATION

The American public school system has always been the focus of much attention and debate. Does the system provide the type of experience needed by today's young people and adults, many of whom will live much of their lives in the twenty-first century? Frequently the critics have been much more vocal than those who have sought to defend public education, and the system has undergone sharp changes in direction from time to time. Our system of education reflects our society and the personal and social needs of its citizens. The continuous and accelerated nature of change in our lives makes it necessary that education, as the chief vehicle for life preparation, be appraised more frequently and intensively than in the past.

Some have said that our system of education stifles initiative, demands conformity with the system, lacks relevance to the real world, is too content-centered, denies equal educational opportunities to all, disregards the needs of learners, and is too costly. Increasingly such discontent, coupled with a shortage of economic resources, has raised some fundamental doubts about the validity of traditional aims and procedures now prevailing in public schools. A well-documented case could be presented for the effectiveness of public education in this country, for the evidence of its success is all around us. However, the demands for alternatives to the present educational system are growing, and policymakers at national, state, and local levels are under pressure to find better ways to develop more relevance, quality, and equality of educational opportunities for students throughout America.

Solutions to the problems of learning are being introduced through competency-based teacher education, community schools, nongraded schools, open schools, computer-assisted instruction, flexible scheduling, systems-oriented curricula, humanized learning, and a plethora of technologically sophisticated approaches for individualizing learning. Proposed prescriptions are numerous and, while there is agreement as to the need for change in the schools, there is no consensus as to how it is best brought about. Nevertheless, there are indications that the need for change is beginning to result in recognized movements that may bring sweeping changes in our system of public education. One such movement is career education.

The term *career education* was first used by United States Commissioner of Education James Allen in 1970. It was described and popularized by Allen's successor, Sidney P. Marland, who undoubtedly deserves credit as the father of modern-day career education. Under Marland's administration, the federal government provided the initial thrust toward career education for all students. Since that time, under the leadership of Commissioner T. H. Bell, and subsequently under Ernest Boyer, career education became a major goal of the Office of Education and a primary concern of educators throughout the nation.

Career education is an evolving concept with both advocates and critics. The range of meanings and the implications of career education are treated in this chapter. Past and present conceptualizations of career education are presented, and the reader is challenged to think creatively about the dimensions of career education. The principles, objectives, and characteristics of career education are treated, and examples of national, state, and local models are reviewed.

Roots of Career Education

Career education revives some educational measures of earlier eras, and it contains some elements that are new. The struggle to introduce vocational education into all educational curricula was identified with the careers of David Snedden, an educational administrator; Charles Prosser, a lawyer; and John Dewey, a philosopher, among others. Snedden was an advocate of integrating occupational education into the general curriculum. Prosser argued for social efficiency and the need for all students to prepare for useful employment. Dewey saw vocational education as a means of liberalizing education (1). In summarizing the historical, philosophical, and conceptual bases of career education, Herr (2) identified five points related to the emergent visibility of career education:

   1. *Virtually every concept which is presently embodied in career education has been advocated at some point in American education.*

2. *Both vocational education and vocational guidance were direct responses to the . . . industrial character of the U.S. in the late 1880s and '90s as well as the first two decades of the twentieth century.*

3. *Advocacy of vocational education and vocational guidance has largely been precipitated by economic and industrial needs. . . . [I]n the last decade, this situation has largely reversed, with individual needs being considered the major base from which educational programming must begin.*

4. *Until approximately 1960, . . . the categories of vocational training were defined by occupational or industrial needs or, in some cases, inertia. Since 1960, however, increased attention has been focused on the needs of special groups of persons—i.e., the disadvantaged, the handicapped, the academically retarded . . . .*

5. *. . . these elements have constituted support for articulating, from the kindergarten through post-secondary education, a series of increasingly complex educational experiences which would be available to all students, to out-of-school youth and to adults. Further these experiences are seen as requiring not only vocational preparation in a continuum from job entry to highly complex technical skills but also vocational guidance in a continuum oriented to pre-vocational and educational awareness, attitudinal development, awareness of personal strengths and potentialities as well as the development of decision-making abilities.*

CONTEMPORARY EMPHASIS ON CAREER EDUCATION

The launching of the contemporary emphasis on career education is attributed to Sidney P. Marland, Jr. In his 1971 address to the convention of the National Association of Secondary School Principals, Commissioner of Education Marland proposed an emphasis on career education so that persons completing school programs at grade 12 would be ready to enter higher education or to enter useful and rewarding employment. He envisioned the blending of the academic and vocational programs into a "totally new system" and placed a high priority on its implementation (3):

> True and complete reform of the high school, viewed as a major element of overall preparation for life, cannot be achieved until general education is completely done away with in favor of contemporary career development in a comprehensive secondary education environment. This is our ultimate goal, and we realize that so sweeping a change cannot be accomplished overnight, involving as it does approximately 30 million students and billions of dollars in public funds.

Although Marland did not attempt to provide a specific definition of the scope of career education, he left little doubt that the full support of his office would be given to fostering changes and programs designed to implement the new system. He proposed a four-fold plan (4) for career development:

1. *major improvements and updating of occupational education emphasizing newer vocational fields and a sound educational base underlying all specific skills training*

2. *more flexible options for high school graduates to continue on to higher education or to enter the world of work*

3. *a closer liaison of vocational education and people from business, industry, and organized labor with more work experience opportunities for students*

4. *a new commitment at all levels—federal, state, and local—toward developing leadership and commitment to the concept of career education*

Commissioner Marland's challenge to the educational community for further discussion and clarification of the concept of career education evoked wide reaction and varying definitions. Some embraced the term to include all of education, whereas others used it to describe "the new vocational education." An individual's view of career education seemed to be much affected by his or her particular vantage point in the educational spectrum.

In 1974 T. H. Bell, who succeeded Sidney Marland as U.S. Commissioner of Education, summarized some of the accomplishments and new directions of career education (5). Addressing the National Conference of State Coordinators of Career Education, he pointed out that for the first time in the history of career education

1. *. . . there is a congressional mandate for career education. By enacting Section 406, Title IV, Public Law 93-380 (Educational Amendments of 1974), Congress made career education a law of the land.*

2. *. . . Congress is favorably considering the appropriation of funds earmarked for career education.*

3. *. . . there will be a National Advisory Council on Career Education.*

4. *. . . an active inter-agency team, representing the Departments of Commerce, Labor, and Health, Education and Welfare, is studying and making recommendations regarding relationships between education and work.*

According to Commissioner Bell, the Office of Education has its own position paper on career education.

While it clearly speaks to relationships between education and work, it leaves States and local school systems free to develop their own specific career education definitions. The centrality of work—both paid and unpaid—in this definition seems to me essential in expressing a set of goals consistent with both the economic and the humanistic need for work in our society today. The paper emphasizes integration within education and collaboration by the formal education system with both the business-industry-labor-professional-government community and the home and family structure. This emphasis provides us with a solid basis for career education . . . that points us toward a bright future.

A policy paper prepared by Kenneth B. Hoyt, Director of Career Education, Office of Education, summarized the conditions calling for educational reform (6). Among the 11 criticisms of present educational systems were these:

Too many people leaving our educational system are deficient in the basic academic skills. . . . American education best meets the educational needs of that minority of persons who will someday be college graduates. . . . Too many persons leave our educational system at both the secondary and collegiate levels unequipped with the vocational skills, self-understanding and career decision-making skills, or the work attitudes that are essential for making a successful transition from school to work.

According to Bell and Hoyt (7), the career education movement has embraced a number of basic concept assumptions. These include:

1. *Since both one's career and one's education extend from the pre-school through the retirement years, career education must also span almost the entire life cycle.*

2. *The concept of productivity is central to the definition of work and so to the entire concept of career education.*

3. *Since "work" includes unpaid activities as well as paid employment, career education's concerns, in addition to its prime emphasis on paid employment, extend to the work of the student as a learner, to the growing numbers of volunteer workers in our society, to the work of the full-time homemaker, and to work activities in which one engages as part of leisure time.*

4. *The cosmopolitan nature of today's society demands that career education embrace a multiplicity of work values, rather than a single work ethic, as a means of helping each individual answer the question "Why should I work?"*

5. *Both one's career and one's education are best viewed in a developmental, rather than in a fragmented, sense.*

6. *Career education is for all persons—the young and the old; the mentally handicapped and the intellectually gifted; the poor and the wealthy; males and females, students in elementary schools and in the graduate colleges.*

7. *The societal objectives of career education are to help all individuals: (a) want to work, (b) acquire the skills necessary for work in these times, and (c) engage in work that is satisfying for each individual throughout his or her lifetime.*

8. *The individualistic goals of career education are to make work: (a) possible, (b) meaningful, and (c) satisfying for each individual throughout his or her lifetime.*

9. *Protection of the individual's freedom to choose and assistance in making and implementing career decisions are of central concern to career education.*

10. *The expertise required for implementing career education is to be found in many parts of society and is not limited to those employed in formal education.*

OVERALL OBJECTIVES AND PURPOSES OF CAREER EDUCATION

There appears to be general agreement that the primary objective of career education is a refocusing of American education (rather than an adding to it) toward a more appropriate goal: education as preparation for work. Career education thus seeks to make preparation for work a major goal of all who teach and all who learn.

Initially, career education was loosely defined; the local school systems were left to arrive at their own definitions and procedures for implementation. An example of the comprehensive definition of career education is presented by Wesley Smith, California State Department of Education (8):

Career Education is a comprehensive, systematic and cohesive plan of learning organized in such manner that youth at all grade levels in the public schools will have continuous and abundant opportunity to acquire useful information about the occupational structure of the economy, the alternatives of career choice, the obligations of individual and productive involvement in the work force, the intelligent determination of personal capabilities and aspirations, the requisites of all occupations, and opportunities to prepare for gainful employment. Career education is the shared and unending responsibility of all professionals in education, and involves input from—and relationship to—all subject-matter disciplines and all supportive educational services. In short, it is a priority objective of public education, with achievement measured by employability in occupations, both gainful and useful, that are a reasonable match of both the talent and the ambition of every citizen.

The USOE Policy Paper (9) written by Director of Career Education Hoyt presents a generic definition of career education:

"Career" is the totality of work one does in his or her lifetime. "Education" is the totality of experiences through which one learns. Based on these two definitions, "career education" is the totality of experiences through which one learns about and prepares to engage in work as part of her or his way of living. "Career" is a developmental concept beginning in the very early years and continuing well into the retirement years. "Education," as defined here, obviously includes more than the formal educational system. Thus, this generic definition of career education is purposely intended to be of a very broad and encompassing nature. At the same time, it is intended to be considerably less than all of life or one's reasons for living.

The Office of Career Education defines career education as "an effort aimed at focusing American education and the actions of the broader community in ways that will help individuals acquire and use the knowledge, skills, and attitudes necessary for each to make work a meaningful, productive, and satisfying part of his or her way of living." (10)

Swanson (11) describes the purposes of career education in terms of helping students to adjust to the labor market. Career education is to provide them with:

1. *an instructive environment which would allow them to relate their education to the world of work—its scope, its significance, and its opportunities.*
2. *an opportunity to engage in occupational exploration including work experience, specialized instruction, and career decision-making leading toward a preferred life-style and career pattern.*
3. *an opportunity to exit and reenter the educational system or the labor force or to be instructed in both, as needed, in order to make initial or subsequent progress toward specific career goals.*

Hoyt and associates (12) cite the following key concepts related to career education:

1. *Preparation for successful working careers shall be a key objective of all education.*
2. *Every teacher in every course will emphasize the contribution that subject matter can make to a successful career.*

3. *"Hands-on" occupationally oriented experiences will be utilized as a method of teaching and motivating the learning of abstract academic content.*

4. *Preparation for careers will be recognized as the mutual importance of work attitudes, human relations skills, orientation to the nature of the workaday world, exposure to alternative career choices, and the acquisition of actual job skills.*

5. *Learning will not be reserved for the classroom, but learning environments for career education will also be identified in the home, the community, and employing establishments.*

6. *Beginning in early childhood and continuing through the regular school years, allowing the flexibility for a youth to leave for experience and return to school for further education (including opportunity for upgrading and continued refurnishing for adult workers and including productive use of leisure time and the retirement years), career education will seek to extend its time horizons from "womb to tomb."*

7. *Career education is a basic and pervasive approach to all education, but it in no way conflicts with other legitimate education objectives such as citizenship, culture, family responsibility, and basic education.*

8. *The schools cannot shed responsibility for the individual just because he has been handed a diploma or has dropped out. While it may not perform the actual placement function, the school has the responsibility to stick with the youth until he has his feet firmly on the next step of his career ladder, to help him get back on the ladder if his foot slips, and be available to help him onto a new ladder at any point in the future that one proves to be too short or unsteady.*

Career education means different things to different people. To some vocational educators, career education represents a new phase in traditional programs of skill development; in addition to the development of job skills, it includes personal and social adaptive skills that are essential to directing one's career life in the face of rapid change. To others, career education is much broader than preparation for one's work role; Keller (13) defines career education as "that part of the school's curriculum and instruction which focuses on the development of individuals for their social and economic roles in life, these roles being the work role, home-community-citizenship roles, as well as the avocational-leisure roles in life."

General educators may interpret career education to mean a special unit or course taught by a social studies teacher. But it is also an infusion into each curriculum area at all educational levels of career-oriented activities. To some educators, career education means a chance to explore the real world of work, to get "hands-on" experience. But, in addition to hands-on experiences, career education should also assist students to interpret such experiences in terms of their career self-images. The elementary teacher may see career education as a concept primarily for the high school, but values, aptitudes, interests, and self-concepts cannot wait until grade 10. The businessperson may view career education as the school's effort to ready students for work. Although the school is responsible for preparing students for a smooth transition to the adult world, career education may fail without the active support of the home and community, which are "learning laboratories" for the skills of adult living.

Career education has been examined for both its *content* and its *process* objectives. Theories of career development that have emerged over the past several decades have significantly affected the conceptualization of career education. Keller (14) perceives the process of career development as both transitional and cyclical, including the following phases:

> *Awareness (of self and career roles); Exploration (to discover self and career roles); Identification (with career roles); Preparation (for career roles); Career Assessment and Recycling.*

An underlying concept of the role of vocational-technical education in career education is that everyone, at every reasonable level, will attain a degree of occupational skill, whether or not that skill represents the ultimate aspiration of the learner. Career education becomes a developmental process of interfacing the individual's life roles with reality—finding out about, deciding on, and preparing for productive participation in life.

PRINCIPLES OF CAREER EDUCATION

For a variety of reasons—including the complexity of the concept of career education and the expenses of operationalizing the concept—the conceptualizations of career education need continuing reassessment. This is necessary to ensure that they possess the philosophical bases, comprehensiveness, and programmatic structures essential for preparing the learner to perform successfully the several roles he or she may have and/or will have in the future. Putting into operation a program of career education without the broadest possible conceptualization could result in a misjudgment of priorities and a misdirected use of available resources.

A properly planned and executed career education program operates as a vital component within a comprehensive school system. The developmental stages in a career education delivery system include conceptualization, design, development, pilot testing, revision, field testing, field revision, installation, and diffusion. As this list suggests, career education aims to improve educational outcomes by relating all teaching and learning activities to the concept of career development. Unfortunately, this concept lacks a systematic philosophical base. What may contribute to the ambiguity of the concept is that it really borrows the traditional concepts of education and attempts to synthesize them with a career-oriented approach.

Among the varied perspectives of students, teachers, school administrators, educational researchers, parents, employers, public policymakers, and others, the various concepts of career education can be characterized, based on their degree of comprehensiveness, into nine categories or levels:

1. Career education focuses on the *performance of manipulative skills* of a practical arts nature, with little, if any, consideration given to the application of those skills to useful employment or to earning a living. Level 1 is thus activity-oriented and present-oriented, and it is unidisciplinary in scope.

2. Career education focuses on the *performance of manipulative skills plus the development of cognitive and affective learnings* essential for successful employment in one or more jobs in an occupational cluster. Learning objectives are derived from task-analysis studies. Level 2 is thus job-oriented and primarily present-oriented. The cognitive and affective learning experiences are provided in such a way as to enable students to perform the manipulative skills. Education for the cluster will proceed so that students can leave school by grade 10 and find employment for which they have the necessary capabilities. The educational system will be organized to permit individuals to return to school at any age for additional training. Strong emphasis will be given to career (job) awareness and exploration to enable students to make wise career (job) selection, prepare for this chosen career (job), and value the dignity of all work. A single field of study provides the manipulative skills and related cognitive and affective learnings essential for the job cluster.

3. Career education focuses on the performance of *manipulative skills plus the development of the cognitive and affective learnings* essential for employment in one or more jobs in an occupational cluster. This level is job-oriented and primarily present-oriented. It is essentially the same as level 2 except that a multidisciplinary approach provides the manipulative skills and related cognitive and affective learnings. That is, the entire curriculum of the school is integrated, with all learning experiences presented in an occupationally relevant manner.

4. Career education focuses on the performance of manipulative skills plus the development of the cognitive and affective competencies needed for employment in a cluster of occupations plus consideration of the relationships between the individual's "off the job" existence and his or her *life as a worker and as a citizen*. Development of the qualities of leadership and citizenship, and of constructive use of leisure time, are provided for. Career education is education for living and for earning a living. It is also concerned with the wise use of leisure time, a satisfactory family life, and

participation in community activities. It is learner-oriented. It seeks to integrate students with their present and immediate future environment. It is taught in a unidisciplinary mode.

5. Career education focuses on the performance of manipulative skills plus the development of the cognitive and affective competencies needed for employment plus competencies needed for family living, participation in community activities, and aesthetic appreciations. It is *education for living and earning a living* in the present and immediate future. It is learner-oriented. It seeks to integrate students with their environment. It differs from level 4 of career education in that *a multidisciplinary approach is used*; that is, the learning experiences are integrated among several subject-matter areas.

6. Career education focuses on development of the individual's *capabilities for coping with the present and the future*. It is *education for living and earning a living now and in a future society*. The individual will prepare for employment in existing jobs as well as in occupations that have not yet emerged, in a society that does not yet exist. Because the job does not yet exist, task analysis cannot reveal the specific skills and learnings it will require. As we move toward "knowledge occupations," less emphasis will be given to psychomotor skills, and increasing emphasis will be given to decision-making competencies involving all levels of the occupational hierarchy. This level of career education is learner-oriented and multidisciplinary. Learning experiences will be organized around problems of *social and economic change*.

7. Career education focuses on *individuals in relation to their physical, social, and technological environments*. Concern will be shown for restructuring the learning and work environments to be supportive of individual life styles in a pluralistic society. This level will be primarily *decision-maker-oriented*, recognizing that decisions are made by all those affected by them. A technology of behavior will provide insights that support behavioral outcomes.

8. Career education focuses on individuals in relation to their physical, social, and technological environments. This level will be *decision-implementer-oriented*, recognizing that decisions are implemented by those who participate in making them. Learning experiences will aim at development of *leadership behavior that recognizes the need to provide learning and work environments that reinforce life styles and evolving world views*. A technology of behavior will support behavioral outcomes as in level 7.

9. Career education focuses on individuals in relation to their total environment, including the political environment. This level of career education will be *public-policy-maker-oriented*. Concern will be given to the development of public policies related to the work ethic, pluralism, welfare,

support of education, and so on. It will be highly future-oriented. A combination of behavioral technology and public policy-making technology will support individual life styles in a pluralistic environment within the framework of evolving world ideas.

To develop and operationalize career education programs from the least comprehensive—level 1—to the most comprehensive, futuristic, humanistic—level 9—will be expensive and demand talent. Crucial decisions must be made as to how to parcel out the work and how to avoid duplication of effort. However, if our citizens are to prosper in the pluralistic society of the year 2000 and beyond, do we have any alternative?

Let us turn at this point to an examination of some basic models that illustrate the conceptual dimensions of career education in the United States.

CAREER EDUCATION MODELS

Career education, according to Herr (15), can be seen as the synthesis of two streams of thought about educational purpose. One uses an occupational model as its stimulus; the other uses a career model. The occupational model has been concerned principally with ensuring that students, when they leave school, have highly developed skills in rather narrowly defined occupations. The career model, on the other hand, conceives of the individual as moving through the educational system along a number of pathways that have differing points of entrance to the work system. This model emphasizes the importance of individuals having the skills that will permit them to choose as freely as possible among the multiple occupational opportunities.

The career model is broader than the occupational model. It includes not only the acquisition of occupational skills but also the factors—attitudes, knowledge, self-concepts—that motivate decision-making styles. This model is concerned with helping students develop preferences and execute plans by which they can implement them. Thus the implications for personal growth found in the career model are not confined only to young people going directly to work. This model maintains that all students, regardless of their ultimate goal beyond high school, need to be helped to find purpose in what they are doing (16).

Most of our school systems currently operate within a subject-centered curriculum. A scope and sequence of skills is identified for each subject, and each student is, theoretically, placed on a continuum according to his or her achievement, abilities, and interests, as shown in Figure 4.1. Little progress has been achieved, however, in cutting across subject lines and integrating these subjects into a meaningful whole for the student. Likewise, there has been only limited success in relating much of the content of these existing courses to student goals.

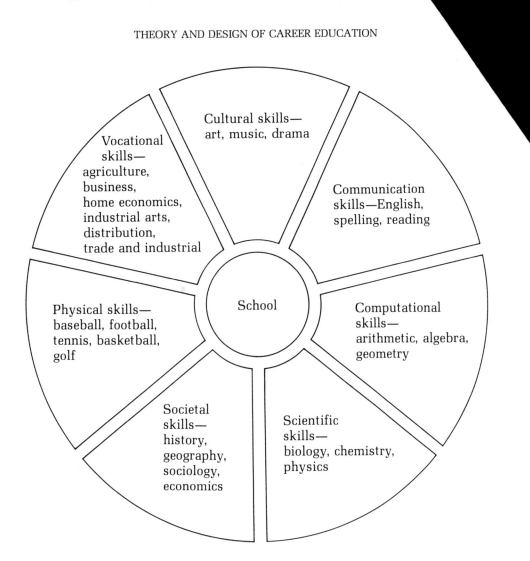

Figure 4.1   The subject-centered curriculum

As reflected in Figure 4.2, however, career education is an educational process, a means to an end, the end being the realization of the individual's economic, political, social, and personal goals. This model illustrates three major principles of career education:

1. There is a continuum of career phases, ranging from career awareness to career preparation, with intermediate stages of career exploration and orientation. Although each phase is identified with a specific time period (K–6, 7–8, 9–10, 11–Adult), there is a progression to the phases, as indi-

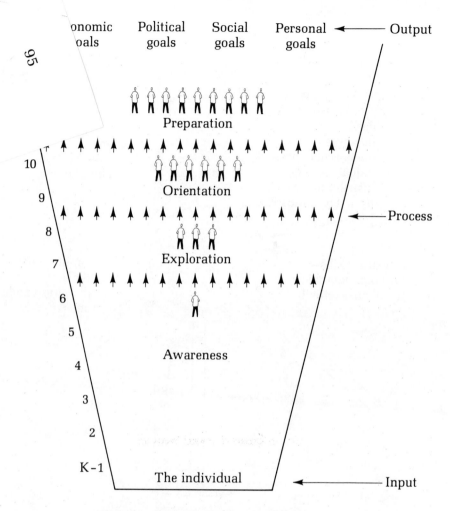

Figure 4.2 Career education model

cated by the upward arrows. The inverse pyramid indicates the continuous and expanding nature of these phases as individuals grow and mature through career education.

2. Learning experiences both within and outside the formal school structure should be selected as a *means* of helping the individual to fulfill his or her economic, political, social, and personal goals. Thus subject matter is selected for its contribution to the student's goals. Learning experiences of more depth are needed throughout life as individuals set and reset goals and as their varying personal roles develop.

3. There is a movement toward an individualized approach to learning. During

the awareness phase, activities are planned for both individuals and groups that focus on general awareness of the world of work, the values of a work-oriented society, and the role of the individual. At this level, all students are exposed to the same concepts, although they practice them in a variety of settings.

As students move through the upper phases of career education, they select clusters, or families, of occupations to explore. As they approach the preparation phase, choices are narrowed to one cluster, and later training provides specialized competency within that cluster. Thus career education becomes more diversified as it advances through the four phases and as individuals select from and experience the multiple career options available, both in the roles toward which they aspire and in the learning experiences available as preparation.

An analysis of federal career education models will set the stage for a more comprehensive understanding of these concepts.

FEDERAL MODELS FOR CAREER EDUCATION

In 1971 the U.S. Office of Education announced its intention to spend $15 million in the development of four experimental models for career education.* Model 1 was to be school based; Model 2, employer based; Model 3, rural-residential based; and Model 4, home-community based. Initial USOE model conceptualization of career education served as a foundation for Model 1.

/. School-Based Model

The Center for Vocational and Technical Education (CVTE) was designated in 1971 by the U.S. Office of Education as the prime contractor for the school-based model. The purpose of the project was to develop, test, and install a Comprehensive Career Education Model (CCEM) by restructuring the existing American educational program around career development needs. The USOE model, shown in Figure 4.3, illustrates the relationship of the broad goals of career education (awareness, exploration, and preparation) to the options of further education or immediate job placement.

The object of Model 1 (CCEM) was to develop and test a career education system (K–12) in six school systems (representing varying sizes, geographic locations, and cultural ethnic populations) that would help students to develop (a) a comprehensive awareness of career options; (b) a concept of self that is in

---

*Simultaneously, 52 "mini-models" of career education, funded as exemplary programs under the Vocational Education Act, were activated in local school districts. United States Office of Education Commissioner Marland further allotted $9 million from discretionary funds to the states for vocational research and development focusing on establishment of career education models.

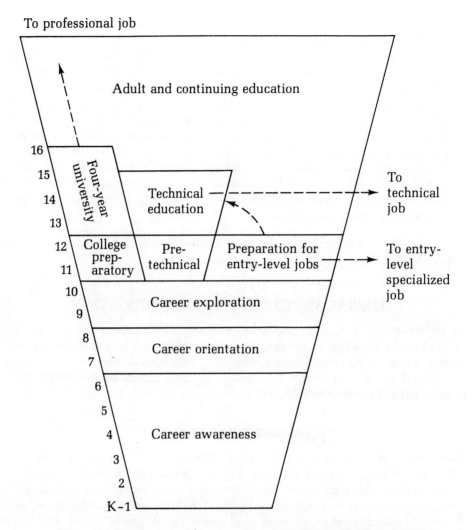

To professional job

Adult and continuing education

16
15
14 Four-year university
13

Technical education → - - - - - - - - → To technical job

12 College prep-aratory
11

Pre-technical | Preparation for entry-level jobs → - - → To entry-level specialized job

10
9   Career exploration

8
7   Career orientation

6
5
4   Career awareness
3
2
K-1

Figure 4.3 USOE comprehensive career education system: school-based model. Source: ERIC Clearinghouse on Vocational and Technical Education, *Career Education Practice,* Information Service No. 65, VT 017 221. Columbus: The Center for Vocational and Technical Education, The Ohio State University, Dec. 1972, p. 19.

keeping with a work-oriented society, including positive attitudes about work, school, and society, and a sense of satisfaction resulting from successful experience in these areas; (c) personal characteristics, such as self-respect, initiative, and resourcefulness; (d) a realistic understanding of the relationships between the world of work and education to assist individuals in becoming contributing members of society; and (e) the ability to enter employment in a selected occupational area and/or to go on for further education.

In conceptualizing the role of career education in a comprehensive school setting, Model 1 drew heavily on theories from the areas of vocational education, guidance, curriculum development, and human growth and development. Eight areas of educational experience were identified as the basic conceptual elements of career education: career awareness, self-awareness, appreciations/ attitudes, decision-making skills, economic awareness, beginning competency, employability skills, and educational awareness.

After the elements were identified, the CVTE staff designated terminal "outcomes" as student-learning goals for each element. These outcomes were designed to equip exiting students with entry-level job skills and to prepare them for further academic or vocational education. The element outcomes were: career identity, self-identity, self-social fulfillment, career decisions, economic understandings, employment skills, career placement, and educational identity. The eight elements and their corresponding outcomes, when placed graphically against the 13 grade levels (K–12), evolved a CCEM Program Goal Matrix, as illustrated in Figure 4.4.

The Model 1 curriculum (K–12) includes all those experiences of the child under the auspices of the school that use both on- and off-campus educational resources to provide the opportunity for, appreciation for, and understanding of the dignity of work and a fulfilling life. It is assumed that Model 1 must:

1. assist youths to choose an individualized personal life style and to establish and discover alternative paths for reaching goals commensurate with that life style
2. prepare students to enter the world of work as contributing members of a productive society
3. assist young people to view education as a lifelong pursuit that is not restricted to schools, classrooms, or traditional institutions of learning
4. assist youths to develop problem-solving skills required to cope with an increasingly cybernated society

2. Employer-Experience-Based Model

The objectives of Model 2, the employer-based model (also called experience-based) (17), were (a) to provide an alternative educational program for students, aged 13–18, in an employer-based setting; (b) to unify the positive elements of academic, general, and vocational curricula into a comprehensive career education program; (c) to increase the relevance of education to the world of work; and (d) to broaden the base of community participation, particularly by involving public and private employers more directly in education.

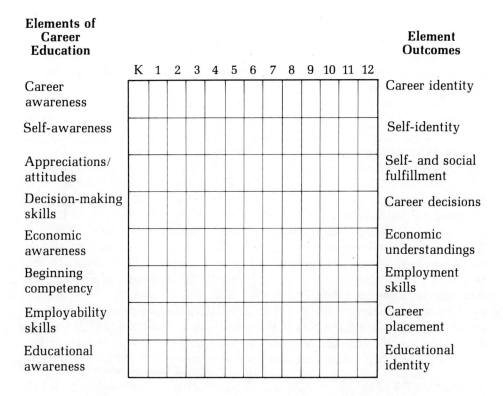

Figure 4.4 Comprehensive Career Education Model: Program Goal Matrix. Source: Center for Vocational Education, The Ohio State University, Progress Report, Project 7−0158, July 20, 1972.

Model 2 advocated year-round operation and open entrance and exit of students, and it offered a new setting for academic studies, which keyed them to job experiences provided by a consortium of local employers, such as banks, publishers, travel agencies, hospitals, and factories. Each consortium encouraged the cooperation of diverse community groups, such as unions, schools, parents, and employers.

Certain stipulations, identified by the U.S. Office of Education, were to be followed in establishing employer-based models; namely, they must provide for the needs of all students; they must allow students to return to a traditional school setting; and they must provide for college-bound students as well as for those who intended to enter the labor force.

An example of the employer-experience-based model is Far West High School, Oakland, California, which served as the original pilot school. Today, students at Far West High School select their own jobs and career fields in community settings. On the other hand, students are expected to respect the rules of campus behavior. Using the resources of the career center, students complete ten career profiles each six weeks and at least one in-depth, work-oriented project per year. These projects bring students into direct contact with lawyers, dentists, welders, and other community resource personnel up to several hours per week (18).

3. Rural-Residential-Based Model

The objective of the Mountain Plains Education and Economic Development Program (MPEEDP) was to develop, through action, research, and experimentation, programs that could be implemented on a widespread basis (19). Model 3, the rural-residential career education model, was committed to improving the personal development and employability of individuals in a six-state region. This experimental demonstration activity involved various individuals, agencies, and other resources in preparing adults and children of rural unemployed and underemployed families in Wyoming, Montana, Idaho, North Dakota, South Dakota, and Nebraska for rewarding employment. The private, nonprofit corporation, MPEEDP, with its core management team located at a former air force base at Glasgow, Montana, engaged in a comprehensive research design, from the initial selection of participants through job placement and follow-up, and trained the staff for each state.

At the Montana site low-income families from the six-state region trained for 6 to 18 months. Each member of each family learned new skills, whether for better jobs, more efficient homemaking, or further education. In 1972, over 100 families were in training in Glasgow. Guiding the research and program development activities was a working definition that viewed career education as the aggregate of processes by which individuals acquired and developed the goals (values), abilities (knowledge, attitudes, skills, and behaviors), and motivation to: (a) contribute to their own growth and to the growth of their society; and (b) make prudent use of their personal as well as their society's resources and energies. The ultimate goal of the residential-based model was to determine whether low-income rural residents could develop career roles through specially adapted in-house experiences.

4. Home-Community-Based Model

The fourth model, a home-community effort, used television and radio programming to encourage unemployed or underemployed adults to take advantage of local retraining programs. Through the use of the home-based model, the U.S. Office of Education hoped to (a) enhance the quality of the home as a learning center, (b) develop educational delivery systems into the home and community, (c) provide new career education programs for adults, (d) establish a guidance and career placement system to assist individuals in occupational and related roles, and (e) develop more competent workers. The home-community-based model thus featured adult education—at home, on the job, in a community center, or wherever it was most convenient or effective.

STATE MODELS FOR CAREER EDUCATION

Various states have developed models and programs for implementing career education. Two federal models, school-based and employer-experience-based, have made significant contributions to theory and practice at the state and local levels.

Wisconsin Model

Wisconsin has an effective approach toward implementing career education. The thrust of the plan is toward integration of career guidance activities into the curriculum. Initially, the state superintendent of public instruction appointed a 35-member career development study committee of teachers, pupil personnel specialists, and school administrators. Over a two-year period, the committee developed and field tested a curriculum-centered career development model. The efforts of the superintendent's study committee resulted in [20]:

1. *a definition of the career development process*
2. *a designed conceptual framework for a career development model*
3. *identification of 16 major concepts in career development*
4. *a scope-and-sequence matrix model for program infusion at appropriate grade levels*
5. *several hundred general objectives that would aid in implementing identified concepts*
6. *local workshop organizational plans, resource aids, and program references*

These products were intended to assist local school staffs in designing their career development programs and to encourage statewide program continuity. Figure 4.5 illustrates the career development model, and Figure 4.6 provides an example of its application.

The program has been carried out in Wisconsin through state-conducted local workshops for teachers; leadership was provided by members of the superintendent's study committee, who had themselves used the workshop approach to validate in-service methods. (Significantly, after developing the model, members of the study committee saw career development as a *process*, whereas each had previously viewed it as a variety of unrelated programs.)

Because the state model covered only general concepts and objectives, members of each local system staff completed their own district guides, including behavioral objectives, teacher methods, student activities, resource

Concept 1

An understanding and
acceptance of self is
important throughout
life

Concept 1

. Example of working
evaluation procedure
cube

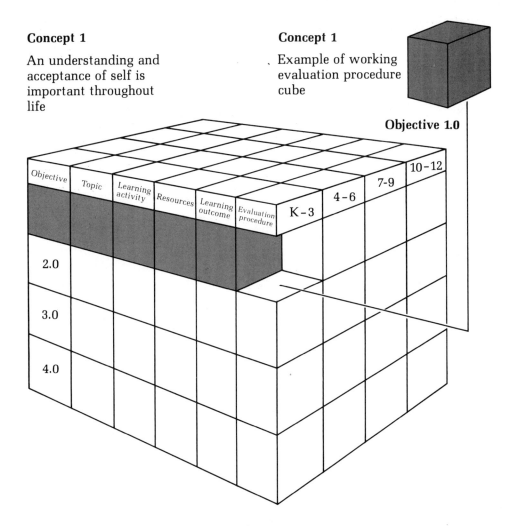

Figure 4.5 Wisconsin model for career development: vertical and
horizontal example for model expansion (21)

materials, curriculum considerations, student outcomes, and evaluation procedures. This strategy ensured maximal implementation of plans that were
uniquely fitted to student and community needs.

Hawaii Model

Hawaii's Career Development Model forms the basis for learning experiences,
grades K-14. The model identifies three basic components essential for
achievement of career development: (a) individual growth and development
through self-realization, economic efficiency, social relationships, and civic

Concepts	Elementary	Middle—Junior High School		High School
	Middle childhood K-3	Late childhood 4-6	Early adolescence 7-9	Adolescence 10-12
1	Introduce	Develop	Emphasize	Emphasize
2	Introduce	Develop	Emphasize	Emphasize
3	Introduce	Develop	Emphasize	Emphasize
4	Introduce	Develop	Emphasize	Emphasize
5	Introduce	Develop	Emphasize	Emphasize
6	Introduce	Develop	Emphasize	Emphasize
7	Introduce	Develop	Emphasize	Emphasize
8		Introduce	Develop	Emphasize
9		Introduce	Develop	Emphasize
10		Introduce	Develop	Emphasize
11		Introduce	Develop	Emphasize
12		Introduce	Develop	Emphasize
13		Introduce	Develop	Emphasize
14		Introduce	Develop	Emphasize
15			Introduce	Develop
16			Introduce	Develop

Code

Introduce

Develop

Emphasize

Career Development Concepts

1 An understanding and acceptance of self is important throughout life.
2 Persons need to be recognized as having dignity and worth.
3 Occupations exist for a purpose.
4 There is a wide variety of careers that may be classified in several ways.
5 Work means different things to different people.
6 Education and work are interrelated.
7 Individuals differ in their interests, abilities, attitudes, and values.
8 Occupational supply and demand have an impact on career planning.
9 Job specialization creates interdependency.
10 Environment and individual potential interact to influence career development.
11 Occupations and life styles are interrelated.
12 Individuals can learn to perform adequately in a variety of occupations.
13 Career development requires a continuous and sequential series of choices.
14 Various groups and institutions influence the nature and structure of work.
15 Individuals are responsible for their career planning.
16 Job characteristics and individuals must be flexible in a changing society.

Figure 4.6 Wisconsin career development scope-and-sequence model (21)(22)

responsibility; (b) an environment in which growth occurs in home, school, work/leisure, and community; (c) a sequence of experiences through awareness, exploration, and preparation-placement. (See Figure 4.7) (23).

South Portland, Maine, Model

As shown in Table 4.1, South Portland's Career Development Design incorporates eight basic elements. Goals at four educational levels—primary, intermediate, junior high, and senior high—are shown for each of the basic elements (24).

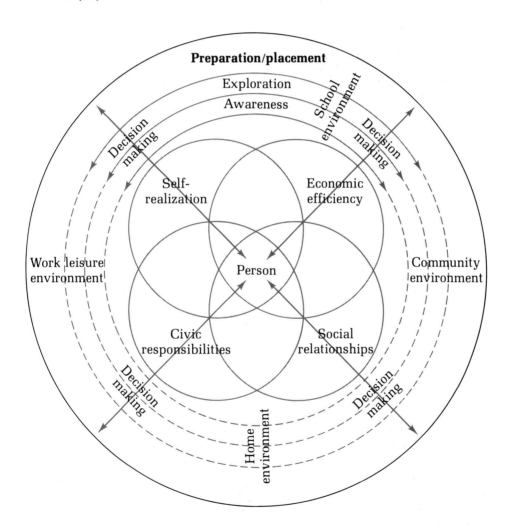

Figure 4.7 Hawaii conceptual model of career development

Table 4.1 Career Development Design, South Portland, Maine

	Goals			
	Primary	Intermediate	Junior high	Senior high
Self-Awareness	Demonstrate an awareness of one's own interests, skills, and feelings.	Demonstrate an appreciation of one's own skills, interests, feelings, and values.	Recognize that one's talents, values, interests, and limitations relate to career goals.	Make goal-oriented choices related to one's career requirements and future employability skills.
Interpersonal Skills	Demonstrate cooperation in social situations.	Develop an appreciation of the differences between individuals or groups.	Develop the interpersonal skills required for work roles, recognizing that trust and respect are factors in human relations.	Demonstrate an understanding of the importance of human relationships in volunteer and part- and full-time work.
Decision Making	Use one's senses to gather data and to develop concepts.	Develop skills in making generalizations, hypothesizing, and predicting.	Develop an awareness of the results of decisions which will give one a sense of control over the future.	Identify realistic alternatives based on education, work experience, and counseling and accept responsibility for career decisions.
Work Awareness	Gain knowledge of workers in the home, school, and community.	Identify the personal and environmental factors which influence a worker.	Explore and analyze the common and unique characteristics of jobs within the 15 USOE job clusters.	Recognize that social, environmental, and technical factors influence career trends and as a result workers must be flexible, adaptable, and mobile.

Manipulative Skills	Develop psychomotor skills.	Improve psychomotor skills.	Identify and use manipulative skills that are essential to many careers and leisure time activities.	Develop competence in use of manipulative skills required in one's future career or educational plans.
Economic Awareness	Understand that people are paid for their work and use that money to satisfy their needs and wants.	Recognize that each individual is a consumer, producer, and citizen, and as such has certain rights and responsibilities.	Develop an awareness of the financial and legal consumer resources as they relate to personal and family economics.	Understand and appreciate, as a worker and consumer, the complexities of the American economic system.
Value of Work	Identify ways that workers are of service to the community.	Recognize that an individual can find satisfaction through work.	Understand impact of one's career on one's lifestyle.	Gain insight into personal and social value of employment through simulated or real work experience.
Relevance of Education	Recognize that school is a place to learn.	Recognize that schooling is necessary for future careers.	Recognize that mental, physical, and communicative skills are basic and applicable to all career fields.	Identify the relation between mastery of content knowledge and educational or vocational plans.

SUMMARY

The continuous and accelerated nature of change in our society brings about frequent and intensive appraisal of education. Career education is a reflection of the continuing need for change in public education. Most of the elements of career education are not new but have their roots in early efforts to implant vocational education and vocational guidance in the public schools. New emphasis, however, was given to the career education concept in 1971 by Dr. Sidney P. Marland, U.S. Commissioner of Education, who advocated a "totally new system," involving the blending of academic and vocational programs. Marland outlined only the broad parameters of a new learner-centered system, preferring that states and local school districts develop and refine their own career education plans and strategies. The challenge to spell out essential aspects evoked a wide and generally positive reaction among educators who formulated a diversity of conceptualizations of career education, ranging from an emphasis on earning a living in the narrowest sense, to an emphasis on the individual in relation to the total environment in the broadest sense. The career education movement received further impetus in 1974 when the Office of Career Education was established by Congress.

There is general agreement that the objectives of career education should be (a) to allow all students to relate their education to the world of work; (b) to provide an opportunity to engage in occupational exploration, including work experience, specialized instruction, and career decision-making, leading toward a preferred life style and career pattern; and (c) to provide automatic exit and reentry to the educational system or the labor force as needed. The transitional phases in career education programs that are most evident are career *awareness,* career *exploration,* career *identification,* career *preparation,* and career *assessment.*

The U.S. Office of Education funded the development of four experimental models for career education: the school-based model, the employer- or experience-based model, the rural-residential-based model, and the home-community-based model. In addition, states have successfully developed and implemented their own career education models. The school-based and employer-experience-based models have made significant contributions to the theory and practice of career education. Most current career education models recognize that learning experiences inside and outside the school should be selected as a means of helping individuals fulfill their economic, political, social, and personal roles. The methodology of career education moves away from a group approach toward an individualized approach to learning.

ACTIVITIES

For review

1. Cite several ways in which career education differs from the traditional subject-centered curriculum.

2. Compare and contrast vocational education and career education.

3. Briefly contrast the four United States Office of Education career education models as to their objectives and organization.

4. Summarize the contributions of career education to the following roles of the individual: economic, personal, social, political.

5. What are the basic reasons for job preparation in terms of occupational clusters as opposed to preparation for a single occupation?

6. What two basic elements are emphasized in the generic definition of career education mentioned by Associate United States Commissioner of Education Kenneth B. Hoyt?

For discussion

1. Which of the nine levels of career education presented in the chapter most closely describes your interpretation of the role of career education?

2. Contrast the basic beliefs of John Dewey and Charles Prosser with the primary objectives of career education as you interpret it.

3. How does career education differ for (a) the high school sophomore, (b) the high school senior, (c) the junior college student, (d) the college senior, (e) you?

For exploration

1. Secure a copy of your state model/plan for career education. How is it similar to or different from the comprehensive career education model and the state models presented in this chapter?

2. Interview one or more of the following individuals for his or her definition of career education: an elementary teacher, a high school teacher of academic courses, a high school teacher of vocational courses, a counselor, a principal, a college teacher of academic courses, a college teacher of vocational courses. How do their conceptualizations differ? Why? What implications can be drawn for future implementation of career education?

3. Prepare a job ladder for the occupational cluster that represents your primary career field of interest. Such a ladder will reflect occupations requiring varying levels of preparation and ability.

4. From the current literature, describe one career education model not discussed in the text.

REFERENCES

1. Gordon I. Swanson, "Facts and Fantasies of Career Education," *The Visitor*, Vol. 69, No. 2, April 1972, p. 2.

2. Edwin L. Herr, *Review and Synthesis of Foundations for Career Education*

(Columbus: ERIC Clearinghouse on Vocational-Technical Education, The Center for Vocational and Technical Education, The Ohio State University, March 1972), pp. 29–30.

3. Sidney P. Marland, Jr., "Career Education Now," in *Vocational Guidance Quarterly,* Vol. 20, No. 3, March 1972, p. 190.

4. Ibid., pp. 190–92.

5. Terrence H. Bell, "Career Education in 1974: A View from the Commissioner's Desk," address to the National Conference of State Coordinators of Career Education, The Center for Vocational Education, The Ohio State University, Oct. 31, 1974. Delivered by tele-lecture.

6. Kenneth B. Hoyt, "An Introduction to Career Education," policy paper of the Office of Education, Nov. 1974.

7. Terrence H. Bell and Kenneth B. Hoyt, *Career Education: The USOE Perspective* (Columbus: The Center for Vocational Education, The Ohio State University, 1974), p. 10.

8. Wesley Smith, "Career Education: A Bridge to Relevancy in the Public Schools" (Sacramento: California Department of Education, n.d.), as quoted in William C. Miller, "Career Education and the Curriculum Leader," *Educational Leadership,* Vol. 31, No. 2, Nov. 1973, p. 154. (Reproduced by permission.)

9. Hoyt, "An Introduction to Career Education."

10. Kenneth C. Hoyt, *A Primer for Career Education* (Washington, D.C.: Office of Career Education, USOE, HEW, 1977), p. 5.

11. Swanson, "Facts and Fantasies of Career Education."

12. Kenneth B. Hoyt, Rupert N. Evans, Edward F. Mackin, and Garth L. Mangum, *Career Education: What It Is and How to Do It,* 2nd ed. (Salt Lake City: Olympus Publishing Company, 1974), pp. 5–6. (Reproduced by permission.)

13. Louise J. Keller, "Objectives for Career Education in Office Education," address to the National Business Education Association, Chicago, Feb. 21, 1973.

14. Ibid.

15. Edwin L. Herr, "Unifying an Entire System of Education Around a Career Development Theme," in *Career Education: Perspective and Promise,* Keith Goldhammer and Robert E. Taylor, eds. (Columbus: Charles E. Merrill Publishing Company, 1972), p. 100.

16. Ibid., p. 101.

17. Keith Goldhammer and Robert E. Taylor, eds., *Career Education: Perspective and Promise* (Columbus: Charles E. Merrill Publishing Company, 1972), p. 8.

18. Robert C. Yeager, "Research for the Real World," *American Education,* Vol. 16, No. 6, July 1980, p. 15.

19. Wesley E. Budke, Glenn E. Beattis, and Gary F. Beasley, *Career Education*

Practice (Columbus: ERIC Clearinghouse for Vocational and Technical Education, The Center for Vocational and Technical Education, The Ohio State University, 1972), pp. 11–13.

20. Harry N. Drier, Jr., "Career Development Activities Permeate Wisconsin Curriculum," *American Vocational Journal*, Vol. 47, No. 3, March 1972, p. 40. (Reproduced by permission.)

21. Ibid., p. 41.

22. Ibid., p. 40.

23. Hawaii Career Development Continuum: Curriculum Guide for Grades 7 through 9 (Office of Instructional Services, Department of Education, State of Hawaii, 1974), pp. 12–13.

24. "Career Development Design," South Portland, Maine, School District. (Reproduced by permission.)

CHAPTER FIVE

■

Implementing Career
Education

INTRODUCTION

In this chapter we shall examine (a) the role and objectives of career education
at the elementary, middle school, secondary, and higher education levels; (b)
the implications of career education for the training of teachers; (c) career
guidance at the elementary, middle school, secondary, and higher education
levels; and (d) the role of the federal government in career education.

THROUGH THE ELEMENTARY SCHOOL

If career education is to attain its goals, then it must begin in the elementary
school. At this level, students must be helped to become aware of the world of
work, of the values of a work-oriented society, and of themselves as individuals
and as members of society.

At the elementary level, career education is conceived as a mélange of
experiences, such as interpersonal relationships, hands-on creative expression,
and problem-solving work. It is most effectively implemented as an integral
part of the existing curriculum. Implementing career education does not mean
adding another course to an already crowded curriculum. Neither does it
suggest that the teacher de-emphasize existing substantive content. Rather, the
implementation of career education involves the modification of present course
outlines to include a career education *emphasis*.

Operating on the broad goals for career education, state and local school systems are identifying specific career education objectives that guide the development and implementation of local programs. For example, the *Career Development Guide for the Elementary School*, developed by the state of Maine, identifies these program objectives (1):

1. *introduce the student to the world of work and career opportunities*
2. *establish the relationship of occupational skills to academic skills*
3. *develop, through exploration, a self realization related to abilities and interest for future career selection*
4. *acquaint students with problem-solving techniques as they prepare themselves for the world of work*
5. *encourage the student to understand that career selection is related to the need and abilities of the individual*
6. *develop an understanding and appreciation of the interrelationship of the various careers in the world of work*

Three basic characteristics were identified in *The Yellow Brick Road* to guide the development and/or selection of career development strategies and resources. First, the strategy must be affectively based; second, the strategy must be action-oriented; finally, the strategy must focus upon examining people in careers, not just jobs or occupations (2).

THROUGH THE MIDDLE SCHOOL

Exploration is a crucial phase in career education. The skills and knowledge acquired during this phase become the foundation for decision making at succeeding levels. The major thrust at the middle school level is toward having the student explore various occupational clusters and become familiar with the preparation requirements and the educational opportunities available for obtaining the necessary training.

The U.S. Office of Education has identified the following occupational clusters as those into which career education will ultimately be integrated at all levels of the educational program:

Business and Office Occupations
Marketing and Distribution Occupations
Communications and Media Occupations
Construction Occupations
Manufacturing Occupations
Transportation Occupations
Agri-Business and Natural Resources Occupations
Marine Science Occupations

Environmental Control Occupations
Public Service Occupations
Health Occupations
Hospitality and Recreation Occupations
Personal Services Occupations
Fine Arts and Humanities Occupations
Consumer and Homemaking Occupations

Within each cluster, specific occupations may be perceived as existing on a particular rung of a career ladder; thus, occupations may be viewed both individually and in relation to each other within the cluster. During the exploratory phase, the student should examine not only the opportunities available within a cluster of occupations but also the life-style implications of each occupation.

The focus of career education at the middle grade level is evident in the objectives identified for the programs. For example, the Hosterman Junior High School Career Development Committee, in Minnesota, has developed a guide to career development in grades 7–9 as it can be facilitated by English, mathematics, science, and social studies units. They formulated a list of assumptions that underlie the development of clusters of occupations and that can be related to specific subject areas (3):

1. *Career exploration, instead of being a difficult and clumsy addition to the teaching process, can actually become an efficient, effective vehicle for all types of learning.*

2. *Curriculum experiences need to be interdisciplinary or, better still, non-disciplinary in nature.*

3. *The student must be allowed to discover through interesting and meaningful (to him or her) activities that planning for career choices and maintenance is an ongoing process.*

4. *Career development is essentially a process of relating self to occupations.*

Along with an examination of occupational clusters, the exploration phase at the middle grades level should provide opportunities for students to examine themselves, their abilities, and their goals. A strong guidance and counseling component is important in the exploration phase of career implementation because it helps students realistically to correlate information about themselves with occupational choices. As students begin to explore a wide variety of occupations, they are also beginning to make very tentative decisions regarding suitable careers that offer possibilities for a life style that they envision as their own. They also continue their analysis of the economic aspects of the world of work and become increasingly familiar with the effects of societal and cultural factors on individual behavior.

THROUGH THE SECONDARY SCHOOL

The career-centered curriculum at the high school level represents a continuation of experiences that are similar to those of the awareness and exploration phases at the elementary and middle school levels. At this level, however, emphasis is placed on occupational preparation activities within occupational clusters.

Integration or interlocking of content is more difficult to achieve at the secondary level than at the elementary levels for obvious reasons: 1. Teacher preparation is presently aimed toward preparing subject-matter specialists. 2. Most teachers, especially those outside the vocational areas, have little or no work experience outside teaching and generally inadequate knowledge of occupational requirements. 3. Many teachers lack the necessary skills and knowledge of occupational clusters needed to relate the curriculum content to the student's career plans. 4. Many school systems are unable to provide the necessary time for teachers of the various disciplines to plan complementary learning experiences.

Increasing numbers of school systems are focusing on revision of secondary school objectives and goals to reflect the integration of curricula that is implicit in career education.

If teachers are to give a genuine career focus to their disciplines, they must have a clear concept of the manner in which career education goals relate to those of their subject areas. According to Suhor (4), certain goals of career education and subject-area instruction should be seen as congruent; others as overlapping; still others as essentially distinctive.

When the goals are congruent, exact fits exist between the subject area and career education goals. Accounting, bricklaying, and auto mechanics illustrate congruent goals in vocational education. In other disciplines, critical thinking skills in English, discovery learning in science, problem solving in mathematics, and inquiry training in social studies illustrate broad types of process-oriented skills that carry over into career.

Subject-based overlapping goals are outgrowths or extensions of units whose primary emphasis is on the subject area. For instance, a unit on nutrition might end with visits by community professionals who discuss careers in health. In a career-based overlapping program, the focus is on careers with a direct tie-in with the discipline. An example would be a math class setting up a miniature "stock exchange."

Some subject-area goals have no apparent career goals except to the person who might later become a specialist in the area. Scanning the meter of a Petrarchan sonnet is of little career use to anyone except the potential English scholar. Many such distinctive goals are an important part of the liberal education of students. Teachers should, however, review the kinds of goals in a given lesson plan or course of study. A large number of distinctive goals might suggest that priorities are focused on the subject, rather than on the student.

A well balanced program in a subject area would probably be strong on congruent goals, reflecting a double orientation towards the cognitive and career development of the student; rich in overlapping goals, reflecting a sense of connectedness between the school and the world of work; and highly selective in distinctive goals, reflecting a thoughtful approach to liberal education rather than indiscriminate dumping of specialized concepts into the curriculum (5).

In summary, career education at the secondary level includes the following objectives: exploring careers within a specific family of occupations; selecting a specific career, making initial preparations, and developing post–high school plans related to it; developing salable skills; continuing development, refinement, and application of basic skills; and developing the attitudes, skills, and understandings that relate to the personal, family, social, and cultural dimensions of one's life.

THROUGH HIGHER EDUCATION

Comprehensive career education has yet to become commonplace in American higher education. However, elements relating to a comprehensive career education effort are evident in many higher education settings. These include open admission, experiential learning, lifelong learning, recurrent education, career development centers, work experience and work-study programs, internships, humanistic education, labor market and employment trends among college graduates, reduction of race and sex stereotyping in educational/occupational decision making, and performance evaluation. Each of these topics shares a number of concerns, assumptions, and research findings with the career education concept, but none of them can be considered synonymous with a comprehensive effort (6).

Career education efforts in higher education should reflect increased efforts to relate what is taught in the classroom to the world of work.

The advantages of a career dimensioned program of integrated education and work are numerous. For students it can mean a more realistic understanding of an occupation's demands and the opportunity to test and deepen or to revise the career commitment. There is also the opportunity to interact with strong role models and to experience involvement as a catalyst for decision-making and a source of higher motivation. Further, such experiences can function to make job hunting less traumatic because of a more realistic view of what to expect (7).

The high proportion of adults who change occupations during their employment points up the necessity for students to acquire skills that are transferable among career choices.

Two-Year Programs

The two-year programs of higher education have a four-fold career-education responsibility: (a) to provide multiple options in career education; (b) to work with secondary schools and postsecondary proprietary schools in the orderly articulation of career education sequences; (c) to work with the major producer and service units in the economy on such issues as desirable pre- and in-service training and work-study programs; and (d) to maintain constant contact with four-year colleges and universities to negotiate the issues of educational philosophy and academic transfer. The two-year college system may well be the fulcrum of career education. As such it has a responsibility to search for balanced, highest-common-denominator agreements about the meaning and direction of the career education movement.

Four-Year Programs

Four-year baccalaureate programs have many contributions to make to the emerging emphasis on career education. The first is to ensure that career education does not slip into the traditional mold of training solely for the vocations and professions. If career education is to become a truly liberating concept, it must subsume definitions of career that go beyond job competency. Most human beings are awake 112 hours a week; only 40 of those hours are spent on the job, leaving 72 hours for social and personal matters. Most four-year higher education institutions attempt to feature those aspects of curricula that relate not just to human technology for the economy but to human conditions. Designers of career curricula must catch the spirit of liberal arts education and meld it with vocational and professional training at all levels.

The second contribution four-year colleges can make to career education is to work with their extension divisions and with external degree programs to provide off-campus remedial programs in liberal arts studies for those who wish to broaden their educational horizons. An individual may come to value the liberal arts components of education later in life, when the tedium of a particular job becomes oppressive.

A third contribution that the four-year college can make to career education is to devise further means of providing wholeness or unity to the total educational program. This task will involve concerted efforts collegewide to provide the basis for multidisciplinary programs and experiences.

Higher education institutions view the emerging concept of career education with mixed reactions. While some deplore the democratization and further vocationalism of higher education, others welcome the shift toward practical training. In the long run, the pluralism of higher education is likely to have a mitigating effect on tensions created by the debate about career education.

But higher education in the United States has always been career-oriented. Harvard University was established in 1636 to train clergy. During the next two centuries a variety of private and sectarian colleges were established for the training of men for spiritual, intellectual, and political leadership. The Morrill Act in 1862 gave thrust to the notion that higher education should be career-oriented in specific and practical terms, and it resulted in a mingling of the liberal arts emphases with occupational professionalism. Consequently, such diverse fields as teaching, law, business, medicine, agriculture, and homemaking have been served both by general education and by specifically occupational courses at the undergraduate and graduate levels.

There is some truth to the contention that most general curricula are designed to cultivate humanistic insights and intellectual capacities that are not specific to careers, hence the assumption that preparation for life is more than narrow job training. In addition the status conferred by degree credentials continues to have bearing on career rewards regardless of the specificity or sophistication of college-level education. Yet automation and specialization have led to the fact that eight of ten jobs in the next ten years will need less than a baccalaureate level of preparation. As the need for technical job skills increases and as the costs of higher education continue to rise, the real and assumed benefits of baccalaureate status may melt away.

The prestigious liberal arts institution tends to deplore these trends toward democratization and further "vocationalization" of higher education. On the other hand, the two-year community college and the comprehensive university and proprietary school tend to welcome the shift toward practical training. The strength of American higher education is its pluralism, and diverse contributions to the concept of career education can be made by even the highest levels of educational institutions: the graduate professional schools and the graduate programs in the arts and sciences.

University of Mississippi

The career education efforts at the University of Mississippi illustrate one approach to implementing career education at the postsecondary level. To cope with increasing student consciousness of and demand for more and better career counseling services, the University of Mississippi appointed a coordinator of career services in 1975 to enhance career counseling in its Student Counseling Center, in the Division of Student Personnel Services. The center performs several major functions: (1) vocational testing and counseling, including making occupational literature available to students; (2) group and individual training in methods of effective study; (3) group and individual training in reading skills; (4) personal counseling on a confidential basis; and (5) administration and interpretation of various standardized achievement tests. Trained counselors are available to help students solve educational, vocational, and personal problems.

Reacting to student demands, the Student Counseling Center is expanding its services. The center is involved in activities that begin prior to admission of students as freshmen and continue beyond graduation. Although the University Placement Office has always assisted students in job placement upon graduation, it is now involved in group and one-to-one counseling and information sessions through courses, office visits, and student organizations.

During freshman orientation there is more emphasis on career development counseling and on making incoming students aware of the resources available at the University to assist them in career decision making. As students become more concerned with their futures and with what their education is doing—or not doing—to prepare them for careers, they rely more and more on the center for help. The center has developed a sophomore-level course in "Career and Life Planning" that carries three semester hours credit. It is designed to give students who are undecided about their career futures a long-term, structured approach to the process of choosing a career through self-assessment, occupational exploration, and decision-making activities. The center serves 150 to 300 students each year through this course.

The center has also been involved in helping academic departments develop career fact sheets for distribution to prospective students. The emphasis in these fliers has shifted from curricula to career opportunities through curricula. The center keeps faculty informed of its activities through memoranda, surveys, and leaflets, and seeks faculty suggestions as to how it can serve the students better.

The School of Education has developed a junior-level course called "Career Education," required of all students preparing to be teachers. Its objective is to prepare them as teachers to assist their students in career development.

Graduate Programs

Graduate professional schools can perform a major role in describing professional careers and in articulating the technical and paraprofessional training needed by those who wish to enter a professional field at a support level rather than at a professional level. The training and certification of paraprofessionals in education is a case in point. Graduate professional schools also bear a heavy responsibility for developing leadership personnel to conduct the research and development aspects of career education.

The quality of intellectual standards involved in research and teaching in graduate schools of arts and sciences has implications for all the professions, ranging from medicine to the newer fields such as oceanography. The multidisciplinary nature of graduate education brings with it a special responsibility to raise profound questions about the social consequences of existing career definitions in order to effect further humanization of the world of work. For example, a graduate school of engineering may work on improving the efficiency of the assembly line, while the graduate school of philosophy raises the question of whether the assembly line is compatible with human dignity. All graduate schools must provide in-service and continuing education for those who wish to shift careers or to upgrade themselves within a specific career. They must continue to collect new knowledge while improving their capacity to disseminate to the world of career education the products of their libraries and laboratories.

The response of higher education toward career education has been attentive, partially critical, and partially supportive. What is needed now is a constructive partnership in which all levels of education work together to create a concept of career education that is both technologically sophisticated and humanistically informed.

TEACHER EDUCATION

Successful implementation of career education requires teachers who are familiar with career education goals, objectives, and concepts. Thus, training of career educators needs to be an integral part of teacher education programs.

Needs of pre-service and in-service teachers should be met in any comprehensive plan for training the three types of personnel that are needed in career education. Staff development opportunities in career education are needed for the already certified teacher. The pre-service prospective teacher must be given preparation to complement his or her specific teacher education program. A career education specialist, whose prior preparation may or may not be in the professional education area, is a third option. The training of all of these personnel would include formal course work and experiences in career development and planning, coordination and public relations, guidance, counseling, and supervision.

Teachers spend a considerable amount of time each day with pupils. Indeed, they may be the only adults that many of the younger students actually observe at work. Thus teachers are in a unique position to serve as models of the working adult. Diagnosing student needs, examining instructional resources, relating content from many disciplines of knowledge, and planning for individual needs all require a continuous flow of decisions. The teacher who works to make reasons, as well as decisions, visible to the class is helping students learn career development skills; they will learn that being human means being capable of making decisions and living with their consequences.

Elementary teachers need preparation for involvement with the self-images of young children, particularly as children project themselves into the future. Technical skills in this area will enable teachers to explore a greater variety of adult roles and models, to bring out the historical and affective dimensions of adult lives, and to focus on the career opportunities that appear to meet needs, interests, abilities, and values. To help children explore the future, elementary teachers need to plan activities around the following concepts: 1. People change their minds about what they like to do with their time, energies, and resources. 2. Dynamic forces shape business, industrial, and government operations. 3. A free society requires that individuals be willing to assume responsibility for part of their own futures. 4. Many of life's activities require cooperation with people of diverse origins, interests, and abilities as well as of varying amounts of individual initiative.

The elementary teacher must understand what support systems are availble to the career education curriculum, in particular: (a) community resources, such as local businesses, parent involvement, and school–community liaison services; (b) administrative and technical support, such as instructional learning centers; and (c) pupil guidance activities and services. For elementary teachers, skills in community development, group dynamics, systems analysis, and human relations will become increasingly important as they become more involved in implementing career development programs.

The readiness and competence of teachers to participate in an organized approach to career planning and decision making is vital to the success of secondary schools in meeting their obligation to help students achieve their developmental tasks. The active involvement of all teachers who are concerned with vocational development should be of immediate concern to school administrators, counselors, and directors of vocational education and of pupil personnel services, because the teacher is in a unique position to reach students in a variety of settings.

Determining what should be taught in the pre-service teacher education setting is logically related to the determination of objectives, content, materials, instructional aids, teaching strategies, and opportunities for individualized learning. Student involvement might well begin with activities planned for an assessment quarter or as part of orientation to the role of the teacher in the beginning stages of the professional education sequence.

To what extent has the prospective high school teacher developed the competence necessary to perform effectively in the classroom, to serve as a group leader, in team with counselors? To what extent does he or she comprehend vocational objectives that might be pertinent for every teacher regardless of subject being taught? Tennyson (8) suggests the following instructional goals for classroom teachers:

1. *to provide experiences which will enable students to gain a fuller awareness and appreciation of the occupational avenues growing out of the particular subject and the nature of the roles played by workers in these occupations*

2. *to contribute to the student's testing of reality by showing the relationship between the requirements of these vocations and the education or training needed to meet them*

3. *to develop attitudes of respect for and appreciation of the social usefulness of all types of work to which the subject may lead*

Questions such as the following might be used to determine the readiness of potential career education teachers: To what extent do they understand that the concept of career increasingly refers to a sequence of occupations that an individual may occupy in his or her lifetime? Are they aware of the job clusters currently identified for study by the U.S. Office of Education? Do they view current technology as leading to preparation for a life of multiple occupations for many future job seekers? What do they know about entry jobs in their immediate labor-market areas? Have they been exposed to the concept of developmental tasks and life stages? Are they aware of research pertaining to the setting of goals by adolescents of various ability levels? Do they view occupational choices as a process of self-actualization?

A helpful discussion with implications for the high school teacher is presented by Super (9). He describes the role of the teacher or the counselor as one of helping individual students to understand themselves and their environment and to find satisfying ways of developing their personal resources. He explains the concept of life stages as they relate to adolescence and the need for planned exploration to continue for several years after the termination of formal schooling. He mentions that vocational maturity involves learning to acquire relevant information and to anticipate choices that will have to be made. These needs of adolescents suggest that schools should develop additional methods for teaching students about the possibilities and pitfalls of planning ahead.

In-service teachers seeking to incorporate career education into their classroom teaching will find themselves heavily involved in producing and using relevant, job-oriented course materials. They will also make more extensive use of the community as a source of teaching materials and learning experiences. Staff development is viewed by Drier (10) as a process encompassing six goals:

> (a) insure that all staff involved with the delivery of career education are continually informed of the rationale and methods of infusing career education into the existing program; (b) provide needed assistance to staff regarding any new career content that is being built into the program; (c) provide ongoing needed assistance to become competent in using specific techniques being designed within the program; (d) provide time and setting to interface with other staff to exchange knowledge, opinions, and questions during the implementation phase; and (e) keep staff advised as to support programs or materials that will assist in meeting their instructional objectives.

Concept of Infusion

The terms *infusion, threading,* and *weaving* are often used to suggest that career education is not separate, but is infused within the total school program—a thread woven throughout the entire curriculum (11). An infusion strategy for career education should be based on at least five principles: 1. Educational leaders must be convinced of career education's value as a conceptual framework. 2. Career education should be integrated into the present curriculum, not treated as a separate additional program. 3. Every teacher should be a career education teacher even though this would require extensive in-service training. 4. Community involvement is an essential part of career education. 5. Teacher involvement is important in the early planning and curriculum development efforts.

Infusion changes, beginning in the elementary school and continuing through postsecondary education, should reflect career implications of subject matter; good work habits; the process of career development; evaluation of student accomplishments; and an increase in the quantity, quality, and variety of vocational and technical education options offered all students.

Most states have developed program guides for the implementation of career education. In addition to goals and objectives, many of the guides include suggestions on how to implement career education, learning activities, and evaluation techniques. Professional organizations such as The National Business Education Association have published handbooks to assist teachers in implementing career education.*

CAREER GUIDANCE

The individual credited with having the strongest influence on early vocational guidance is Frank Parsons. His theory of vocational choice, proposed at the beginning of the twentieth century, has continued to influence vocational guidance to the present day. According to Parsons, the wise choice of a vocation involved three factors (12):

> (a) a clear understanding of yourself, your aptitudes, abilities, interests, ambitions, resources, limitations, and their causes; (b) a knowledge of the requirements and conditions of success, advantages and disadvantages, compensations, opportunities, and prospects in different lines of work; (c) true reasoning on the relations of these two groups of facts.

The outcome of vocational guidance, using Parsons's theory, was the matching of an individual to an occupation that was most suitable. This emphasis on the matching of the two sets of data, individual traits and job factors, illustrates that Parsons viewed guidance as an event that took place in a person's life, rather than as a process.

The work of Parsons and of others who expanded and elaborated on his ideas became known as the *trait-and-factor theory*, which subsequently formed

---

*See the section on the federal role in career education, later in this chapter.

the basis for the development of several popular instruments currently used in vocational guidance. These include the Strong Vocational Interest Blank, the Kuder Preference Record, the Differential Aptitude Test, and the Guilford-Zimmerman Aptitude Survey.

DEVELOPMENTAL THEORY AND CAREER GUIDANCE

After the 1950s the emphasis in counseling shifted away from an occupational choice to an analysis of *why* and *how* a person chooses a particular occupation.

Super and Ginzberg, leaders of the developmental period, advanced the theory that vocational development is a lifelong process. They shifted the focus of vocational guidance from the concentration on a single occupational choice at some point in one's life to a recognition that vocational development is a process that takes place over a period of time. The *developmental theory* thus involves an understanding of vocational behaviors occurring at different life stages. Super redefined vocational guidance as (13):

> the process of helping a person to develop and accept an integrated and adequate picture of himself and of his role in the world of work, to test this concept of reality, and to convert it into a reality, with satisfaction to him and to society.

Since the turn of the century, theories underlying vocational guidance have resulted in major changes in its practices (14):

1. *The single occupational-choice-at-a-point-in-time focus of the early practitioners of career guidance has given way to a broader, more comprehensive view of the individual and his or her development over the life span.*

2. *The specific age focus of traditional career guidance is not valid. Instead of the notion that a permanent occupational choice is made at some point, usually during late adolescence, we now understand that occupational choice is a process which takes place over a period of time and is a result of a combination of interacting determinants.*

3. *Career guidance activities are important over the life span of the individual; therefore, educational personnel at all levels, kindergarten through adult, have a part to play. When viewed as a continuous process, career guidance is a program in the mainstream of education rather than an ancillary service.*

4. *People at work are no longer seen only as objects through which occupations are analyzed and classified. Rather we now understand that a work setting can be used as a medium to help people better understand themselves.*

5. *Career guidance is more than a simple process of matching people to jobs; it is a complex process of human development and should be treated as a major educational goal.*

The emerging programs of career education draw on the developmental theory of vocational development, building on the classifications of the life span made by Havighurst, Ginzberg, Super, and others.

It is an underlying goal of career education to enable every person to make *informed* choices about his or her career. Every person has certain career options, and the real question is whether that person is able to perceive those options and to make effective decisions regarding them. Being able to make wise decisions about available options is the result of knowledge. As O'Hara suggests (15): "Students must have knowledge of the elements involved in the educational and vocational actions they are about to take."

As opposed to the earlier concept of guidance, in which the counselor assisted the individual to assess his or her aptitudes in the light of skill requirements for specific jobs, career guidance is concerned that each individual *understand* the process of decision making and the gradual unfolding of vocational possibilities and consequences. Career guidance is concerned not with matching individuals and jobs but rather with providing the individual with the tools needed to arrive at decisions in light of the options that are available.

Ginzberg points out (16) that persons with higher incomes have more opportunity than the poor to make mistakes and recover from them in career planning. Youth from higher income families can remain in school for longer periods and can revise their career plans if they become dissatisfied with their initial choices. They learn about themselves and their strengths, interests, values, and limitations as related to the world of work in a process that begins at birth and extends over a long period, with input from family, friends, peers, and society at large.

For the poor, however, many paths have been closed or narrowed at birth by family or neighborhood poverty, minority status, poor schooling, and the like. The job-exploration process is considerably shortened among the disadvantaged because early in life they frequently must settle for a job—a way to support themselves and their families.

We have said, then, that an individual moves along one of a number of pathways through the educational system and into the world of work. Moreover, these pathways depend on a number of factors—economic, social, psychological, and educational—as well as on the decisions made by the individual.

Career guidance, as a vital component of career education, is concerned with providing individual students with the tools to make informed choices. To choose a career is to select among available alternatives. The individual learns to narrow the field of choices by discarding the undesired options.

If we accept the importance of decision making in career development and the fact that the ability to make effective decisions is crucial to the healthy development of every human being, then we must ask ourselves whether learning to make good decisions should be left to chance or should be taught. Such decision-making skills can be taught in varying degrees of sophistication beginning in the elementary grades. But the optimal time for formal decision-making training seems to be in the middle school years, before attitudes become too firmly fixed.

Decision-making skills closely parallel the steps in scientific problem solving (17), including (a) how to identify the decision to be made; (b) how to identify the alternatives to the decision and where to find information about each alternative; (c) how to predict one's success in each alternative; (d) how to estimate the degree to which each alternative will accord with one's values, interests, and abilities; and (e) how to construct a plan of action. Without training, an individual usually completes the first two steps in the process, but less frequently is each of the remaining completed.

CAREER GUIDANCE AT THE ELEMENTARY LEVEL

Beginning in kindergarten, career development should focus on expanding the perceptual base of the individual with relation to self, education, and the world of work. Experiences should be planned that help students to develop positive self-concepts—finding out who they are, how they are alike and different from others—and healthy interpersonal relationships. In addition to the self-related goals, elementary career guidance should focus on developing a broad occupational information program that will serve as a foundation for career decisions. The career guidance emphasis at this level, as reflected in the career education models in Chapter 4, is on awareness; this is not a time when definite occupational choices should be made.

Use of the team approach to career guidance at the elementary level is essential for success. Effective programs do not operate solely within the confines of the counselor's office; rather they permeate the entire educational process. One way of encouraging total school involvement is through the use of a guidance committee, including counselors, teachers, students, and administrators. Parents and representatives from the local business community can also make valuable contributions to such a committee. The use of advisory committees is not new to vocational educators who, through the years, have recognized the contributions of lay persons and other educators to vocational education.

In designing career activities for elementary guidance programs, several characteristics of the learning habits of elementary pupils should be kept in mind:

1 Imitation is a major method of learning

As Campbell and associates state (18): "Children use role modeling as a basis for developing their own behavior." A career guidance technique is to bring into the child's world adults who represent a variety of role models, thus exposing the child to occupational roles outside his or her immediate environment.

2 Learning is enhanced through physical activities because verbal skills are still in the process of being developed

A visit to an elementary school, especially during the children's play periods or free time, will demonstrate the importance of physical activities as learning techniques. From early years, children engage in role-playing activities as they play doctor, nurse, teacher—modeling the roles they know about. Through planned, play-type experiences, including dramatics, role-playing, games, and simulations, students can effectively explore the occupational world.

3 Concrete rather than abstract concepts are more readily learned

Especially at the early elementary levels, children have trouble attempting to think abstractly. Therefore, guidance activities should be planned that give children the opportunity to learn through direct experience.

CAREER GUIDANCE AT THE MIDDLE SCHOOL LEVEL

The exploration level that follows the awareness level in the career education models basically corresponds to the middle school years within the educational framework. Matheny believes that (19):

> urging middle school youth to make vocational decisions would appear untimely, but furnishing them with opportunities to explore work both as observers and as participants would seem highly desirable. Exploring broad occupational areas contributes to the student's understanding of the nature of work, the characteristics of workers, the differences in work settings, and his own preferences and distastes.

As at the elementary level, career guidance at the middle school level is most effective when it is a product of the total school program. Whenever possible, community resources should be used in conjunction with school activities to offer realistic career development experiences for students. The objective of these experiences is to promote an understanding of the skills needed in a job, not to teach specific job skills. Games, problem-solving exercises, and other stimulation activities are increasingly available to supplement or, in some cases, to replace, first-hand, on-the-job exploration. Developing decision-making skills, described earlier in this chapter, is also an important objective for the middle school level.

In summary, career guidance objectives for the middle school level should include the following (20): (a) exploring the relationship between student characteristics and occupational and educational requirements; (b) learning the processes involved in planning and implementing occupational goals; (c) learning educationally and vocationally related behaviors; and (d) beginning to develop tentative plans for the future.

CAREER GUIDANCE AT THE HIGH SCHOOL LEVEL

The high school years are significant in our society. During this time students are expected to make important decisions concerning the future. Should they enter the labor market on completion of high school, or before? Should they seek further training in vocational-technical school, in a community college, or in a university? Through programs of career awareness and exploration, students have narrowed their area of interest and have begun developing skills within occupational clusters of their choice. Career guidance assumes an important role as a conditioner of occupational preferences at the secondary level.

Hansen suggests some basic assumptions that might undergird a secondary career guidance program (21):

1. that an integrated cross-disciplinary program of career guidance as part of the regular school curriculum, grades K–12, is more consonant with new and emerging contemporary knowledge about career development

2. that it is possible to plan a series of vocationally relevant experiences which have meaning for the career development of adolescents, and that certain kinds of appropriate experiences can be defined for students at various levels of their growth

3. that the curriculum needs to be interpreted broadly to include kinds of experiences that extend beyond the school walls and beyond traditional subjects

4. that an integrated program has as its goal not to encourage the student to make a specific vocational choice but rather to foster an understanding of the process of decision-making—the relevant factors in self and society and the variety of potentialities which might be fulfilled

5. that an effective program of career guidance must involve the cooperation of total staff and community in planning meaningful experiences to meet the emerging needs of students

Several goals may be identified as appropriate for the implementation of career guidance at the secondary level: (a) to continue practice and refine expertise in decision-making skills introduced in the middle grades; (b) to acquaint students with a variety of options available during high school and after high school; (c) to assist students in evaluating short-term and long-term effects of selecting various options; (d) to assist students in evaluating occupational opportunities in relation to self needs, interests, values, and aptitudes; (e) to train students to locate and use information such as employment bulletins and school catalogues; (f) to help students interpret and evaluate occupational, and/or educational information. To realize these goals, counselors will need to employ both group and individual guidance activities, using direct and indirect contact, thereby expanding the role of counseling at the secondary level.

In most career education models, students select two or three occupational clusters for thorough exploration, and then they begin preparation in one of those clusters. An interesting alternative to this approach—examining clusters *vertically*—is a *horizontal* examination of job clusters, that is, an examination of a job cluster that would include functional job groupings related to a person's abilities, achievement areas, and personal aspirations. In the vertical approach the jobs that are examined are related by similar identifications and field characteristics. In the horizontal approach, a student might consider a group of jobs that are, professionally, almost totally unrelated, as compared with normally classified, or vertical, job clusters. Thus each student would develop a set of job clusters that, because of personal abilities or aspirations, he or she wishes to explore.

An important aspect of career counseling at the secondary level is job placement and follow-up. Follow-up programs provide important input to the school program by (a) indicating needed curriculum revisions; (b) identifying areas for staff development and growth; (c) pointing up equipment and facilities needed for career education; (d) evaluating the effectiveness of instructional methods and procedures; (e) providing additional information about the requirements and opportunities of various jobs; and (f) evaluating the effectiveness of placement programs.

Follow-up activities are helpful in assisting individuals to acquire jobs, and they provide an effective summative evaluation of instructional programs. They are of little value, however, if the process of follow-up ends with the collection and tabulation of data. Only when the data are examined in light of program objectives and when teachers, students, counselors, administrators, and advisory council members *use* data for program improvement do follow-up activities take on real meaning.

CAREER GUIDANCE
AT THE POSTSECONDARY LEVEL

Many students who are enrolled in postsecondary schools or colleges have postponed specific career decisions and are in need of career counseling. The role of postsecondary education, especially in vocational-technical schools and community colleges, presents a challenge to counselors. It is not unrealistic to anticipate that most of the citizens of our society will benefit from some form of postsecondary education in the near future. The open-door policy of the two-year post–high school institution has resulted in the attendance of a heterogeneous group of students, with widely different needs, values, interests, abilities, and achievement levels. The Educational Amendments of 1972 determined that equal access to postsecondary education for all citizens was a national goal.

The community college, or junior college, serves a wide range of students through its multiple programs. At least six major services may be identified: (a) transfer programs—two-year programs for students planning to transfer to four-year colleges or universities; (b) occupational training—pre-employment training, retraining, or updating of skills of present and potential workers; (c) adult basic education—programs of basic survival skills for persons of less than eighth-grade education; (d) adult civic education—high school equivalency programs (General Educational Development Programs); (e) workshops, seminars, and special-interest mini-programs for various groups within business, industry, and the community; and (f) avocational and cultural education—instruction in a wide range of leisure activities.

Consequently, student personnel services at the postsecondary level are confronted with a student population consisting of recent high school graduates, minority groups seeking new educational opportunities, homemakers seeking new or updated skills to enter or reenter the labor market, and older workers seeking retraining for jobs changed by technology. Other enrollees include school drop outs who are deficient in basic education; various groups from business and industry who are enrolled in mini-courses, workshops, and seminars; and individuals of all ages and walks of life who enroll in a variety of courses for personal interest and development.

Career guidance at the postsecondary level is a function of a broader area—student personnel services—which is concerned with total student development. Because a community college must be responsive to the needs of the society it serves, and must offer many levels of learning experiences to its heterogeneous population, it requires a strong student personnel program. The activities of the student personnel program, including career guidance, may be classified into 14 functions (22): precollege information, registration and records, appraisal, counseling, orientation, remediation, cocurricular activities, health services, financial assistance, placement services, housing, food services, research and evaluation, and community services.

CRITICISMS OF CAREER EDUCATION

Critics of career education have raised a number of concerns about the theory and practice of career education. Professors Robert J. Nash and Russell M. Agne of the University of Vermont identify what they regard as three questionable assumptions of career educators about the teaching-learning experience (23). They then explore the ramifications of these assumptions for teacher-education reform.

■ ■

1 Career educators assume that because special-ization is the key to occupational success, then the learning experience itself must be highly specialized.

■ ■

Professors Nash and Agne point out that excessive specialization of education around job clusters is restrictively utilitarian and that students gain insight only into the nature of the marketplace and so neglect the intuitive, spiritual life of the arts, humanities, and religion. Similarly, they advance the view that teacher-education reform risks excessive specialization in its emphasis on practical, demonstrable, measurable competencies (24):

> To alleviate the catastrophes of "career overload," teacher educators will have to provide a vision of life for prospective teachers where human beings are continually learning to integrate all kinds of knowledge—liberal, spiritual, instrumental, expressive, political, scientific, and sexual. We might develop paratactical models for enabling persons to . . . identify professions barren of personal growth possibilities . . . and to receive new ideas and experience throughout their lives without becoming paralyzingly overloaded or indiscriminately selective.

Is it possible that people will become more obsessed with jobs and economics and less concerned with constructing a truly democratic, participating social order?

■ ■

2 Career educators assume that learning must take place in one sequential order.

■ ■

It is suggested that the rationale that views career education in terms of sequential stages is merely an administrative convenience for doling out training in stages over periods of time for increased educational productivity and lower unit-cost learning. Similarly, performance-based teacher education is seen as an administrative device to keep track of and control over a student's progress through teacher-determined stages. Rigid sequencing in conjunction with external vocational goals and behavioral objectives can be an overwhelming learning impediment for some students. Introspection, experimentation with different forms of affiliative relationships, and withdrawal from institutionalized learning represent different forms of student disengagement from the educational structure. Teacher education should do more, it is contended, than give lip service to the rhetoric of "individual differences."

■ ■

> 3 Career educators assume that a specific body of skills and knowledge should be required of all students.

■ ■

The current emphasis on designated marketable skills—vocabulary, mathematical, and attitudinal competencies—appears to Nash and Agne to be incomplete and shortsighted because the knowledge and behaviors that will be required in the future have yet to be determined. The emphasis on maintaining the economic system as it is could be viewed as effecting a deadening standardization in learning (25): "Strikingly absent from career education programs thus far is training in skills which enable people to become more probing, analytical, and politically astute." Teacher educators, it is suggested, will have to encourage students to explore and challenge not only their own value systems and those of the corporate state, but also the underlying ideological purposes of their studies—with the objective of making explicit the sociopolitical values embedded in the infrastructure of each curriculum (26). This can happen only when students understand the structural realities of the institutions where they will work and when they can effectively consider and act upon workable alternatives to those institutions (27).

Although the criticism of exclusionary organizations is admirable, educators must still recognize the realities of all corporate systems: workers in today's world perceive a direct relationship between their work and their worth, and this perception arbitrarily designates some careers as high or low in status. Despite their efforts to replace teaching credentials with teaching performance, career educators are still in danger of perpetrating, it is suggested, a meritocracy of professions: workers will continue to make status designations about their jobs based on the number of years spent in training, the extent of their technical skills, and the financial supremacy of some clusters over others. From a teacher education standpoint, the deinstitutionalization and despecialization of careers is suggested. Nash and Agne advance the belief that educators can change the traditional meaning of work by stressing what both the individual and the society require in order that each may realize its best possibilities. The reconceptualization of work involves two basic questions: how will a career best fit my life style? and, how can I help to create a society where every human being can live a satisfying, autonomous, and creative life?

The key to personal fulfillment in the future will be the ability to undergo a variety of work experiences and still be able to integrate the diverse facets of existence through continuing education and personal reflection.

FEDERAL ROLE IN CAREER EDUCATION

Federal support of career education began in the early 1970s. In 1972, when the National Institute of Education (NIE) officially came into being, career education model development was an important area of emphasis. In 1973 the National Council on Educational Research, NIE's policy-making body, approved the relationship between education and work as one of five priority areas. The four career education models (school-based, employer-experience-based, rural-residential-based, and home-based) described in Chapter 4 were implemented under the direction of NIE. But new federal legislation was in the offing that would put career education clearly on its own.

Education amendments of 1974

Title IV, Section 406 of Public Law 93-380 gave federal recognition to career education. In this act, Congress enumerated three basic policies that gave new impetus to the concept of career education (28):

1. *Every child should, by the time he has completed secondary school, be prepared for gainful or maximum employment and for full participation in our society according to his or her ability.*

2. *It is the obligation of each local educational agency to provide that preparation for all children (including handicapped children and all other children who are educationally disadvantaged) within the school district of such agency; and*

3. *Each State and local educational agency should carry out a program of career education options which are designed to prepare each child for maximum employment and participation in our society according to his or her ability.*

Career Education Incentive Act

The Career Education Incentive Act (PL 95-207), which authorized an expanded program, replaced the Education Amendments Act of 1974. The purpose of the Career Education Incentive Act is (29):

to assist states and local educational agencies and institutions of postsecondary education, including collaborative arrangements with the appropriate agencies and organizations, in making education as preparation for work, and as a means of relating work values to other life roles and choices (such as family life), a major goal of all who teach and all who learn by increasing the emphasis they place on career awareness, exploration, decision making, and planning, and to do so in a manner which will promote equal opportunity in making career choices through the elimination of bias and stereotyping in such activities, including bias and stereotyping on account of race, sex, age, economic status, or handicap.

PL 95-207 indicates a major shift in emphasis for career education, with major leadership responsibilities moving from the Office of Career Education to the state departments of education across the nation. States apply for the funds by submitting state plans. Funds are prorated on the basis of school-age population. The state departments, then, determine the amounts of money local school systems will receive. Most states use the money primarily to improve career education curricula and counseling techniques and to establish cooperative arrangements between schools and business, labor, and industry. Funding for 1980 was $20 million for use at K–12 levels only. The Office of Career Education is now under the assistant secretary for elementary and secondary education.

Career Education Project

Professional organizations have been recognized by the Office of Career Education as prime channels for assisting teachers in the infusion of career concepts. In 1978 the U.S. Office of Education awarded contracts to seven professional education associations for retraining educational personnel in career education. The associations were American Alliance for Health, Physical Education, Recreation, and Dance; Council for Exceptional Children; National Art Education Association; National Business Education Association; National Council for the Social Studies; National Council of Teachers of English; and National Science Teachers Association.

The National Business Education Association project (30) focused on two major objectives: (a) to help its members understand the need for career education reforms and the importance of these reforms to the teaching of business, and (b) to assist its members in implementing those reforms in their classroom teaching. A number of special activities and publications resulted from this project, including *A Classroom Teachers Handbook* (31) containing examples of teaching materials illustrating career education concepts such as occupational and economic awareness, self-image and self-awareness, awareness of work values and habits, human relationships, career decision making, and job seeking and maintaining; three monographs, *Methods for Involving the Business Community* (32), *Strategies for Implementation* (33), and *Current Status and Future Direction* (34); a national training seminar and five regional training seminars in career education; four newsletters describing project activities; and a column in the *Business Education Forum*.

SUMMARY

Career education efforts at the elementary school level have focused on activities designed to help pupils to become *aware* of the world of work, of the values of a work-oriented society, of themselves as individuals, and of their potential roles in society. *Exploration* of various occupational clusters is emphasized at the middle grades and junior high school level. At the high school level, career education emphasizes occupational *preparation* activities within occupational clusters. Programs of higher education have a responsibility to provide *multiple options* in career education, to work with high schools in articulating the career education sequence, and to provide pre- and in-service training and work-study programs. A key factor in the success of career education at the local school level is the active involvement of all who are affected in planning, implementing, and evaluating the program.

Vocational guidance, as we know it today, has been affected by changes in our education system as well as the economy itself. Historically, several theories of vocational counseling have given direction to the process of career guidance. The first of these was the *trait-and-factor theory*, generally attributed to the work of Frank Parsons in the early part of the twentieth century, which viewed guidance as an event that matched an individual's traits to the job factors.

Leaders such as Super and Ginzberg advanced the idea that vocational development is a lifelong process involving an understanding of vocational behaviors occurring at different life stages. The focus on a single occupational choice at a point in one's life gave way to a broader, more comprehensive view of the individual and his or her development over the life span. Career guidance became recognized as a complex process of human development, best treated as a major educational goal.

Theories of career guidance today, as opposed to earlier concepts in which the counselor assisted the individual in assessing aptitudes in the light of skill requirements for specific jobs, are concerned that each individual understand the process of decision making and the gradual unfolding of vocational possibilities and consequences.

Strong and definite leadership for career education has developed at the national level. The U.S. Office of Career Education, now under the wing of the assistant secretary for elementary and secondary education, serves primarily as a coordinating agency for funding at the K–12 level. A reduction in the level of career education funding, and a shift of this agency from the Office of Vocational and Adult Education, may indicate that the federal government sees the public schools absorbing career education into the mainstream of the curriculum.

ACTIVITIES

For review

1. Explain the primary functions of career education at the following levels: elementary, middle grades, high school, college.
2. Define "infusion" as related to career education implementation.
3. Explain the contribution made by Frank Parsons to vocational guidance.
4. Compare the trait-and-factor theory with the developmental theory of counseling.
5. Contrast the career guidance role at each educational level: elementary, middle grades, high school, college.
6. Explain the impact of the Educational Amendments of 1974 and the Career Incentive Act on career education.

For discussion

1. Who should be in direct charge of career education at each level of the educational ladder: (a) the regular teacher(s), or (b) a specialist in career education? Why?
2. Some members of the community have expressed an opinion that career education is not needed for the college-bound student. How would you justify career education for *all* students?
3. It has been said that the two-year college system may well be the fulcrum of career education. What reasons can you cite to support this statement?
4. At what level of the educational continuum would you expect to find most opposition to career education? Why?
5. How is guidance related to career education?

For exploration

1. Assume that you are an administrator in a local school system that is planning to incorporate career education in grades K–12. Outline a staff development plan to prepare teachers for the change.
2. Prepare a report describing the current scope and progress of career education in the school where you are employed or one in which you would like to work.

REFERENCES

1. Charles W. Ryan, *Career Development Guide for the Elementary School* (Augusta, Me.: Bureau of Vocational and Adult Education, State Department of Education, July 1971).

2. Ellen S. Amatea, project director, *The Yellow Brick Road,* A Source Book of Career Guidance Strategies for the Elementary Counselor and Teacher (Tallahassee, Fla.: Department of Education, State of Florida, 1975), p. 15.

3. Hosterman Junior High School Career Development Committee, *Career Development* (Robbinsdale, Minn.: Independent School District 281, Robbinsdale Area Schools, Aug. 1971).

4. Charles Suhor, "Goals of Career Education and Goals of Subject-Area Instruction: A Model," *Journal of Career Education,* Vol. 5, No. 3, March 1979, pp. 215–19. (Reproduced by permission.)

5. Ibid., p. 219. (Reproduced by permission.)

6. Kenneth B. Hoyt, *Application of the Concept of Career Education to Higher Education: An Idealistic Model,* Monographs on Career Education (Washington, D.C.: Dept. of Health, Education and Welfare, 1976), p. 2.

7. D. A. Casella and S. Samples, "Career Education in Universities," *Journal of Career Education,* Vol. 3, No. 1, Summer 1976, p. 6.

8. W. Wesley Tennyson, "The Teacher's Role in Career Development" (Washington, D.C.: National Vocational Guidance Association, 1965); quoted in Milton Kiesow, "Career Education for High School Teachers," *Journal of Teacher Education,* Vol. 24, No. 2, Summer 1973, p. 104.

9. Donald E. Super, "Career Development," in *Psychology of the Educational Process,* J. R. Davitz and Samuel Ball, eds. (New York: McGraw-Hill Book Company, 1970); quoted in Kiesow, "Career Education for High School Teachers," p. 105.

10. Harry N. Drier, Jr., "In-Service Preparation: Key to Career Education Delivery," in *Implications of Career Education for Teachers' Preparation,* Anna M. Gorman and Joseph F. Clark, eds. (Columbus: Center for Vocational and Technical Education, March 1972), p. 165.

11. Barbara S. Preli, *Career Education and the Teaching/Learning Process,* Monographs on Career Education (Washington, D.C.: Dept. of Health, Education and Welfare, n.d.), p. 14.

12. Frank Parsons, *Choosing a Vocation* (Boston: Houghton Mifflin Company, 1908), p. 5.

13. Donald E. Super, "Vocational Adjustment: Implementing a Self-Concept," *Occupations,* Vol. 30, Nov. 1952, p. 92.

14. Norman C. Gysbers, Harry N. Drier, Jr., and Earl J. Moore, *Career Guidance* (Worthington, Ohio: Charles A. Jones Publishing Company, 1973), pp. 6–7. (Reprinted by permission of the publisher.)

15. Robert P. O'Hara, "Guidance for Career Development," in *Guidance for Education in Revolution,* David R. Cook, ed. (Boston: Allyn and Bacon, 1971), p. 195.

16. Eli Ginzberg, "A Critical Look at Career Guidance," *Manpower,* Vol. 4, No. 2, Feb. 1972, p. 3.

17. Kenneth B. Matheny, "Facilitating Career Development in the Middle School," in *Contemporary Concepts in Vocational Education,* Gordon F. Law, ed. (Washington, D.C.: American Vocational Association, 1971), p. 244.

18. Robert E. Campbell, Garry R. Waltz, Juliet V. Miller, and Sara F. Kriger, *Career Guidance: A Handbook of Methods* (Columbus: Charles E. Merrill Publishing Company, 1973), p. 19.

19. Matheny, "Facilitating Career Development," p. 242. (Reproduced by permission.)

20. Campbell et al., *Career Guidance,* p. 27.

21. Lorraine S. Hansen, "A Practitioner Looks at Career Guidance in the School Curriculum," *Vocational Guidance Quarterly,* Vol. 16, No. 2, Dec. 1967, p. 99.

22. Charles C. Collins, *Premise: Planning Student Personnel Facilities* (Washington, D.C.: American Association of Junior Colleges, 1967). (Reproduced by permission.)

23. Robert J. Nash and Russell M. Agne, "A Case of Misplaced Relevance," *Journal of Teacher Education,* Vol. 24, No. 2, Summer 1973, p. 88.

24. Ibid. (Reproduced by permission.)

25. Ibid., p. 90. (Reproduced by permission.)

26. Ibid.

27. Ibid.

28. "Educational Amendments of 1974," Public Law 93-380 (Washington, D.C.: Government Printing Office, 1974), p. 68.

29. "Career Education Incentive Act," PL 95-207 (Washington, D.C.: Government Printing Office, Dec. 13, 1977).

30. "Retraining Business Teachers in the Development and Dissemination of Career Education Concepts in Business Education," national career education project, Calfrey C. Calhoun, project director (Reston, Va.: National Business Education Association, 1978–79).

31. Alton V. Finch, *A Classroom Teachers Handbook* (Reston, Va.: National Business Education Association, 1980).

32. Robert Poland, *Methods for Involving the Business Community* (Reston, Va.: National Business Education Association, 1980).

33. Robert Ristau, *Strategies for Implementation* (Reston, Va.: National Business Education Association, 1980).

34. Calfrey C. Calhoun, *Current Status and Future Direction* (Reston, Va.: National Business Education Association, 1980).

CHAPTER 6

■

Organization of Vocational-Technical Education

INTRODUCTION

All countries have organizational mechanisms of some sort (usually ministries of education) for planning and administering the regular education system. But relatively few have any organized way of seeing to it that employing establishments throw their full weight into the task of training qualified personnel to meet their own needs and to promote the country's development. Nor is there usually any organized way of promoting desirable linkages between the employment system and the education system so that each will aid the other in their particular responsibilities for OET [occupational education and training]. Likewise lacking, in the usual case, are organized means for joint planning and for enlisting mutually reinforcing efforts of the education system and employing establishments and also of the numerous other institutions . . . [engaged in occupational education and training] (1).

The preceding paragraph points to a problem so complicated that it staggers the imagination. Since its beginnings the United States has wrestled with the problem of establishing responsibility for education and of providing competent structures for carrying out that responsibility.

This organizational problem has affected vocational as well as academic education. Staley (2) recommends the following structure for an occupational training organization: an autonomous, quasi-public entity with a governing body representing:

1. *employers, public and private*
2. *workers, through representatives of trade unions and professional associations*
3. *government agencies concerned, usually the labor and education ministries, but also perhaps other ministries or agencies concerned with manpower, planning, economic affairs, industry, commerce, or agriculture*
4. *special education and training institutions or development services actively engaged in work related to the OTO's [occupational training organization] functions.*

Getting such an organization established and functioning in our society is a difficult task, even though it would undoubtedly result in much increased efficiency, by bringing together all the segments of society that are involved in occupational education and training. Many national conferences have been held on this issue, resulting in various recommendations and resolutions to alleviate the problem. But then each participating agency has been left on its own to develop its programs as it sees fit, with no established means of coordinating or comparing efforts. Burkett (3) points up the hopelessness of comprehensive workforce planning at the national level and suggests that the situation cries out for a coordinated effort that can be successful.

The purpose of this chapter is not to propose a national plan; rather, it is to outline national efforts, as well as state and local organizational efforts, for vocational and technical education in the United States. Although these efforts are undergoing constant reorganization, the changes are slow enough and the need to understand them is great enough that we must become well acquainted with these efforts. Knowing the influences working on organizational structures is essential to understanding, evaluating, and improving the administrative leadership and thus the quality of vocational and technical education. Examining the status quo provides a basis for making improvements.

NATIONAL EFFORTS

Although no single organizational structure at the national level is solely responsible for vocational and technical education, the Department of Education in the executive branch of the federal government is looked to for leadership in educational development, including vocational education and career development. The United States Department of Labor also provides national direction for vocational and technical education. Although this department has long been involved with the support of vocational training, the Comprehensive Employment and Training Act of 1973 (Public Law 93-203) extended its role. This act (4) assigned to the secretary of labor the responsibility of encouraging and supervising the development and administration, at state and local levels, of programs to provide job training and employment opportunities for economically disadvantaged, unemployed, and underemployed persons so that they could compete for, secure, and hold jobs. But, for purposes of this discussion, our primary attention will be on the Department of Education and the Office of Vocational and Adult Education, which is the operating branch of the federal government for vocational education.

Many national organizations influence the area of vocational and technical education. They include professional organizations such as the following: American Vocational Association, National Education Association, National Business Education Association, American Industrial Arts Association, American Home Economics Association, National Association for Practical Nurse Education and Service, American Occupational Therapy Association, Board of Certified Laboratory Assistants, Council of Dental Education, American Medical Association, American Registry of Radiologic Technologists, The Vocational Industrial Clubs of America, Inc., Future Business Leaders of America, Inc., Future Homemakers of America, Future Farmers of America, Distributive Education Clubs of America, Future Secretaries of America (National and International Secretaries Associations), Office Education Association, Future Data Processors, National Association of Secondary School Principals, and the National Science Foundation. Other agencies exerting influence nationally include such organizations as the AFL-CIO, Joint Council on Economic Education, American Association of Colleges for Teacher Education, National Council for the Accreditation of Teacher Education, National Congress of Parents and Teachers, National Association of Manufacturers, United States Chamber of Commerce, and National Retail Merchants Association. In addition many agencies from business and industry are influential, and there are many agencies and commissions that grow out of or are affiliated with organizations already mentioned.

United States Department of Education

History was made on October 17, 1979, when President Jimmy Carter signed the legislation creating a separate Department of Education (5). The creation of a separate Department of Education represented the culmination of a long struggle on the part of education leaders to remove the federal government's involvement in education from the Department of Health, Education and Welfare. On December 6, 1980, Shirley M. Hufstedler took the oath of office as the nation's first secretary of education (6). The Department of Education opened its doors officially on May 4, 1979, one month earlier than required by the legislation establishing it and five months after Hufstedler was sworn in (7). With the advent of a conservative administration early in 1981, Terrel H. Bell was appointed to replace Hufstedler as secretary of education—portent of a decreasing role of the federal government in the education of Americans.

Before the creation of the Department of Education, the education affairs of the United States government were administered by the Education Division of the Department of Health, Education and Welfare, composed of the United States Office of Education and the National Institute of Education. Inasmuch as the major responsibility for education has traditionally been left to the state governments, the influence of the United States Office of Education was limited. It traditionally acted as a clearinghouse for educational information, collected statistics on the condition of education, disseminated the information to school systems, and promoted efficient methods of teaching. With the increase in federal legislation, in federal funding, and thus in the need for controls, the influence of the United States Office of Education increased dramatically during the last two decades. It administered far-flung and multifaceted education programs funded by the United States government. Even so, particular care was taken to avoid federal control of education; the historic tradition of vesting primary responsibility for education in state and local governments was upheld. The increasing federal role in education made effective and efficient administration difficult within the framework of the Department of Health, Education and Welfare. The creation of the Department of Education was long overdue.

The organizational structure of the United States Office of Education was not static; neither will be the structure of the new Department of Education. Its structure will change as the educational needs of the nation change, as determined by Congress and the president. However, to understand the role of the federal government in vocational education, it is necessary to discuss the organization of this office. Being newly created, the department is still undergoing organizational changes necessary for its new status and responsibilities and duties. Even though its structure will continue to change, discussing its original structure will give us a sense of how it goes about achieving its objectives.

The department is headed by the secretary of education, who is appointed by the president with the approval of the United States Senate. There is an undersecretary of education and two deputy undersecretaries, one for intergovernmental affairs and one for interagency affairs. There is an Office of Regional Liaison, under the deputy undersecretary for intergovernmental affairs, which administers the ten regional offices into which the United States is divided. The department has 15 major divisions, 12 of which are administered by assistant secretaries. They are Nonpublic Education, Public Affairs, Education for Overseas Dependents, Congressional Relations, Elementary and Secondary Education, Civil Rights, Planning and Budget, Vocational and Adult Education, Postsecondary Education, Management, Special Education and Rehabilitative Services, and Educational Research and Improvement. In addition, there are the offices of Inspector General, General Counsel, and Bilingual Education and Minority Languages Affairs, headed by a director. The relationships among the various components of the Department of Education are shown in Figure 6.1 (8).

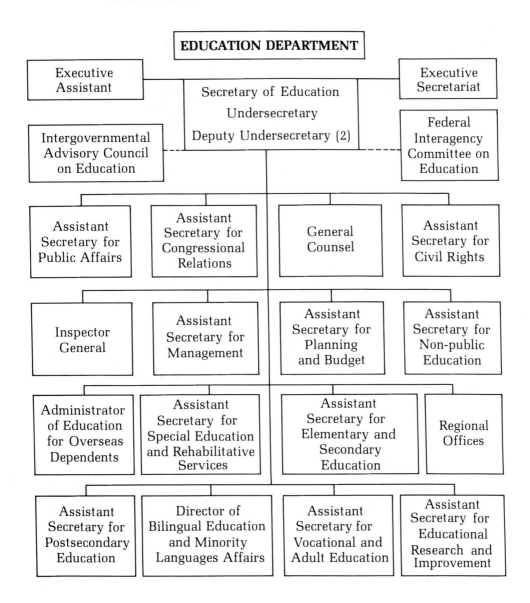

Figure 6.1 United States Department of Education. Source: *Update,* Vol. 2, No. 8, May 1980 (Arlington, Va.: American Vocational Association), p. 3.

The department was established to meet the following objectives: (1) to strengthen the federal government's commitment to access to equal educational opportunity for every individual; (2) to supplement and complement efforts by states, local school systems, community organizations, students and other individuals, public and private educational institutions, and others to improve the quality of education; (3) to improve the quality and usefulness of education through federally supported research, evaluation, and sharing of information; (4) to improve the coordination of federal education programs; (5) to improve the management and efficiency of federal education activities so as to reduce duplication of efforts; and (6) to increase the accountability of federal education efforts to the president, the Congress, and the public.

Vocational and technical education is the responsibility of the Office of Vocational and Adult Education, administered by an assistant secretary. It currently has two major subdivisions: (1) Adult Learning and School-Community Relations, and (2) Education and Employment. Adult Learning and School-Community Relations is divided into two offices: Adult Education and the Community Education Branch. Adult Education is divided into Field Operations Services and Program Development. Education and Employment currently has three subdivisions: (1) Research and Demonstration, (2) State Vocational Program Operations, and (3) Vocational and Technical Education. Research and Demonstration is divided into Curriculum Development, Demonstration, Personnel Development, and Research. Vocational and Technical Education is divided into Postsecondary Adult Occupational Programs, Program Support, and State Programs and Services (9). The organizational structure is shown in Figure 6.2.

National Institute of Education

On the organizational chart of the Department of Education, the National Institute of Education is an entity within one of the 15 major divisions—Educational Research and Improvement. Created by the Education Amendments of 1972, the National Institute of Education was formed to carry out the following policies (10):

> The Congress hereby declares it to be policy of the United States to provide to every person an equal opportunity to receive an education of high quality regardless of his race, color, religion, sex, national origin, or social class. Although the American educational system has pursued this objective, it has not yet attained that objective. Inequalities of opportunity to receive high quality education remain pronounced. To achieve quality will require far more dependable knowledge about the processes of learning and education than now exists or can be expected from present research and experimentation in this field. While the direction of the education system remains primarily the responsibility of State and local governments, the Federal Government has a clear responsibility to provide leadership in the conduct and support of scientific inquiry into the educational process.
>
> The Congress further declares it to be the policy of the United States to:

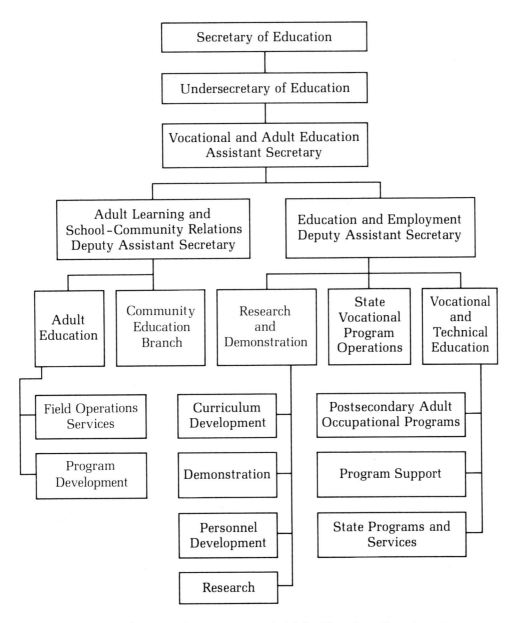

Figure 6.2 Office of Vocational and Adult Education, Department of Education. Source: *The Chronicle of Higher Education*, July 14, 1980, p. 8.

1. *help to solve or to alleviate the problems of, and promote the reform and renewal of American education*
2. *advance the practice of education, as an art, science, and profession*

3. *strengthen the scientific and technological foundation of education*
4. *build an effective educational research and development system*

The 1972 amendments further provide that the institute shall consist of a National Council of Educational Research and a director of the institute. The council is composed of 15 members appointed by the president, by and with the advice and consent of the Senate, the director, and such other ex officio members who are officers of the United States as the president may designate. The council establishes general policies for and reviews the conduct of the institute. It also makes recommendations for strengthening educational research and improving methods of collecting and disseminating the findings of educational research. The director is authorized through the institute (11):

> to conduct educational research; collect and disseminate the findings of educational research; train individuals in educational research; assist and foster such research, collection, dissemination, or training through grants, or technical assistance to, or jointly financed cooperative arrangements with, public or private organizations, institutions, agencies or individuals; promote the coordination of such research and research support within the Federal Government; and may construct or provide (by grant or otherwise) for such facilities as he determines may be required to accomplish such purposes. As used in this subsection, the term "educational research" includes research (basic and applied), planning, surveys, evaluations, investigations, experiments, developments, and demonstrations in the field of education (including career education).

NIE conducts three basic activities (12):

1. *Research* NIE supports research concerning the relationship of education and work. These include studies of the changing economic and noneconomic returns to individuals and society from the investment in education, and policy analyses examining assumptions about the match between educational experience and world of work experience. These studies assist students, parents, teachers, school boards, administrators, and legislators in making the many decisions they face regarding the improvement of educational practice.

2. *Program development* Based on the findings of research and policy analyses, NIE supports design and development projects, from prekindergarten to adult levels, to evaluate a range of suggested improvements. While ultimately intended for implementation within state and local educational settings, these developmental activities characteristically are too high-risk or too expensive for states and localities to undertake. The outcomes generally will be programs and ideas that have proven themselves successful, but will from time to time include the finding that proposed solutions or improvements do not improve education.

3. *Dissemination* NIE has the mandate to improve educational practice by learning how best to assist states and localities in applying the results of research and development activities. NIE is developing a variety of ways to provide information on products from its successful R&D. On a limited scale it is providing appropriate technical assistance to help school districts, colleges, and other institutions use career education products.

National Advisory Council on Vocational Education

This advisory council was created by Congress through the Vocational Education Act of 1963 and amended through the Vocational Education Amendments of 1968 and 1976. It is composed of 21 persons, appointed by the president, from diverse backgrounds in labor, management, and education. It is charged by law to advise the commissioner of education concerning the operation of vocational education programs, to make recommendations concerning such programs, and to make annual reports to the president, the secretary of education, and Congress.

The council is charged with advising the federal government on the administration of, preparation of general regulations and budget requests for, and operation of, vocational education programs. It reviews the effectiveness of these programs and of labor force training programs in meeting the purposes for which they are established and operated. In consultation with the National Commission for Manpower Policy, it identifies the nation's vocational education and employment and training needs. It is charged with conducting studies, hearings, or other activities as necessary to formulate appropriate recommendations. It is required to provide technical assistance and leadership to state advisory councils and to assist them in carrying out their responsibilities.

Professional Organizations

A number of professional organizations are concerned with promoting vocational education, its programs, research, and legislation. Many of the organizations, such as American Home Economics Association, National Vocational Guidance Association, and National Business Education Association, are concerned specifically with one field of vocational education. ⁀ organizations that encompass all of the vocational areas are briefly describ⌐⌐ below.

American Vocational Association

The American Vocational Association (AVA) is a national organization with state affiliates, composed primarily of teachers, supervisors, teacher educators, administrators, and counselors. Divisions have been established in these areas: Administration, Agriculture, Business Education, Distributive, Guidance, Health Occupations, Home Economics, Industrial Arts, Manpower, New and

Related Services, Technical, and Trade and Industrial. Special organizations are maintained for members in most of the divisions.

consumer homemaking is one division

The board of directors of AVA includes the president, president-elect, past president, vice presidents of the 12 divisions, vice presidents of the 5 regions, and an executive director. The expansion of the organization to include vice presidents in 12 areas, as opposed to 6 a decade ago, is an indication of responsiveness to growth, changes resulting from legislation, and special needs relating to vocational education.

AVA promotes research through its various divisions and committees. It carries on a program of publication and provides leadership in promoting national legislation relating to vocational education. *Voc Ed,* published monthly September through June with a combined November/December issue, is the official organ of this organization, which presently has a membership of over 55,000. *Update* is the organization's newspaper, published monthly except June, August, and December.

National Education Association

The National Education Association (NEA), with state and local affiliate groups, is the nation's largest professional organization for teachers, supervisors, teacher educators, administrators, counselors, and educational secretaries in all fields of education. NEA maintains numerous divisions, associations, councils, and commissions. Many of these have active organizations that hold local, state, and national meetings, and publish journals, yearbooks, and other volumes of interest to their members. Like AVA, the NEA is actively involved in research, publication, and promotion of legislation relating to education. The headquarters of the organization, with over a million members, is in Washington, D.C.

Duplication of effort

For practically every type of vocational and academic program, one or more national organizations exert influence on that program. Such efforts may tend to strengthen programs, by virtue of analysis from different points of view, or they may tend to weaken programs, through lack of cohesion. Duplication and multiplicity of effort in national organizations are exemplified in business education, an area in which many national organizations exert an influence. Some effort is made to provide means for these organizations to work together, but for the most part they work independently and thus weaken the effect they might have if more unity were achieved. The National Business Education Association, probably the strongest national group working to improve all levels of business education, has some of its efforts duplicated by the Business Education Division and the National Association of Teachers for Business and Office Education of the American Vocational Association, as well as by the American Assembly of Collegiate Schools of Business.

STATE EFFORTS

Organization at the state level

The organization of vocational education at the state level is more unified than it is at the national level because the Vocational Education Act of 1963 required that each state have its own plan. Even though the various state organizations are uniquely different, having a state plan, as specified by the Vocational Education Act of 1963 and subsequent amendments, tends to unify the various state influences.

In addition, it is much easier to influence individuals within the confines of a limited geographical area, such as a state, than it is to pull the various nationwide influences together.

Each state has an administrative unit to plan, organize, supervise, and administer education, including vocational education. Whereas the federal government's role has been largely advisory, fact finding, and information disseminating in nature, the state government's role has been much more administrative and supervisory. The state government supervises local programs closely and sets specific standards to which each local unit must adhere. But as is true at the national level, the state-level organizational structure of vocational education is not static; it changes to meet changing needs within the state and to meet changes that are reflected in federal legislation.

There are significant differences in philosophies within the various states for the administration and control of vocational education. Wisconsin has a unique program that emphasizes vocational education at the postsecondary level, with little emphasis in the high schools. In Ohio, the State Division of Vocational Education has primary responsibility for secondary school programs, whereas postsecondary programs are under the direction of the State Board of Regents. California's program includes a well developed community college system, which provides free postsecondary vocational education within commuting distance of 90 percent of the state's residents. Colorado has a state board for vocational education and community colleges, which administers both secondary and postsecondary education.

The vocational and technical program in Mississippi provides educational experiences in both the secondary schools and postsecondary junior colleges. The program is administered by the State Board of Education— a pattern that is followed by many states. The organizational chart for the Vocational-Technical Division of the Mississippi State Department of Education is shown in Figure 6.3, as taken from the state plan. This chart identifies the state director of vocational-technical education as the executive officer responsible for vocational education. He or she reports to the assistant state superintendent, who in turn reports to the state superintendent of education, whose responsibilities include vocational education as well as all phases of public education of less than baccalaureate-degree level. It should be noted that the state superinten-

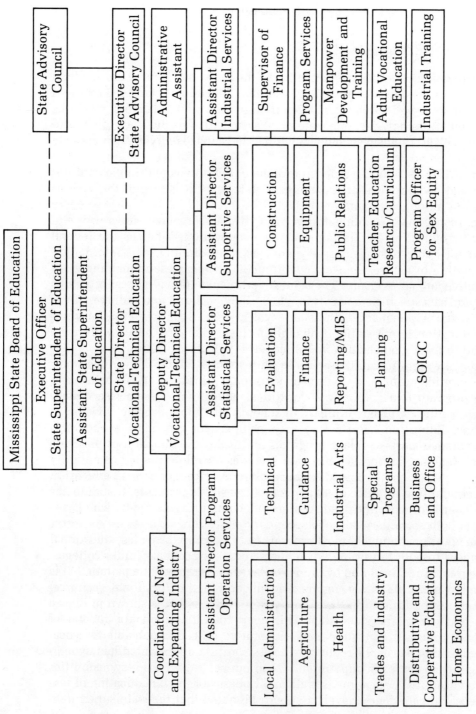

Figure 6.3 Organizational chart for vocational-technical education in Mississippi. Source: 1980 Mississippi State Plan for Vocational Education, p. 116.

dent reports to the Mississippi State Board of Education. The state plan specifies that the Mississippi State Board for Vocational Education is responsible for the administration of the state plan and has the necessary power to administer vocational and technical education under the state plan.

The state plan also quotes a portion of the Mississippi Code of 1942, which specifies that the State Board of Education shall constitute the State Board for Vocational Education. Although there are some disadvantages to this organization, it does tend to facilitate action. As the executive officer of the State Board of Education, the state superintendent is responsible for the administration of the state's vocational education programs. The staff of the vocational division is also responsible to the state board through the executive officer. In Mississippi, the state board is composed of three members: the state superintendent, the state attorney general, and the secretary of state. Each is elected to office by popular vote (13). The composition and method of acquiring members of state boards of education vary widely from state to state.

The Vocational-Technical Division of the Mississippi State Department of Education has four subunits for administrative and supervisory purposes, each headed by an assistant director. The units are: Program Operation Services, Statistical Services, Supportive Services, and Industrial Services. The purpose of Program Operation Services is to administer and supervise the state's vocational programs, which include components in agriculture, health, business and office occupations, distributive and cooperative education, home economics, technical, guidance, industrial arts, special programs, and trade and industry as well as local administration.

State advisory council

The relationship among the federally required state advisory council, the state superintendent of education, and the state director of vocational education is illustrated in Figure 6.4. The Mississippi State Advisory Council is composed of 15 members appointed by the governor (14). The Vocational Education Amendments of 1968 (15) require representation on such state advisory councils as follows: persons who are (a) familiar with vocational needs and problems of management and labor in the state; (b) from community and junior colleges and other institutions of higher education, area vocational schools, technical institutes, and postsecondary or adult education agencies; (c) familiar with, although not directly involved in, the administration of state and local vocational education programs; (d) familiar with programs of technical and vocational education, including programs in comprehensive secondary schools; (e) representative of local educational agencies and school boards; (f) representative of labor and vocational education agencies in the state, including representation from the Comprehensive Area Manpower Planning System of the state; (g) representative of school systems with large concentrations of academically, socially, economically, and culturally disadvantaged

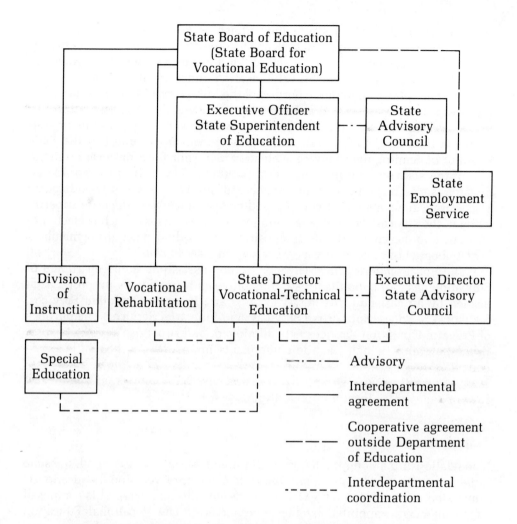

Figure 6.4 Relationships among the vocational division of the Mississippi State Department of Education and other state agencies. Source: 1978–82 Mississippi State Plan for Vocational Education.

students; (h) knowledgeable or experienced with respect to the special educational needs of physically or mentally handicapped persons; and (i) representative of the general public, with knowledge of the poor and disadvantaged, who are not qualified for membership under any other category.

The amendments further require that the state advisory council (a) advise the state board on the development of policy matters arising in the administration of the state plan; (b) evaluate vocational education programs, services, and activities assisted under this title and publish and distribute the results; and (c) prepare and submit an annual evaluation report of the effectiveness of vocational education programs, services, and activities, recommending any necessary changes.

An example of the relationship that might be required between the state administrative unit for vocational education and other agencies is illustrated in Figure 6.4. Cooperative agreements are maintained by the Division of Vocational Education of the Mississippi State Department of Education with the Mississippi Employment Service. The state plan calls for a liaison committee with representatives from both agencies and local institutions to provide a continuous discussion of information available and actions necessary to meet objectives. The agreement with the State Employment Service requires the state board and local vocational agencies to (16):

1. *make available to the Mississippi State Employment Service information regarding training programs being planned in the public schools and junior colleges of the State*

2. *collaborate with the Mississippi State Employment service in determining needs for vocational and technical programs*

3. *cooperate with the Mississippi State Employment Service in providing counseling, testing, and placement service*

4. *provide lists, including occupational qualifications, of students having completed various vocational-technical programs to the Mississippi State Employment Service*

5. *provide lists of the schools and classes that are being conducted by the local educational agencies*

6. *provide Mississippi State Employment Service a list of vocational-technical dropouts; qualifications at the time of termination will be included*

The Mississippi State Employment Service is required to (17):

1. *provide information regarding job opportunities in the communities and elsewhere to the State Board and local educational agencies*

2. *provide information regarding job requirements of occupations to the State Board and local educational agencies*

3. *cooperate with the State Board and local educational agencies in giving aptitude tests and other assessment instruments*

4. *cooperate with the State Board in conducting studies to collect information not otherwise available about jobs in fields of work for which vocational training is deemed to be practical*

5. *provide the State Board with information in regard to exceptional persons available for training*

6. *give special attention to counseling, testing, and placement services to school dropouts*

7. *assist in placement of students who have left or completed training*

The Vocational Education Division also maintains working agreements with the state's institutions of higher education to see that there are adequate programs to prepare teachers and adequate facilities and personnel for curriculum research and development. The Vocational Division supervises these activities as well as vocational programs and activities at the local level.

LOCAL EFFORTS

The organization of vocational education at the local level is influenced by its organizational counterparts at the state and national levels. The influence of the federal government is felt primarily through legislation that affects the state organization, which in turn establishes guidelines and controls that affect local organization. Such influence over local units is effected by the federal and state governments' control of funds, which are issued on the basis of the local units' compliance with established guidelines.

It seems important at this point to define *local level*. It might refer to a countywide system of vocational education, a citywide system, or even a combination city-county system. It might involve one school, or a number of classes taught in a number of places in a city or county, or it might even occur within the physical facilities of the state department of education. With all these different possibilities, it seems most appropriate to think of *local level* as applying to those conditions where vocational education brings learner and teacher together in a single administrative system, even though a single administrative system might comprise two or more subsystems. A local-level system thus generally includes all programs that are administratively prepared as a local plan to be submitted for approval to the state department of education.

In the following pages, we shall discuss local-level organization of vocational education in the public schools and consider the facilities used to carry out the programs. We shall first discuss college preparatory school organization and facilities, then the comprehensive school and the vocational school.

/. Organization and Facilities in College Preparatory Schools

In college preparatory schools, vocational teachers are likely to report to the school principal just as all other teachers do. There will not be a full-scale program of vocational education, but there might be selected programs designed to help the college-bound student. For example, typewriting is a skill that may prove valuable both in course preparation and as the source of part-time employment while the student is in college. That it might help him or her earn a living later is incidental. For the college preparatory school, the same kind of reasoning would apply to classes in home economics, industrial arts, and other vocational areas.

Career education exists in college preparatory schools only as it applies to the college-bound student. Guidance and counseling are therefore designed to help students make choices for college entrance; little attention is given to ultimate career decisions. As a result, many students in the college preparatory school enter college with no conception of their future career.

As a result of this focus, facilities for vocational education in the college preparatory school are limited. There will probably be few schools that do not offer typewriting, home economics, or industrial arts. But the quality of the equipment will depend on the financial situation of the school and the interest and competence of the teacher.

2. Organization and Facilities in Comprehensive Schools

Comprehensive schools are organized to meet the needs of both the college preparatory student and the vocational student. Vocational curricula theoretically receive as much attention as academic curricula, depending on the kinds of jobs that secondary-school graduates are being prepared to fill. The vocational program, as well as other programs, might be loosely organized under a *head*. Such organization provides vocational teachers a framework through which curricula can be developed by teachers in the particular vocational field; it also provides a structured arrangement for determining school objectives that are in agreement with student and community objectives. In large schools, where enrollment in several vocational areas requires more than one teacher in each area, there should be a head for each area as well as a head for the total vocational program. The head teacher reports to the principal, who in turn reports to the superintendent.

The layout of the up-to-date physical plant of the comprehensive Valdosta High School in Georgia is shown in Figure 6.5. The two-winged diamond-shaped plant is designed to serve a comprehensive curriculum. The objectives of the school include preparing individuals for college or for work immediately following graduation. Although one diamond wing is primarily for academic courses and the other for vocational courses, the plant is actually designed so that subject matter areas are in the physical areas best suited to them. For example, note in Figure 6.5 that homemaking is located in the academic wing with science, math, social studies, foreign language, and English, whereas art and music are located in the vocational wing with business education, driver education, and trade and industrial education.

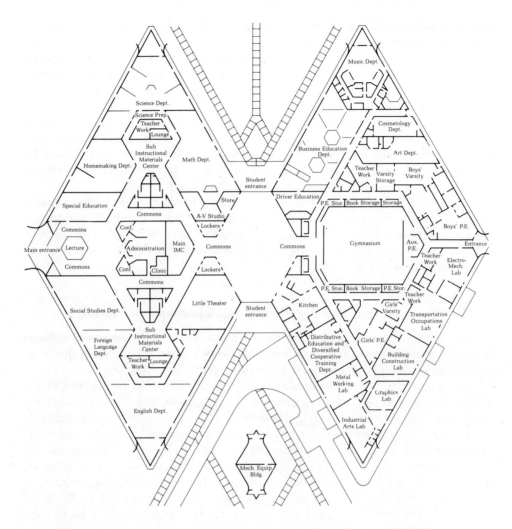

Figure 6.5 Physical plant of the Comprehensive High School, Valdosta, Georgia. Source: Superintendent of Schools, Valdosta, Georgia.

Each subject area in this "open" school takes up the equivalent space of one to five or six classrooms in a traditional school. Areas are designed to accommodate the latest equipment, materials, and teaching techniques. Facilities in each area are designed to accommodate large-group instruction (open space planning), small-group instruction, and individualized instruction. Students can work independently, and teachers can easily move from tutorial-type instruction to team teaching. Flexibility and adaptability are key characteristics of this plant.

The planners envisioned that individuals would be able to proceed at their own level of progress in their area of interest and aptitude and at the same time have opportunities to interact with students in other areas of interest.

Career education in the comprehensive high school takes on a much broader meaning than is the case in the college preparatory school. It includes preparation for careers requiring college education and for careers not requiring a college education. The organizational structure of school personnel must thus be such that career counseling, guidance, and instruction are provided for both college-bound and work-bound students. Subject matter instruction and learning must be coordinated toward career objectives. Facilities and personnel must be so organized and developed that integration of learning activities is implemented. Guidance and counseling for students preparing to go to work immediately following high school and for students preparing to go to college receive equal attention. Personnel, usually referred to as career coordinators or counselors, are available to work with teachers in various disciplines to plan curricula and activities that are career-oriented and to provide opportunities for team teaching among teachers with special skills in various disciplines. For example, a career coordinator might stimulate the planning of a series of lessons for a buildings class that might be team taught by the buildings trade teacher and the English teacher.

3. Organization and Facilities in Vocational and Technical Schools

Some public secondary vocational schools, usually found in large metropolitan areas, operate with one objective—preparing individuals to enter the world of work. In such schools, the traditional college preparatory courses receive secondary emphasis to courses that are structured to give students the understandings, skills, and attitudes necessary for job competency. Programs should be structured even in the vocational school so that individuals might be qualified to continue their education at the college level, should they decide to go to college rather than to work. However, English, math, science, and social studies should be planned to support preparation for work in agriculture, business and office education, distributive education, health education, home economics education, and trade and industrial education. Preparing individuals to enter college should be incidental to preparing them for work.

The organizational structure of the vocational school is similar to that of the college preparatory school and the comprehensive school. Where there is more than one teacher in a vocational area, a head teacher should be designated. The head teacher usually reports to the school principal, who reports to the superintendent. The superintendent reports to the board of education, which reports to the people of the community being served by the school. The superintendent might be elected to the position or appointed, and he or she might or might not be a member of the board of education, which establishes policies under which schools operate. The board is sometimes responsible to the people and so might be elected by popular vote, or the board might be appointed by a governing body of the community being served by the schools.

A school participating in federally funded programs is required to have an overall advisory committee of community leaders to help determine policy with respect to objectives, curricula, finances, and other matters. In addition, each occupational area is required to have a craft committee to advise teachers in planning, organizing, and conducting the program.

Frequently, a vocational and technical secondary school serves one or more high schools. An example of such a school is the Oxford–Lafayette County Business and Industrial Complex located in Oxford, Mississippi. This school serves two high schools, each under separate administration. Figure 6.6 shows the relationships among the organizational structures of the three schools.

Oxford High School is governed by a board of trustees as part of the Oxford Municipal Separate School District in Lafayette County (so designated because it includes the geographical city limits of Oxford as well as some outlying areas of the county, which are administratively organized as part of the city schools). The board is made up of five members, three of whom are appointed by the Oxford city council and two of whom are elected by the registered voters in the outlying areas.

Lafayette County High School is governed by a board of trustees elected by the registered voters in the county on a rotating basis.

Oxford–Lafayette County Business and Industrial Complex is governed by a board of trustees made up of six members, three from each of the two boards of trustees of the school systems being served.

Vocational students spend half the school day at their parent high schools, taking general education courses on a traditional schedule of 50-minute periods. The other half of the student's school day is spent on a block schedule at the complex, preparing for work in a specific vocational area. In addition, each of the parent schools being served by the complex has vocational programs, some of which receive funds under the state plan for vocational education. For example, distributive education, which is reimbursed, is taught in Oxford High School rather than in the complex. Both parent schools also offer nonreimbursed secretarial courses.

Teachers in the Oxford-Lafayette County Business and Industrial Complex are responsible to the director, who is responsible to the board of trustees of the complex. The director has equal status with the principals of the two parent schools. The principals report directly to their respective superintendents, who report to their respective boards of education.

Three advisory councils are maintained, one for each of the two high schools and one for the Business and Industrial Complex. Members of the councils for the parent schools are appointed by the respective superintendent for an indefinite term. Members of the council for the complex are recom-

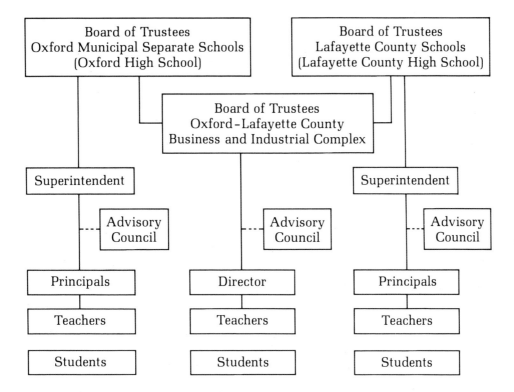

Figure 6.6 Vocational education in Lafayette County, Mississippi. Source: Adapted from the Local Plan for Vocational Education for the Oxford Municipal Separate School District and the Lafayette County School District.

mended by the director and appointed by the board. They advise the schools on employment trends and needs in the community, make suggestions for improvement of vocational programs, and serve as public relations liaisons. They are also involved in preparing the local plan for vocational education. Each member on the advisory councils serves as a member of the craft (advisory) committee in his or her occupational area.

Facilities in vocational schools necessarily depend on the kinds of programs to be operated, the organization of these programs, and the availability of funds. Figure 6.7 illustrates plant facilities of vocational centers established to serve parent schools (as compared to Figure 6.5, which shows plant facilities of the vocational program in a comprehensive school). Such facilities must be designed to accommodate specific programs, but they must also be flexible enough to be adapted easily to other vocational uses.

The kinds of vocational programs to be found in vocational schools should be determined by the needs of the students and the community to be served.

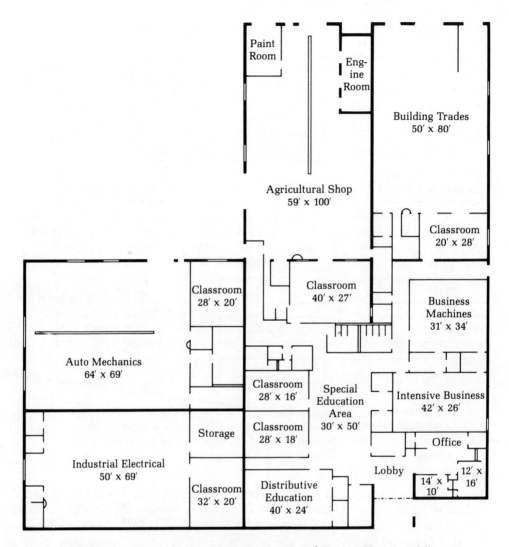

Figure 6.7 Floor plan for Houston Vocational Center, Houston, Mississippi. Source: Superintendent of Schools, Houston Separate School District.

For example, one would think that in the primarily rural setting of Lafayette County, agricultural education would be a major program in the vocational complex. In the initial stages of planning, agricultural education was included. It remained in the planning until a survey was taken of students who would be using the facilities. Not one expressed an interest in vocational agricultural education, so the program was dropped from the curriculum before the facility was completed.

STATE AND LOCAL TAX SUPPORT FOR SCHOOLS

In the long run, educating young people for employment costs society less than educating them for college, which they may never reach, and then providing remedial training thereafter. But the federal government invests nearly four dollars in remedial labor programs for each one dollar it invests in preventive vocational programs. And in the short-run budget of a school district, because it costs more in equipment and facilities to prepare a student for a job than to prepare him or her for college, vocational education usually receives less than adequate support.

As a result, it is at the state level that vocational education receives most support. Each state is responsible for guaranteeing that all its citizens are provided with opportunities for quality education and that the resources of the state are allocated to maximize educational development and economic efficiency. Recognition of such responsibility by state education leadership appears to be a major factor leading toward state-increased coordination, control, and financial support of new efforts in vocational-technical education.

State and local taxes provide 92 cents of every school dollar; the remaining 8 cents comes from federal sources. Local school districts use their tax funds to pay salaries of teachers, administrators, and support personnel; maintain and operate school plants; purchase goods and services necessary for school operation; and pay interest on school debts. Capital improvement and new construction expenses normally come from the sale of bonds issued by the school board with approval of the district voters. Recent court decisions at both state and federal levels have shown the nation is headed toward major changes in the pattern of support of public elementary and secondary education. But it is not clear, at this point, just what the direction will be.

State laws generally provide for school support through public taxation. State school funds come from a wide range of tax sources, including personal income taxes, sales taxes, use and occupation taxes, franchise and license fees, inheritance and gift taxes. Some states designate certain taxes for education; others draw on the general tax funds to meet their obligations to local districts. The states vary considerably in the machinery used to channel state tax funds to local districts.

Two funding devices that are commonly used by states are the flat grant and the equalization grant. State flat grants generally go to districts on the basis of average daily attendance during the previous school year. Some states provide for adjustments of attendance bases during the current year to account for rapid increases in school enrollments. The grants, computed on district reports, are paid to the local school units periodically during the fiscal year.

Equalization support is a method used by some states to bring a degree of equality to district school funding. With the nation's increased urbanization has come a polarization of schools into rich and poor districts. In some states where this has happened, state funds are allocated on the basis of local need.

Achievement of equality of educational opportunity in a given state depends on the effectiveness of the tax-allocation system among the school districts.

The state may encourage local taxation for education by setting minimum tax rates to qualify the district for state support. These qualifying tax rates are expressed either in mills (tenths of a cent) per dollar, or in cents per $100 of assessed valuation. State law or state constitutions may also set upper limits on local school taxes; if the district's tax rate is below that limit, the voters of the district may authorize an additional amount to be levied on all taxable property. But many local districts are near their upper limits of taxation and so face severe school-finance problems.

Local taxes are imposed under taxing power granted to the district by the state legislature. Whenever the state laws grant local school districts the power to tax, the statute will be construed strictly. Generally the districts' tax objects are real and personal property, although some states extend local school taxes to other objects and sources.

Subject to constitutional or statutory limitations, the local school board determines its budget in advance of the fiscal year, estimates the assessed valuation of the district's taxable property, and computes the rate necessary to raise the needed revenue. The board may be fiscally dependent or independent; if dependent, the board must seek budget approval from some other public body, such as the city, county, or intermediate governing body. Fiscally independent boards determine their own budgets and tax rates. The law generally provides opportunity for the public to inspect the school budget and to make objections and suggestions at a public hearing.

The school tax may be coupled with other government units and a single tax bill prepared for property owners. In some states the tax-assessment and tax-collection functions are performed by different public officials. Regardless of the scheme, the local school districts ultimately receive local tax funds for school use. The payments may come to the district in periodic installments, and the local board may then have the power to invest excess operating funds in certain types of securities until the funds are needed. However, state laws generally restrict the board's power to invest school funds, to safeguard the public against the board's speculation and possible reduction or loss of tax monies. The management of school-tax funds is a technical matter, and reference to specific state laws is necessary for an accurate understanding of the procedures and limitations.

Most states provide for public participation in decisions about school taxes. The upper limits of school taxation may be determined by statute; periodic referenda to registered voters in the district are common forms of public participation. Tax increases are presented to voters in the form of referenda, which are conducted under statutory authority and specified procedures. If a referendum fails, the board must adjust projected expenditures downward to stay within its school income.

Tax funds generally must be used for current operating expenses, that is, for expenses incurred during a given fiscal year, such as for salaries, supplies, materials, utilities, and maintenance costs. Accumulation of excess operating funds is generally limited by statute. The purpose of this limitation is to hold school-tax income to a level near school needs and to minimize "overtaxation" for school purposes.

A board's authority to issue bonds for capital improvement and new construction must be granted by state law; such authority will not be implied. Bonds are certificates evidencing a debt by the school district and generally must be approved by the voters in a special election. On approval by the voters, the school district sells the bonds and uses the proceeds for the purpose specified in the bond referendum.

SUMMARY

Organization of vocational and technical education for public educational institutions at the local level is affected by a number of factors generated at the national level, the state level, and the local level.

At the national level the most influential factor is the role the federal government assumes, a role that is expanding through increased funding of state and local vocational education programs.* The administration of funds is primarily a responsibility of the United States Department of Education. Although the major activity of the federal government has traditionally been that of collecting and disseminating information, it is now supervising vocational activities and conducting research that affects local-level programs. Another national influence on vocational education is professional and non-professional organizations. Such organizations affect programs through policy statements and through activities such as making project grants.

At the state level the most influential factor is the role of the state government, operating through the state department of education and the state board of vocational education. Political and social attitudes of the people of the state toward vocational education influence the organizational structure. Organization at the state level is much more unified than at the national level. Goals and objectives at the state level are more easily defined because of the smaller geographical area and the more homogeneous nature of the needs being served. Each state receiving vocational funds from the federal government is required to prepare a state plan for vocational education under guidelines established by federal legislation.

---

*At the time this publication is going to press, a conservative federal government is attempting to decrease the role of the federal government in all phases of life of the United States citizens. Thus, it is possible that we are about to enter into a period of decreased funding thus decreasing "the total" involvement of the federal government in education, including vocational education.

At the local level the most influential factors are the needs of the people in the community being served and the willingness of the community to provide for those needs. The kinds of organizational structures are numerous and varied, but there is usually an elected or appointed board of education that establishes policy. This policy is administered by officials most often identified as superintendents, who are members or ex officio members of the board. Individual schools are administered by principals and/or directors. Vocational programs are found in comprehensive schools, which also provide programs to meet the needs of the college-bound student, and are increasingly located in vocational complexes adjacent to the comprehensive school or on a separate campus. Vocational high schools are found in large metropolitan areas; their primary objective is to prepare individuals for work immediately upon graduation. The vocational school is responsible for all phases of education and does not look to another school for general education. In the college preparatory school, vocational courses are secondary to the basic purpose of the curriculum, and are intended to aid the college-bound student.

Organization and facilities change as goals, objectives, curricula, and activities are reexamined and as new technological developments are made. Examples of school plants have been discussed in this chapter to illustrate the need for flexible learning areas that provide for a wide variety of activities, both academic and vocational. The plant, equipment, and supplies must be adequate to provide learning activities for students with varying abilities, interests, and aptitudes.

Advisory councils, advisory committees, and craft committees at the national, state, and local levels are increasingly important in the organization of vocational and technical education. Made up of both professional and lay persons, they influence, through their policy statements, recommendations, and suggestions, the planning and implementation of programs, as well as the acquiring of necessary facilities and equipment. They provide greater assurance that vocational education meets the needs of individuals working and preparing to work in the business and industrial sector of the nation.

ACTIVITIES

For review

1. What factors influence the organization of vocational and technical education at the national level? state level? local level?

2. Describe the organizational structure of vocational education at the national level.

3. What are the major functions of the United States Department of Education and the National Institute of Education?

4. What federal legislation created the National Institute of Education?

5. Is vocational education more unified or less unified at the state level than it is at the national level? Explain.

6. Describe the organizational structure of vocational education at the state level.

7. What are the criteria set forth in the Vocational Education Amendments of 1968 for the composition of a state advisory council for vocational education?

8. What are the responsibilities of a state advisory council as set forth in the Vocational Education Amendments of 1968?

9. What state agencies might be involved in vocational and technical education other than the state department of education?

10. Define the term *local level* with respect to the organization of vocational education.

For discussion

1. Discuss the need for and the problems involved in joint planning between the employment system and the educational system in organizing and actuating vocational and technical education in the United States.

2. Do labor organizations influence the organization of vocational education? Explain.

3. Discuss the feasibility of establishing a national agency responsible for developing a national program of vocational education, with goals, objectives, activities, and procedures for implementing the program throughout the United States. Who would make up this agency? How would it function? What would be its relationship with states and local-level programs? What would be the advantages of such an agency? the disadvantages? What kinds of problems would be encountered?

4. Compare the extent of the federal government's control over vocational education with that of the state government.

5. Discuss the advantages and disadvantages of providing vocational education in each of the following types of schools:
   (a) college preparatory school
   (b) comprehensive school
   (c) vocational school

For exploration

1. Study the constitution and bylaws of the American Vocational Association. Is the organization planned to provide the most effective leadership for your occupation? Are all segments of vocational education adequately represented? Is the association organized to bring about the most effective influence and leadership? How are offices determined? What are their

duties and responsibilities? What projects and services are rendered to members? Be prepared to report on the organizational structure to the class. Invite an active leader in the American Vocational Association to talk to your class about the role of the association in vocational education.

2. Study the constitution and bylaws of your state's vocational association; follow the same procedures that are called for in Item 1 above.

3. Study the constitution and bylaws of the national organization for teachers in your occupational specialty. Follow the same procedures for this organization that are called for in Item 1.

4. Study the constitution and bylaws of the state organization for teachers in your occupational specialty. Is there more than one? Follow the same procedures for this organization that are called for in Item 1.

5. Study the organization of vocational education at the state level in your state. How does it compare with the organization discussed in this chapter? What is the makeup of your state board of vocational education? How are members placed in office? Are they elected? appointed? Be prepared to present your findings to the class. Invite a state vocational leader to talk with your class about the role of the state in vocational education.

6. Study the organization of vocational education in your community. How does it compare with the organizational structures discussed in this chapter? What is the makeup of the governing body of vocational education in your community? How are members placed in office? Are they elected? appointed? Be prepared to present your findings to the class. Invite a local leader to talk with your class about the organization of vocational education in your community.

7. How should the physical facilities needed to carry out the objectives of vocational education in a local system be determined? Study the literature in your college library on physical facilities for vocational education. Study physical plants (buildings and grounds) and equipment, furniture, teaching materials, and so on, required in your occupational specialty. If possible, visit one or more vocational facilities. Talk with administrators and teachers. What do they think is good about their facilities? What is bad? Why? Compare what you see and hear with what you find in the literature. How do you account for differences?

8. Explore the advantages and disadvantages of having school officials (superintendents and members of boards of education) elected and appointed. Take a position and be prepared to defend this position in class. Invite an official who is elected and one who is appointed to come to the class to discuss how they feel about this issue.

9. Invite a vocational education official to come to the class to discuss the purposes of and similarities and differences between an advisory council and a craft committee.

10. What are the sources of funding for vocational education in your community? Are the programs supported primarily through taxes? How does the system of financial support for education in your community compare with the ideas presented in this chapter?

11. Write to the secretary of education of the United States Department of Education for an updated organizational chart showing the organizational structure of vocational education at the national level. Compare the updated chart(s) with the charts in this chapter. Be prepared to present and to discuss the changes in class.

REFERENCES

1. Eugene Staley, *Planning Occupational Education and Training for Development* (New York: Praeger Publishers, 1971), p. 152.

2. Ibid., p. 153.

3. Lowell A. Burkett, "It's Impossible, Period," *American Vocational Journal*, Vol. 46, No. 3, March 1971, pp. 25-27.

4. "Comprehensive Employment and Training Act of 1973," Public Law 93-203, *United States Statutes at Large*, 1973, Vol. 87 (Washington, D.C.: Government Printing Office, 1974).

5. "Education Department Signed by Carter," *Legislative Briefs*, Vol. 5, No. 8, Oct. 1979 (Washington, D.C.: American Association of Colleges for Teacher Education, Association of Colleges and Schools of Education in State Universities and Land Grant Colleges and Affiliated Private Universities, and Teacher Education Council of State Colleges and Universities), p. 1.

6. "New Cabinet Post Filled," *Update*, Vol. 2, No. 4, Jan. 1980 (Arlington, Va.: American Vocational Association), p. 1.

7. "New Department Opens for Business with Fanfare," *Update*, Vol. 2, No. 8, May 1980 (Arlington, Va.: American Vocational Association), p. 1.

8. Ibid., p. 3.

9. "Organization Chart of the Department of Education," *The Chronicle of Higher Education*, July 14, 1980, p. 8. (Reproduced by permission.)

10. "Education Amendments of 1972," Public Law 92-318, Section 405, *United States Statutes at Large*, 1972 (Washington, D.C.: Government Printing Office, 1972), pp. 93-94.

11. Ibid., p. 95.

12. Office of Public Information, National Institute of Education, *NIE: Its History and Programs* (Washington, D.C.: Department of Health, Education and Welfare, 1974).

13. *1978-1982 Mississippi State Plan for Vocational Education* (Jackson, Miss.: Mississippi State Department of Education, 1974), Part I, p. 1.

14. *1980 Mississippi State Plan for Vocational Education* (Jackson, Miss.: Mississippi State Department of Education, 1980), p. 116.

15. "Vocational Education Amendments of 1968," Public Law 90-576, Section 104(b)(1), United States Congress (Washington, D.C.: Government Printing Office, 1968).

16. *1978-1982 Mississippi State Plan for Vocational Education*, Part III, p. 20.

17. Ibid.

■

CHAPTER 7

Vocational-Technical Education Programs

INTRODUCTION

The *curriculum,* originally conceived as consisting of a series of courses leading toward a definite goal or objective, should be regarded as all of the educational experiences that an individual encounters under the direction of the school. The vocational component of the curriculum is a body of prescribed educational experiences under school supervision designed to prepare the individual for a role in society and to qualify him or her for a trade or profession.

Providing an adequate curriculum is the most important function of the school system. Numerous factors affect the curriculum, including the administrative policies of the school, philosophy of the school, teacher competence, school equipment and facilities, findings of educational research, instructional materials, school personnel policies, parent–teacher relationships, community culture and environment, socioeconomic trends, public opinion and support, and federal, state, and local laws.

APPROACHES TO CURRICULUM DEVELOPMENT

A variety of approaches have been used in curriculum development, including (a) *activity or job analysis approach,* which determines needed skills for adult use; (b) *adult needs approach,* which prepares the learner for adult life; (c) *student needs approach,* which attempts to satisfy essential needs of individuals; (d) *creative values approach,* which encourages each individual to develop latent abilities; (e) *current practices approach*, which surveys the best practices in present curricula and incorporates them into the new curriculum; (f) *educational shortages approach*, which readjusts the curriculum if students do not reach desired standards; and (g) *interest studies approach*, which takes its direction from analysis of the interests of individuals and groups.

Teske Program Planning Model

Dr. Philip R. Teske, vocational agriculture teacher educator and U.S. Office of Education vocational program planning specialist and research advisor, developed a comprehensive model for curriculum design that has been successfully used in vocational education. The model, shown in Figure 7.1, is a comprehensive one that is well adapted for use in planning a total curriculum or any one or a combination of its individual components. The Teske model illustrates a sound approach toward systematic development, implementation, and revision of vocational curricula.

Foundations of Curriculum Development

The aims and objectives are the most important factors in the school program because all other factors (equipment, materials, methods, and so on) depend on the teachers' beliefs regarding what should be done. Tentative aims should be determined early in the process of curriculum development because they (a) locate the ends toward which effort should be directed; (b) act as guiding principles throughout a course of action; (c) serve as criteria for the selection of materials to be presented to students; and (d) serve as standards by which the outcomes of instruction may be finally evaluated.

The selection, organization, and presentation of subject matter should follow a psychological order; that is, activities, experiences, and materials should be planned and then taught at the time when the need for their use is most apparent. Among the criteria for selection of subject matter are the following:

1. Subject matter should be related to the student's interests.
2. It should make a definite contribution to the student's objectives.
3. It should give the learner that development which is most helpful in making decisions and in meeting and controlling life situations.
4. It should be assembled primarily for the needs of the learner, not according to content and boundaries of existing subject matters.

A thorough study of the curriculum should involve the following:

1. philosophy of the school
2. objectives of the program

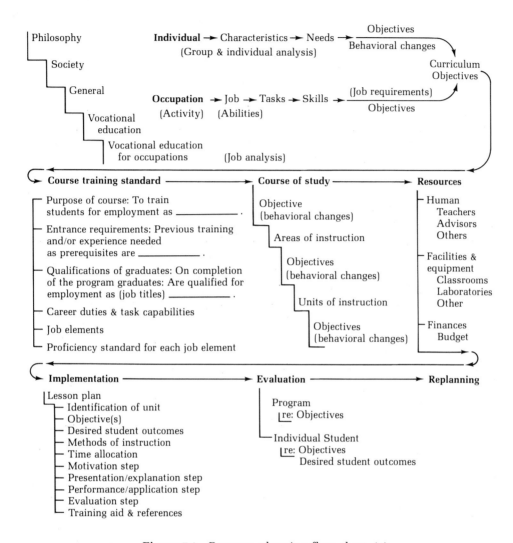

Figure 7.1 Program planning flow chart. (1)

3. relationship of curriculum to community and occupational life

4. characteristics, growth, and development of target population

5. learning theory

6. student–teacher planning

7. student–teacher relationships

8. articulation among the divisions of the school system, home, community, industry, professions, and higher education

9. organization, time, schedule, grade allocation or level

10. general scope and sequence of the curriculum
11. content, activities and experiences
12. sample units, modules, and operation sheets
13. methods, forms, records, classroom management
14. instructional materials, including equipment, supplies, and multimedia
15. building facilities necessary to carry out curriculum objectives
16. plans for evaluating and testing
17. materials for students and teachers

Principles of Curriculum Construction

Traditionally, the following procedures have been used in curriculum development:

1. Consult with students, parents, teachers, and the school guidance counselor to determine the interests, needs, and abilities of the students
2. Conduct job analyses to determine
    (a) number and type of jobs available in employment area
    (b) necessity for, amount of, and type of training
    (c) employment conditions
    (d) additional training necessary for advancement
3. Conduct surveys to determine
    (a) probable number of students who will be enrolled in the program, in relation to community size
    (b) probable number of jobs that can be filled each year
    (c) employment trends in area for which training is planned
    (d) pupil mobility
4. Set up advisory committee to work cooperatively with school administration and vocational teachers in building an effective and realistic program; this advisory committee should include
    (a) employers
    (b) outside curriculum specialist
    (c) nonbusiness representative
5. Include in the content of the curriculum the following elements
    (a) technical job information
    (b) vocational skills
    (c) occupational intelligence
    (d) integration of job information, job skills, and occupational intelligence to complete the job preparation and make the student a finished worker
    (e) development of attitudes, appreciations, and personality

6. "Sell" the proposed program to ensure
   (a) a favorable attitude among the administration, faculty, parents, and students
   (b) the ability of the school to support the program in terms of equipment and teaching personnel

7. Make decisions concerning
   (a) selection of students—based on interest, aptitude, and ability
   (b) credit or recognition for satisfactory completion of course
   (c) standards of achievement
   (d) length of the course
   (e) transfer of credit should student be unfitted for such work
   (f) type of work experience—simulated, directed, cooperative, or other
   (g) the portion of the total program to be taught by the laboratory method and the portion to be mastered by outside study
   (h) the method of instruction—individual, class, or both
   (i) the method of learning—"learning by doing" or discussion, question-answer method

8. Draw up guides for evaluating effectiveness of program, looking especially at
   (a) achievement (accomplishment of changed behavior) versus objectives
   (b) relevance of subject matter
   (c) effectiveness of teaching methods

9. Provide for study and revision through
   (a) occupational surveys
   (b) changed social and economic conditions
   (c) follow-up studies of students placed
   (d) research, both formal and informal
   (e) discovery of new and relevant resource materials
   (f) periodic checkup on all facets of program

Modern Curriculum Design Using Systems Approach

A systems approach to curriculum development is a rational, problem-solving method of analyzing the educational process and making it more effective. The system is this process taken as a whole, incorporating all of its aspects, including the students, teachers, curriculum content, instructional materials, instructional strategy, physical environment, and evaluation of instructional objectives.

Educational effectiveness is defined in terms of desired changes in student behavior, and it is tested accordingly. Implicit in this definition of effectiveness is the understanding that these changes will be achieved within the context of minimal cost and feasible allocation of resources without imposing unacceptable limitations on any other elements within the total system. Systems analysis attempts to increase educational effectiveness by clarifying educational objectives with precision and then by redesigning the entire educational process to ensure student achievement of these objectives. Both the student and the teacher know exactly what is expected on completion of an instructional unit. General statements of purpose become operational only when they are specified in terms of behavioral changes in skills, knowledge, attitudes, and values on the part of the student, as shown in Figure 7.2.

Flow-Chart Explanation

Step 1   Gather input data on students

Exactly what is known about the population of students for whom this curriculum will be developed? New tests will be developed to supplement the existing information provided by currently standardized tests and school records. Results of these tests will help to establish more accurately the level of skill development, knowledge, and attitudes that each student will bring to the classroom. A full-time school psychologist will assist in acquiring relevant information about these students and in handling special problems as they arise.

Step 2   Formulate student performance objectives

All course, unit, and lesson objectives will be stated in terms of student performance. Students will know exactly what is expected of them and how they will be evaluated. The objectives are concerned with skill development in reading, writing, listening, speaking, and viewing.

Step 3   Construct pretests

Each student will be pretested to determine to what degree he or she has already mastered the unit objectives. The results of each pretest will enable the teacher to diagnose learning requirements and to prescribe the proper learning packet.

Step 4   Select course content

Course content will be selected only after the objectives have been determined and on the basis of the contribution it will make toward helping the student achieve the stated objectives.

Step 5   Select the instructional strategy

Once the content has been chosen, the media considered most suitable for its presentation will be selected, to include printed materials, films, audiotape, filmstrips, and other audiovisual media.

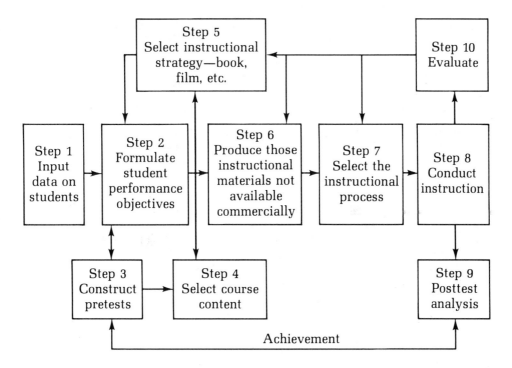

Figure 7.2 A systems approach to curriculum design: strategic areas.

Step 6 Produce those instructional materials not available commercially

Although a great variety of instructional materials are available commercially, many cannot match specific teaching objectives. Therefore, a media production and duplication center should be established locally to help develop the kinds of materials necessary to ensure achievement of the objectives.

Step 7 Select the instructional process

After the objectives, content, and media have been chosen, the instructional process thought to be most effective will be determined. This learning environment includes large-group instruction, small-group interaction, independent research, and individualized instruction.

Step 8 Conduct instruction

As the function of the teacher in this curriculum differs from that of his or her more conventional role as dispenser of information, there will be little "talk and chalk." The new functions of the teacher will be to diagnose learning problems, to prescribe the best learning sequences, to conduct small-group discussions and train the students to engage independently in similar discussions, and to assist via individual conferences.

Step 9 Analyze posttest

On completion of the instructional units and after consultation with the teacher, the student will be tested. If there is a significant gain between the pre- and posttest scores, the student will then go to the next learning sequence.

Step 10 Evaluate

Every phase of the instructional process will be constantly evaluated so that more effective procedures and strategies can be developed. This continuing evaluation is the key element in the entire process. It will be performed in conjunction with leading consultants in the field and will provide the necessary data to revise the course, unit, and lesson objectives. The students who participate in the pilot program will be involved throughout the entire evaluation process by means of interviews, attitude surveys, and questionnaires.

MODELS FOR CURRICULUM DESIGN

One of the major problems confronting vocational educators is that of developing and maintaining curricula that are attuned to rapid social and technological changes. Since the early 1960s, the rate of change has been accelerating. Thus, maintaining a relevant curriculum is a continuing task for vocational educators at all levels. Techniques, content, and methods that have served satisfactorily in the past are not necessarily adequate to present and emerging needs.

Each generation has debated the question of what should be taught in the schools. The following discussion reviews some of the basic characteristics of curriculum models as they have been practiced.

Subject-Centered Curriculum

A traditional organizational pattern that has been widely used at the secondary level separates students into two or three separate tracks—college-bound, general, vocational—an organizational pattern that has tended to penalize all students. The college-bound students are directed toward those courses that will enhance their performance on standardized tests, such as college entrance exams, and in college courses. However, there is little opportunity for them to acquire entry-level employment skills or to learn about the business and industrial community and how it functions. In contrast, students enrolled in the vocational track develop employment skills, but they have limited opportunity to develop basic competencies needed in present-day society or to enroll in college preparatory courses that would allow them a later option for college training. Students in the general programs often graduate without occupational preparation or specific plans for the future.

The most common organization of content within the traditional curriculum is the isolated subject, a curriculum in which individual subjects are stressed. Consideration is given to the vertical arrangement of courses, but little attention is given to horizontal relationships of courses offered during a particular year or semester.

Core Curriculum

Traditionally, curricular offerings at the high school and college level have been divided into those courses required of all students, those required of some students, and those electives required of no students. The group of separate subjects required of all students is commonly known as the core. Establishing a core that is required of all students is common practice in high schools and colleges. Generally, vocational education subjects are not included as part of the common core required of all students, but are treated as electives.

Other types of core curricula emphasize the separate subjects but provide for informal and formal correlations among the subjects around a theme. Alberty, in his discussion of the six types of core curricula, suggested that the Type V core provides the most promising curriculum design for transforming general education in the high school into a program suited to the challenging times in which we live (2).

The Type V core, known as the adolescent needs or problems core, is concerned with treating broad categories covering areas in which students are likely to encounter problems. The content of the Type V core is not a fusion of two or more subjects; rather, it consists of materials from whatever fields bear on the solution of student problems. Thus, fields such as vocational education, which have heretofore not been regarded as part of general education, are included in the development of appropriate teaching-learning units. This organizational pattern makes use of large blocks of time and encourages the use of problem-solving techniques and decision-making skills in attacking problems (3).

Cluster-Based Curriculum

Through the years vocational education has tended to be organized around a single-occupation concept. That is, within a given vocational area, a student would select one occupation and follow a planned program in preparation for it. Today we live in an age characterized by mobility and the changing nature of jobs. Persons who are prepared with a broad base of skills that apply to more than one occupation tend to have more flexibility in adapting to the needs of the labor market. Thus, the cluster concept evolved as an alternative to the single-occupation concept.

The cluster concept is based on the premise that certain occupations have common learning and skill requirements and that students who have mastered these skills have more employment options. There are critics, however, who point out that such an approach may not develop the depth required for specialized job performance in single occupations.

During the 1960s, several projects were funded by the U.S. Office of Education in which clusters were identified in areas such as building trades, child care, mechanical technology, merchandising, and office occupations. In one such project involving building trades work, ten trades were selected for study: bricklaying, carpentry, cement finishing, electrical work, iron work, painting, plastering, plumbing, roofing, and sheet metal. From the analysis of data, seven clusters of knowledge widely used in the ten building trades were identified: construction types, methods, and materials; tools and machines; mathematics; science; communication; safety; and worker welfare. Specific skills and knowledge were identified in each cluster (4).

In a project at the University of South Florida under the direction of Calhoun, 12 units of instruction were found to be common to the functional aspects of business and office education: computational skills, filing, grooming, human relations, keeping records, mail handling, office machines, problem-solving, processing forms, proofreading, using the telephone, and typewriting (5).

Organic Curriculum

In the late 1960s, Morgan and Bushnell proposed a curriculum design that would lead to options permitting the maximum self-actualization of each individual. Students leaving school either before or following graduation would have useful tools for employment. For example, a student might enter college and pursue a professional degree program; he or she might enter a community college or technical school for advanced occupational training. The student would have entry-level skills, which would permit access to the labor market, or he or she might continue training through adult education.

Figure 7.3 illustrates the options available in an organic curriculum. A key feature in the organic curriculum is that the student is able to decide which option to take after graduation instead of three or four years before. The organization of this curriculum design was based on a systems concept, hence the name "organic," or systemic.

The first step in implementing the organic curriculum model is to identify the behavioral requirements needed for entry into the several postsecondary options. The next step is the construction of a high school program that will provide students with the skills and knowledge needed to attain these objectives.

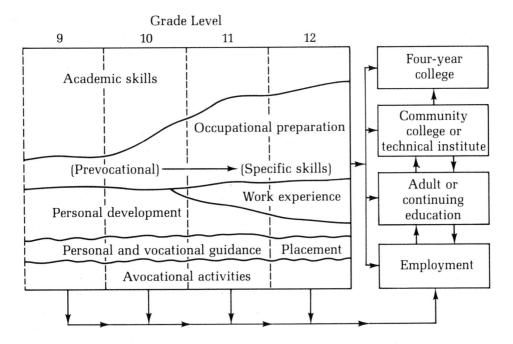

Figure 7.3   Organic curriculum options (6)

The financial costs of such a curriculum discouraged all but the most enthusiastic supporters. Nevertheless, the organic curriculum became a forerunner of current career education concepts.

Competency-Based Curriculum

One trend in vocational education at all levels is competency-based instruction. A competency-based program specifies the desired objectives or competencies in an explicit form, identifies the criteria to be applied in assessing the learner's competencies, and holds the learner accountable for meeting these objectives. Such a program, however, must be based on two major technologies that only recently became available to education. The first of these is a systems design that permits the employment of a sophisticated management schema. Only through such a management plan can the program really be controlled, evaluated, and renewed. The second technology is the modularization of the instructional program. The individualization of the program has been made possible through the development of learning modules whose use permits self-pacing by students and instructors.

Traditionally the competencies needed for employment have been defined ambiguously. An examination of curriculum and courses of study at the high school, technical school, junior college, and college/university reveals that indicators of expectancies are stated in terms of required courses and time spent in them, such as one year of cosmetology, three quarters of shorthand, one year of horticulture. In competency-based education programs, the demonstration of competencies replaces course "passes" and specific amounts of time spent in class as indicators of subject mastery. In other words, in a traditional program, the time is held constant and the achievement varies from student to student. In competency-based programs, the time varies from student to student and the competencies are more nearly constant.

The absence of clearly defined expected outcomes hampers the instructional process. Even when sufficient time is provided, the lack of specific criteria makes it difficult to measure whether the programs (courses) have resulted in desired outcomes.

Two conditions must be met if competency-based programs are to be implemented: (a) identification of specific competencies, and (b) procedures for assessing competencies in terms of appropriate criteria.

The systems-oriented curriculum-instruction design process can be construed as a series of functions that must be performed to achieve the objectives of the subsystem. Each function includes identifiable processes and products. The functions are:

1. specification of assumptions, tasks, goals, and objectives
2. generation and selection of objective criteria
3. identification and design of assessment strategies
4. specification of instructional philosophy
5. development of instructional strategies
6. selection and/or development of instructional resources
7. development of feedback mechanisms

Individualized Instruction

Contemporary curriculum designs are characterized by a trend toward learning that is student-centered rather than teacher-centered. Objectives, which are based on task analysis, communicate the anticipated outcomes to the learner. The emphasis in instructional programs has shifted away from concern for the group norm toward concern for the individual. Individualized instruction thus requires that vocational educators make decisions that are relevant to each student.

Basically, a curriculum model for individualized instruction includes the following elements:

1. selection and sequencing of instructional tasks and objectives

2. development and/or selection of instructional materials and activities needed for teaching each objective, or for achieving each objective

3. evaluation for placing each student at the appropriate point in the curriculum

4. plan for developing individualized programs of study

5. procedure for evaluating and monitoring individual progress

The term *individualized instruction* is frequently used in education and has numerous interpretations. It is characterized by at least three levels of sophistication, thus allowing considerable flexibility in designing programs.

■ ■

Level one—self-paced The simplest form of individualization to implement is one in which students are expected to acquire the same skills and knowledge with the same material, but the rate or pace at which each student progresses through the material varies.

■ ■

Level two—alternate modes The next level of individualization consists of providing more than one instructional mode for acquiring each competency. For example, this level involves the use of a variety of instructional modes for presenting the same concepts—tapes (auditory), sound-slides or filmstrips (auditory-visual), print (visual), and so on.

In the initial stage the teacher usually recommends the mode that each student should follow, based on observation and knowledge of the student's ability and learning style. In the next stage, two or three alternate modes are identified, and the student is allowed to choose the one he or she wishes to use. The final stage in level two (same competencies for all students, but different routes and rates) permits students to determine on their own the instructional mode best suited to their individual styles of learning.

■ ■

Level three—independent learning One of the most important goals in education is to help each student

acquire the competencies necessary to become an
independent learner, one who can assume personal
responsibility for learning. If the teaching-learning
process is teacher-centered, if students are limited to
what the teacher explains or demonstrates, if students never learn "how to learn" or how to become
independent learners, then students are severely
handicapped when they leave school. The changing
nature of jobs makes it imperative that students
know how and where to acquire necessary new
skills. They must not be limited by what the instructor knows or presents in the classroom.

■ ■

After leading the student through the first two stages of individualization,
the teacher is now ready to introduce level three, in which the learner selects
the competencies to be acquired and the instructional modes to be used, and
determines the length of time to be devoted to each.

There are, of course, many basic competencies that all students must
master and that the student cannot elect to omit. However, at the application
level, students who demonstrate sufficient maturity can embark on independent learning.

Open-Access Curriculum

In the early 1970s, a number of key ideas triggered an interest among educators
in what has become known as the *open school*. These ideas stemmed generally
from a realization that change had created a wide gap between the theory and
practice of curriculum design. The bases for educational reform, founded in
social, philosophic, economic, and psychological developments of the times,
have been discussed elsewhere in this text. New knowledge stimulated questioning of old practices and established new assumptions about the role of
education. The volume of new knowledge brought with it a realization of the
impossibility of education's "being all things to all people." The possibility of
attacking any discipline from a variety of entry points gained credibility when
it became apparent that pupils could not only learn things out of sequence but
could move at a faster pace and increase their apparent capacity for knowledge
in the process. The publication of Bruner's *The Process of Education* (7)
stimulated a reconsideration of the *structures* of knowledge in all fields and
raised serious questions regarding previously held assumptions concerning
curriculum scope-and-sequence patterns. The creativity movement paved the
way for acceptance of the idea that virtually anything may be taught, on some
level, to children of any age. Knowledge and learning viewed from this

perspective emphasized the need for building within each learner a competence in "learning to learn" and extended relearning throughout a lifetime of
encounters with relativistic, changing "truth."

The open school, as a form of curriculum design, represents an innovative
approach to making education serve the learner. Although in operation in
relatively few schools, it possesses potential for wider use as problems
connected with its implementation are solved. The open school is characterized by:

1. an individually established success formula for each student

2. creation of large clusters of content

3. multiple entry points

4. open-exit

5. emphasis on learning as opposed to teaching

6. personalized intensive study in large blocks of time

7. discretionary grouping and scheduling

8. differentiated teacher roles

9. open-spaced teaching services and learning centers

10. individualized, multimedia instructional packages

The open-access curriculum rejects all of the following: the isolated-
subject schedule, the idea of tracking students, grouping in the school's master
schedule, sequencing content beyond absolute essentials, permitting more than
one-fourth of the curriculum to be defined as a core of common learnings,
labeling any legitimate body of knowledge as a "frill," use of behavioral
changes in students or teachers as an exclusive measure of program effectiveness, "intellectual closure" as a primary teaching method, restricting what the
student learns to what the teacher knows, and requiring teachers to work alone
and unassisted by related specialists or unchallenged by competing disciplines
or philosophies.

Open-school advocates rely heavily on involvement of students, teachers,
administrators, members of the school board, and the community to gain acceptance. Visitations to schools in the "open" design and in-service experimentation are an important part of the process of adoption. Computers are
frequently used to program individual student data such as test scores, personality traits, strengths and weaknesses; to differentiate teacher roles; and to
provide individualized curricula based on computerized data. Careful planning and the acceptance of key publics are vital to the success of the open
school.

The teacher is the key to the potential success of the open classroom.
Teachers must understand the open classroom concept personally and then
develop the desire to explore it. They must be encouraged to try many different

avenues with their students, including a variety of teaching techniques. They must be provided with an abundance of instructional materials, many of which they have developed themselves. Such an approach will result in many teachers customizing education for their students as well as for themselves.

Vocational and other teacher education programs are likewise indispensable to the success of the open school. Those programs, which are themselves in a competency-based format, will be able to:

1. help teachers to understand and internalize the concepts of open education: teaming, nongradedness, continuous progress, and unified media

2. provide intensive training in techniques of open education: contracts, learning centers, individualized packets

3. show teachers how to individualize instruction in the content areas

4. provide training in management techniques of open education: scheduling, organizing, recordkeeping, control and management, parent involvement, and reporting

5. help teachers identify the proper use of media in the schools of the future

6. help teachers identify and provide a unique learning experience for students

The open-access classroom is being used in many vocational programs where individualized instruction is emphasized. In one school, all business education courses are taught by a team of three instructors in a classroom laboratory that operates daily during all class hours. Students may schedule their courses at any period their schedules permit, with the help of an advisor. All three instructors are available to teach any course to individuals or small groups.

This flexible-scheduling feature permits many more students to enter the business program than could under the fixed-class schedules of previous years. Instructors can increase the number of students they can efficiently teach from a previous level of 100 to as many as 300.

All courses are taught on a completely individualized basis, with emphasis on individual interests and abilities. Work programs for each student replace the large-group lecture methods of the past. Many more opportunities for personal career counseling are possible between individual students and the instructor. During unscheduled study periods, students use the lab and its facilities to work on project assignments with the help of an instructor who is always on duty in the laboratory.

A similar example may be found in home economics education. Within a large laboratory, equipment and materials relating to various specializations are grouped together. For example, the foods learning center may be located at one end of the laboratory, whereas learning centers related to clothing, child care, or arts and crafts are arranged throughout the lab. Such an open-space arrangement facilitates individual and/or small-group instruction in several learning centers simultaneously. Instructional teams (teachers and aides) work cooperatively with students in formulating and realizing their objectives.

CURRICULAR NEEDS ASSESSMENT

Although there would be no disagreement among vocational educators over the importance of maintaining a relevant curriculum, actually putting such a curriculum into effect is difficult. Vocational education, probably more than any other area in the school, is attuned to the needs of its students and of the business and industrial community because of its use of such techniques as advisory committees, cooperative work programs for students, internships in business and industry for teachers, and identification of specific skills needed for employment; however, there remains a need for systematic efforts in curriculum revision.

One strategy for curriculum updating is the use of needs assessments. A need may be defined as a discrepancy between what is desired and what exists. The greater the discrepancy observed, the greater or more critical the need.

Consider this example: suppose an analysis of test data reveals that students enrolled in a given vocational area score lower than the school norm (or total vocational norm) in mathematics. A survey of students, parents, teachers, and business/community leaders reveals agreement on the need for students to improve their math skills because this is one of the basic skill components of vocational programs. A need has now been defined. The test data provided evidence of *perceived level* of performance; the survey data revealed a *desired level,* which is higher than the current level.

The example shows that two types of needs are generated by the assessment process—felt needs and validated needs. Felt needs reflect the ideas, attitudes, and beliefs of people—the students, staff, parents, and community/ business leaders. Validated needs are generated from relevant data (or hard data) gathered about current conditions in the school—student enrollment in vocational education, available instructional materials, library resources, test results, and so on. These are the facts on which a successful needs assessment depends. For vocational education, systematic needs assessments serve to gain support for a quality program by involving staff, students, parents, and community/business leaders in identifying the student needs the program should fill; to identify critical student needs most likely to benefit from concentrated improvement programs; and to identify those student needs that students, staff, parents, and community/business leaders value as having highest priority.

These procedures may be used to determine the critical needs and the priority among them:

1. determine the desired student outcome objectives that the school seeks to achieve

2. collect, analyze, and interpret data that reflect the extent to which the objectives are now being achieved

3. using the identified needs as a basis, and with the help of an advisory committee, develop a questionnaire to which students, parents, teachers, and business/community representatives might respond by
   (a) indicating omission of major needs
   (b) indicating extent of agreement with identified needs
   (c) indicating which needs are most critical

THE VOCATIONAL EDUCATION FAMILY

Vocational education today consists of a number of interrelated fields, programs, and curricula, with the primary objective of preparation for gainful employment. The distinction between vocational and general education is rapidly being replaced by an educational system, reflected in career education, that integrates both vocational and general education aspects through curricular programming.

The following section focuses on the unique contributions of the fields that comprise the vocational education family. A brief treatment of the nature of each field, curricular content, trends, and employment opportunities is provided.

Agricultural Education

The passage of the Smith-Hughes Act in 1917 inaugurated a period in which vocational education focused on the training of farmers. The Federal Board for Vocational Education, in its 1931 report, proclaimed that "the primary aim of vocational agriculture is to train present and prospective farmers for proficiency in farming." Subsequent editions of the publication reaffirmed this aim (8).

During the past quarter-century major changes have taken place in the field of agriculture. Advances in science and technology have transformed agriculture into a complex industry. In addition, along with the increase in the total population of the nation, there has been a decrease in total farm workers needed to produce food to meet increasing consumer needs. The decrease in numbers of farm workers has been accompanied by an increase in the number of off-farm workers engaged in agricultural supply, services, and marketing. To provide for these changing educational needs, the scope of agriculture education programs has been extended to include training in agri-business, natural resources, and environmental protection.

Two decades ago, the vocational agriculture curriculum was essentially the same throughout the nation. In keeping with expanding on-farm and off-farm occupations and vocational agriculture objectives, subject matter is now adapted to individual needs and interest within local school districts.

The content of the instructional program in agriculture was classified as follows by the U.S. Office of Education in Handbook VI, *Standard Terminology for Curriculum and Instruction in Local and State School Systems* (9):*

01.01 Agricultural Production

01.02 Agricultural Supplies and Services

01.03 Agricultural Mechanics

01.04 Agricultural Products (Processing, Inspection, Marketing)

01.05 Ornamental Horticulture

01.06 Agricultural Resources (Conservation, Utilization, Services)

01.07 Forestry

As can be seen from this classification, the majority of opportunities are in nonfarm occupations. The employment outlook points to a continuation of this trend, with the number of farm workers expected to decrease and the significant source of job openings being job replacements. The replacements, however, will need to be more highly trained than their predecessors because of improvements in technology and the increasing mechanization of farm operations.

The curriculum in agricultural education includes courses related to both farming and nonfarming occupations. The trend at the high school level is to offer basic instruction—including units such as plant science, animal science, soil science, and agricultural mechanics—and occupational exploration during the first two years. In the last two high school years, specialized courses such as agricultural mechanics, forestry, and ornamental horticulture are offered. Because persons entering occupations in agricultural businesses and industries need vocational competencies other than technical agriculture, programs of study frequently incorporate content from other vocational areas, such as from business education, distribution and marketing, and trades.

Contemporary programs, which are outgrowths of the Vocational Education Act of 1963 and the Vocational Education Amendments of 1968, emphasize broadened objectives, including: (a) preparation and advancement in *any* occupation involving knowledge and skill in agriculture; (b) occupational exploration, guidance, and counseling; and (c) development of abilities essential for effective citizenship.

Roberts (10) lists seven major objectives of vocational agriculture to meet the aim of training present and prospective farmers for proficiency in agriculture: (1) make a beginning and advance in farming, (2) produce farm commodities efficiently, (3) market farm products advantageously, (4) conserve soil

---

*This taxonomic source has been used throughout this chapter to classify occupations within the various vocational fields.

and other natural resources, (5) manage a farm business effectively, (6) maintain a favorable environment, and (7) participate in rural leadership activities.

Designed primarily for secondary school students, the preceding objectives may be adapted to other levels of instruction in vocational agriculture. An example of specific objectives in agricultural education is provided by the Omaha Public Schools (11):

1. *to develop an appreciation of the role of agriculture on the part of all students. This would involve units of agricultural information in elementary grades, exploratory and pre-vocational junior high courses for girls and boys, and courses in general agriculture such as economics and livestock and livestock products*

2. *to prepare persons for off-farm agricultural employment*

3. *to provide a course in agricultural science professions for seniors*

4. *to contribute to the solution of agricultural-rural migrant adjustment problems*

5. *to provide facilities for training and retraining of workers, including adults, in agricultural industries*

These objectives go far beyond the vocational aspects of the subject and provide all students with the opportunity to become knowledgeable about agriculture as a part of their general education.

Like all other fields of education, agricultural education is changing rapidly. Hunsicker (12) describes the transitions in vocational agricultural education as leading to an entirely new concept. He says that the names "agricultural education" and "vocational agriculture"—which for half a century have connoted chiefly production agriculture, such as farming and ranching—are giving way to the broad concept of vocational education for agri-business occupations, increasingly referred to as "agri-business education." Hunsicker emphasizes that this new title includes the preparation of individuals for employment in both agricultural production and the off-farm-related business. He defines agri-business as being a blend of agriculture and business and a combination of the producing operations of a farm, including the services associated with them; the manufacturing and distribution of farm equipment, fertilizers, and supplies; the processing, storage, marketing, and distribution of farm commodities including food and fiber; and the conservation, preservation, and use of renewable natural resources.

Thompson (13), state superintendent of public instruction in Wisconsin, expressed similar ideas in her address to the general session of the Agricultural Education Division of the American Vocational Association in 1976. She described the farmer as being bombarded by an array of farm machinery, pesticides, mutated seeds, hormones, antibiotics, grain dryers, storage units, prefabricated housing for hogs and chickens, credit arrangements, and the expanding nature of agri-business. She emphasized the need for vocational programs designed to prepare young people and adults for these emerging occupations—programs that go far beyond preparation for production agriculture, that include an international as well as a domestic outlook. She described these programs as including women, minorities, handicapped, and urban students.

Full-time and part-time postsecondary programs provide the student with opportunities to specialize in the various phases of vocational agriculture as listed in the USOE classification. Short-term specialized programs and workshops are available for adults through secondary and postsecondary institutions.

In 1928 the Future Farmers of America (FFA), a youth service organization for present and former students enrolled in vocational agricultural programs, was organized. Its major aims and purposes include leadership and character development, opportunity for self-expression, cooperation, service, and sportsmanship. There are four types of membership in FFA—active, associate, collegiate, and honorary—with four grades of active membership ranging from Green Hand to American Farmer. In 1969 girls were first made eligible for membership in FFA on the national level. The organization publishes an official magazine, *The Future Farmer*. Collegiate FFA chapters have been active for many years, primarily for agricultural teacher education students. The National Postsecondary Agricultural Student Organization is a newly formed student organization, primarily for agricultural students in junior-community colleges. In its formative stages, this organization looks upon its present name as temporary. It no doubt will select a permanent name more suitable to its purposes and objectives.

Business and Office Education

Business education has been a part of this country's educational system from its earliest years, with training in accounting, commercial law, and business arithmetic included in the early high school curriculum. In present-day curricula, business education is recognized as having both general and vocational education objectives. It has been defined as education that will equip the student with skills necessary to perform particular functions in an office or data processing occupation; it will also provide him or her with the understandings and knowledge needed for conducting personal affairs and for using the services of the business world.

A review of the major objectives of business education helps to develop an understanding of its role in the school program. The *vocational objective* relates specifically to the preparation of students for initial employment, to upgrading existing skills, and to retraining in new and/or related business and office occupations. The *exploratory objective*, aimed primarily at the middle grades and early high school, provides opportunities for students to gain information about careers in business. The *occupational intelligence objective* recognizes that all citizens should have an intelligent understanding of the various areas of work in which they earn a living. The *economic understanding objective* is related to developing economic literacy in all citizens. The *consumer education objective* serves a dual role; it promotes both the discriminating use of services and resources by consumers and a corresponding understanding of the consumer viewpoint and how best to serve the consumer. The *personal use objective* relates to those business courses designed to prepare students for proper execution of their personal business affairs. The *semivocational objective* recognizes that many business skills lead to advancement in professions or occupations other than those directly related to business. The *college preparation objective* recognizes that high schools have an obligation to provide background preparation in business as well as to develop skills that provide students with tools to cope more effectively with college demands.

Changing objectives in business education are reflected in a review of the philosophical statements in *This We Believe about Business Education in the High School,* prepared by the Policies Commission for Business and Economic Education. The first statement, published in 1961, was written by 12 national leaders in business education, who represented two of the most prestigious organizations in the field—the National Business Education Association and Delta Pi Epsilon, a national honorary fraternity. The commission's first statement described the purposes of business education as being concerned with two major aspects of the education of youth: (a) the knowledge, attitudes, and nonvocational skills needed by all persons to be effective in their personal economics and in their understanding of our economic system, and (b) the vocational knowledge and skills needed for initial employment and for advancement in a business career. The statement asserts that business education has an important contribution to make to the economic literacy of every high school boy and girl; business education must provide an adequate program of vocational preparation for those boys and girls who will enter business upon completing high school; and business education courses should be available as electives to those high school students planning to go to college and should be accepted by the colleges and universities as meeting part of the college entrance requirements (14).

Within ten years a third organization had been added to the sponsorship of the Policies Commission—the American Vocational Association. The commission's second statement (15) regarding the role of business education in the high school reflected the increasing importance of vocational preparation through business education. Although there might be no significance attached, the commission rearranged the order of expressing its philosophy regarding the role of business education in the high school. It stated that business education is an effective program of occupational instruction for secondary students desiring careers in business; business education has an important contribution to make to the economic literacy of all secondary school students; and business education is desirable for students who plan programs requiring postsecondary and higher education in business.

A complete reading of the two statements reveals only one mention of the word *career* in the first statement and repeated use of the word in the second statement, clearly indicating a change in the attitude of business educators. They are no longer preoccupied with the academic acceptability of business education at the secondary level; they are more concerned with the need for business education to provide all students with the knowledge, skills, and attitudes necessary for them to function effectively as business and office workers and as citizens. Another difference in the two statements that indicates a change in attitude on the part of business educators is the orientation of the second statement around the needs of individuals, the business community, and the community at large, suggesting the need for a flexible curriculum to meet those needs. In comparison, the earlier statement describes a rather rigid and highly structured subject matter curriculum.

The Policies Commission for Business and Economic Education has prepared a number of statements reflecting the objectives, roles, and needs of business and office education. Its first pamphlet, "A Proposal for Business-Economic Education for American Secondary Schools," was directed to school administrators. Its purpose was to ensure that administrators were focused on the need to begin, to continue, or to reinforce business education programs in the secondary schools. Since then, the commission's statements have reflected changing attitudes of business educators. "This We Believe about Implementing Individualization of Instruction in Business Education" is a statement that reveals a new focus on the part of business educators—on the needs of students as individuals rather than on a desire to teach certain subjects or to gain acceptability from peers in doing so.

The objectives of business education in the high school should be written collectively by business teachers, with the advice of students, other teachers, school administrators, and representatives of the business community. The objectives should reflect the philosophy of the school and business community being served. The objective might be (a) to prepare students for careers in business; or (b) to help students assume their economic roles as consumers, workers, and citizens; or (c) to assist students in preparing for professional careers requiring advanced study. A school might have all three of these objectives, or just two.

Learning experiences in business and office education are designed to lead to employment and/or advancement of individuals in occupations related to the facilitating function of the office. "Facilitating function," as used here, refers to the expediting role of office occupations as the connecting link between the production and distribution activities of an organization. Included are a variety of activities, such as recording and retrieval of data, supervision and coordination of office activities, internal and external communication, and the reporting of information.

The U.S. Office of Education classified the business and office education instructional program into nine areas:

14.01 Accounting and Computing Occupations

14.02 Business Data Processing Systems Occupations

14.03 Filing, Office Machines, and General Clerical Occupations

14.04 Information Communication Occupations

14.05 Materials Support Occupations

14.06 Personnel, Training and Related Occupations

14.07 Stenographic, Secretarial and Related Occupations

14.08 Supervisory and Administrative Management Occupations

14.09 Typing and Related Occupations

The business curriculum, aimed at realizing both vocational and general education objectives, is usually divided into two areas of instruction:

1 Basic or general business

These courses contribute to the primary understandings and knowledge needed by all students. Examples include Introduction to Business, Basic Business, Business Law, Economics, Economic Geography, Consumer Problems, Business Management, Business Principles, and Business Psychology.

2 Vocational business education

These courses equip students with entry-level skills in the various business and office occupations. Examples include Advanced Typewriting, Bookkeeping, Accounting, Shorthand, Office Machines, Office Practice, Cooperative Business Education, and Vocational Office Training.

Data processing is one of the most rapidly growing aspects of business education. It may be classified as vocational business education, especially at the postsecondary level. Courses related to this phase of the business curriculum include Key Punch, Introduction to Computers, Unit Recordkeeping, Basic Computing Machines, Computer Mathematics, COBOL, and Computer Programming.

The business function in our society continues to expand, and as it does, it develops new jobs, uses new machines, and designs new systems. The broad occupational categories in the field of business include the following:

1. *Clerical*—clerk typist, file clerk, shipping and receiving clerk, dispatcher,

information clerk, office machine operator, title searcher, switchboard operator, post office clerk, receptionist

2. *Secretarial*—stenographer, court reporter, executive secretary, legal or medical secretary

3. *Bookkeeping and accounting*—credit analyst, estimator, auditor, bank teller, bookkeeping machine operator, cashier, tax specialist, junior accountant, treasurer

4. *Data processing*—systems analyst, programmer, computer and console operator, keypunch and coding equipment operator, tape librarian, project planner

5. *Management*—administrative assistant, budget management analyst, administrative secretary, clerical and office supervisor, chief clerk, credit and collection manager, personnel manager

6. *Business teaching*—middle school or high school level, vocational-technical schools, independent business schools, community and junior colleges, college or university level, educational assistant, training specialist, school supervisor or administrator

One of the most recent developments in office occupations is word-processing systems, in which secretarial jobs are organized according to functions related to correspondence and to administrative support. Administrative and corresponding secretaries are the primary specialists in the word-processing center. Remotely located, linked by recorders and dictation devices, and supported by automated typing and copying equipment, these information-production professionals now require a new set of tools and facilities (frequently linked to a computer) to provide administrative services. Similar dramatic changes are occurring in other aspects of the office occupations.

Several youth organizations are available to students enrolled in business and office education. The largest of these is Future Business Leaders of America (FBLA) with its collegiate counterpart, Phi Beta Lambda. FBLA offers three levels of active membership: assistant, supervisor, and leader. The programs and activities of FBLA are aimed at helping students to prepare for business careers, increasing understanding of the business education program, and developing leadership abilities. The official publication of FBLA is *Future Business Leader*. Future Secretaries Association (FSA) is an international student organization for prospective secretaries designed to promote interest in secretarial careers. A similar organization for students interested in electronic data processing is Future Data Processors (FDP), sponsored by the Data Processing Management Association. Several colleges also sponsor chapters of Pi Omega Pi, a youth organization for business and office education. Another organization is the Office Education Association (OEA), founded in 1967 for office occupations students. Students who are members of FBLA, FSA, and FDP may also join OEA.

Distributive Education

Distributive education is charged with the responsibility of preparing persons for employment in marketing. Thus it is concerned with activities such as selling, buying, transporting, storing, promoting, financing, research, and management. Instruction in distributive education is offered at the high school, postsecondary, and adult levels; it includes preparatory and supplemental training to prepare persons for initial employment as well as to update existing skills or provide new ones.

The Distributive Education Publications Committee of the American Vocational Association describes the purposes of distributive education as follows (16):

> The major purpose of distributive education is to prepare people for employment in distribution. Three goals, which describe the responsibility and functions of distributive education, are generally accepted.
>
> The first goal, to offer instruction in distribution and marketing, emphasizes the educational contribution of distributive education. This primary aim provides instruction, which is essential for entrance or advancement in distributive occupations, for youth and adults, regardless of their previous educational achievements, their social, economic, cultural, or ethnic backgrounds.
>
> The second goal, to aid in the improvement of the techniques of distribution, is economic in nature. Our high standard of living is based upon the efficient distribution of goods and services. Distributive education makes a further economic contribution in terms of human resources by helping to provide people with the wide range of competencies necessary for successful employment.
>
> The third goal is a social one because distributive education has a commitment to help prepare workers who understand their responsibilities to society—workers who will strive to secure equal rights and opportunities for all, and who will recognize that only through proper work habits and responsible actions can a fine and competitive society be maintained.

The objectives of distributive education have changed since it was first introduced to the secondary school program in Boston in 1912. At that time, the objective was to provide cooperative training in retail store work for the purpose of improving the lot and quality of work of sales personnel (17). During its early years it was often under the supervision of persons in business education, trade and industrial education, and agricultural education.

With the passage of the George-Deen Act in 1936 and later through the George-Barden Act of 1946, distributive education became officially recognized as a part of reimbursed vocational education. Training under these acts, however, was limited to employed persons above the age of 16 and to cooperative plans in the high school distributive programs. Major provisions of the Vocational Education Acts of the 1960s included removal of the employment requirement for participation, thus enabling schools to develop preparatory programs. Postsecondary programs were stressed under these acts.

Distributive education has become increasingly important in recent years because of the role of marketing and distribution in the economic growth of the nation. As technological advances are made, as society becomes more complex, as changes occur in producer-consumer relationships, distributive education must adjust. Distributive education is thus concerned with creating and managing change in the area of marketing and distribution, but its real task is to bring about change that will best serve the customer.

The content of distributive education may be classified into five areas of competency, including marketing competency, technology competency, social competency, basic skill competency, and economic competency. These areas are included, in varying degrees of difficulty or concentration, in programs ranging from the high school through the adult level.

Jobs within the distributive area fall within one of the following occupational categories, as identified by the U.S. Office of Education:

04.01 Advertising Services	04.10 Home Furnishings
04.02 Apparel and Accessories	04.11 Hotel and Lodging
04.03 Automotive	04.12 Industrial Marketing
04.04 Finance and Credit	04.13 Insurance
04.05 Floristry	04.14 International Trade
04.06 Food Distribution	04.15 Personal Services
04.07 Food Services	04.16 Petroleum
04.08 General Merchandise	04.17 Real Estate
04.09 Hardware, Building Materials, Farm and Garden Supplies	04.18 Recreation and Tourism
	04.19 Transportation

Occupational opportunities in marketing and distribution range from basic jobs, usually filled by graduates of high school programs, to top management positions, usually filled by college graduates. Present and projected employment opportunities in the distributive field are strong.

Students enrolled in distributive education classes at the high school and post-high school levels are eligible for membership in Distributive Education Clubs of America (DECA). Organized in 1947, DECA is primarily concerned with leadership development. There are three types of membership: active, associate, and honorary. In addition to the student organization, there is an adult organization—DECA, Incorporated—which was established to serve as the legal body for the student organization. The official publication of DECA is *The Distributor*.

Mason (18) emphasizes that DECA is not extracurricular but cocurricular and, as such, some of its activities should take place during school time. He believes that both high school and college students have been motivated toward careers in distribution, primarily through competitive activities and conferences.

Corbin (19) formulated 12 major goals for DECA through a survey of national leaders, distributive education teachers, and DECA members. He reported these 12 goals in descending order of importance: 1. Develop leadership characteristics. 2. Develop self-confidence. 3. Develop greater understanding of our free, competitive enterprise system. 4. Further develop occupational competencies needed for careers in marketing, merchandising, and management. 5. Develop high ethical standards in personal and business relationships. 6. Develop effective interpersonal relationships. 7. Develop a greater awareness of career opportunities in marketing and distribution. 8. Develop greater proficiency in communication. 9. Develop greater appreciation of the responsibilities of citizenship. 10. Develop a healthy competitive spirit. 11. Develop social and business etiquette. 12. Participate in planned social activities.

High school instruction is organized either under the *cooperative plan* or under the *project plan*. The cooperative plan involves a combination of classroom instruction and supervised on-the-job training. The project plan combines classroom instruction with coordinated laboratory experiences. The distributive education curriculum at this level provides pre-employment courses, generally offered at grades 9 and 10, focusing on topics such as introduction to the nature of business, job interviews, and introduction to the field of distribution. Technical and related instruction, correlated with the cooperative training, is offered during the last two years.

Distributive education at the postsecondary level is concerned primarily with specialized areas of distribution and marketing for students preparing for specialist and middle management positions. Postsecondary programs, which combine class experiences plus internship, include such courses as human relations, mathematics, communication, marketing, management, and supervision. Whereas the primary focus of high school and postsecondary programs is on preparation for employment, adult programs are designed for those seeking greater job proficiency and specialized skills as well as for those desiring entry-level skills. Consequently, both general and specialized courses are offered in the adult program. Donnell (20) suggests that the qualifications for a retail employee are undergoing greater changes than ever before, and that increased sales volume, along with escalating costs, is forcing many changes in business. He suggests that the computer and increased complexity of business require better educated employees to handle computer-related activities, and to serve a more alert citizenry.

Numerous factors may be identified that contribute to the changes in the distributive occupations. Samson (21) lists six factors that he considers to be of primary importance in influencing change, including archaic material handling, new life styles of consumers, electronic computers, changing business structure, job creation for the disadvantaged, and the service emphasis.

Health Occupations Education

Labor problems in the health occupations have mounted over the past decade. A number of factors may be identified as contributing to the demand for health services, including population growth, rising income levels, increased awareness of the importance of health education, expanded health insurance coverage, and government financing of health care for the aged and for low-income families. One solution for meeting increasing labor demands is the training of technicians and aides at less than professional level to remove the more routine duties from the professional medical worker.

A limited number of programs in practical nursing were in operation after the Smith-Hughes Act of 1917, under which nursing was broadly defined as a trade and thus included under the trade and industrial provisions of the act. Health occupations were first mentioned in federal legislation in the George-Barden Act of 1946, which made available funds for teaching practical nursing. A decade later the Health Amendments Act established this area as a new subsystem within vocational education. As a result, programs in practical nursing were developed at the secondary and postsecondary levels. The Vocational Education Act of 1963 and the subsequent Vocational Education Amendments of 1968 allowed states considerable flexibility in developing health occupations programs.

Not only are the numbers of health workers increasing sharply, but new occupations and specialties are continually emerging in medicine, dentistry, and nursing. Techniques for the regulation of workers in health occupations have been developed and administered, either by appropriate professional organizations or by legally constituted authority in the respective states, as a means of safeguarding the public against unqualified and/or unscrupulous persons. Therefore, regulatory practices such as licensing, certification, and/or registration in certain of the health occupations have been established.

The U.S. Office of Education included the following classification of instructional programs in its taxonomy of the health occupations:

07.01 Dental

07.02 Medical Laboratory Technology

07.03 Nursing

07.04 Rehabilitation

07.05 Radiologic

07.06 Ophthalmic

07.07 Environmental Health

07.08 Mental Health Technology

07.09 Miscellaneous Health Occupations Education

There are a wide range of job opportunities in the health occupations. Approximately 250 such job titles are listed in the *Dictionary of Occupational Titles*, including a variety of technicians, nurses, aides, office assistants, and maintenance workers. Job requirements vary within these occupations, with most preparation programs ranging from one to four years. Instructional programs in health occupations education are found at both high school and postsecondary school levels. The majority of the programs, however, are at the postsecondary level and involve a combination of classroom instruction and supervised field experience.

Some of the more common health occupations are practical nurse, assistant, and technician. Practical nursing programs generally are 12 months in length and involve classroom work and supervised hospital experiences. The curriculum includes topics such as first aid, family life, geriatric nursing, needs of children, the human body, nutrition, medication and treatment, and human relations.

Health occupations assistants work in various occupations, such as dental, medical laboratory, occupational therapy, and medical office. Training programs and curricula are designed for the specific occupation; for example, the curriculum for laboratory assistants includes hematology, bacteriology, serology, parasitology, chemistry, and blood banking, whereas the curriculum for medical office assistants focuses on topics such as typewriting, accounting, filing, records management, communication, medical terminology, and instruments.

Health occupations technicians apply technical knowledge to a specific health occupation; thus they work primarily with instruments. A number of technical occupations are related to health occupations, including dental laboratory technicians, dental hygienist, medical technician, optical technician, and X-ray technician. Specific curricula and supervised laboratory experiences are designed for each specialization.

The development of new programs for extending nursing roles to include work that would otherwise be performed by a physician is one of the most important current trends in the nursing profession. Other trends include the use of health teams (paramedics) to replace the doctor and nurse as the sole health workers, thus allowing the physician to use his or her professional skills in a more efficient manner.

Health occupations education is becoming a viable program at the secondary school level. Traditionally, preparation for work related to health occupations has been left to hospitals, private schools with advanced programs requiring a high school diploma for admission, higher education institutions, and other agencies. With these institutions unable to meet the increasing need for preparation of medical workers at reasonable costs, demands are being made more and more on public education systems, including the secondary school. It is now recognized and accepted that many paramedical tasks can be learned and performed by high school–age individuals.

What are the objectives of such a program? Sands (22) discusses the four main issues in health care that have influenced the development of health occupations education at the secondary level. They are "unequal availability of health care, questionable quality of health care, skyrocketing costs, and responsibility for or control of health services." It should be the objective of secondary health occupations programs to help cope with these issues.

Rachel K. Winer (23), Chief of Health Occupations, Division of Occupational Education, Massachusetts Department of Education, proposed a secondary curriculum in health occupations that would allow for numerous career options with exposure to a variety of experiences in the world of work. The program makes it possible for students to enroll in a health continuum where exposure to a variety of semispecialized skills builds up in vertical fashion. Or, a student may choose a single elective in the continuum and still remain in a regular program of study. A single elective might prepare a student to become qualified for employment as a nurse's aide in a nursing home or in a primary care facility. In the ninth grade a student receives a concentrated introduction to the world of work in health occupations. In the tenth grade, a 20-week course in nursery school aide/child care and a 20-week course in dietary aide are available. In the eleventh grade the program is designed to prepare the student to function as a nurse's aide, hospital assistant, or health service assistant. At the twelfth grade level, the student has three options: medical assistant aide, dental assistant aide, or work-study program. These courses equip students with a beginning skill to function as an aide in a doctor's office, clinic, or medical library, or as a ward or unit clerk in a health agency. At this level, the student acquires the facility to maintain patient records, handle forms for Blue Cross/Blue Shield and Medicare, and prepare case histories, as well as acquire skills in telephone communications, medical communication, initial medical transcription, and other office tasks. In addition, upon graduation students can gain entrance, with advanced standing, into a postsecondary program. The program designed to meet these objectives is shown in Figure 7.4. A similar program described by Hill (24) is designed for essentially the same objectives. The curriculum was planned to include instructional content common to all health occupations, a thorough study of health careers, and on-the-job skill development.

Gunby (25) describes what he calls the most exciting high school in America, the Houston (Texas) High School for Health Professions. Students combine traditional courses such as English and math with a health-oriented curriculum. Students are permitted to go as far as their interests and abilities in the health field will allow. Upon graduation some students go directly to work as nurse aides, medical records clerks, research aides, pharmacy assistant

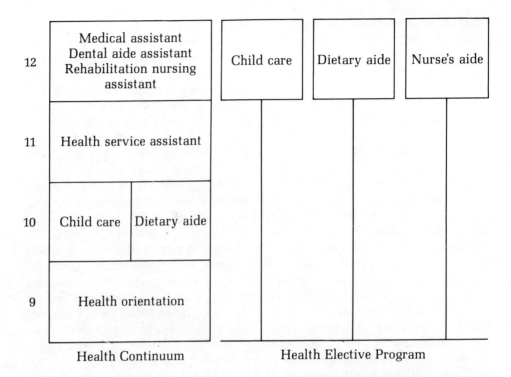

Figure 7.4 A program in health careers for secondary schools

aides, medical secretaries, blood bank associates, and in other, similar positions. Others will go on to either two-year or four-year colleges for further study; some of these go on to graduate school. In this unique secondary school teachers of the traditional courses work in medical aspects of the careers for which students are preparing. Students are given laboratory sessions in patient care and clinical and research areas at Baylor College of Medicine. They also have on-the-job work experiences in Houston hospitals.

Further evidence of the growth of secondary health occupations programs in Texas is provided by Haddad (26). He states that programs are offered in many high schools in Texas, as well as in Texas junior colleges. The increased growth in such programs in publicly supported schools has permitted many hospitals to use more of their resources for patient care and less for education. Programs include health care, science classes offering an introduction to health care, pre-employment laboratory programs, and vocational education for the handicapped. Experienced health professionals are employed as teacher-coordinators. The cooperative programs offer students introductory information along with practical experience and skills. The students gain on-the-job experience and at the same time relieve professional personnel of some of their menial tasks.

Texas is also responsible for establishing a national organization for students in health occupations education. It established the Texas Association of Health Occupations Students of America, out of which the national organization developed. Each chapter plans activities for students on the local level and provides an outreach through area, state, and national affiliations (27). The Health Occupations Student Association (HOSA) serves a rapidly expanding membership. Currently the national office is located in Wilmington, Delaware (28).

Home Economics Education

Home economics consists of the related courses or units of instruction that are organized to enable students to acquire knowledge and develop understanding, attitudes, and skills relevant to (a) personal, home, and family life; and (b) occupational preparation using the knowledge and skills of home economics. The subject matter includes concepts that are drawn from the natural and social sciences and humanities as well as those that are unique to the field.

Home economics classes are offered at high school, postsecondary, and adult levels, with the majority of enrollments being at the high school level. Federal aid for home economics began with the Smith-Hughes Act of 1917, with programs for home and family living. The Vocational Education Act of 1963 and the Vocational Education Amendments of 1968 and 1972 placed more emphasis on training for gainful employment. The Education Amendments of 1976 expanded and redirected consumer and homemaking education programs and services to meet current economic, social, and cultural conditions. Emphasis in such programs was to be placed on consumer education, food and nutrition, parenthood education, and resource management. The legislation emphasized the preparation of both males and females for the combined role of homemaker and wage earner. Webb, Siegel, and Jones (29) suggest that it was not the intent of Congress through this legislation to change radically consumer and homemaking education; rather, the intent was to expand the scope and outreach of federally funded programs, services, and activities. The legislation specifically identified consumer education with home economics as a discipline.

The U.S. Office of Education taxonomy of occupations identified two major instructional areas in home economics education:

09.01 Homemaking: Preparation for Personal, Home, and Family Living; these programs are not specifically directed toward preparation for gainful employment

09.02 Occupational Preparation: Care and Guidance of Children; Clothing Management, Production and Services; Food Management, Production and Services; Home Furnishings, Equipment and Services; and Institutional and Home Management and supportive services

Home economics instruction includes a combination of directed projects, course offerings, and related group experiences in areas such as home management, family economics, family health, family relations, child care and development, nutrition, clothing, and textiles. Home projects are an essential part of home economics instructional programs, as are occupational experiences a component of all vocational programs. The content of home economics curricula lends itself to a variety of organizational patterns and curriculum models, thus allowing students to select topics or areas of concentration for personal and professional use.

Hill (30) suggests that home economics educators should be alert to situations such as the following: a reversal of present trends toward care of children outside the home; an acceleration of communal living; invention of new food products; and development of yet-unknown designs for urban living. Home economics educators have a major responsibility for instruction to help all workers make consumer decisions that will be compatible with individual goals and community welfare. They need to join with business educators and social science educators, and with other fields with a particular responsibility for consumer education, to develop a more effective consumer program in the public schools. Emphasis needs to be given to such areas as the influence of consumer decisions on environment, consumer protection, the effects of international trade practices and tariffs on quality and cost, and the ethics involved in buying services.

Technological advances in our society and the resulting changes in agriculture, business, and industry have been reflected in twentieth-century family life. The primary responsibility of the home is no longer the provision of food, clothing, shelter or the rearing, education, and employment of its members. Increasing numbers of women are employed at some time during their lifetime, with about three of every five serving in multiple roles of homemaker, wife, mother, and wage earner. This fact suggests the importance of joint programs in occupational areas such as home economics, business education, health occupations, and distributive education to prepare women for their multiple roles.

Reflecting the changing roles of women in society, the objectives of vocational home economics have been expanded (31) to include an increased emphasis on management; greater concern for educating the individual for self-understanding and for family membership; a lessening, but not the abandonment, of manipulative skills; and education for assuming the dual role of homemaker and wage earner.

The directions for home economics as described by Hatcher and Halchin in the following statement are just as appropriate for the eighties as they were for the seventies (32):

The charge to home economics for the seventies is to help all people to improve their quality of life. All people is not to be loosely interpreted. . . . The signs of the times as manifested in the identification of discriminatory practices involving sex, race, age, religion, and ethnic background, and the accompanying social action and federal legislation, have added impetus to making home economics more generally available to groups of people and individuals who have been neglected, not willfully, but because of limitations within the discipline itself. The old home economics, consisting principally of foods and clothing instruction with a little consideration given to family relationships, family health, child rearing, and management, was limited in its potentiality for serving all people of all ages in all walks of life. With increased emphasis on human development and relationships, nutrition, consumer education, decision-making, concern for adequate housing, and environmental control, it is generally recognized that the home economics concepts are needed by everyone. Then, too, a shift in sex roles has some additional implications for home economics. Women working outside the home (and an increasing number of them are) are carrying responsibility for the dual or even multiple roles of homemaker, wife, mother, and wage earner. By the same token men and boys are becoming more and more involved in the work of the home.

Girtman identifies the following specific objectives of home economics, which reflect both the general and vocational emphases (33):

1. *to improve the quality of family living and to help youth and adults develop the abilities needed for the occupation of homemaking*
2. *to prepare individuals for gainful employment in occupations involving home economics knowledge and skills*
3. *to provide preprofessional education for students who will enter colleges and universities*
4. *to help prepare individuals for responsible citizenship, with special emphasis on consumer responsibility*
5. *to help transmit the American culture from one generation to another and to develop heritage appreciation*

Blankenship and Moerchen (34) identify three major professional organizations for home economics teachers: the American Home Economics Association (AHEA), the Home Economics Education Association (HEEA), and the Home Economics Division of the American Vocational Association (AVA). Open to all home economists, the AHEA publishes the *Journal of Home Economics*, the *Home Economics Research Journal*, *AHEA Action* (the newspaper), and other special publications. AHEA has established a foundation that initiates and sponsors educational and research programs as well as service projects. The Center for the Family was established by AHEA in 1972 to coordinate research and other programs for the family. An affiliate of the National Education Association, HEEA draws its membership primarily from home economics teachers, supervisors, and home economics education faculty. Its purpose is to contribute to the growth and development of home economics education. The purpose of the Home Economics Division of AVA is to promote, support, and contribute to the growth and strength of vocational home economics in particular and of vocational education in general. Membership in AVA is made up primarily of teachers and teacher educators representing all the vocational areas. Membership in the Home Economics Division includes home economics teachers, teacher educators, and supervisors. They join to work out problems and advance the interests of vocational home economics programs through meetings, legislation, publications, and research.

Hill and associates (35) describe a Vocational Education Coalition of AHEA, AVA, and HEEA established in 1977 for the purpose of increasing communication and projecting a unified thrust and focus on issues related to vocational home economics education. The coalition is made up of two representatives from each association. Its purpose is to serve as a clearinghouse for policy or position statements developed by any one of the organizations. The coalition will maintain continuous dialogue among the professional organizations concerned with vocational home economics education. It will identify existing and potential issues of vocational home economics education. It will review positions on current issues relating to vocational home economics education and facilitate development of consensus among the organizations.

The Vocational Education Coalition describes the scope and definition of vocational home economics education as being to prepare

> *males and females for the occupation of homemaking and paid employment in home economics occupations. . . . The term vocational homemaking education is used as a generic term for programs now designated in legislation as "consumer and homemaking" programs. Vocational home economics education is used as a more general term to include both wage earning and homemaking programs and to describe professional educators (36).*

The coalition describes the occupation of homemaking as requiring knowledge and skills that are interrelated and necessary for optimum quality of life for individuals and families. Values, management, and interpersonal relationships are specified as major concepts that unify the content of the subject matter areas of child and family development, clothing and textiles, foods and nutrition, consumer education and resource management, and housing. The essential skills of homemaking are described as including (a) providing for personal and family development at various stages of the life cycle and establishing satisfying personal and family relationships, (b) nurturing children, (c) providing nutritious food for family members, (d) selecting and maintaining housing and living environments for family members, (e) providing and caring for family clothing, and (f) managing financial and other resources (37).

The home economics youth organization, Future Homemakers of America (FHA), was founded in 1945 and is open to any individual who has taken or who is taking a course in home economics. FHA is concerned with developing cooperative and intelligent leadership and with helping individuals to improve personal, family, and community living. The official FHA publication is *Teen Times*. The Florida state chapter handbook (38) describes two types of chapters: the Future Homemakers of America emphasizes consumer education, home and family life education, and job and career opportunities in home economics; HERO (Home Economics Related Occupations) emphasizes preparation for jobs and careers with recognition that workers fill multiple roles as family members and community members. Although the organization is a single entity at the national level, in some states FHA and HERO are organized separately. Some schools may have a single chapter of FHA/HERO or have separate chapters of each or have either kind of chapter and not the other. FHA/HERO is sponsored by AHEA, HEEA, the Home Economics Division of AVA, and the Division of Vocational and Technical Education of the United States Department of Education.

Trade and Industrial Education

Vocational industrial education is considered the broadest of all the vocational fields, with training programs designed to prepare skilled and semiskilled workers in a wide range of trade and industrial occupations. The U.S. Office of Education defined trade and industrial education (39) as (a) any craft, skilled trade, or semiskilled occupation that directly functions in the designing, producing, processing, fabricating, assembling, testing, modifying, maintaining, servicing, or repairing of any product or commodity; and (b) any other occupation, including service occupations that are not covered above, which is usually considered to be technical, or trade and industrial in nature.

A relevant program in industrial education, as in all vocational education, is one that is attuned to current and projected trends in business and industry. To be so attuned, industrial educators must maintain a close relationship with business and industrial leaders and workers and must see that changes are reflected in the curriculum.

Industrial education is offered at high school, postsecondary, and adult levels in part-time and full-time programs, with the largest enrollment being in adult programs. Curricula are aimed at preparing persons for initial employment, at upgrading their existing skills, and at retraining them in a new or related occupation. The increasing number of comprehensive high schools throughout the nation has resulted in an increase in industrial education programs at the secondary level.

Instruction in trade and industrial education is provided in (a) basic manipulative skills, (b) safety judgment, and (c) related areas such as mathematics, drafting, communications, and science, as required to perform successfully in a given occupational cluster. Instructional programs aim at developing attitudes and concepts basic to all industrial occupations in addition to developing specific skills and knowledge applicable to the various occupational clusters. Supervised work experience is an integral part of many programs, whereas simulated laboratory experiences are an alternative in other programs.

Vocational industrial occupations are found in a variety of job categories, such as manufacturing, construction, mining, transportation, and public utilities. Industrial education programs had their beginning in 1917, with the passage of the Smith-Hughes Act, and were expanded through the George-Barden Act of 1946, the Vocational Education Act of 1963, and the 1968 and 1972 Vocational Amendments.

The wide range of occupations covered in industrial education is evident in the U.S. Office of Education classification of instructional programs, as indicated below:

17.01 Air Conditioning

17.02 Appliance Repair

17.03 Automotive Services

17.04 Aviation Occupations

17.05 Blueprint Reading

17.06 Business Machine Maintenance

17.07 Commercial Art Occupations

17.08 Commercial Fishery Occupations

17.09 Commercial Photography Occupations

17.10 Construction and Maintenance Trades

17.11 Custodial Services

17.12 Diesel Mechanics

17.13 Drafting

17.14 Electrical Occupations

17.15 Electronics Occupations

17.16 Fabric Maintenance Services

17.17 Foremanship, Supervision, and Management Development

17.18 General Continuation

17.19 Graphic Arts Occupations

17.20 Industrial Atomic Energy

17.21 Instrument Maintenance and Repair

17.22 Maritime Occupations

17.23 Metalworking

17.24 Metallurgy

17.26 Personal Services

17.27 Plastic Occupations

17.28 Public Service Occupations

17.29 Quality Food Occupations

17.30 Refrigeration

17.31 Small Engine Repair, Internal Combustion

17.32 Stationary Energy Sources Occupations

17.33 Textile Production and Fabrication

17.34 Leathermaking

17.35 Upholstering

17.36 Woodworking

Roberts (40) uses the term *vocational industrial education* to include machine shop, carpentry, electrical appliance servicing, millwork and cabinet making, radio servicing, sheet metal, auto mechanics, printing, air conditioning, barbering, practical nursing, foundry, needle trades, plastics, plumbing, upholstering, and watchmaking.

Trade and industrial education is concerned with preparing students at the secondary and postsecondary levels to (a) make wise career choices; (b) attain the attitudes, skills, and knowledge necessary for job entry employment; and (c) upgrade existing skills or retrain for a new job in a wide range of semi-skilled, skilled, and technical occupations.

Roberts (41) describes the following objectives as basic to the establishment of the vocational industrial education program:

1. *to provide instruction of an extension or supplemental type for the further development of performance skills, technical knowledge, related industrial education, safety, and job judgment for persons already employed in trade and industrial pursuits*

2. *to provide instruction of a preparatory type in the development of basic manipulative skills, safety judgment, technical knowledge and related industrial information for the purpose of fitting persons for useful employment in trade and industrial pursuits.*

Some states classify their postsecondary occupational programs into two main categories: technical and trades. Technical programs consist primarily of two-year programs in such areas as engineering technology, office-related technology, nursing, and forest technology. Trade education generally consists of one-year programs in curricula such as auto mechanics, drafting, welding, practical nursing, and machine shop. The following discussion provides a more detailed treatment of the concept of technical education.

Technical Education

As our technology becomes increasingly complex, engineers and scientists have to become more highly trained. These demands are also reflected in training programs for technicians. Instructional programs must of necessity be flexible, responding to the changes brought about by technology.

The majority of programs in technical education are located in public and private postsecondary institutions. Junior colleges, vocational-technical schools, technical institutes, engineering schools, and technical high schools offer instructional programs of a technical nature.

The main thrust of technical education can be traced to the 1940s, when the U.S. Office of Education recognized and proclaimed the need to train technicians who would work on jobs that required more limited competencies than those of a professional engineer but more than those needed by skilled mechanics. As industry mushroomed during and after World War II, there were increasing demands for technical workers.

The definition of technical education is still somewhat unclear, with technical institutes, colleges, and vocational-technical schools formulating their own objectives. McMahon (42) suggests that

> *preparation for a technical occupation requires an understanding of, and ability to apply, those levels of mathematics and science appropriate to the occupation. And in those occupations that can be properly defined as technical, the mathematics and science required is more advanced than that required for a middle-type craft or skilled-trades occupation.*

Such a definition tends to view technical education as a level of training as well as an occupational field.

Technical curricula include preparation in supporting sciences and mathematics in addition to an emphasis in the field of technical specialization, such as in electronics, mechanics, chemistry, or aeronautics. Instructional programs generally combine classroom instruction, laboratory experiences, and supervised work experiences. The U.S. Office of Education classified instructional programs of technical education as follows:

16.01 Engineering-related Technology

16.02 Agricultural-related Technology

16.03 Health-related Technology

16.04 Office-related Technology

16.05 Home Economics–related Technology

16.06 Miscellaneous Technical Education

Technicians are frequently employed in direct support of the professional engineer. For example, engineering technicians are capable of assisting in engineering functions such as designing, developing, testing, and modifying of products and processes; production planning, writing reports, and preparing estimates; analyzing and diagnosing technical problems that involve independent decisions; and solving a wide range of technical problems by applying their background in the technical specialties.

There is no national youth organization exclusively for students in technical education. Secondary students enrolled in vocational industrial education (trade, industrial, or technical courses) are eligible for membership in the Vocational Industrial Clubs of America (VICA). Organized in 1965, VICA provides four types of membership: active, professional, associate, and honorary. Six national goals have been identified by VICA: professional growth, community understanding, safety, teacher recruitment, cooperation, and good public relations. Educators recognize the importance of VICA, and of all vocational service organizations, as a significant teaching tool in realizing the objectives of the various occupational programs.

Industrial Arts Education

Before 1973, industrial arts was recognized primarily as general education for students. It offered opportunities for exploring various vocational areas and for instruction in leisure-time activities and home-repair skills. Through the past half-century, indusrial arts curricula have included a variety of units, such as woodworking, drafting, metalworking, plastics, graphic arts, power mechanics, and electronics. Instructional units are frequently organized around four levels: introductory, basic, intermediate, and advanced, as offered at the middle and high school levels.

In December 1973, industrial arts was added to Public Law 92-318 and officially became part of the group of vocational education programs eligible for federal aid. Industrial arts is defined in the *Federal Register* as (43):

> *those education programs which pertain to the body of related subject matter, or related courses, organized for the development of understanding about the technical, consumer, occupational, recreational, organizational, managerial, social, historical, and cultural aspects of industry and technology including learning experiences involving activities such as experimenting, designing, constructing, evaluating, and using tools, machines, materials, and processes which provide opportunities for creativity and problem solving and assisting individuals in the making of informed and meaningful occupational choices.*

In the Vocational Education Act the following objectives are identified for industrial arts instructional programs:

1. to assist individuals in the making of informed and meaningful occupational choices by
   (a) providing occupational information and instruction pertaining to a broad range of occupations
   (b) providing laboratory experiences in shops and laboratories in business or industry to acquaint students with jobs
   (c) providing guidance and counseling for students enrolled in the industrial arts program
   (d) employing industrial arts teachers who have qualifications as provided in the state plan
2. to prepare individuals for enrollment in advanced or highly skilled vocational and technical education programs by
   (a) providing individuals with occupational information and exploratory experiences for enrolling in such programs

(b) providing occupational information and exploratory experiences directly related to current practices in industry

After the inclusion of industrial arts as a federally reimbursed field of vocational education, the curriculum was expanded to include transportation, construction, graphic communication, and American industry. Not all courses in industrial arts can (or perhaps should) be reimbursed through vocational funds because they do not all fit into the prevocational or vocational categories. The United States Office of Education classified instructional programs in industrial arts education as follows:

10.01 Construction	10.11 Industrial Arts Science (Applied Physics)
10.02 Crafts (Industrial)	
10.03 Drafting	10.12 Industrial Materials and Processes
10.04 Electricity and Electronics	
10.05 Elementary School Industrial Arts	10.13 Manufacturing
	10.14 Metals
10.06 General Industrial Arts	10.15 Plastics
10.07 Graphic Arts	10.16 Power/Automotive Mechanics
10.08 Home Mechanics	10.17 Research and Development
10.09 Industrial Arts Mathematics	10.18 Service Industries
10.10 Industrial Arts Science (Applied Chemistry)	10.19 Woods

White (44) describes part of the basic goal of industrial arts as enabling students to use technology efficiently for their personal benefit in a variety of life roles (family, occupational, recreational) and to use their skills and knowledge about industrial technology to improve the world. He further describes industrial arts as being liberal education needed by all citizens in an industrialized democracy and distinguishes between industrial arts as general education and vocational education. Industrial arts programs may qualify for vocational funds through the Education Amendments of 1976 when, under a state's vocational plan, industrial arts is considered as assisting in meeting the purposes of vocational education.

Along with the Health Occupations Students Association and the National Postsecondary Agricultural Student Organization, the American Industrial Arts Student Organization (AIASO) is a newly organized student organization for secondary industrial arts students. It was incorporated in December 1977 and is considered an indispensable part of any quality industrial arts program by the American Industrial Arts Association, Incorporated (45). The purposes of AIASA (46) are: (1) to provide opportunities for the development of leadership in social, civic, scholastic, and community activities; (2) to encourage scholastic motivation by providing opportunities to integrate and use the knowledge and skills of other educational disciplines in a practical way; (3) to increase the knowledge and broaden the understanding of all students living in our industrial-technological society; (4) to assist in the making of informed and meaningful occupational choices; (5) to provide opportunities to promote industrial arts in school, community, state, and nation; and (6) to inspire students to respect the dignity of labor and to appreciate craftsmanship.

SUMMARY

The curriculum of a school may be regarded as a product of its environment. It is affected by community culture, by laws, by the philosophy of society, and by socioeconomic trends. Although a variety of techniques have been developed for constructing curricula, vocational educators draw heavily on activity and job analysis. Objectives are, in a sense, the most important factor in planning the curriculum because they determine what will be done. Traditionally, curriculum planning in vocational fields has relied on community surveys to determine what employers needed in the workforce. More recently, however, the emphasis in job preparation has shifted toward developing the capabilities and meeting unique needs of individuals.

Selection and organization of experiences and curriculum materials should follow a developmental psychological order. The modern method of curriculum building uses a systems approach, which emphasizes the development of precise educational objectives and the redesign of the educational process to ensure appropriate student achievement of objectives. A systems approach to total curriculum design involves (a) gathering input data on students; (b) formulating student performance objectives; (c) constructing pretests; (d) selecting course content; (e) selecting instructional strategy; (f) developing instructional materials; (g) selecting the instructional process; (h) conducting instruction; (i) analyzing posttest results; and (j) evaluating student learning.

Numerous models or designs have been used over the years in the attempt to keep curricula relevant. The *subject-centered curriculum* groups students on the basis of their objectives into college preparatory, general, and vocational programs. The *core curriculum* design advocates a large block of time in which all students employ problem-solving techniques to solve felt problems and to meet needs. The *cluster-based curriculum* in vocational education is based on the premise that certain related occupations have common learning and skills requirements and that students who have mastered these skills have more options available for employment.

The *organic curriculum* has been proposed as a design that would provide a student with a variety of options after high school. It emphasizes the integration of academic and vocational learning and more field-centered experiences. The *competency-based curriculum* specifies the desired outcomes in explicit form, identifies the standards to be applied in assessing learner competencies, and holds the learner accountable for meeting those outcomes. Such *systems-oriented curriculum* provisions are based on a procedure that includes (a) specification of assumptions, tasks, goals, and objectives; (b) generation and selection of objective criteria; (c) identification and design of assessment strategies; (d) specification of instructional philosophy; (e) development of instructional strategies; (f) selection and/or development of instructional resources; and (g) development of a feedback mechanism. Competency-based curricula make heavy use of *individualized* approaches, which adjust the pace of learning to the learner, vary the instructional modes, and promote independent learning.

Most recent in the list of curriculum design strategies is the *open-access curriculum*, which creates large clusters of content to replace lesser courses; emphasizes easy access and exit; deemphasizes traditional teaching in favor of active involvement of the student in learning; uses large blocks of time, large open instructional spaces (classrooms without walls), and multimedia instructional packages. Needless to say, these models or designs are not mutually exclusive but rather have some features in common. The open lab in vocational education is a relatively recent adaptation of the relatively old idea of individualized instruction.

Needs assessments constitute a strategy for updating the curriculum and staff of the school by generating two types of data from appropriate publics: *felt needs* are generated from students, staff, parents, and the community; *validated needs* comprise hard data gathered internally about current conditions in the school—enrollments, materials, resources, test results, and so on. Needs assessments constitute a valuable tool for identifying critical needs of the school, for improving the quality of the instructional program, and for gaining support for education.

The vocational education family consists of a number of interrelated fields, programs, and curricula, including agricultural education, business and office education, distributive education, health occupations education, home economics education, trade and industrial education, and technical and industrial arts education. A brief treatment of content and employment opportunities in each field is provided in this chapter. The integration of vocational and career education concepts is being reflected in the fusion of career-oriented activities into existing curricula at all levels. Vocational education uses both formative (informational, diagnostic) and summative (terminal assessment) forms of evaluation to improve curricula.

ACTIVITIES

For review

1. Explain the steps in Teske's curriculum planning model and illustrate how they apply to your field.

2. What criteria would you use in selecting subject matter to implement a curriculum?

3. Compare the procedures in the systems-based curriculum model and the Teske curriculum model. How are they alike? How are they different?

4. Identify some basic principles of curriculum construction that have traditionally been used in vocational education.

5. Identify each of the following curriculum models and specify the advantages and/or disadvantages of the use of each in vocational education:

Subject-centered curriculum
Core curriculum
Cluster-based curriculum
Organic curriculum
Competency-based curriculum
Open-access curriculum

6. What is *needs assessment*, and what is its role in vocational education?

7. Discuss the effects of automation and technology on each of the vocational education fields, with regard to the nature of the field, employment trends, and curriculum.

8. For each of the vocational fields, identify the primary federal legislative act that provided initial funding of the program.

9. Name the youth organizations associated with each vocational field. What contributions do these groups make toward realizing the goals of vocational education?

10. Explain and/or differentiate three levels of individualization of instruction and give specific examples for implementing each.

For discussion

1. What are the components that make up an instructional system?

2. What will be the role of vocational education within the broader career education scheme? Will all students be provided with employable skills at the end of high school or whenever they exit school? What "employability" skills should be taught to ensure maximum future adaptability and potential?

3. Is it realistic to propose that every high school student be equipped with an entry-level job skill? Is it possible, for example, for a student to enter the health occupations at an assistant level and move up the career ladder to become a physician? Are there more direct ways of ensuring student mobility and advancement?

4. Vocational education has a negative image among some educators and members of minority groups. How can vocational education demonstrate

that it deserves the prestige accorded the academic subject areas and that it offers hope for all groups?

5. The centrality of work in determining an individual's future life style is well known. However, how can educators prepare people for work roles and also accommodate those for whom a career may not be the sole or major determiner of life style?

6. Vocational education challenges the concept that the basic function of the school is the transmission of knowledge. However, this challenge does not negate the importance of providing a base of knowledge and skills to support an individual's preparation for a career and to enable him or her to deal effectively with problems. What bodies of knowledge are of the most importance? How can a truly interdisciplinary curriculum be developed?

7. Identify the problems that might be encountered, both at the secondary and at the postsecondary level, in implementing the (a) core curriculum, (b) competency-based curriculum, (c) organic curriculum, (d) open-access curriculum.

8. What role should parents and students play in curriculum construction?

9. Which curriculum model would best fit your vocational field, school, and community needs? Justify your choice.

10. Compare the curriculum organization and content of vocational education in the 1960s with the changes suggested by career education models at the elementary, middle, high school, and post-high school levels.

11. What are some of the means through which the principles and concepts of open schools and individualized instruction could be implemented in a traditional school setting?

12. Select three or four of the forces affecting curriculum as listed below. Briefly discuss how each has affected (a) education in general, and (b) vocational education in particular:
    (a) Sputnik
    (b) technological developments
    (c) attack on poverty
    (d) civil rights movement
    (e) rising aspirations of populace
    (f) growing prosperity
    (g) rising education level of populace
    (h) more extensive and accessible performance records
    (i) change in methods and content of education
    (j) change in social setting and social functions of educational institutions
    (k) Vocational Education Act of 1963
    (l) Elementary-Secondary Education Act
    (m) National Defense Education Act

(n) move from rural-agrarian to urban-industrial society
(o) mobility of the population
(p) more extensive and wider variety of current instructional materials
(q) rise in humanism
(r) rise of controversy over cognitive person vs. mentally healthy person
(s) shift in character of job openings
(t) expanding bank of current scientists and scientific data
(u) more leisure time
(v) speed in communication of ideas and data; mass media explosion
(w) increasing imperative that all citizens possess reading skill
(x) demands for involvement in decision processes
(y) space exploration
(z) accountability

For exploration

1. Examine the course offerings of a vocational-technical school or junior college in one of the vocational fields. Compare this listing with the instructional areas identified by USOE. Which instructional areas are included in the curriculum you reviewed?

2. Under the Vocational Education Act of 1963 and the Amendments of 1968 and 1972, monies were allocated for programs for the disadvantaged and the handicapped. Interview a vocational education instructor at a post-secondary institution and find out what provisions are being made for recruitment, instruction, placement, and follow-up of these students.

3. Construct a needs assessment instrument that could be administered to teachers, parents, students, administrators, and business community representatives. Administer the instrument to a sample of these groups and prepare a report of the findings to share with the class. Did the groups tend to agree? Which groups were most diverse in their views about the needs of the schools? How could you use these data in curriculum planning and revision?

4. Prepare a diagram of an open-space laboratory that would be ideal for your vocational area in your school setting.

5. Read several definitions of curriculum and select or adapt one with which you most nearly agree.

6. Select a vocational field, preferably one other than your area of concentration, and prepare a report on its history and development.

7. Prepare a speech that you might give to seventh- or eighth-grade students on job opportunities in your vocational field. Include employment trends, educational prerequisites, and major changes—both present and projected.

8. Interview a student enrolled in a cooperative occupational program in a field other than your own. What is the student's impression of the pro-

gram? What types of experiences are being provided on the job? How is the classroom instruction related to the on-the-job experiences? You may wish to tape record the interview and share it with the class.

9. Select one youth organization with which you are unfamiliar. Interview a student member and find out his or her impressions of the contributions of the club to its individual members, the department, and the school.

10. Interview an industrial arts instructor and prepare a report for the class about the changes in the program resulting from federal funding.

11. React to each of the following points as it relates to individualized learning in vocational education. Is each point true or false?
    (a) The teacher makes the assignment—the student does the work at his or her own pace.
    (b) Levels replace grades.
    (c) Provisions are made for large-group, small-group, and individual teaching.
    (d) Team teaching necessitates curriculum revision.
    (e) Nongradedness can function without change of facilities.
    (f) Individualization of instruction significantly improves achievement levels of students.

REFERENCES

1. Philip R. Teske, "Models for Curriculum Design," unpublished paper, 1969.

2. Harold Alberty, *The Core Program in the High School* (Cincinnati: South-Western Publishing Company, 1955), p. 25.

3. Ibid., p. 24.

4. William A. Bakamis, Robert E. Kuhl, Edwin K. Hill, Beverly Swarthout, and Dale L. Nish, *Identification of Task and Knowledge Clusters Associated with Performance of Major Types of Building Trades Work* (Pullman: Washington State University, 1966), pp. 2, 12.

5. Calfrey C. Calhoun, Project Director, *Purpose Centered Curriculum for Florida Office and Business Education* (Tampa: University of South Florida, 1970).

6. Robert M. Morgan and David S. Bushnell, "Designing an Organic Curriculum," *National Business Education Quarterly*, Vol. 35, No. 3, March 1967, p. 11. (Reproduced by permission.)

7. Jerome S. Bruner, *The Process of Education* (Cambridge, Mass.: Harvard University Press, 1960).

8. J. Robert Warmbrod and Lloyd J. Phipps, *Review and Synthesis of Research in Agricultural Education* (Columbus: Center for Research and Leadership Development in Vocational and Technical Education, 1966), p. 2.

9. U.S. Office of Education, *Standard Terminology for Curriculum and Instruction in Local and State School Systems*, State Educational Records and Report Series: Handbook VI (Washington, D.C.: Government Printing Office, 1969).

10. Roy W. Roberts, *Vocational and Practical Arts Education: History, Development, and Principles*, 3rd ed. (New York: Harper & Row, Publishers, 1971), p. 158.

11. James T. Horner, "Agricultural Education from Kindergarten to Senior High School," *The Agricultural Education Magazine*, Vol. 42, No. 11, May 1970, p. 286.

12. H. N. Hunsicker, "Transition in Agricultural Education," *The Agricultural Education Magazine*, Vol. 45, No. 5, Nov. 1972, p. 103.

13. Barbara Thompson, "Cultivating Vo-Ag's Future," *American Vocational Journal*, Vol. 52, No. 2, Feb. 1977, pp. 32-35.

14. Policies Commission for Business and Economic Education, *This We Believe about Business Education in the High School* (Washington, D.C.: National Business Education Association; St. Peter, Minn.: Delta Pi Epsilon, 1961).

15. Policies Commission for Business and Economic Education, *This We Believe about Business Education in the Secondary School* (Washington, D.C.: National Business Education Association; St. Peter, Minn.: Delta Pi Epsilon, 1970).

16. Distributive Education Publications Committee, *Distributive Education & You* (Washington, D.C.: American Vocational Association, March 1970), pp. 2-3.

17. Kenneth B. Haas, "The Origin and Early Development of Distributive Education—Parts I, II, and III," in *The Origin and Development of Distributive Education*, Susan S. Schrumpf, ed. (Hightstown, N.J.: McGraw-Hill Book Company, Inc.,1972), p. 9.

18. Ralph Mason, "Evaluating Instructional Objectives in Distributive Education," in *Evaluation and Accountability in Business Education*, Donald J. Tate and Robert E. Hoskinson, eds. (Washington, D.C.: National Business Education Association, 1978) , p. 250.

19. Steven B. Corbin, "Integrating DECA Goals into the Distributive Education Program," *Business Education Forum*, Vol. 31, No. 4, Jan. 1977, p. 29.

20. Edward S. Donnell, "Consumers and Youth, Keys to the 70's," *American Vocational Journal*, Vol. 45, No. 2, Feb. 1970, p. 33.

21. Harland Samson, "The Changing Nature of Distributive Occupations," in *The Emerging Content and Structure of Business Education*, Ray G. Price, Charles R. Hopkins, and Mary Klaurens, eds. (Washington, D.C.: National Business Education Association, 1970), p. 60.

22. William F. Sands, "The Health Care Crisis: Can Vocational Education Deliver?" *American Vocational Journal*, Vol. 46, No. 9, Dec. 1971, p. 24.

23. Rachel K. Winer, "Rung by Rung up the Health Career Ladder," *American Vocational Journal*, Vol. 48, No. 7, Oct. 1973, pp. 47–49.

24. E. Joy Hill, "Kentucky Pacesetters for Health Careers Education," *American Vocational Journal*, Vol. 47, No. 5, May 1972, p. 32.

25. Phil Gunby, "The Most Exciting High School in America," *Phi Delta Kappan*, Vol. 61, No. 5, Jan. 1980, pp. 356–57.

26. John Haddad, "Health Manpower and Vocational Education: The Texas Connection," *American Vocational Journal*, Vol. 53, No. 4, April 1978, pp. 37–38.

27. Ibid.

28. "Divisions Gather to Give Honors, Assess Progress and Make Plans—Health Occupations," *Update*, Vol. 2, No. 4, Jan. 1980 (Arlington, Va.: American Vocational Education Association), p. 6.

29. Anita Webb, Judith Siegel, and Fran Jones, "Responsiveness of Consumer and Homemaking Education Programs," *Journal of Home Economics*, Vol. 72, No. 1, Spring 1980, p. 16.

30. Alberta D. Hill, "Don't Stop! But Look and Listen," *American Vocational Journal*, Vol. 46, No. 4, April 1971, p. 43.

31. Hester Chadderdon and Alyce M. Fanslow, *Review and Synthesis of Research in Home Economics Education* (Columbus: Center for Research and Leadership Development in Vocational and Technical Education, 1966), p. 2.

32. Hazel M. Hatcher and Lilla C. Halchin, *The Teaching of Home Economics*, 3rd ed. (Boston: Houghton Mifflin Company, 1973), pp. 48–49. (Reprinted by permission of the publisher.)

33. Carolyn J. Girtman, "The Program, the Teacher, and FHA," *American Vocational Journal*, Vol. 43, No. 3, March 1968, p. 26.

34. Martha Lee Blankenship and Barbara Dommert Moerchen, *Home Economics Education* (Boston: Houghton Mifflin Company, 1979), pp. 26–27.

35. Alberta D. Hill, Twyla Shear, Camille G. Bell, Aleene A. Cross, Enid A. Carter, and Leora N. Horning, "Vocational Home Economics: A Statement by the Vocational Education Coalition," *Journal of Home Economics*, Vol. 71, No. 4, Winter 1979, p. 12.

36. Ibid., p. 13.

37. Ibid.

38. *Especially for Advisors*, 1974–75 Florida Association, Future Homemakers of America/Home Economics Related Occupations (Tallahassee, Fla.: Florida Department of Education, Vocational Division, Home Economics Section), pp. 3–5.

39. *Administration of Vocational Education—Rules and Regulations,* Vocational Education Bulletin No. 1, U.S. Office of Education (Washington, D.C.: Government Printing Office, 1966), p. 46.

40. Roberts, *Vocational and Practical Arts Education,* pp. 281-82.

41. Ibid., p. 271.

42. Gordon G. McMahon, "Technical Education: A Problem of Definition," *American Vocational Journal,* Vol. 45, No. 3, March 1970, p. 23.

43. *Federal Register,* Document 73-24594 (Washington, D.C.: Government Printing Office, filed November 20, 1973).

44. Michael R. White, "Industrial Arts and Voc Ed Looking Ahead to the Eighties," *American Vocational Journal,* Vol. 53, No. 4, April 1978, pp. 57-58.

45. "Association Notes," *Man/Society/Technology,* Vol. 37, No. 4, January 1978, p. 5.

46. "President's Corner," *Man/Society/Technology,* Vol. 38, No. 3, December 1978, p. 6.

CHAPTER EIGHT

■

Research and Development in Vocational-Technical Education

INTRODUCTION

In society's preparation for the future, educational research is generally accepted as crucial and, in the long run, indispensable. From the viewpoint of program planning and development, the objective of research is to facilitate change and improvement in vocational-technical education.

> *It is clear that research is in a state of evolution. The research function is broader than ever before, encompassing both research (R) and development (D) activities. Vocational education has been proactive in this evolution. In fact, in vocational education, the "D" appears to be as important as the "R" (1).*

Therefore, research is used interchangeably with *research and development* (R&D) in this chapter.

Until the sixties, most of the theoretical research in vocational education was done in the form of master's theses and doctoral dissertations. Federal legislation of the early 1960s, however, triggered a national awareness of the need to expand such research and to unify and organize the scattered fragments of already existing research.

In few areas of the educational spectrum have new knowledge, research, and development occurred more dramatically than in the vocational subjects in

223

the 1960s and 1970s, if one accepts the term *vocational* as the umbrella under which may be included all education and preparation for occupations and careers. Few areas of formal education have contributed more to the advent and development of the technologies (or, conversely, have been more affected by them) than have the various vocational fields. The technician frequently is employed in direct support of the professional and applies his or her specialized background to the solution of a wide range of supporting technical problems. Likewise, the products and inventions from fields such as agriculture, business and industry, and health have improved the productivity of the technician.

In this chapter we shall deal with the focus of vocational research and with four types of research that have made a contribution to vocational education. Research competencies of vocational education teachers are reviewed. Attention is given to research centers and organizations along with the special problem of disseminating the results of research. General problems related to vocational education research and problem areas needing investigation are discussed. Special sections are devoted to analysis of research, funding of research, preparation of research proposals, and examples of current vocational education research.

The Focus of Vocational Research and Development

Despite the apparent lack of vocational research until the 1960s, vocational education pioneered in the use of community occupational surveys, recommendations of local advisory committees, and occupational analyses. It is unlikely that those responsible for any other aspect of the secondary education program have planned their program on as sound a research base as that of vocational education. Brandon (2) uses a paradigm developed by Clark and others and makes some adaptations for vocational research. Evans (3) in particular emphasizes the categories of (a) investigation of educationally oriented problems, (b) classroom experimentation, (c) field testing, and (d) demonstration and dissemination, but with the reservation that unless the results of research in basic scientific investigation are known to vocational researchers, their work will be seriously handicapped or completely worthless.

In the context of reporting research performed in vocational, technical, and practical arts education, Wenrich and others (4) point out that research is highly compartmentalized, that industrial sociologists and psychologists are not aware of work done in vocational and practical arts education, and that there are glaring deficiencies in the treatment of principles of teaching and learning and curricular experimentation. They further indicate the need for research that deals with the sociological and psychological implications of work, with specific community labor needs, and with the organization and administration of the vocational education program.

There are numerous other suggestions about needed research, many of which are concerned with funded research and so have categories of priorities that the funders will recognize. This practice of "prioritizing" research is typical of the federal agencies, as necessitated by controlling legislation, by the recommendations of advisory committees, or by the ultimate decisions of administrative officers. Private foundations also tend to support research of a particular viewpoint or orientation. It is evident that state educational agencies with the research coordination units acquired under the amended Vocational Education Act have also framed priority lists in compliance with the federal agency or with their own designs and purposes.

Brandon (5) identifies three prevalent positions among vocational educators with respect to research priorities. At one end of a continuum, practitioners (teachers, administrators, supervisors) wish to see more of the applied and action-type research, with more actual practitioners conducting or directing the research. Research results, accordingly, would be quickly interpreted, disseminated, applied, and evaluated. At the other end of the continuum, scholarly researchers advocate more basic research related to the psychological and social foundations of education. They indicate a need for much more freedom, fewer earmarks and priorities, more long-term grants, and fewer obligations to interpret and apply research findings.

A third voice, smaller yet not necessarily weaker, is that of the advocate of interdisciplinary research, who demands the involvement of educators, economists, engineers, and others in vocational-technical research. Such an approach would thus involve numerous research methodologies. Research related to the economics of education in general and to vocational education in particular illustrates this approach. Current efforts in cost-benefit analysis, systems analysis, operations analysis, and information management and analysis for decision making are all related to this trend in research and research administration.

Obviously, research activities from these three positions, as well as from others, will continue. That their extreme positions must be reconciled is clear, if research and development are to contribute to the meaningful education of youth and adults for vocational and career education.

TYPES OF EDUCATIONAL R&D

Educational research in vocational education may be classified into four basic types, each of which serves its unique function in the development and improvement of vocational education. *Basic research* is primarily concerned with producing scientifically exact knowledge, whereas *applied research* starts with the facts and propositions established in basic research and tests them in actual situations. *Research and development* programs focus on projects that result in finished products, such as textbooks and supplementary print and nonprint materials; these projects are usually too demanding, expensive, and time-consuming to be completed by one individual. *Action research* is concerned with obtaining specific knowledge about a particular group of respondents with results that are not generalizable to other situations.

RESEARCH COMPETENCIES

Vocational education teachers have varying responsibilities that require special research competencies. Typically they are called on, individually or as members of a group, to assist in the development and/or implementation of proposals affecting their school.

Vocational Education Teacher

There are certain basic research skills and knowledges that vocational teachers need to possess, whether they are interested in conducting research or in implementing research findings. Such research and development skill is useful to the teacher in a personal sense. Then, too, without a vocational research and development effort, such knowledge and skill could not be developed. Specifically, they should be able to (6):

1. *use the language of research*
2. *locate sources of resource information*
3. *recognize the commonly used modes of research in education*
4. *enunciate a research problem*
5. *formulate well-constructed hypotheses, tentative solutions or predictive statements which incorporate theory into testable form*
6. *develop the research design for solving the problem*
7. *execute research with precision so that its purposes can be accomplished*
8. *draw conclusions that are based on accurate and valid interpretation of the findings*
9. *use the techniques and tools of research*

TRANSLATING RESEARCH INTO PRACTICE

The translation of research findings into classroom practice is, in most instances, a slow process. For example, it may take one or more years to complete a research study, some time to write the report, from two to six months for journal editors to review it, and then, after acceptance, a lag of six months to a year before it is published. Thus, there may be a gap of 18 months to two years from the time a research report is completed until its publication.

A significant development that is helping to alleviate this problem is the creation of the Educational Resources Information Center (ERIC), an acquisition, storage, retrieval, and dissemination system for education. There are 19 ERIC Clearinghouses throughout the nation, each responsible for a particular educational area. The ERIC Clearinghouse for Vocational and Career Education is currently at Ohio State University, Columbus, Ohio. In addition to the ERIC Clearinghouses, the U.S. Office of Education has funded research and development centers, a network of curriculum centers, and regional laboratories, which are concerned not only with the production of educational research but also with its dissemination and implementation.

One method of dissemination used by ERIC is *Research in Education,* a monthly publication made up of résumés and indexes. The résumés highlight current research reports, curriculum studies, instructional materials, conference proceedings, speeches, position papers, and bibliographies. The content of each issue is indexed according to subject, author, institution, and accession numbers. Documents summarized in *Research in Education* are available from the ERIC Document Reproduction Service in microfiche or hardcopy.

Another source of current information is *Abstracts of Instructional and Research Materials* (AIM/ARM), compiled and published several times each year by the Center for Research in Vocational Education, Ohio State University, Columbus, Ohio. Each publication is divided into three subsections: abstracts, subject index, and author index. In addition to résumés of completed projects, the publication also includes abstracts of projects in progress. Documents cited in AIM/ARM are generally available in full text or in microfiche either from the publisher or from the supplier.

The research consumer should also investigate the series of review and synthesis of research papers in vocational and technical education and related fields published by the Center for Research in Vocational Education. These publications assist in identifying substantive problems and methodological approaches for researchers, and they provide practitioners with a summary of research findings. This series includes *Review and Synthesis of Research* in the various content areas of vocational education as well as in problem areas common to all the content fields.

The reevaluation of vocational education by the Panel of Consultants appointed by President Kennedy in 1961 and the supportive position adopted by the American Vocational Association were primary influences leading to the establishment of a national research center in vocational-technical education at Ohio State University. Its seven purposes include three objectives related to research plus the study of the role of vocational and technical education, the improvement of leadership, foreign assistance, and retrieval of information. The center cooperates with the Education Research Information Center (ERIC) of the U.S. Office of Education. It became the first official clearinghouse for vocational and technical education, a function that it still performs.

An active effort at the University of Wisconsin includes three research focuses that are intimately related to vocational and technical education. These include the Industrial Relations Research Institute, the Center for Studies in Vocational and Technical Education, and the Institute for Research on Poverty. The activities of the Wisconsin center are an example of those research efforts funded by private foundations, in this case the Ford Foundation.

Several centers on the international level are active in vocational and technical education. The International Education Act is an American effort to provide for a center of this nature. The International Labour Organisation (ILO), with headquarters at Geneva, Switzerland, maintains centers for vocational training and research. The center at Geneva puts out a training periodical and has a continuing abstract service, both available by subscription directly from ILO, Geneva, or from its Washington, D.C., office. A more recent establishment of the ILO is the International Centre for Advanced Technical and Vocational Training, at Turin, Italy, which began its operation in 1965. It is a forum for study and research by (a) the fellows in the center, in the form of study and evaluation; and (b) various organizations interested in the different aspects of economic development, of a sociological, psychological, or pedagogical nature. Languages of instruction are English, French, and Spanish.

Annual reports of the U.S. Department of Labor's Office of Manpower Policy, Evaluation and Research (OMR), as illustrated in *Manpower Research Projects*, provide valuable reading for researchers in vocational-technical education. OMR's research program has covered the social, cultural, educational, and economic aspects of unemployment and the underutilization of labor. Much of its research has centered on the young, the nonwhite, the poorly educated, the handicapped, the older worker, and those in chronically depressed communities, regions, and industries. In its role as a coordinator of research in the Labor Department, OMR was instrumental in the passage of an amendment that authorized the secretary of labor to make grants to strengthen labor programs in colleges and universities and to stimulate the study of labor problems. This action has been implemented through the small-grants program and an institutional-grants program, the latter to support long-term programs of research, to provide technical assistance to organizations interested in labor policies and programs, to recruit and train needed research personnel, and to develop interdisciplinary research concerned with the use of human resources. Many doctoral students have received research support through the small-grants program.

The National Science Foundation's interest in the education of scientific and engineering personnel has led to some research activities on its part and to its cooperation with others in studies that relate to the engineering technician. It cooperated with the U.S. Employment Service in examining technical occupations in research, design, and development. Its grant and contract studies are usually reported in the literature and in its *Publications of the National Science Foundation* in "Manpower and Education Studies."

The various military services are very active in research that is invaluable to vocational and technical education. Training, testing, curriculum construction, personnel research and analysis, and many other activities are being conducted on a large scale in various branches of the military. Ready access to military research information is now possible through (a) the computerized Defense Documentation Center; its publication, the *Technical Abstract Bulletin*, provides brief research descriptions and numbers by which copies of research reports may be ordered; and (b) the Clearinghouse for Federal, Scientific, and Technical Information, which provides information retrieval. Its semimonthly journal, *U.S. Government Research and Development Reports*, is available from the U.S. Department of Commerce.

In 1963 the Ford Foundation and its Fund for the Advancement of Education became interested in vocational and technical education in the United States. The status of its support program is reported in *Ford Foundation Grants in Vocational Education*, published periodically by the foundation. The report indicates that grants are supporting work in secondary schools, technical institutes, community colleges, research organizations, universities, and teacher education institutions in four categories: (a) curriculum improvement, (b) research, development, and information, (c) vocational-technical teacher education, and (d) cooperative work-study education. The foundation supports work at the University of Wisconsin and at the American Institutes for Research.

Graduate students are now, under the Vocational Education Act, producing studies related to the total field of vocational and technical education. For the most part, however, the subject matter of graduate education is not structured to produce research of this nature. Acknowledged weaknesses are in dissemination, application, and evaluation. But numerous completed projects and others currently in progress are worthy of examination.

Despite all of these research efforts, adequate study of new and emerging occupations and their educational implications is not taking place. Instead, there is undue emphasis on the industrial and engineering technician and relatively little on the emerging occupations in agriculture, business and distribution, and health and medicine. This indicates that public school curriculum planners may be generally content to develop existing programs in depth, but at the expense of experimental programs to train people for promising new occupations and to awaken student interest.

Research conducted by state agencies, regional educational laboratories, curriculum development centers, and consortia is now beginning to increase. Several interesting new agencies now include research among their objectives. Among these are: (a) the regional consortia of educational laboratories of state agencies and universities; (b) the state research coordinating units; (c) the five curriculum development centers; and (d) the Educational Commission of the States, which established a sounding board for educational discussion and an inquiry base for the improvement of education.

At the international level, vocational-technical research has been far less actively undertaken than has instruction itself, although an increasing receptiveness toward research appears to be emerging. This attitude is not reserved to the developed countries of Western Europe, the Soviet Union, Japan, or the few countries that have received the bulk of foreign assistance. The developing countries in Latin America and Southeast Asia are also interested in research in vocational and technical education. The Agency for International Development of the U.S. Department of State assists hundreds of active projects throughout the world. Similar projects are supported on a smaller scale by UNESCO, the United Nations Educational, Scientific and Cultural Organization.

PROBLEMS IN VOCATIONAL-TECHNICAL RESEARCH

Brandon (7) has identified a number of general problems related to research in the vocational and technical fields. First, vocational and technical administrators are frequently not "research prone"; that is, they are often inexperienced as to the problems of organizing, operating, and evaluating a research program. The sensitivity between researcher and administrator is always present, because the former wishes to study what he or she pleases, and the latter wishes to direct the attention and study to demonstrable ends. A desirable balance is thus difficult to maintain.

Second, research in vocational and technical education is of relatively recent origin. Before some degree of sophistication could be achieved in and among the various specializations of this field, considerable research had become interdisciplinary. Regardless of the merit of the interdisciplinary involvement, communication and understanding are highly problematical. Research techniques, methods, and the terminology and jargon of one discipline are not always well understood by or readily acceptable to workers in another discipline. This condition is clearly reflected in the economics of vocational education. No doubt the economist has justifiable interest in the analysis of expenditures and benefits if they are related to the decision-making process. The educator, on the other hand, cannot tolerate the hanging of a price tag on the many intangible purposes and contributions of educational programs. Again, if research is to be interdisciplinary in nature, it will need to be accompanied by education at many levels and not restricted to any one of the disciplines, even if the necessity of such education is not immediately evident to those who are counting the costs.

Third, the ratio of supply to demand of research personnel is critically out of balance in the vocational and technical areas. It is hoped that the increased availability of funds for the preparation of research personnel is a step in the right direction.

To what extent can research help to solve the problems of vocational education? Through the years vocational educators have recognized that research is one means of helping to provide answers to problems at the local, state, and national levels.

Tyler (8) describes several functions of educational research that should help the vocational educator to recognize the role of research in answering questions and finding the solution to problems:

1. *to provide answers to operational questions*

2. *to assess educational programs, practices, and materials*

3. *to build up a body of information about the educational enterprise*

4. *to provide the outlook, stimulation and guidance for innovation*

5. *to develop valid theory about educational processes*

Participants at the National Conference of Research listed the following items as critical problem areas for most states (9): (a) the methodology of curriculum development; (b) the formation of broad labor policies; (c) the relative efficiency of various organizational structures for guiding occupational education; (d) building curriculum for the disadvantaged; (e) teacher education processes; (f) student selection procedures and devices; (g) the development of an informational system that will keep practicing teachers up to date; (h) the indexing of staff and personnel throughout the state who are competent in research techniques; and (i) the extent of vocational education in the private sector.

An AVA publication (*Research and Implementation in Vocational Education,* 1969) identified six topics relating to vocational teaching that call for investigation: philosophical foundations of vocational education; the process of vocational instruction; the preparation of professional personnel; reorganizing the high school curriculum; postsecondary vocational development; and vocational guidance and career development.

If vocational educators are to use educational research to improve classroom practice and to find answers to problems in the field, then they must realize that:

1. educational practices need to be continually challenged, evaluated, and redesigned

2. to effect progressive change, schools and departments need the ability to adapt meaningfully to proven innovative practices

3. the most crucial single factor is the competence of the teacher; little progress can be made until more professionally competent and committed teachers give priority to their role as agents for change

4. research and development, to change vocational education for the better, must involve researchers, educators, and citizens working together to build a profession of education relevant to the times

RESEARCH UNDER THE VOCATIONAL EDUCATION
AMENDMENTS OF 1976

Public Law 94-482 set aside 20 percent of the basic grant to states for program improvement and supportive services, which included research. Under section 131(a) of the amendments, funds available to the states may be used for support of state research coordination units and for contracts by those units in line with comprehensive plans for program improvement involving:

1. *applied research and development in vocational education;*

2. *experimental, developmental, and pilot programs and projects designed to test the effectiveness of research findings, including programs and projects to overcome problems of sex bias and sex stereotyping;*

3. *improved curriculum materials for presently funded programs in vocational education and new curriculum materials for new and emerging job fields, including a review and revision of any curricula developed under this section to insure that curricula do not reflect stereotypes based on sex, race, or national origin;*

4. *projects in the development of new careers and occupations, such as*
    (a) *research and experimental projects designed to identify new careers in such fields as mental and physical health, crime prevention and correction, welfare, education, municipal services, child care, and recreation, requiring less training than professional positions, and to delineate within such career roles with the potential for advancement from one level to another;*
    (b) *training and development projects designed to demonstrate improved methods of securing the involvement, cooperation, and commitment of both the public and private sectors toward the end of achieving greater coordination and more effective implementation of programs for the employment of persons in the fields described in subparagraph (a), including programs to prepare professionals to work effectively with aides; and*
    (c) *projects to evaluate the operation of programs for the training, development, and utilization of public service aides, particularly their effectiveness in providing satisfactory work experiences and in meeting public needs; and*

5. *dissemination of the results of the contracts made pursuant to paragraphs 1 through 4, including employment of persons to act as disseminators, on a local basis, of these results (10).*

A final requirement of the amendments was that no contract shall be made under subsection (a) unless the applicant can demonstrate a reasonable probability that the contract will result in improved teaching techniques or curriculum materials that will be used in a substantial number of classrooms or other learning situations within five years after the termination date of the contract.

With this brief background of funding support, let us examine the ways in which the federal government has sponsored various types of educational research and development.

Office of Vocational and Adult Education

Until 1970 most federal support for educational research was administered by the U.S. Office of Education, a division of the Department of Health, Education and Welfare. Various agencies within USOE supported research activities. In 1969 the Bureau of Research was reorganized and became the National Center for Educational Research and Development (NCERD). The new title was intended to reflect the USOE commitment to research and development as an approach to improving American education. The center contained five divisions: (a) Educational Laboratories, (b) Elementary and Secondary Education Research, (c) Comprehensive and Vocational Education Research, (d) Higher Education Research, and (e) Information Technology and Dissemination.

The Division of Comprehensive and Vocational Education Research was formed to support research related to vocational education at the high school and junior college levels. It was composed of branches for basic research, instructional materials studies, and studies on organization and administration. An additional branch, the Career Opportunities Branch, was established to support research concerned with identifying and developing careers in new and growing subprofessional fields.

NCERD was dismantled in a USOE reorganization in 1972, and its responsibilities were absorbed largely by program personnel of the Bureau of Occupational and Adult Education, now the Office of Vocational and Adult Education.

On May 7, 1980, the new U.S. Department of Education went into operation. President Jimmy Carter named Daniel Taylor, a former West Virginia chief state school officer, to be the Education Department's first assistant secretary for vocational and adult education. The new bureau's vocational and adult education budget approximated $889 million.

The Vocational Education Amendments of 1976 consolidated into the basic grant existing authorization for work-study, cooperative education, residential schools, and new energy education programs. It is up to each state to determine which, if any, of these programs it wishes to fund in addition to the basic vocational education programs. Eighty percent of the basic grant authorization is to be used for these consolidated programs. The remaining 20 percent is allocated to the second area of consolidation—program improvement and supportive services—which includes research, exemplary and innovative programs, curriculum development, guidance and counseling, teacher education, and grants to overcome sex bias. Not less than 20 percent of the funds under the program improvement consolidation must be used for guidance and counseling.

The purposes of the complementary efforts described above are to improve and extend the vocational education process at the elementary-secondary, postsecondary, and adult levels; to promote the development and diffusion of vocational education curriculum materials; and to demonstrate the results of these efforts to educators and the public, including new ways to create a bridge between school and the world of work for young people. The bureau's Division of Research and Demonstration administers these three programs.

Projects and programs supported by the bureau are carried out through individual contracts or grants awarded in response to proposals submitted by colleges and universities, by state and local education agencies, by other public or nonprofit private agencies or institutions, as well as by profit-making groups. Competitions for new grant awards, including priority or program statements, are announced in the *Federal Register*. Requests for Proposal (RFPs), which result in contracts, are announced in the *Commerce Business Daily* when proposals are being sought for a specific product.

Various groups advise the Office of Vocational and Adult Education concerning the establishment of priorities for the applied research, exemplary demonstration, and curriculum programs each fiscal year. Counsel is sought from the Research Committee of the National Advisory Council on Vocational Education, from the National Network for Curriculum Coordination in Vocational-Technical Education, from the National Research Coordinating Unit Directors Association, and from other groups or individuals concerned with improving the quality of vocational education.

In 1972, at the request of President Richard M. Nixon, Congress created the National Institute of Education (NIE). Operating within the Department of Health, Education and Welfare and independent of USOE, NIE was created as a vehicle for supporting educational research and development. Its first director, Thomas Glennan, developed an organizational structure composed of the following units:

1. *The Office of Research Grants* was vested with responsibility for stimulating research in five study areas: human development, social thought and processes, learning and instruction, objectives and evaluation, and the educational system.

2. *The Office of Research and Exploratory Studies* was charged with a broad range of policy research issues, including exploratory studies leading to program commitments in curriculum and instruction and responsibility for assessment of regional educational laboratories and research and development centers (formerly a USOE responsibility).

3. *The Office of Programmatic Research and Development* was named to administer major research and development initiatives undertaken by NIE,

including short-range programs oriented toward development and demonstration as well as toward integrated programs of longer duration.

4. *The Office of Research and Development Resources* was formed to improve the effectiveness of educational research, including a research program on the research and development system itself, in addition to training and dissemination services for linking the institute with the research and development community.

5. *The Office of Planning and Management* was charged with five major responsibilities: planning and evaluation, budget, management systems, organization development, and staff support to the National Council on Educational Research.

6. *The Office of Administration* was given responsibility for five divisions: grants and contracts, finance, general services, personnel, and information resources.

The National Council on Educational Research is responsible for formulating general policies for the institute. Council members advise the director of NIE on program development; recommend improved methods of collecting, disseminating, and implementing education research findings; and submit annual reports to the president and Congress on the institute's activities, education research, and education in general. Congress intended that the National Institute of Education would exercise a major role in directing educational research and development at all levels.

Research priorities established by the National Council on Educational Research directed NIE's efforts toward: (a) basic research into the learning process; (b) problems of education for the disadvantaged; (c) educational financing; (d) improving the education of educators; (e) linkage between research and development institutions and schools and universities; and (f) emerging approaches to education: continuing education, nonformal and extra-institutional education, and the relationship of public and nonpublic education.

The NIE was authorized (11) "to assume responsibility not only for the development of educational materials and practices, but also for their dissemination (previously vested in the Office of Education) to students, teachers, administrators, and other potential users."

Current research

The National Institute of Education undertook a four-year study of vocational education that could lead to basic changes in some of the most venerable programs in federal education assistance legislation. The study was mandated by Congress in 1977 in preparation for the required reauthorization of the Vocational Education Act in 1982. Federal support of vocational education, begun in 1917, is the second oldest form of direct federal assistance to schools.

The NIE study is primarily concerned with the four major subjects specified in the legislation mandating it:

How are federal, state, and local funds for vocational education currently distributed in terms of services, occupations, target populations, enrollments, and educational levels, and what should that distribution be in order to meet the greatest human resource needs for the next ten years?

How well are states and localities complying with federal laws applicable not only to vocational education programs but also to equal opportunity, sex discrimination, and related issues?

How are the quality and effectiveness of vocational education programs evaluated?

How effective are federally funded consumer and homemaking programs?

The study, funded by statute up to $1 million per year for four years, also examines other issues not specifically mandated but necessary for an understanding of vocational education—particularly the role of federal policy. The intent of these substudies is to help answer questions that have been raised about the levels, purposes, uses, and effects of federal support for vocational education.

The institute is also conducting a number of smaller studies including the effectiveness of consumer and homemaking education programs, vocational education for the incarcerated, vocational education in rural and sparsely settled areas, coordination between Comprehensive Employment and Training Act (CETA) and vocational education programs, and issues and problems of compliance in grant-in-aid programs, for purposes of comparison with vocational education.

PREPARATION OF RESEARCH PROPOSALS

The use of project proposals as vehicles for the development, implementation, and funding of new educational programs has become standard practice. As a result, proposal writing is a valuable skill for both the teacher and the administrator. This section looks at the mechanics of preparing a proposal. Suggestions are made about the various components and procedures, including the rationale, related research, objectives, hypotheses, design, evaluation, dissemination, facilities, personnel, and budget.

Practical Considerations Prior to Proposal Writing

Some of the factors that will influence the timing of proposals are the following:

1 Availability of funds at the funding level

Some agencies commit the bulk of their funds long before the end of the fiscal year in June, so that an application submitted in May, for example, does not have much of a chance during that fiscal year. On the other hand, sometimes there are monies left over in June, which may cause accelerated action on proposals already submitted by that time.

2 Personnel availability

Many districts have had great difficulty finding project directors and other important project staff if they have not begun their search early enough. New job hunting begins in the winter, and most regular staff are committed by April or May.

3 Local budgeting

For those projects that require matching funds or cooperative support at the school district level, provisions must be made for this consideration in the budget. Budgets are approved at different times of the year, but most are drawn up in the winter and voted on or otherwise approved in April or May. If a proposal requires local funds, this circumstance must be known before budget time.

4 Student schedules

Although school is in session from September to June, neither of those months is worth much as far as instructional programs are concerned. Therefore, the beginning date for a project directly affecting students over several months should be between October and February.

5 Procedural delays

Proposals cannot be written in a day, nor can approval on most projects be obtained in a week. Considering all the factors involved in preplanning, consultation, obtaining local approval, revision, incorporation of state and national suggestions, and preparation of manuscript, a district will need months to bring a proposal to final form.

Review procedures on some kinds of research projects at the USOE or NIE require two to six months. If state approval is also needed, an additional few weeks should be added. After approval, two or three days are taken up in notifying the district's member of Congress, so he or she can pass the information on to the local newspaper. Then negotiation of budgets may require four to six weeks.

Writing the Proposal

Application and proposal forms vary in complexity, from the "fill-in-the-blank" type to the proposal for a competitive research grant that will be scrutinized by panels of specialists. The writing of research proposals has become a high art. Every foundation and agency that dispenses research funds requires a statement of the nature of the proposed project. Sometimes these statements must adhere rather rigidly to a standard format; in other instances the format is quite flexible.

In the actual writing of a research project proposal in which careful account must be made of rationale, procedures, and evaluation, these sections will usually be included:

1. rationale; statement of the problem
2. review of the literature
3. objectives
4. hypotheses
5. the design
6. procedures
7. evaluation
8. dissemination
9 facilities
10. personnel
11. budget

Not all components are relevant to all agencies, but it is important to keep in mind the nature and requirements of each. Also, the format of experimental, pilot, and developmental proposals may vary considerably depending on the scope of the project.

For several reasons, it is not possible here to give complete instructions on how to design a research proposal. Each project varies from others in such ways that different procedures are needed in every case. A thorough analysis of research design and statistical analysis would take several hundred pages. Moreover, within each project and design there are alternate paths that may be taken. However, there are points of similarity in most proposals, and some of the major points are outlined in this section.

Rationale; statement of the problem

The rationale section should explain why the project is needed and the general theory on which the procedures rest. The outline of the statement of the problem may run somewhat as follows:

1. State the problem in terms intelligible to someone who is generally sophisticated but who is relatively uninformed in the area of the problem.
2. Define and delimit the specific area of the research.
3. Indicate the broad questions or hypotheses to be tested.

4. Indicate briefly the significance of the study.

5. Include a single clear statement of the purpose of the research.

The section on significance is often the one that the researcher finds hardest to write. The following suggestions should prove helpful:

1. Indicate how your research will refine, revise, or extend existing knowledge. This applies to both content and method.

2. Almost all studies have two potential audiences—practitioners and professional peers. Statements relating the research to both groups are in order.

3. Indicate what the research means for your institution.

Review of the literature

Almost every proposal includes a review of the literature, which serves at least two purposes:

1. It demonstrates to the reader that the writer has a comprehensive grasp of the field and is aware of recent developments.

2. It explains how the study will refine, revise, and/or extend what is currently known about the problem.

It is not easy to decide where to put the review of literature because it can describe research related to all phases of the project, from rationale to procedures. Probably the best place is after the rationale. The review is an essential part of the proposal, for it will convince the reader that the investigator is not duplicating previous research on the same subject and it shows that the investigator is aware of the findings of related research. The review should show (a) the uniqueness of the proposal, (b) previous discoveries, if any, related to the proposed research, and (c) gaps in previous research to be filled by the proposed project.

As a starter, the uninitiated reviewer may wish to look for related research in sources such as the *Encyclopedia of Educational Research*, the *Review of Educational Research*, the *Education Index*, the *Psychological Abstracts*, the yearbooks of professional associations in the vocational service areas, specialized books and periodicals, research available through ERIC microfiche, the *Research in Education* abstracts, *Abstracts of Instructional Materials AIM/Abstracts of Research Materials* (ARM).

The organization of the review will vary according to the purpose of the project, but one possible sequence is: (a) historical reviews of the topic in brief style, as in the *Review of Educational Research*; (b) a sufficiently detailed summary of several closely related experiments so that the reader can understand procedures and results; and (c) analysis of previous research, showing its relevance to the current proposal.

Objectives, hypotheses, questions

Research seeks to test hypotheses or to answer questions. Hypotheses are stated when the researcher wants to test the implications of a theory. In instances where a theory cannot be stated, it is appropriate to ask questions or to pose objectives. The reader of the proposal should be able to connect a particular objective with activities in the procedure section. He or she should also be able to judge whether the evaluation method will indeed determine whether the objectives have been obtained.

Procedures (design, treatment, and evaluation)

As the instructions from the USOE or the NIE imply, projects vary so much that no suggested prescription for procedural design will be universally useful. Most proposals, however, contain the following sections:

1. *Design:*   This section should make it clear whether the basic technique employed is that of a controlled experiment, a case study, an opinion survey, or whatever. In the case of the experiment, it must be shown that the project staff will be able to identify and control variables such as treatment and control procedures.

2. *Population:*   In the case of a design calling for the study of subjects, these persons should be described in terms of their age, sex, training, special characteristics relative to the study, and the method to be used to select the population as a sample of a larger group.

3. *Treatment:*   If there is a subject population and its members are to be taught in some special way or given an experimental treatment, the procedure must explicitly describe what will be done to the experimental group and to the control group. One common weakness to avoid is the brief reference to the control group as receiving "conventional instruction"; more detail is needed.

4. *Instrumentation:*   Instrumentation is a point at which many research designs break down. Fundamentally sound ideas can fail to produce fruitful findings if instruments not relevant to the variables are used. The writer should be careful to describe the instruments to be used in the study and the process of development, if the instruments are to be constructed.

5. *Sampling:*   The sample should identify the population to which the results will be appropriate and the type of data to be collected.

6. *Data collection:*   The proposal should include the general plans for collecting the data plus the anticipated time schedule.

7. *Data analysis:*   The analysis of data usually involves some type of statistical treatment. The proposal should thus specify the statistical or analytical

procedures to be used and the tools, such as a computer program, that are to be employed.

Evaluation

The evaluation section is commonly the weakest part of proposals. It may be helpful to define the term *evaluation* as that process by which some persons pass judgment on the degree to which the aims of an enterprise were successfully achieved. This judgment is usually based on the collection of data and then its analysis and interpretation.

In this section the investigator should explain as explicitly as possible how he or she will determine the degree to which the objectives of the project have been realized (instrumentation, data collection, and data analysis are discussed above). Strengthening the evaluation section means paying closer attention to basic procedures such as (a) listing objectives in measurable form; (b) describing the method of collecting data; and (c) outlining the techniques of interpreting the data.

Dissemination

Another of the weaker sections of many proposals, the dissemination part should clearly indicate a workable plan for spreading project information to other organizations to aid them in the process of imitation. Possible techniques include demonstration, publicity in professional publications and in news media, state education department publicity, lectures and reports at conventions, and the final report that can be made available through ERIC microfiche or hard copy. The criteria for judging dissemination plans include clarity, validity, pervasiveness, impact, timeliness, and practicality.

Facilities

Granting authorities are naturally interested in knowing whether a local district has the building, equipment, laboratories, etc., necessary for the successful conduct of a project. The proposal should include a description of pertinent facilities, such as space available, subjects available, staff talent, sources of consultative help, data processing center, and library and instructional media resources.

Personnel

The agency also wants to know who the people are who will conduct the project activities. Of course, these people may not be known at the time of application—another argument for appointing a local person as project director in advance. A description of a person's background includes his or her education, professional experience, publications, and honors. This is no time to be modest, because the reviewing field readers and/or consultants are wary of persons without degrees and college affiliations.

Budget

Budget preparation is tiresome and difficult, especially for the novice. Yet it is important because it shows whether the author really understands the practical requirements of the proposed project. Careless budget preparation may suggest that the applicant would be unable to support a needed operation in the later phases of the project.

PARTS OF THE BUDGET.   It is important at the outset to investigate the budget requirements of one's institution and those of the granting agency. Explain in detail how estimates are determined. Do not pad and do not overlook overhead and other entitlements. Budget forms differ from one department to another, but they are likely to contain provision for the following expenditure categories:

1. *Personnel:*   Specify how total amounts were calculated. For example:

Consultant, statistical, ten days at $100 a day	$ 1,000
Ass't. Project Director, two years half-time at $10,000 per year plus $550 annual increment	$10,275
Secretary, four months at $500 per month	$ 2,000

    Note that the U.S. Office of Education does not ordinarily approve amounts greater than $100 a day for consultants unless the organization requesting funds customarily pays more or unless there is a special reason for a higher fee.

2. *Benefits:*   The grantee may elect to pay benefits. Otherwise do not forget these categories: retirement, social security, health benefits. The business office in your organization or the state accounting office can provide the percentage to be used for estimation of professional and nonprofessional retirement, social security, and health benefits.

3. *Travel:*   There has been a general tightening up on travel allowances in the past few years. However, it is still reasonable to ask for money to make reports at one or two important conferences, to travel to visit consultants and other projects of a similar nature, and to pay for consultant travel and for local travel of project personnel on official business. The rate for the latter should be at the level of the organization sponsoring the proposal; for example, 18 cents per mile.

4. *Supplies:*   It takes paper to run the project. There are reports, correspondence, memorandums, and so on, for which supplies will be needed. Film, audiotapes, and other materials of this type will be needed if students are to be instructed through the project.

5. *Equipment:*   Some agencies will permit the purchase of research equip-

ment; others will not. Some will buy 20 percent the first year, 20 percent of the remaining costs the second year, and so forth. In general, the purchase of office equipment is not encouraged, although it is not unusual to allow rental of typewriters or other office equipment.

6. *Communications:*   Telephone costs to be included are the regular trunk costs plus long distance calls. This category also includes the cost of postage.

7. *Services:*   These include items such as the development of film, computer rental, and data processing.

8. *Rental:*   Rental of office space may be budgeted, but it will normally be charged to overhead. Find out the cost per square foot of renting space in your area, estimate the number of square feet needed, and figure a total. Utilities and custodial service charges will increase if more space is required. Some of these costs may be paid from local money in order to make the local contribution a real one.

9. *Indirect costs:*   The allowance varies from one agency to another and the policy varies from one year to the next. Some large organizations, such as universities, have determined a flat percentage charge for overhead, based on estimates obtained by their auditors. Smaller organizations may have to negotiate the overhead percentage or budget separate items as direct cost expenditures. Some agencies allow a flat percentage; others allow no overhead at all.

   The overhead is an estimate of the additional expense an institution will incur if it supports a grant project. Project administration adds many hours of time and many headaches to administrators who are not on the project budget. The business office has bills to pay and the superintendent has phone calls and visits to make in connection with the project. One method of arriving at an estimate of overhead is to obtain the total budget figure for the administration of a district and take a fixed percentage of it.

LOCAL CONTRIBUTION.   Some vocational education projects require the local district to make a 50 percent contribution to costs of the project on the premise that the federal or state government should not be the only agency willing to support projects at the local level. Typical local contributions are for secretarial help, travel, consultation, employee benefits, office materials, telephone, postage, rental, utilities, and estimated administrative overhead not reimbursed by the government.

DEVIATIONS FROM BUDGET.   It is unlikely that anyone will stay exactly on the budget to the last dollar. A common rule of thumb is that deviations from the line item expenditure estimates may be made to the extent of 15 percent, except for sensitive items such as travel and equipment. In other words, transfer from one item to another may be made without notifying the agency if the amounts do not exceed 10 percent of the budget item from which the transfer is to be made. Each agency should be consulted about its policy.

Evaluation of Proposals

After the proposal is received by the funding agency, it is usually circulated to reviewers who are experts in the field under investigation. Reviewers normally employ about four basic criteria or questions in judging the worth of a proposal:

1. Is the problem educationally significant, as measured by
    (a) the importance of the problem
    (b) a sound theoretical basis for the problem
    (c) the extent to which results can be generalized
    (d) the relationship to similar known research
2. Are personnel and facilities adequate, as measured by
    (a) professional competence and experience of the investigator
    (b) necessary space, personnel, and equipment for performing the work
3. Is the research design sound, as measured by
    (a) clear and logical statements and relationships among the problem, objectives, and procedures
    (b) information in the statement of procedures including, where applicable, sampling techniques, controls, data to be gathered, instruments to be used, and statistical and other analyses to be made
4. Is the proposal economically efficient, as measured by a favorable relationship between the probable outcome of the project and the total effort expended

The following inadequacies may be identified (12) as among the most frequent and serious that occur in research proposals:

1. *The problem is trivial.*
2. *The problem is not delimited.*
3. *The objectives, hypotheses, or questions are stated too broadly.*
4. *The procedures are lacking in detail.*
5. *The design is not appropriate for the problem; that is, a simple design is frequently used to investigate a complex problem.*
6. *Relevant variables are not considered or are lightly dismissed.*

SUMMARY

The objective of research, as a function of program planning and development, is to encourage change and improvement in the field. In the past, the focus of research efforts in vocational education has been largely developmental.

Four types of research activities may be identified in vocational education: basic research, applied research, research and development, and action research. Certain well-defined competencies are necessary for the vocational educator who engages in such research, whether he or she is a teacher, a supervisor, or a teacher educator. These competencies emphasize research-mindedness and the ability to plan, execute, and evaluate the findings of research.

The ERIC Clearinghouse for Vocational and Career Education (its publication, *Research in Education*) and the Center for Research in Vocational Education (AIM/ARM documents) have been highly effective in disseminating the results of research and development in vocational and technical education. Research centers, such as those at the Ohio State University and the University of Wisconsin, have actively promoted and conducted a wide variety of research in this field.

The 1976 Vocational Education Amendments authorized research for program improvement involving applied research and development; experimental, developmental, and pilot programs; improved curriculum materials; projects for the development of new careers; and dissemination of the results of such activities.

A key factor in the improvement of education is the amount and quality of research that is undertaken. Despite the long-range increase in the level of financial support by all agencies for educational research and development, the total remains low. Experts recommend that support should be increased until at least 1 percent of the national expenditure for education is devoted to research and development.

The primary vehicle for contract and grant support to research in vocational education is the Office of Vocational and Adult Education. Under the Vocational Education Act, the bureau carries out a wide variety of research and training projects.

The newest federal research agency is the National Institute of Education. Created in 1972 as a vehicle for supporting research and development in education, NIE adopted priorities related to basic research into the learning process, problems of education for the disadvantaged, educational financing, improving the education of educators, linkage between research and development institutions and schools and universities, and emerging approaches to education.

It is important for the vocational educator to develop a degree of competence in the preparation of research and development proposals. The components of such proposals normally include the rationale and statement of the problem, review of the literature, objectives, hypotheses (if applicable), the design, procedures, evaluation, dissemination, facilities, personnel, and budget. Detailed suggestions provided in this chapter relate to the preparation of each of these components. The four basic criteria that are usually applied to the evaluation of proposals include educational significance, economic efficiency, soundness of the research design, and adequacy of personnel and facilities.

ACTIVITIES

For review

1. What is the function of the ERIC Clearinghouse?
2. Identify at least three functions of educational research.
3. What positions are taken by practitioners, professional researchers, and proponents of interdisciplinary research regarding the focus of research?
4. Why is there a lag between the completion of vocational research and its use in the classroom?
5. Explain the research function of the Office of Vocational and Adult Education with regard to the Vocational Education Act of 1963, as amended.
6. What are the usual components of a research proposal?
7. Why is a review of literature needed in a research proposal?
8. What are the criteria used by reviewers to evaluate research proposals?
9. How might vocational education research be improved?
10. Identify at least four weaknesses of research proposals.

For discussion

1. Do you agree with the list of competencies suggested for vocational teachers? Are there others that you would add to the list? Would a teacher with a four-year degree possess these qualifications? In the undergraduate and graduate programs, should more emphasis be placed on developing research consumers?
2. What are some of the means that could be used to make research findings in vocational education more readily available to the consumer?
3. Cite some examples of changes in vocational education that are the result of research.
4. How may local school systems work with colleges and universities in conducting and/or implementing vocational research?
5. Identify some problem areas that, in your opinion, need to be researched in vocational education.
6. What research studies have made the greatest impact on your vocational field?
7. What sources available in your campus library include summaries or abstracts of vocational research?
8. Explain how research can help a teacher to change classroom practices.

For exploration

1. Compare your research competencies with those suggested for a person in your position (teacher, supervisor, teacher educator). Identify areas of weakness that you need to strengthen.

2. Bring to class one example of each of four types of research. Explain the basis on which you classified each.

3. Interview one vocational teacher, one supervisor, and one teacher educator. Ask each one to read the list of recommended research competencies and to make suggestions for revision.

4. Evaluate a research study, using the criteria suggested in this chapter or a comparable reference. Write up your review and report it to the class.

5. Select an area of concern and survey the research literature for solutions.

6. Examine the guidelines for proposal preparation provided by the U.S. Department of Education or other funding agency. How do they differ from the guidelines suggested in this chapter?

7. Invite a vocational supervisor, state department representative, or USOE representative to discuss the outlook for funded research.

8. Invite a publishing company representative to discuss how research findings are used in textbooks and supplementary materials.

9. Outline a research study that you could implement on your job.

10. Select an area of interest or concern to you. What research, reported in *Research in Education* (ERIC) or in AIM/ARM, is related to the topic? Examine the *Review and Synthesis of Research* series in various vocational fields for further information.

REFERENCES

1. William B. Richardson and Gary E. Moore, "Using Research Findings to Improve Instruction," in *Vocational Instruction*, Aleene A. Cross, ed. (Arlington, Va.: The American Vocational Association, Inc., 1980), p. 88.

2. George L. Brandon, "Vocational and Technical Education," in *Encyclopedia of Educational Research*, 4th ed., Robert L. Ebel, ed. Copyright ©1969, American Educational Association. (Reprinted by permission of Macmillan Publishing Company, Inc.)

3. Rupert Evans and George L. Brandon, "Research in Vocational Education," in *Vocational Education 64th Yearbook*, NSSE, Melvin L. Barlow, ed. (Chicago: University of Chicago Press, 1965), pp. 263–80.

4. Ralph C. Wenrich et al., "Vocational, Technical and Practical Arts Education," *Review of Educational Research*, Vol. 32, 1962, pp. 363–423.

5. Brandon, "Vocational and Technical Education." (Reprinted by permission.)

6. Geraldine M. Farmer, "Research Competencies of the Business Educator," in *Contributions of Research to Business Education*, Calfrey C. Calhoun and Mildred Hillestad, eds. (Washington, D.C.: National Business Education Association, 1971), pp. 353–54. (Reproduced by permission.)

7. Brandon, "Vocational and Technical Education," p. 1519. (Reproduced by permission.)

8. Ralph W. Tyler, "The Field of Educational Research," in *The Training and Nurture of Educational Researchers*, E. Guba and S. Elam, eds. (Bloomington, Ind.: Phi Delta Kappa, 1965), pp. 8–9.

9. Carl J. Schaefer and Gordon F. Law, "Research on Teaching Vocational Skills," in *Second Handbook of Research on Teaching*, Robert W. Travers, ed. (Chicago: Rand McNally College Publishing Company, 1973), p. 1304.

10. Public Law 94-482, Education Amendments of 1976, 90 Stat. 2193, Oct. 12, 1976.

11. House of Representatives, 92nd Congress, First Session, Report No. 92-554, Oct. 8, 1971, pp. 65–66.

12. Gerald R. Smith, "A Critique of Proposals Submitted to the Cooperative Research Program," in *Educational Research: New Perspectives*, Jack A. Culbertson and Stephen P. Hensley, eds. (Danville, Ill.: Interstate Printers and Publishers, Inc., 1963), pp. 281–85.

■

CHAPTER NINE

Public Relations for Vocational-Technical Education

INTRODUCTION

American schools have extended their mission and services until they touch more lives than ever before. But, paradoxically, many of the "whys" of education have, to an increasing extent, eluded the public grasp. Schools appear to move from one crisis to another, sometimes following and sometimes leading in the race to keep abreast of change. Education must deal with many problems, but its most fundamental challenge is to justify itself in the minds of those who finance it.

Education has suffered from a failure to understand the community and to develop the community's understanding of the school, its services, objectives, problems, and successes. In too many instances, the school has failed to create a climate conducive to an exchange of views between the school and its publics. Administrators and teachers have been too absorbed in the immediate problems to give adequate attention to the problems of informing the public and enlisting its cooperation. Too frequently, school administrators, including vocational administrators, have assumed that "if we run a good school," the public must necessarily approve, even though conceptions may vary widely as to what constitutes a "good school."

The 1960s were years of rapid change and shifting social patterns, years in which the nation's schools were caught up in a web of difficult relationships. News of public education and its problems moved to the front pages of newspapers, with headlines reporting teacher strikes, school bond defeats, parental opposition to busing, and student riots. Growth in news coverage of education in part reflected the public's increased awareness of schools and their impact on society. The events and circumstances of the sixties—the civil rights movement, protests in the streets, discovery of the poor, acceleration of industrial technology, and swiftly changing social patterns—all served to establish firmly in the public mind the social urgency of public education.

The 1970s saw public demands for accountability and a reluctance, in the face of declining student enrollments, to raise levels of financial support. In combination with the poor economic conditions of the mid-1970s, these pressures have resulted in a retrenchment in education and a demand that the need for and quality of existing and proposed programs be reviewed. These developments have led to significant changes in the structure of educational programs and an increasing sensitivity to the role of the school as a cooperative agency in the educational enterprise.

The 1980s see continued public demands for accountability—both financial and in the quality of educational programs. When public education fails to meet the expectations of parents and students, they frequently seek alternative sources of education. As a result of planned public relations efforts, educational institutions should reflect increased joint efforts between schools and their publics.

Vocational education must continue to adapt to the processes of change and progress. It is the consensus of many educators that the public schools will make progress about as rapidly as the general public will support change. Thus public relations becomes an essential facilitator of change.

> *Changes in regard to purpose, content and teaching method, along with the increasing size and costs of schools have tended to confuse the general public and leave them without adequate information. Today's complex and urbanized society demands that public school pupils be provided educational experiences quite different from many of those which present-day parents themselves received in school (1).*

For this reason, it is more important than ever that the public be intelligently informed about what schools are attempting to do. The public will continue its support of the best in education only when it is kept well informed of the progress of its schools, when it is involved in promoting the total school program, identifying concerns, and seeking solutions to problems.

Public opinion—the state of the public's education on a given subject—is not stable. Changes are especially marked in a highly competitive society. The instability of public opinion is manifested on such diverse subjects as the actions of particular foreign countries, conservation of natural and human resources, or the varying uses of the tax dollar. This particular feature of public opinion is the reason why a good public relations program must be continuous and consistent.

During recent years there has been a general awakening to the importance and possibilities of an intelligent school public relations program. However, there has been a tendency to give this information to the public only when a new bond issue was to be passed or other financial assistance was to be secured. Thus the program assumed a somewhat selfish aspect and was not inclined to add to the confidence of the general public.

Educators are gradually coming to understand that every person who is in any way connected with the educational program is a public relations agent, whether or not that person knows it. Students, by virtue of their role as the most direct beneficiaries of educational programs, become the schools' most important public relations agents; the impressions they transmit to their parents are frequently accepted without question. Therefore, public relations must take on an in-school as well as an out-of-school emphasis. Teachers undoubtedly are the most important official agents in school public relations. Nonteaching personnel including secretaries, custodians, food service personnel, and bus drivers are important communicators of a school program. They should be aware of their roles in public relations and, consequently, should be included in the in-school public relations activities of a school or school system. It is important, too, that various community groups be made aware of the part they play in the important task of making good schools better.

That the American public has great faith in its schools is evidenced by their continuous support over the years. As long as the great majority of people believe in education, sporadic attacks in the press or from pressure groups will not defeat the schools. However, in some communities where programs have been developed without adequate explanation and without participation of the community, progress has been retarded, and ill-advised changes have been made because of opposition from uninformed groups.

The public school system receives its support from the people. Just as the stockholders in a business enterprise have a right to know the facts concerning the status of the business they own, so also the people of any community have a right to know what is going on in their schools, which belong to them and are operated for the benefit of their children and the community. Therefore, educators need to take the public into their confidence, providing them with the information they need to understand the total school program. Such information programs should not be deferred until a crisis arises.

Philosophy in the field of public relations is often more advanced than is practice. But it is generally believed that a sound curriculum is the basis on which a public relations program should be founded. Students' development and growth furnish the standard. For the school administrator, however, the question is how to proceed beyond this point. It is only natural that he or she should turn for guidance to private business, which has had such successful experience in public relations work.

American education has lagged far behind business and industry in the acceptance, development, and refinement of public relations techniques. But just because public relations cannot qualify as an exact science, its processes should not be rejected. Whatever is known, with reasonable sureness, about public relations should be studied by all who deal with and depend on the public. Because the schools have been created for service and not for profit, however, the methods should be adapted for use in education. It would be worse than a mistake for any public institution to adopt outright the methods that have been successful in private enterprise.

PUBLIC RELATIONS IN THE CHANGING EDUCATIONAL SCENE

Public relations has been defined (2) as "that field of action which concerns itself with the relations of an individual, an idea, an institution with the publics upon which it depends for its visibility." An earlier but still highly relevant description of school public relations was provided by Kindred (3) in 1957:

> School public relations is a process of communication between the school and the community for the purpose of increasing citizen understanding of educational needs and practices, and encouraging intelligent citizen interest and cooperation in the work of improving the school.

A decade later, Jones (4) reaffirmed the two-way relationship between the school and the community when he stated that "public relations designates all the functions and relationships that pertain in exchange of ideas between school and community that establish the basis for joint understanding."

Because school public relations is a two-way process, it involves *listening* as well as talking, and it should not be confused with publicity, a one-way process of giving information that does not necessarily ensure understanding. The question confronting educators is not whether they want public relations, but whether they want *planned* or *unplanned* public relations, favorable or unfavorable public relations.

Importance of School Public Relations

The development of good public relations is impossible without good communication. In the absence of communication, there is no public relations, because relations with people are established only by communicating *with* them. Public relations, as a process, involves an interchange of facts, viewpoints, and ideas.

Basically a school or vocational department communication program should be organized on the basis of its internal and external publics. *Internal publics* may be described as those within the environs of the school; that is, students, teachers, administrators, guidance personnel, and nonteaching personnel. *External publics* include those beyond the environs of the school; that is, parents, alumni, merchants, and people engaged in business, civic and service groups, the news media, feeder schools, postsecondary vocational schools, colleges, and universities. Both these types of publics represent persons with varied backgrounds, experiences, and interests. Consequently, the communication process must be tailored to fit the characteristics of each group. To think of "the public" as one massive assemblage is a common mistake, and efforts to communicate effectively with the "general public" are on the whole unsuccessful and ineffective.

Several principles may be identified as being fundamental to the establishment of effective two-way communication between the school and its publics:

1. There must be a genuine willingness to share information.
2. Communication should not be deliberately distorted or misleading, but should be factual, accurate, and temperate.
3. Information should be timely and messages transmitted quickly to avoid misunderstanding.
4. Repetition is essential. Information should be repeated in different terms and through different media to make it clearly understood.
5. Information should be communicated in small amounts for clear understanding.

The sole justification for any segment of the school system is to provide appropriate educational opportunities for all students, a process that is best achieved through the coordinated efforts of the school and its publics. The effectiveness of the school is conditioned by the amount of confidence it enjoys. Confidence is built on understanding, trust, and appreciation. To bring about better understanding between the school's internal and external publics, to meet attack and criticism, to understand the broader community so that the school can adapt its program to changing conditions, and to foster a more adequate program of financial support, a planned and systematic approach to public relations is essential. Although public relations is intangible, its efforts clearly contribute to the work of the school.

Need for Effective Public Relations in Vocational Education

Because vocational education is an integral part of the educational continuum, vocational educators face the continuous and challenging task of interpreting the objectives and purposes of their field to publics both inside and outside the school. In addition, vocational educators are particularly concerned with relationships arising from existing or potential contact with employers in business, industry, and government, as an important facet of their educational program.

At least eight types of problems faced by vocational educators have strong implications for a public relations program:

1. the need to develop a strong liaison between vocational educators and members of Congress and state legislatures, to maintain and extend federal and state support for vocational education

2. the need to define vocational education, to point out its relationship to academic and career education, to identify its objectives and goals

3. the need to define the standards desired by and expected of vocational education

4. the need to interpret methods of designing, teaching, and evaluating vocational curricula

5. the need to change the stereotypes that have become so deeply rooted in the minds of some people about vocational education

6. the need to point out the accomplishments and the problems of vocational education

7. the need to interpret what is being done to improve the quality of vocational programs

8. the need to justify the role of vocational education as an essential component in the education of all students

A closer relationship is developing between the business and academic communities. Vocational educators are finding that many of the problems and techniques discussed in the classroom have reality in business, and they are looking more to business and industry for counsel and advice. On the other hand, business leaders are recognizing their responsibility to schools and colleges as sources of educated labor, scientific knowledge, a more favorable business climate, instructional materials, and on-the-job instruction.

The vocational educator is an important link between the school and the employer, as illustrated in Figure 9.1. The strength of that link will determine, in large measure, whether the school is keeping abreast of the needs of the community and whether the school is actually fitting its graduates to take their places in the world of work. In making a positive effort to know the needs of local business, such as by promoting cooperative vocational work experience programs, follow-up studies of graduates, field trips, and informal contacts with business employers, the school can adjust its curriculum to meet the needs of its employment community and of its graduates. These liaison-with-business activities of the vocational educator, if properly coordinated, will do much to bring into proper focus the school, the student, and the business and industrial community.

Because of this unique relationship between vocational educators and the community, vocational teachers should be leaders in the field of public relations. They should keep their perspective by remembering that there are

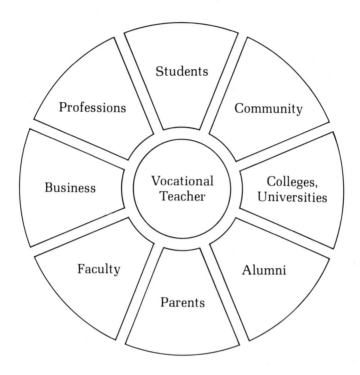

Figure 9.1   Public relations through cooperative endeavor: a two-way relationship

weaknesses in every school system; they should not shut their eyes to these problems but rather should indicate a willingness to work on them. They should take the initiative in securing more meaningful cooperation of internal and external school publics.

Students are the most significant and important force in the public evaluation of a school program because they are the focal point of the educational process. Experiences of students after graduation reflect their former experiences within the school and thereby color the school's reputation. High school graduates who enroll in postsecondary institutions are representatives of their particular high schools. Likewise, students entering the labor market mold public attitudes toward the school by their dress, manner of speech, general conduct, and job performance.

Communication Needs in Vocational Education

One of the dilemmas confronting vocational educators is how to satisfy the diversity of opinions and demands of the various groups constituting their publics. It becomes necessary for vocational educators to operate on the same principle that all other public institutions must operate on—that is, in accordance with the wishes of the majority. How can vocational educators know that their programs are being operated according to the wishes of the people? First, enlightened public opinion cannot be developed unless people have full access to the facts; they must know *what* vocational education is trying to accomplish, *how* it is going about achieving its objectives, *how well* it is succeeding, and the *problems* it is encountering. Merely dispensing such information to the public does not ensure understanding. Second, through needs assessments, opinion polls, advisory committees, and other public relations activities, the people can make their opinions known and vocational educators can use the information to make more effective decisions.

Communication between the schools and local industry can be improved by (a) schools increasing their efforts to maintain close contact with business and industry to gauge training requirements; and (b) business and industry taking a greater interest in the schools, learning their capabilities, and informing the schools of skills required today and of those needed in the future.

Bagin (5) suggests these steps for improving public relations and communication between schools and their publics:

1. Take a serious look at your programs. *An image reflects that which is. If your graduates of vocational programs are unable to compete with other vocational graduates in the labor market, should some changes be made in these programs?*

2. Provide inservice communications and public relations help for all employees. *Insist that all employees use comfortable language (usually about ninth grade) when preparing materials. Work with curriculum personnel and teachers to help them communicate better with parents.*

3. Involve the community in the schools. *Be sure you mean it though. Involvement for the sake of a grant requirement that misuses or underuses people will be resented. Solid involvement pays off. Don't, for example, have the community assist in setting goals for your programs and then continue to establish the same priorities you had before the goal-setting groups pointed out new ones.*

4. Improve morale through better internal communication. *Discuss internal communications and establish priorities for improvement. Encourage every staff member to improve the place where he or she works. People who work there have a dramatic impact on the opinions that others hold about your vocational programs.*

5. Personalize the schools more. *Every staff member should remember that people are more important than things. This means returning phone calls and a general caring about students. A good catalyst is to pretend the voucher system is in effect. If employees might lose their*

jobs if no students selected their school, would they go out of their way to show "customers" that they care?

6. Don't over-react to criticism from a vocal few. *Build a data base of opinions from the community. Develop an instant feedback system that provides community thinking.*

7. Make the communications/public relations functions a vital part of every management decision. *When school officials reflect on the three major crises of any given year, usually at least two of them are attributable to a poor communications or public relations effort.*

8. Keep a log of your time. *See if the way you are investing your hours is consistent with the goals of your school and your program. Perhaps you are using too much time on things you enjoy, but these are not paying off.*

9. Work with zero-base budget for your PR effort each year. *Start over, asking the tough questions: Is this worth the money and time? Would it be better to use that time another way?*

10. Keep up in your field. *Read the journals and newsletters that can help you to improve your efforts. Capitalize on what others have done that has worked for them.*

Advisory Committees in Vocational Education

Advisory committees can be effectively used to establish closer contact between schools and business and industry. Such committees have been important to vocational education for many years, especially in job-training programs for young people and adults. Four groups appear to have particular relevance to programs of vocational education: school administrative personnel, labor and management segments of business and industry, labor organizations, and students.

Although the literature about industry–education cooperation recommends the use of advisory committees, it is concerned largely with the use of formally organized advisory committees to achieve the desired cooperative participation of industry. Unfortunately, only occasionally is there provision for the use of specially assigned school staff for industry- or community-liaison purposes.

In addition to long-term advisory committees, short-term advisory committees that are formed for a specific purpose are an effective means of broader input and participation from parents and the business-industrial community. For example, an advisory committee could be formed for two months to investigate types of equipment used in the employment community for a certain vocational field. After the committee makes its report, it is then disbanded.

Consulting or advisory committees should be carefully selected. Among the more important characteristics of committee members are that

1. they are able, intelligent people
2. they are public-spirited people, willing to contribute to the betterment of the community
3. they possess outstanding personal qualities of responsibility, integrity, open-mindedness, cooperativeness, and insight
4. they are representative of all elements of the community or special program interests they serve; consideration is given to sex, experience, age, religion, politics, and organizational affiliation
5. if they represent a special program area, they bring the needed expertise and interest to the committee; of great importance is keen interest and insight into their specialty

The specialized committee for vocational-technical education has also been referred to as an occupational advisory committee. Some of its functions are to:

1. serve as a communications channel between colleges and community occupational groups
2. list the specific skills and suggest related and technical information for the course
3. recommend competent personnel from business and industry as potential instructors
4. help evaluate the program on instruction
5. assist in recruiting students, in providing work training stations, and in placing qualified graduates in appropriate jobs
6. keep the school informed about changes in the labor market, specific needs, and surpluses
7. provide means for the school to inform the community of occupational programs
8. assess program needs in terms of the entire community
9. suggest ways of improving the public relations program of the school

PRINCIPLES OF PUBLIC RELATIONS

The soundness, consistency, and defensibility of a school public relations program are dictated by the assumptions and principles underlying it. However, the development and acceptance of principles do not in themselves guarantee that a program will be effective. Principles must be translated into policies and plans for implementation.

The following assumptions underlie the development of a sound public relations program:

1. Good public relations is a necessary and desirable aim of public schools.

2. The activities or techniques employed in a school's public relations program are necessarily subordinate to and in line with the school's philosophy and objectives.

3. Public relations begins with certain types of activities.

4. Some activities and media are more effective than others as interpretive and communicative agents.

5. The positive identification of activities and practices that have public relations value contributes to a more successful school program.

6. Vocational education is only a part of the total school program; consequently, any formal public relations activity undertaken on behalf of vocational education must be coordinated with the overall school public relations program.

The place and role of public education in a democratic society dictate the principles that underlie an effective school public relations program. The following are examples of principles on which a good public relations program may be organized and operated:

1. The school as a social institution is inaugurated by the people for the achievement of their purposes and has no value apart from the purposes and wishes of the people.

2. The role of education is unchanged; however, the organization and implementation of formal education must be considered transitory.

3. The school as a democratic social institution rests on public confidence, which, in turn, depends on the honesty and sincerity of institutional functioning.

4. The school, as an impartial democratic agency, operates on the tendency of public opinion to form favorable attitudes toward it.

5. The theory of democratic institutional authority limits the purpose and method of the school public relations activity because enlargement or contraction of institutional activity is recognized as being a function of the people. The interests of all the people are superior to those of the teaching profession or of any other minority interest group.

6. The public school exists as an agency for harmonizing cultural differences.

7. The cooperative partnership concept of public education is contingent on the active, intelligent participation of parents, citizens, business/community leaders, and other social agencies.

8. The legal responsibility for determining the school's public relations policy and approving methods of implementation rests with the board of education.

School public relations programs are characterized by standards generally agreed on by researchers and public relations specialists. These include dimensions of honesty, positiveness, comprehensiveness, and sensitivity to publics represented. Elements of repetitiveness, continuity, and follow-through are also important. The school public relations program should be well planned, staffed by competent personnel, adequately funded, well coordinated and continuous, and sensitive to the changing needs of its publics. In addition, the program should provide opportunities for involvement by all publics, should communicate its ideas simply, and should be appraised continuously and improved through study, research, and experimentation.

The preceding characteristics of effective public relations programs show that vocational educators cannot depend on incidental, hit-or-miss efforts to ensure desired results. An effective public relations program for vocational education must be systematically planned, developed, implemented, and evaluated. Figure 9.2, a vocational education public relations model, illustrates a systematic approach toward planning and implementing a public relations program.

PUBLIC RELATIONS CHECKLIST FOR VOCATIONAL EDUCATION

What are the public relations activities, procedures, techniques, and media that have been used to promote vocational education? Who are the publics to be reached?

A number of internal or in-school publics exist through which better public relations for vocational education may be promoted. These publics include the following: school administrators; teachers; guidance personnel; clerical and secretarial personnel; custodial, maintenance, and service personnel; paraprofessional personnel; and students. There exists also an almost unlimited number of external publics, those beyond the environs of the school itself, including merchants and people engaged in business, parents, community organizations, professional education associations, middle and junior high schools, high schools, post–high school vocational-technical schools, junior colleges, and colleges and universities.

The Public Relations Checklist for Vocational Education, which appears on the following pages, is a modification of a doctoral research study completed by the author (6) at Ohio State University. It answers the primary question, What are the nature and scope of public relations practices used in vocational education as shown by research studies and the general literature? It classifies public relations activities and media into three principal categories: (a) those that may be used by vocational educators to reach *external* school publics; (b) those that may be used to reach *internal* school publics; and (c) *school-sponsored* activities that, of themselves, may promote good public relations for vocational education.

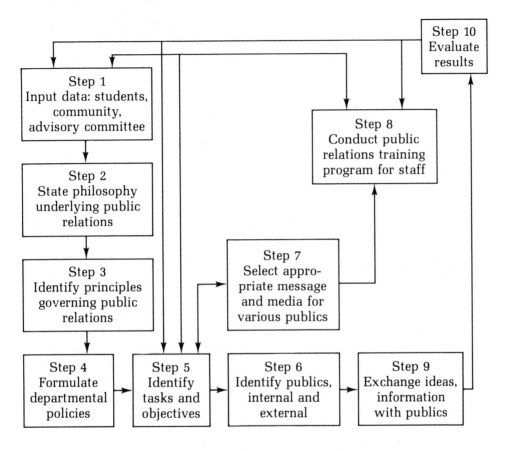

Figure 9.2 Vocational education public relations model

Originally designed for high school vocational teachers, the checklist has been modified so that vocational educators at any level may use it to evaluate their public relations activities against those that are recommended by researchers as being effective. A qualitative appraisal of the relative value of these activities and media would do much to increase the effectiveness of public relations efforts in the field. With a view toward facilitating such an evaluation, the categorized activities have been arranged into a checklist under a coded column headed "Value of Activity" (Limited = L; Average = A; and Excellent = E). An additional column headed "Have Used" (Yes or No) is designed to determine whether the respondent has had experience with the activity or media under evaluation. A qualitative evaluation of the items by vocational educators would point up those activities believed to be most effective as public relations tools. To accomplish such a result, one could administer the instrument to one or more groups, assign a numerical value to each possible response on the checklist, then rank the items on a scale from most effective to least effective.

Public Relations
Checklist for Vocational Education

Directions Listed below are some activities and media that have been identified through research as having possibilities for promoting vocational education with its internal and external publics. The purpose of this appraisal sheet is to secure an evaluation of the worth of the following items as public relations instruments for vocational education.

In the first group of columns ("Value of Activity"), please *circle one letter value* (L = Limited; A = Average; or E = Excellent) for each item. In the second group of columns ("Have Used"), indicate by *circling the appropriate letter* (Y = Yes; N =No) whether you have ever used this idea or technique in your vocational education program or have had any first-hand experience with it that would aid you in evaluating its effectiveness.

Activities	Value of Activity	Have Used
	(Circle 1)	(Circle 1)

Activities used by the vocational educator to reach external publics

A Public relations contacts of vocational educator with business and industry

	Value of Activity	Have Used
1 Career day activities	L A E	Yes No
2 School advisory committee(s)	L A E	Yes No
3 Job analyses made by vocational teacher	L A E	Yes No
4 Personal contacts with persons in business	L A E	Yes No
5 Cooperative work experience program .	L A E	Yes No
6 Vocational teacher receives occupational training through summer business job .	L A E	Yes No
7 Vocational teacher provides local firms with publicity and information about the program	L A E	Yes No
8 Vocational teacher patronage of local stores	L A E	Yes No
9 Junior achievement organization (local firm sponsors temporary student-operated business ventures for educational purposes)	L A E	Yes No

Activities	Value of Activity (Circle 1)			Have Used (Circle 1)	
10 Persons in business serve as resource people to the school (consultants, speakers, etc.)	L	A	E	Yes	No
11 Business surveys conducted by vocational teacher (job survey, equipment survey, or needs assessment)	L	A	E	Yes	No
12 Vocational teacher serves as consultant to business firms (employee training, systems and procedures)	L	A	E	Yes	No
13 Business-sponsored instructional materials	L	A	E	Yes	No
14 Business machines show staged in school	L	A	E	Yes	No
15 Adult vocational education program (short courses, workshops, training or retraining for vocational or avocational purposes)	L	A	E	Yes	No

B Public relations contacts of vocational educator with community organizations

   1 Membership and active participation in business-related groups

(a) Administrative Management Society	L	A	E	Yes	No
(b) Better Business Bureau	L	A	E	Yes	No
(c) Chamber of Commerce	L	A	E	Yes	No
(d) Community Improvement Association	L	A	E	Yes	No
(e) National Secretaries Association ..	L	A	E	Yes	No
(f) Retail Merchants Association	L	A	E	Yes	No
(g) Other (List) _____	L	A	E	Yes	No
2 Membership and participation in community councils, forums, and committees dealing with education and school planning	L	A	E	Yes	No
3 Membership and participation in civic-service club activities (Civitan, Kiwanis, Lions, Rotary, etc.)	L	A	E	Yes	No
4 Membership and participation in church groups and activities	L	A	E	Yes	No

Activities	Value of Activity			Have Used	
	(Circle 1)			(Circle 1)	
C Public relations contacts of vocational educator with parents					
1 Evaluation of students' work through report cards, letters, parent–teacher conferences	L	A	E	Yes	No
2 School open-house event	L	A	E	Yes	No
3 Bulletins and informational reports sent to parents concerning the school program	L	A	E	Yes	No
4 Personal contacts with parents outside the school	L	A	E	Yes	No
5 Invitations to parents to visit the school and vocational program	L	A	E	Yes	No
6 Reception of visitors at school	L	A	E	Yes	No
7 Back-to-school night (parents attend abbreviated sessions of their student's classes)	L	A	E	Yes	No
8 Parent-Teacher Association activities ..	L	A	E	Yes	No
9 Parental involvement in curriculum planning, evaluation, and determination of program needs and priorities	L	A	E	Yes	No
D Public relations through vocational educator membership, attendance, and participation in professional groups					
1 National and state *education* associations	L	A	E	Yes	No
2 National and state *vocational education* associations	L	A	E	Yes	No
3 Local *education* associations	L	A	E	Yes	No
4 Local *vocational education* associations	L	A	E	Yes	No
E Public relations through vocational educator contacts with middle school/junior high school					
1 Serving as speaker or consultant for career exploration classes	L	A	E	Yes	No
2 Providing instructional materials/media for career education program	L	A	E	Yes	No

Activities	Value of Activity	Have Used
	(Circle 1)	(Circle 1)
3 Providing information to prospective students about the vocational program through interviews, conferences, or direct mail	L A E	Yes No
4 Vocational teacher as assembly guest speaker	L A E	Yes No
F Public relations contacts of vocational educators with area vocational-technical schools and junior colleges		
1 School open-house event	L A E	Yes No
2 Joint programs (high school with vocational-technical school or junior college; junior college and vocational-technical school)	L A E	Yes No
3 Shared services and facilities	L A E	Yes No
G Public relations through vocational educator contacts with colleges and universities		
1 Cooperation in guidance of student teachers assigned to vocational program for pre-service training	L A E	Yes No
2 Cooperation in advanced research conducted by graduate students and colleges	L A E	Yes No
3 Attendance and participation in vocational education conferences, clinics, workshops, institutes, and staff development activities sponsored by the college	L A E	Yes No
4 Attendance at summer schools	L A E	Yes No
5 Attendance at campus and in-service classes	L A E	Yes No
H Public relations contacts of vocational educator with alumni		
1 Surveys of alumni, requesting information, evaluation of experiences or of the vocational program	L A E	Yes No

Activities	Value of Activity	Have Used
	(Circle 1)	(Circle 1)
2 Providing placement services for school alumni	L A E	Yes No
3 Furnishing departmental publications and reports to alumni (new personnel, equipment, curricula, etc.)	L A E	Yes No
4 Alumni reunions sponsored by vocational education department	L A E	Yes No

I Public relations contacts of vocational educator with the community

1 Sharing instructional materials, tests, films, etc., with vocational programs of other schools	L A E	Yes No
2 Contacts with newspaper and magazine editors through news stories about the vocational programs	L A E	Yes No
3 Providing information regarding student qualification for jobs when requested by employment bureaus and employers	L A E	Yes No

School-sponsored activities, practices, and media that promote good relations for vocational education

A School clubs enrolling vocational students

1 Distributive Education Clubs of America	L A E	Yes No
2 Future Business Leaders of America, Phi Beta Lambda	L A E	Yes No
3 Future Farmers of America	L A E	Yes No
4 Future Homemakers of America	L A E	Yes No
5 Future Secretaries Association	L A E	Yes No
6 Office Education Association	L A E	Yes No
7 Vocational Industrial Clubs of America	L A E	Yes No
8 Other (List) _____	L A E	Yes No

B Student publications involving vocational students

1 School newspaper (including news of vocational programs and students)	L A E	Yes No

Activities	Value of Activity			Have Used	
	(Circle 1)			(Circle 1)	
2 School news section of community newspaper (featuring copy on vocational programs and activities)	L	A	E	Yes	No
3 School yearbook (sales, advertising, and vocational education content handled by vocational students)	L	A	E	Yes	No
C School assemblies depicting vocational education					
1 Demonstrations by vocational students	L	A	E	Yes	No
2 Plays illustrating business situations ...	L	A	E	Yes	No
D School displays and exhibits featuring vocational education					
1 Class work displays on school bulletin boards	L	A	E	Yes	No
2 Exhibits of departmental work displayed in stores	L	A	E	Yes	No
3 Exhibits of departmental work displayed at fairs and festivals	L	A	E	Yes	No
4 Schoolwide exhibits of materials and equipment used in classes	L	A	E	Yes	No
5 Photographic displays	L	A	E	Yes	No
E School celebration of special days and weeks					
1 Parent Visitation Day	L	A	E	Yes	No
2 Business-Industry-Education Day	L	A	E	Yes	No
3 High School Day (students operate local firm for a day)	L	A	E	Yes	No
4 Vocational Education Week	L	A	E	Yes	No
5 Career Week (outside speakers discuss job opportunities and requirements with students)	L	A	E	Yes	No
F Special services by vocational students to teachers, administrators, and community					
1 Information attendant and school guide to visitors	L	A	E	Yes	No

Activities	Value of Activity			Have Used	
	(Circle 1)			(Circle 1)	
2 Office assistant to administration or school faculty	L	A	E	Yes	No
3 Host or hostess at school or departmental open house	L	A	E	Yes	No
4 Student tutorial program (advanced students coach other students needing extra help)	L	A	E	Yes	No
5 Volunteer community service work ...	L	A	E	Yes	No
6 Guest speaker representing vocational education before community groups ...	L	A	E	Yes	No

Activities used by vocational educators to reach internal (in-school) publics

A Effective public relations through vocational educator contacts with students

1 Cooperative teacher-student planning ..	L	A	E	Yes	No
2 Maintain quality of the school instructional program	L	A	E	Yes	No
3 Use of individualized, multimedia materials	L	A	E	Yes	No
4 Teacher guidance of students (in program planning, choosing an occupation, with personal problems, etc.)	L	A	E	Yes	No
5 Use of a simulated or open laboratory in vocational programs	L	A	E	Yes	No
6 Recognize outstanding student achievement (through awards, commendation, news releases, honor roll, etc.) .	L	A	E	Yes	No
7 Sponsoring and participating in student organizations and programs	L	A	E	Yes	No
8 Teacher visitation of students on cooperative part-time job (work under joint supervision of school and business employer)	L	A	E	Yes	No
9 Teacher follow-up of graduates (through job, evaluation, or placement follow-up)	L	A	E	Yes	No
10 Teacher provides in-service training and retraining for former graduates and employees	L	A	E	Yes	No

Activities	Value of Activity	Have Used
	(Circle 1)	(Circle 1)
B Public relations contacts of vocational educators with school administrators and supervisors		
1 Keeping administrators informed through the annual report	L A E	Yes No
2 Special reports of vocational education programs and activities	L A E	Yes No
3 Reporting newspaper and magazine articles published by departmental staff . . .	L A E	Yes No
4 Departmental booklets and brochures describing the programs	L A E	Yes No
5 Furnishing samples of outstanding work done by vocational students	L A E	Yes No
C Vocational education relationships with school faculty		
1 Faculty meetings	L A E	Yes No
2 Interdepartmental materials and methods conferences and committees	L A E	Yes No
3 Exchange of professional literature and/or instructional materials	L A E	Yes No
4 Sponsoring in-service courses for teachers	L A E	Yes No
5 Maintaining a service pool from which teachers may requisition student services	L A E	Yes No
6 Participating in school and/or department staff development activities	L A E	Yes No
D Vocational educator contacts with school guidance personnel		
1 Cooperating in instructional and job placement of students	L A E	Yes No
2 Cooperating in administering and analyzing tests for students (aptitude, achievement, etc.)	L A E	Yes No
3 Keeping counseling staff informed of latest developments in vocational fields	L A E	Yes No

Activities	Value of Activity			Have Used	
	(Circle 1)			(Circle 1)	
4 Cooperating in preparation and maintenance of literature dealing with job opportunities and requirements in vocational fields	L	A	E	Yes	No
E Vocational educator contacts with clerical, secretarial, and administrative staff workers of the school					
1 Serving as consultant on systems and layout	L	A	E	Yes	No
2 Using school offices as training stations	L	A	E	Yes	No
3 Providing current information about courses and curricula to staff	L	A	E	Yes	No
F Vocational educator contacts with school maintenance, custodial, and service personnel					
1 Voluntary assistance to school service personnel	L	A	E	Yes	No
2 Invitations to visit the department during open house, displays, exhibits, and other special events	L	A	E	Yes	No
G Vocational educator relationships with the school as a whole					
1 Informal conversations with school personnel	L	A	E	Yes	No
2 Invitations to participate in department events	L	A	E	Yes	No
3 Making department equipment, facilities available	L	A	E	Yes	No
4 Intraschool communications	L	A	E	Yes	No
5 Voluntary services by the vocational staff	L	A	E	Yes	No

The Public Relations Checklist for Vocational Education identifies a broad scope of public relations practices and media. Such a checklist, developed from the general literature and from research studies, provides the basis for an effective evaluation of a comprehensive cross section of techniques used for public relations purposes in the area of vocational education.

To evaluate the theoretical worth of these activities and media, the checklist might be adapted to a local situation and administered to a jury of persons who are especially competent in public relations practice. Such a jury might be divided into three groups: public relations directors or consultants in business, school public relations directors, and vocational education authorities.

To test the practical value of the activities and media that the jury has judged effective, it is further suggested that the opinions of a sample of outstanding vocational teachers be surveyed. The ratings assigned to individual activities, by both the jury and the teachers, could then be assigned arithmetic weights and the items ranked from high to low. The lower-value items might then be dropped from the checklist.

A final step might involve an on-the-spot examination of a number of schools that have excellent vocational education programs. A study could be made to determine whether the checklist activities are used in these schools and, if so, to what extent they are felt to be effective. A definite tendency among the schools surveyed toward the effective use of the checklist activities and media would serve to validate the items.

The checklist and the flowchart (Figure 9.2) presented earlier in the chapter suggest how schools may go about developing, implementing, and evaluating a program of public relations. The ultimate objective is, of course, the improvement of vocational education through the cultivation of a pattern of highly recommended activities and media, designed to increase public confidence and support for the program. Such activities should result in better performance of vocational teachers by improving cooperation between the various vocational programs and their internal and external publics.

SUMMARY

This chapter has considered the fundamentals of public relations as they affect the development of positive relationships with internal and external school publics. Principles, problems, techniques, and media affecting public relations have been examined as they apply to the implementation of school programs, including vocational education. Public relations has been viewed as a two-way process, a cooperative effort for mutual understanding and effective teamwork between the community and the school. Emphasis was placed on developing a continuous program of interpretation, involvement, and cooperation as the school seeks to serve the individual and vocational needs of its publics.

The effective school public relations program should be well planned, staffed by competent personnel, adequately funded, coordinated, continuous, and sensitive to the changing needs of its publics. It should provide opportunities for involvement by all publics, communicate its ideas simply, and be appraised continuously.

A vocational education public relations model involves the following components: (a) collecting input data from students, community, and advisory committee; (b) formulating philosophy underlying public relations program; (c) identifying principles governing public relations; (d) formulating departmental policies; (e) identifying public relations tasks and objectives; (f) identifying appropriate internal and external publics; (g) selecting appropriate message and media for various publics; (h) conducting public relations training program for staff; (i) exchanging ideas and information with publics; and (j) evaluating results.

A checklist for vocational education identifies a wide range of public relations activities and media and classifies them into three principal categories: (a) those that may be used by vocational educators to reach external school publics; (b) those that may be used to reach internal school publics; and (c) school-sponsored activities that promote good public relations for vocational education. The checklist is arranged so that vocational educators may evaluate their public relations efforts against those recommended by the literature as being effective.

ACTIVITIES

For review

1. Differentiate between "public relations" and "publicity."
2. Summarize the principles underlying effective communication between the school and its internal and external publics.
3. Discuss the role of the student in the public relations program of (a) the school and (b) the vocational education department.

For discussion

1. If a vocational department has no planned program of public relations, what responsibilities should the individual classroom teacher assume?
2. This chapter gives numerous reasons why a school or vocational department should be concerned about its public relations. What are five of the most important reasons for vocational educators to be concerned about their public relations program?
3. Explain the underlying philosophy that you think should support a public relations program in your vocational field.
4. How can state supervisors in the various vocational fields provide leadership for public relations programs?
5. What are some activities that teachers can use to improve their communication with parents?
6. It has been suggested that teachers are their own worst enemies in lowering

the status of the group to which they belong. They do not keep professional business to themselves or within their own ranks, but rather they talk about their disputes and disagreements in the community. Do you agree or disagree? If you were a vocational department chairman, what steps would you take to prevent such an occurrence?

7. In planning the curriculum, should top priority be given to public opinion or to the professional opinion of the vocational educator?

For exploration

1. Review your local newspaper for several days. Summarize the articles that relate to (a) the total school system and (b) vocational education.

2. Interview one or two business or industrial leaders in the community. Find out how much they know about local vocational education programs; for example, objectives, courses, equipment.

3. Report cards are one means of communicating with parents of students you teach. Evaluate the effectiveness of report cards you use or with which you are familiar. What changes would you recommend to improve the reporting system?

4. Using the checklist provided in this chapter, evaluate the public relations program in your department. Invite other vocational educators to evaluate their programs.

5. Identify the internal and external publics for your vocational program. Select one internal group and one external group. Prepare a public relations plan for each group to include goal, objective(s), procedures or activities, resources needed, timeline, and means of evaluation.

REFERENCES

1. James J. Jones, *School Public Relations* (New York: Center for Applied Research in Education, Inc., 1966), pp. 2-3.

2. Edward L. Bernays, "Parity for Public Relations in Higher Education," *College and University Journal*, Vol. 11, No. 4, Sept. 1972, p. 7.

3. Leslie W. Kindred, *School Public Relations* (Englewood Cliffs, N.J.: Prentice-Hall, Inc., 1957), p. 16.

4. Jones, *School Public Relations*, p. 2.

5. Don Bagin, unpublished mimeographed material, Public Relations Workshop, Barrow County Schools, Winder, Ga., Aug. 14-15, 1980. (Reproduced by permission.)

6. Calfrey C. Calhoun, "The Identification, Classification and Evaluation of Public Relations Activities and Practices in Secondary School Business Education" (Doctoral dissertation, The Ohio State University, Columbus, 1960), pp. 316-19.

CHAPTER TEN

■

Evaluation in Vocational-Technical Education

INTRODUCTION

Evaluation of vocational programs is a prime requirement of the Vocational Education Amendments of 1976, which mandated a national vocational education data reporting and accounting system that went into effect October 1, 1977. This management information system, which has been implemented in each state, includes information regarding students, programs, program completers and leavers, staff, facilities, and expenditures.

Every important aspect of vocational education needs assessment. How may the effectiveness of instructional programs be increased? How accurately has the occupational competency of students been determined? How appropriately do the materials and methods of instruction reflect students' abilities and needs? How do students perceive themselves, their teachers, and the educational process? These kinds of questions provide direction to those involved in measuring the success of vocational education.

Evaluation is in a period of crisis and change. Parents, teachers, administrators of public schools and technical institutes, college and university personnel, and the critics of education in general are questioning the validity of time-honored evaluation procedures. What is the impact of an evaluation program on those whom it is designed to serve? Do evaluation measures illuminate and guide, or do they obscure and confuse? It is difficult to conceive of effective vocational teaching without procedures for determining students' interim and terminal skills and the degree to which their educational progress parallels that of their peers.

Planning for the evaluation of vocational programs takes place at all levels of the educational system and is tailored to the objectives defined for each level. Such an approach yields an evaluation system that is built on an individual student record system and that makes possible the measurement of program effectiveness in terms of the individual's ultimate employment, taking into consideration continued education beyond the job-entry level. Program evaluation also involves consideration of resource-allocation and cost-effectiveness factors.

This chapter outlines some of the guiding principles on which an effective evaluation of vocational education is built. Benefits of evaluation are discussed in terms of individual student growth, program operations, credibility, cost effectiveness, and other uses. Two evaluation models are presented and their characteristics explained. Attention is given to overall program evaluation in relation to vocational curricula, personnel, and facilities evaluation. A special section covers measurement and data collection, including criterion-referenced and norm-referenced tests, informal evaluation measures, questionnaires, and needs assessment. A discussion of the cognitive, affective, and psychomotor classification of behaviors as a basis for evaluation is summarized. The chapter concludes with a discussion of the consultative role that accrediting agencies perform in the evaluation process.

GUIDING PHILOSOPHY OF EVALUATION

This section defines evaluation and presents some of the basic principles that direct evaluation in vocational education and other fields.

Definition and Scope

The necessity for evaluation of vocational programs is generally accepted in principle. However, the method of evaluation is difficult and complex, for several reasons. First, vocational education programs are widely divergent in nature. Second, the present state of the methodology of evaluation is inadequate to serve as the basis for determining program effectiveness. In essence, evaluation is the process of securing value judgments concerning a condition or a process. Such value judgments should be based on a critical consideration of the best evidence available concerning the given condition or process.

Bloom, Hastings, and Madaus (1) view evaluation of learning as "the systematic collection of evidence to determine whether in fact certain changes are taking place in the learners as well as to determine the amount or degree of change in individual students."

A management-oriented view of curriculum evaluation is expressed in the following statement by Taylor and Maguire (2):

Curriculum evaluation can be viewed as a process of collecting and processing data pertaining to an educational program, on the basis of which decisions can be made about that program. The data are of two kinds: (a) objective description of goals, environments, personnel, methods and content, and immediate and long-range outcomes; and (b) recorded personal judgments of the quality and appropriateness of goals, input, and outcomes. The data—in both raw and analyzed forms—can be used either to delineate and resolve problems in educational programs being developed or to answer absolute and comparative questions about established programs.

Ammons (3) sees evaluation as the description of student progress toward educational objectives. She notes that, in contrast to testing, evaluation is directed more to individuals than to groups; it seeks to describe the progress of the individual student toward certain school-defined objectives.

Evaluation is viewed by Harris (4) as

the systematic process of judging the worth, desirability, effectiveness, or adequacy of something according to definite criteria and purposes. The judgment is based upon a careful comparison of observation data with criteria standards. Precise definitions of what is to be appraised, clearly stated purposes, specific standards for the criteria traits, accurate observations, and measurements, and logical conclusions are hallmarks of valid evaluation.

Guba and Stufflebeam (5) view evaluation as the "process of . . . obtaining and providing . . . useful . . . information for making . . . educational decisions." Tyler (6) presents evaluation as related to instruction, seeing it as a "process for finding out how far the learning experiences as developed and organized are actually producing the desired results."

A similar definition that reflects the changing role and purpose of evaluation has been formulated by the Phi Delta Kappa National Study Committee on Evaluation (7) as follows: "Educational evaluation is the process of delineating, obtaining, and providing useful information for judging decision alternatives."

In summary, evaluation may be viewed as a systematic process of obtaining information for judging the effectiveness of vocational programs in relation to acceptable criteria or objectives.

Principles of Evaluation

An effective approach toward evaluation is based on principles that reflect a clear sense of direction, flexibility, and an honest desire to improve and upgrade all persons, programs, and processes involved in vocational education.

The following are fundamental considerations involved in implementing an evaluation process.

1. Evaluations must have a *definite frame of reference;* that is, meaningful evaluations must be made in terms of specific values, goals, or objectives. Evaluative procedures that fail to take into account the self-determined goals of the individual or institution are not only worthless, but may actually be harmful in their distorting or coercive effects.

2. Evaluations should be *continuous and cumulative.* Any evaluation as of a given moment is likely to be erroneous or incomplete in certain particulars. Furthermore, because goals change as conditions change, it is necessary for sound evaluative procedures to take such changes into account. The predictive significance of a given evidence of excellence may vary in such a way as to make that evidence of greatly unequal value on different occasions. Thus evaluations should be made regularly over a period of time.

3. Evaluations should be *comprehensive and conclusive.* Because in any given situation multiple goals are usually being sought, it is necessary to find out the extent to which each of the goals is being attained. It is clear that, in certain instances, success in achieving certain goals may be offset by losses with respect to other goals. Whereas individuals or institutions should be evaluated on the basis of a "total pattern" of characteristics, it should be recognized that superiority in some characteristics may be regarded as compensating, to some extent, for deficiencies in others.

4. The primary purpose of all evaluative procedures is that of *encouraging and promoting improvement* with respect to the condition or activity being evaluated. Consequently, all evaluative procedures should provide for specific, constructive suggestions for improvement. In general, effective evaluation will make slight and incidental, if any, use of inter-individual or inter-institutional comparisons; rather it will compare the record of the given individual or institution at successive time intervals and always in the light of the individual's or institution's unique needs and purposes.

5. In view of the essential nature of evaluation (making value judgments of the progress being made toward specific objectives) and of the basic purpose of evaluation (improvement of a condition or a process), it is clear that sound evaluative procedures will involve the *actual participation* of the person or institution concerned; that is, effective evaluation will emphasize self-appraisal activities. However, this statement does not exclude the use of outside persons or agencies who, on invitation, may be prepared to serve in a resource or consultant capacity on various technical aspects of the evaluation program.

6. All evaluations should involve *three fundamental processes:*
   (a) the formulation and acceptance of specific values or goals
   (b) the securing of specific evidence relative to the existence, quantity, and quality of a condition or a process

(c) the act of making a judgment, in light of available evidence, concerning the extent to which the desired values or goals have been attained

It is obvious that evaluative techniques will be sound and effective in proportion to the accuracy and precision with which each of these three processes is carried out. For example, evaluations may be imperfect because of an inadequate formulation and analysis of objectives; that is, objectives may be stated in such value-laden or general terms that it is difficult or impossible to secure appropriate evidence concerning their realization. Because all evaluations are based on evidence of some sort, it is clear that evaluations will tend to be successful in proportion to the quantity and quality of the evidence available. In the same way, the worth or soundness of an evaluation will depend on the extent to which critical, reflective thinking has been employed in relating the obtained evidence to the objectives sought.

Among the criteria that Swanson (8) applies to vocational education are the following. If evaluation is to be meaningful, it must be considered in the context of principles such as these.

1. *Vocational education programs must develop and maintain input standards.*
   (a) *The student must have the aptitude, the ability and motivation necessary to succeed in the assigned program.*
   (b) *The teacher must have extensive training and experience in the occupation or technology to be taught.*
   (c) *The equipment and supplies must be similar to the equipment and supplies used by the student when employed.*
   (d) *Instruction materials must be organized in a manner to give an adequate curriculum for the specific program of instruction.*
2. *Vocational education must develop and maintain output standards.*
3. *The content of vocational programs must be realistically related to the requirements of the labor market.*
4. *The number of persons in training must be related to the number of persons who will be needed by business, industry, commerce, and government.*
5. *Vocational education must involve business, labor, industry, and government as well as schools.*

BENEFITS OF EVALUATION

The benefits of evaluation may be applied to the overall vocational education program, to individual curricula, to single courses, or to experiences and activities within individual courses.

The Center for Research in Vocational Education developed the *Innovations Evaluation Guide*, which provides criteria to aid educators in evaluating programs. The format of this guide allows the evaluator to do a step-by-step analysis of benefits and costs. Potential users include classroom teachers, school administrators, state supervisors, local education agency project directors, state department personnel, teacher educators, and research and development personnel. By providing information for the applicable characteristics, the evaluator can gain support and approval from those who are affected by his or her decision.

The following checklist from the guide (9) summarizes benefits as they relate to programs affecting individual pupil growth, program operations, cost effectiveness, and so on.

Individual student growth

1. What effect does the program have on the rate of student learning? 2. How does the program affect the number and type of learning experiences and/or skills to which the students will be exposed? 3. What effect on attitudes can be attributed to the program? Are there experiences that assist students in the development of their self-concepts and their abilities to relate to other individuals?

Program operations

1. What information is available that will allow a cost benefit analysis of the program? How does this analysis compare to the present status of other alternatives? 2. What evidence indicates the program is achieving the required objectives to our satisfaction?

Society and the economy

1. What effect does the program have on increasing the opportunities to acquire job-entry skills? 2. What effect does the program have on productivity and costs to society in relation to such items as wages, occupational mobility, and school drop-out rates? 3. What attempts are made to create an awareness of society through the teaching of concepts concerning institutions, laws, cultures, and social problems? 4. What benefits accrue to the school and community from the program? What effect does the program have on school and community relations and the public image of the school?

Credibility

1. What evidence indicates that the program is achieving its objectives? 2. Where has the program been tested previously? How similar are these settings to our situation?

Costs

1. What is the cost per unit over time? Does the program involve a savings? 2. How is the program funded? Is the cost borne locally, or is assistance avail-

able wholly or in part from state, federal, or public sources such as foundations? What are the possibilities of reallocating present budget items to accommodate installation? 3. What processes and/or procedures are followed to acquire the necessary funding? Is the local educational agency in a position to expend its own money and be reimbursed later, or are funds from other sources available prior to expenditure? 4. In what proportion are funds available from other sources? Do matching funds have to be local funds? 5. What limitations are placed on the use of other funds? Are funds used for instruction only, equipment and instruction, or equipment, supplies, and instruction? Are funds used for items such as construction, food, transportation, or consultants?

Time considerations

1. How much time does it take to get the program working? 2. What deadlines are placed on activities prior to the operating date? How much time is necessary to order and receive items such as texts and materials? How much time is needed to order, receive, and install equipment? Does the program require teacher orientation or advanced teacher planning time? 3. How much time must be devoted to planning by a teacher, coordinator, or administrator during each week? 4. What amount of time is required by the teacher in daily preparation, classroom activities, meetings, etc.? 5. What characteristics of the program dictate that it be installed at a particular time during the calendar or academic year?

Installation considerations

1. What barriers can be anticipated from the community, school personnel, or students concerning the program? 2. What is the extent of involvement necessary to install the program? How many staff members, students, schedules, classrooms, laboratories, or schools are involved? 3. What are the requirements concerning extent of installation? Can it be trial tested by the adopting unit before complete installation of the total product? 4. What changes in policy on the state and local level are necessary in order for the program to be successful? 5. Is the program in an installable form or does it require more development? Are additional materials or training activities necessary? 6. What evidence is there to indicate that the program will work in our situation? 7. What adjustments can be made to meet local conditions without damaging the authenticity of the program?

Organizational change

1. What interruption of routine is required by the program due to rescheduling of classes, retraining of teachers, sharing of facilities, etc.? 2. What effect will the program have on the present school or department structure? Does it create a need for a separate division or department? 3. What changes in duties and/or responsibilities are necessary for successful operation of the program? 4. What

new kinds of relationships among departments or grade levels will be necessary for successful operation of the program?

Personnel needs

1. What additions to the staff are required? How many part-time or full-time people per unit are needed? 2. What staff experiences are necessary for successful operation of the program? Do leaders need to have a knowledge of the community? 3. What requirements are necessary for the development of certain roles, attitudes, skills, and competencies not presently possessed by personnel? Is the present staff capable of, and willing to handle, the personnel development necessary for the success of the program? Are consultants available?

Space requirements

1. Are present facilities sufficient? If not, what physical facilities are necessary to house the program? 2. What acreage is necessary for installing the program? 3. Does the success of the program require close proximity to ongoing programs or present facilities? On the other hand, is a separate location desirable? 4. What are the options to acquiring needed space for the program?

Equipment requirements

1. What are the major items of equipment or their components necessary for the operation and success of the program? 2. What supplies are necessary for the operation of the program?

EVALUATION SYSTEMS AND MODELS

Characteristic of the 1980s is the increased interest in evaluation by lay persons, legislators, and government agencies, as well as by school districts. The days of free spending and almost unlimited tax-dollar resources are coming to an end. Taxpayers and legislators are asking educators and other public agencies for justification of both proposed and existing expenditures. The increased use of systems in various facets of the educational process, such as curriculum construction and development of instructional materials, focuses additional attention on evaluation because it is built into systems models.

In view of the current interest in evaluation, various models have been introduced throughout the country. Two representative evaluation models will be considered briefly; each of these could be helpful in evaluating vocational programs or in developing other models. Before each model is discussed, however, an examination of the systems approach and its application to evaluation is in order.

Systems are made up of sets of interrelated components that function together. A systems approach, then, is a way of thinking about the overall system and its components. Systems analysis includes the evaluation of alternative means to accomplish a particular objective. Mushkin and Pollak (10) refer to systems analysis as a "process of comparing and assessing costs and benefits of competing programs to support choice."

Characteristics of Evaluation Systems

McCaslin (11) describes six desirable characteristics that an evaluation plan in vocational education or any other field should possess if it is to be useful and effective.

> *The first desirable characteristic of an evaluation system is that* realistic objectives *should be formulated. The formulation of these objectives should be realistic and involve both program and evaluation personnel. If there is basic agreement on these objectives, many misunderstandings can be avoided at a later time. However, it should be noted that mutual objective setting is not a panacea for avoiding conflict. In a practical sense, people operating programs have to believe in what they are doing; evaluation personnel, on the other hand, have to question what vocational education programs are doing. Both of these points must be reconciled in conducting the evaluation.*
>
> *Secondly, a sound basis for measuring these objectives must be established. In some cases, appropriate measurement techniques may already exist. In other cases, these techniques may require modification. In still other cases, development of new measurement techniques may be required. A caveat is necessary; there is often a tendency to measure those items that are easy and to ignore the most difficult ones. For example, information on the number of students completing a program may be collected when information on the students' job performance (after completing the program) should be included. The objective to be measured should dictate the type of information to be collected.*
>
> *A third desirable characteristic of an evaluation system is that of* clear and immediate feedback. *Feedback, in this instance, is considered a two-step process. First the administrator needs to inform the evaluator and/or program personnel of the adequacy of the evaluation results to meet decision-making needs. Secondly, the evaluation and program personnel need to provide information to those programs from which the data were collected. All too often, evaluation has been a one-way, upward flow of information. People at all levels of the education community resist filling out forms and providing data. Some procedures must be provided to insure that those who complete the forms understand the reasons for the collection of and use of the information. For example, local schools should have a summary of the information they submitted returned to them. Perhaps a comparison of the results with the comparable state figure would be helpful. It is also important that the information should be summarized in a manner easily understood and as brief as possible. If the*

evaluation feedback is voluminous, chances are it will be ignored. Certainly, all of the information needed by a state will not be the same type of information needed by a local educational agency. Whenever possible, these requirements should supplement one another.

A fourth characteristic is that the information collected by an evaluation system should reflect the original purpose(s) of the evaluation. In this regard, planning and budgetary information should be future-oriented. Information on performance factors and motivation can be present and/or past oriented. The major problem has been that the administrator did not develop clear purposes for the evaluation initially. This results in information that is not relevant to the administrator's decision-making requirements. Given that the evaluation results are relevant, evaluation reports should include the negative as well as the positive effects of the programs. Evaluation results should also include suggestions for potential alternative courses of action for decision-makers. Additionally, both the advantages and disadvantages of each alternative would be specified by the evaluator. The administrator must realize that both the alternatives and advantages and disadvantages will undoubtedly reflect the biases of the evaluator. Therefore, these must be interpreted in that regard.

A fifth characteristic of a desirable evaluation system is involvement of personnel interested in, and affected by, the program to be evaluated. Many evaluations have encountered problems due to apparent misunderstandings that have arisen due to the noninvolvement of personnel. It is important that program evaluation reflect a consensus of these personnel on a number of issues, including (a) the goals of the program; (b) the nature of the program services; (c) measures that indicate the effectiveness of the program in meeting goals; (d) methods of selection of participants and controls; (e) allocation of responsibilities for participant selection, data collection, descriptions of program input, etc.; and (f) the decisional purposes that evaluation is expected to serve. Although total agreement on each of these points will not remove all the problems, it is likely to minimize them.

A sixth, and final, characteristic to be discussed is that an effective evaluation system must be reasonable in cost. Administrators need to be aware of ongoing evaluation efforts and their cost in order that realistic budgets can be prepared. Typically, evaluation studies range from approximately 5–10 percent of the program budgets. As a general rule, the larger the program budget, the smaller will be that required for evaluation. It has not been uncommon for some personnel to think that evaluation can be conducted for as little as 1 percent or less of total budgets. Personnel costs alone make it extremely difficult to conduct meaningful evaluations for most programs at this rate of funding. Again, anything less than a total effort is a waste of resources.

Burnham (12) suggests five steps that are common to any systems approach to evaluation. The emphasis given to each step varies among the models and the headings differ, but the procedures are basically the same. The common steps are the following:

1. State the system objective *This refers to the outcomes of the system or subsystem being evaluated.*

2. Establish a criterion measure *The objective should be measurable or quantifiable to some extent. The more specific the objective, the better the measure, and the more rigorous the evaluation.*

3. Define the relevant variables *These are usually categorized as uncontrollable and controllable variables.*

4. Explicate the interactions between variables *How are the variables (men, material, money, tasks, time) interrelated?*

5. Analyze the interrelated variables in some technical model and enter the values each variable can assume *This involves input–output ratios, the extent of goal attainment, or simply the logic of the flow chart through the use of some decision rule.*

The final task of the evaluator, in any model, is to evaluate the evaluation. The criteria recommended by Stufflebeam (13) are closely related to those used to assess research:

Scientific Criteria	*Practical Criteria*	*Prudential Criterion*
Internal validity	Relevance	Efficiency
External validity	Importance	
Reliability	Scope	
Objectivity	Credibility	
	Timeliness	
	Pervasiveness	

In selecting an evaluation model, the vocational educator should consider at least two questions: 1. Is the model appropriate for the situation to be evaluated? 2. Are the evaluators capable of handling the complexities of the model? Evaluation models vary considerably in the complexity of design and intent. Some of the more complex models are not appropriate for use by persons who are untrained in evaluation.

CIPP Evaluation Model

The Context-Input-Process-Product Evaluation Model (CIPP), developed by Stufflebeam, is built on the theory that educational decisions may be classified

into four categories: planning, programming, implementing, and recycling—
and that for each there is an evaluation procedure (14).

> Planning decisions are those which focus needed improvements by
> specifying the domain, major goals, and specific objectives to be served.
> Programming decisions specify procedures, personnel, facilities, budgets,
> and time requirements for implementing planned activities. Recycling
> decisions include terminating, continuing, evolving, or drastically
> modifying activities.

Table 10.1 summarizes the four kinds of evaluation—context, input,
process, product—recommended to assess educational decisions and the relationship of each to decision making.

Stufflebeam (15) suggests that the structure of evaluation design is the
same for all types of evaluation. He outlines six major components that com-
pose the logical structure of a design.

1. *Focusing the evaluation*
   (a) *Identify the major level(s) of decision-making to be served, e.g.,
       local, state, or national.*
   (b) *For each level of decision-making, project the decision situations to
       be served and describe each one in terms of its locus, focus, timing
       and composition of alternatives.*
   (c) *Define criteria for each decision situation by specifying variables
       for measurement and standards for use in the judgment of alterna-
       tives.*
   (d) *Define policies within which the evaluation must operate.*

2. *Collection of information*
   (a) *Specify the source of the information to be collected.*
   (b) *Specify the instruments and methods for collecting the needed in-
       formation.*
   (c) *Specify the sampling procedure to be employed.*
   (d) *Specify the conditions and schedule for information collection.*

3. *Organization of information*
   (a) *Specify a format for the information which is to be collected.*
   (b) *Specify a means for coding, organizing, storing, and retrieving in-
       formation.*

4. *Analysis of information*
   (a) *Specify the analytical procedures to be employed.*
   (b) *Specify a means for performing the analysis.*

5. *Reporting of information*
   (a) *Define the audiences for the evaluation reports.*
   (b) *Specify means for providing information to the audiences.*

Table 10.1 The CIPP Evaluation Model: Strategies for Evaluating Educational Change (16)

	Context evaluation	Input evaluation	Process evaluation	Product evaluation
objective	to define the operation context, to identify and assess needs in the context, and to identify and delineate problems underlying the needs	to identify and assess system capabilities, available input strategies, and designs for implementing the strategies	to identify or predict, in process, defects in the procedural design or its implementation, and to maintain a record of procedural events and activities	to relate outcome information to objectives and to context, input, and process information
method	by describing individually and in relevant perspectives the major subsystems of the context; by comparing actual and intended inputs and outputs of the subsystems; and by analyzing possible causes of discrepancies between actualities and intentions	by describing and analyzing available human and material resources, solution strategies, and procedural designs for relevance, feasibility, and economy in the course of action to be taken	by monitoring the activity's potential procedural barriers and remaining alert to unanticipated ones	by defining operationally and measuring criteria associated with the objectives, by comparing these measurements with predetermined standards or comparative bases, and by interpreting the outcome in terms of recorded input and process information
relation to decision-making in the change process	for deciding on the setting to be served, the goals associated with meeting needs, and the objectives associated with solving problems, i.e., for planning needed changes	for selecting sources of support, solution strategies, and procedural designs, i.e., for programming change activities	for implementing and refining the program design and procedure, i.e., for effecting process control	for deciding to continue, terminate, modify, or refocus a change activity, and for linking the activity to other major phases of the change process, i.e., for evolving change activities

(c) *Specify the format for evaluation reports and/or reporting sessions.*

(d) *Schedule the reporting of information.*

6. *Administration of the evaluation*

    (a) *Summarize the evaluation schedule.*

    (b) *Define staff and resource requirements and plans for meeting these requirements.*

    (c) *Specify means for meeting policy requirements for conduct of the evaluation.*

    (d) *Evaluate the potential of the evaluation design for providing information which is valid, reliable, credible, timely, and pervasive.*

    (e) *Specify and schedule means for periodic updating of the evaluation design.*

    (f) *Provide a budget for the total evaluation program.*

Phi Delta Kappa Model

The Phi Delta Kappa National Study Committee on Evaluation proposed an evaluation process that comprises three major aspects—delineating information needs, obtaining information, and providing information—as illustrated in Figure 10.1.

Implementing this approach to evaluation calls for a logical series of steps, including (17):

1. *the determination of what is to be evaluated: for what kinds of decisions are evaluative data needed?*

2. *the kinds of data needed in making these decisions*

3. *the collection of the data*

4. *defining criteria for determining the quality of the matter being evaluated*

5. *analysis of the data in terms of these criteria*

6. *providing information for decision makers*

The Phi Delta Kappa evaluation design (Figure 10.1) does not include decision making as a component of the model itself, but rather stops at the point of providing information needed to make decisions. The designers of this model do not view decision making as a part of the evaluation process. Others, however, see decision making as an integral part of the evaluation process and as an obligation of the evaluator.

PROGRAM EVALUATION

In this section we shall discuss the elements involved in evaluating the curriculum, facilities, personnel, and teaching. Special consideration will be given

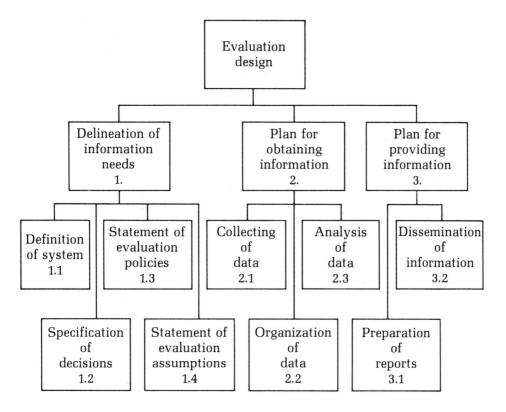

Figure 10.1 Phi Delta Kappa evaluation model (18)

to the use of needs assessment as a technique for getting at formative and summative evaluation of vocational education programs.

Formative-Summative Evaluation

An evaluation may be described as formative or summative, that is, process- or product-oriented. Summative (product) evaluation is concerned with judging the effectiveness of a curriculum, grading students, or assessing the effectiveness of personnel. Because it takes place at the culmination of a unit, course, or semester, it is frequently administered too late to provide remedial help for a particular person or program. Such data are valuable as assessments of overall effectiveness and as a basis for change in program elements. The most valuable summative-type evaluation is in the form of periodic follow-ups of the effectiveness of graduates in their jobs. Another example of summative evaluation is the annual evaluation report of vocational programs required of state advisory councils under the Vocational Amendments of 1976.

To be of value, however, evaluation must take place not only at the termination of a process but also during the formative stages, when the person or program is more susceptible to modification. Thus, formative (process) evaluation is concerned with collecting data to use as a basis for improving a program or process currently underway. Formative evaluation, as related to student assessment, for example, focuses on determining the degree of mastery of a given task, not on gathering data for grading the student. One of the basic objectives of formative evaluation is to provide feedback to students, informing them of both their accomplishments and their deficiencies. Such an evaluation provides clues to the teacher and student and allows them better to adjust the teaching-learning process.

Evaluation has two major purposes—accountability and program improvement. Accountability is an attempt to determine whether the results achieved can be equated to the resources expended. Evaluation for program improvement attempts to determine changes that will result in greater achievement of the objectives of the program. Obviously, the objectives of these two types of evaluation are not mutually exclusive.

Evaluating the Curriculum

In evaluation for program improvement, criteria can be divided into two categories—those items that *cause* quality (process evaluation) and those items that *show* quality (product evaluation). There must be a demonstrated relationship between the two types of items.

It has been said that a primary defense against an undesirable reaction to the many good programs in vocational education is careful evaluation of results to ensure the elimination of defective programs. To accomplish this end, there must be a climate of mutual trust and concern among administrators, evaluators, and teachers. Supervisory personnel can find in individual program evaluations some specific suggestions that, if used, can lead to program improvement.

Value judgment plays an important role in program evaluation. For example, selecting objectives and placing them in the order of priority involves the cooperative judgment of professionals and, to a certain degree, of parents, students, and community representatives. Judgments are involved at many different points during the completion of an evaluation study. However, the lack of completely objective measures should not hinder educators in their efforts to evaluate programs. Whenever programs are not evaluated, it becomes easy to lose sight of goals and to operate without change. Program evaluation requires the identification of program goals and a systematic, critical look to determine to what degree and in what ways the goals are being met. Figure 10.2 illustrates in more detail a typical model of curriculum evaluation.

Several elements should be considered in program evaluation. Plans for the evaluation itself should be made when the program is planned and begun.

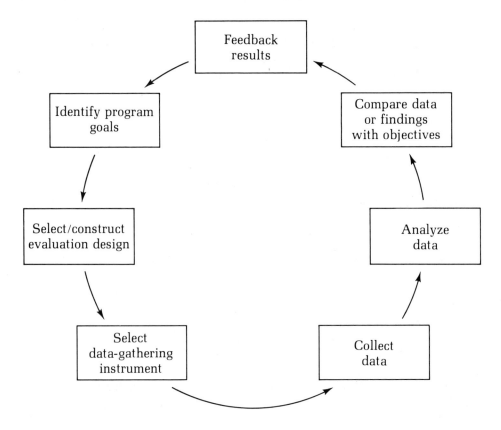

Figure 10.2 Model for curriculum evaluation

After goals are determined, these questions should be asked: 1. What means will be used to measure progress toward the goals? 2. What information will be needed to measure progress? 3. What data will be collected and maintained, and what steps taken, from the outset of the program, to ensure adequate information at a later time?

All persons who participate in vocational education should be involved in its evaluation. Such evaluation should provide for assessment of all goals of the program, both quantitative and qualitative. Evaluation should include a heavy emphasis on progress being made; that is, *where we were* versus *where we are* versus *where we want to be,* as well as comparisons with other programs and norms. Finally, program evaluation should be concerned with both long-term and short-term goals.

There have been extensive changes in vocational education curricula over the years, changes that have resulted in increased course offerings, expanded program objectives, new teaching strategies, a variety of instructional materials and media, and an emphasis on individualization. Through such means, voca-

tional educators are continuously seeking to find new ways to improve programs. Program changes, however, are sometimes judged by the wrong criteria.
For instance, frequency of use is often confused with effectiveness. In other
words, we tend to judge an innovation in terms of material, organization, and
how many schools employ it rather than in terms of the effectiveness of the
practice itself.

As the emphasis on evaluation and accountability continues, evaluation
instruments continue to be developed by vocational educators at national,
state, and local levels, at colleges and universities, through funded projects, by
individual researchers, and by accreditation agencies. Figure 10.3 provides
some abbreviated examples of evaluation instruments that may be used to
assess the organization of an individual classroom in vocational education.

Evaluating Student Progress

One measure of the effectiveness of the vocational curriculum or of institutional programs is the performance of students. The assessment of student
mastery of skills and knowledge is also a measure of teacher effectiveness.
Thus, student evaluation may be conducted for reasons other than those relating specifically to the student. At least three additional purposes for assessment of individual student progress may be identified. First, the individual
student is evaluated to determine his or her readiness to pursue the next step of
learning; this type of mastery test samples the concepts that are basic to the
next step in the learning sequence. A second basic purpose for assessment is
diagnosis, which is used either to place the student properly at the onset of
instruction or to discover the underlying causes of deficiencies in student
learning as instruction unfolds. A third purpose of assessment is to provide
individual guidance; a problem the guidance person faces is to identify enough
of the student's background to help him or her to take the next step.

Bloom et al. (19) summarize the function of diagnostic, formative, and
summative evaluation of student learning as follows:

Diagnostic

1. *Placement: Determining the presence or absence of prerequisite skills.*
   Determining the student's prior level of mastery.
       Classifying the student according to various characteristics known
   or thought to be related to alternative modes of instruction.
2. *Determination of underlying causes of repeated learning difficulties.*

Formative

1. *Feedback to student and teacher on student progress through a unit.*
2. *Location of errors in terms of the structure of a unit so that remedial*
   alternative instruction techniques can be prescribed.

Learner Characteristics	To high degree	To moderate degree	To slight degree	To no degree
Physiological				
• Are special sensory needs of learners met?				
• Are adequate safety measures carried out?				
• Do learners have sufficient opportunities for movement?				
Social				
• Is student-direction of learning situations encouraged?				
• Are students' group roles clearly defined?				
Affective				
• Is a reasonable opportunity for success insured?				
• Is stigmatization avoided?				
• Can the varied interests of students be met?				
Cognitive				
• Are the experience backgrounds of students utilized?				
• Can difference of learning rates be accommodated?				
Educational				
• Are planned experiences to meet specific skill needs possible?				
• Are sufficient opportunities provided for diagnosis?				

Figure 10.3 Checklist for evaluating classroom organization for vocational education instruction

Summative

1. *Certification or grading of students at the end of a unit, semester, or course.*

Current emphasis in student evaluation is focused on comparisons that are *intra-individual* rather than *inter-individual*. This emphasis represents a change from normative comparisons (that is, comparisons with other persons,

Instructional Goals

(This section would, of course, vary with the course objectives.
Sample questions might include:

	Always	Usually	Sometimes	Never
• Are a variety of teaching-learning methods practiced?				
• Are opportunities available for students to practice what they have learned? Etc.)				

Implementation

Teacher Personnel

• Is teacher expertise maximally utilized?
• Are teacher preferences and interests considered?

Data Collection

• Can adequate samples of student behavior (as applied to content) be obtained?
• Can information regarding growth in specific skills be obtained?

Materials

• Can a variety of materials be employed?
• Are the requisite materials within the school's financial resources?

Figure 10.3 *(continued)*

such as through use of standardized tests) to absolute comparisons (comparison with absolute standards, as in a teacher-made criterion test). Intra-student evaluation is concerned with measuring *what* rather than *how much* the student has learned.

The increased emphasis on evaluation has resulted in an increased use of tests and, consequently, a need for good testing procedures. The first step in attempting to evaluate students enrolled in vocational-technical programs is to write a set of measurable objectives. Next, appropriate evaluation instruments must be selected or constructed. A variety of instruments are available, such as achievement tests, aptitude tests, criterion-referenced tests, interest inventories, attitude scales, checklists, teacher-made tests, and observation. The instrument that is used must measure the objectives previously determined and must be of the appropriate level of difficulty for the students being evaluated. Measurement instruments will be treated in more detail later in the chapter.

Evaluating Vocational Personnel

The increased emphasis on evaluation strongly suggests that vocational educators should develop appropriate systems for evaluating system personnel. To an extent, the design will depend on the purpose of the evaluation. Some of the more commonly recognized purposes of teacher evaluation have been identified by Bolton (20):

1. *to improve teaching, including out-of-classroom activities as well as classroom instruction*
2. *to supply information for modification of assignments*
3. *to reward superior performance*
4. *to protect individuals or the school system in legal matters*
5. *to validate the selection process*
6. *to provide a basis for career planning and individual growth and development of the teacher*

One of the key factors in the success of personnel evaluation is the involvement, from the beginning, of all staff to be evaluated. It is essential that all persons be aware of and understand the purposes of the evaluation. "Morale cannot be high if staff members are fearful or hostile" (21).

To be effective the personnel evaluation system should provide for continuous feedback, with an emphasis on improvement rather than on fault-finding. Figure 10.4 illustrates a typical personnel evaluation model that vocational educators may employ.

Several different methods are used for evaluating vocational personnel. Teacher effectiveness is often measured by the degree of skill exhibited by the student, such as his or her accuracy in blueprint drawing, competency in automotive body repair, or speed in transcribing dictation. A more recent approach to personnel evaluation is the use of a job-target approach, or management by objective, in which the evaluator and evaluatee jointly agree on the desired or target job performance, the kinds of evidence to be accepted, and the initial level of performance.

As a means of measuring personnel effectiveness, competency-based approaches are also being used and are receiving increasing attention (see Chapter 8, Research and Development in Vocational-Technical Education). Vocational educators may be evaluated on the basis of competencies that generally fall into one of three categories: (a) in-classroom behavior of the teacher, (b) out-of-classroom behavior of the teacher, and (c) student accomplishment. Input into performance in these areas may come from peers, students, administrators, supervisors, paraprofessionals, and nonteaching personnel. Evaluative instruments for assessing the performance of teachers, department chairmen, supervisors, administrators, and aides have also been developed.

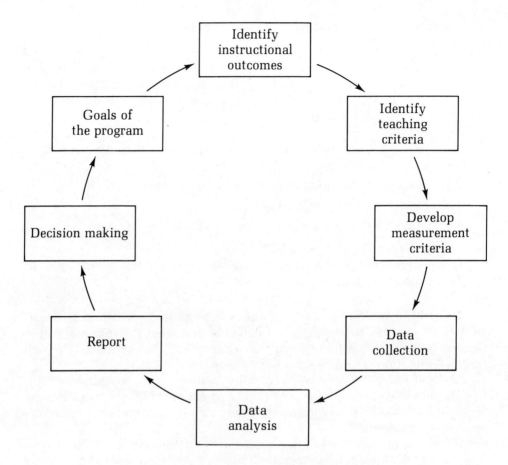

Figure 10.4 Personnel evaluation model (22)

Evaluation of Teaching

Teacher evaluation serves a dual purpose: it provides a comprehensive guide for diagnosis and for constructive supervision, and it makes possible reliable ratings of teaching effectiveness. The collective judgment of administrators and supervisors as to the relative effectiveness of individual teachers must not be an end in itself, but rather must serve the broader purposes of evaluation. At the same time, if the best teachers are to be selected, given tenure, and otherwise recognized, it is obvious that a sound basis must be established for determining the best teachers.

Criticisms of procedures and devices used in rating teachers focus largely on their subjectivity. Most rating scales are not only limited in content, but they call for a record of opinion only. Some of the newer instruments, however, are constructed so as to require actual observation of those practices, behaviors, and conditions that give concrete evidence of the quality of teaching. Subjective opinion is thus reduced to a minimum, and observed objective evidence becomes the basis for evaluation.

Much experimentation has been done to determine the amount of observation time necessary for an adequate evaluation of teacher effectiveness. Supervisors and administrators of vocational programs should recognize the importance of observing a teacher systematically, over a representative period of time and under a variety of conditions.

Many school systems follow the practice of setting up a presupervisory conference between the teacher and his or her immediate supervisor. Held early in the school year, such a conference may focus on identifying both short-range and long-range goals of the teacher. It also establishes baseline data against which the progress of the teacher may be measured during or at the end of the school year.

Teacher evaluation, if it is to serve both a guidance and a merit-rating function, must be a cooperative process. Although the actual practices and conditions being observed and the learning content being presented will vary from teacher to teacher, instructors should be allowed to familiarize themselves with the evaluation scale. If formal observation and rating is conducted, composite evaluations by two or more competent persons will increase the reliability of results. Also, as a morale factor, teachers will more willingly accept the joint ratings of two or more persons.

At this time, research on classroom evaluation of teachers reveals little statistical relationship between teacher effectiveness (as measured by student behavioral change) and subjective classroom observation. However, the following sample items from *The Teaching Evaluation Record* (23), a teacher-rating scale developed by Dwight Beecher for Educators Publishing Company, illustrates evaluation of performance based on actual observed evidence.

1. The teacher is fair and impartial   *The teacher's behavior is consistently unbiased.*

   Sample evidence   *Shows no favoritism or partiality; praise and criticism are based on fact; all criticism constructive; no pets; appraisal of students fair and reliable; no extensive criticism of individual students; maintains confidence of students.*

2. Teacher employs a variety of approaches in presenting new materials *Teacher shows adaptability and broad understanding of techniques in presentation of new methods.*

   Sample evidence   *Teacher uses many illustrations; utilizes suggestions from pupils as to methods and procedures; changes method quickly when it is obvious that methods being used are not effective;*

encourages students to try out several solutions; teacher and students discuss the relative merits of the various solutions.

Evaluating Facilities

The evaluation of vocational education facilities must take into consideration the total physical environment. The term *facilities* includes not only the building and its equipment and furnishings, but also its dimensions, types of surfaces (color of walls, type of floor, window coverings), amount of lighting, noise control and acoustical materials, air conditioning, and ventilation. Human beings are greatly influenced by their environment whether it is the classroom, the athletic field, or an office. Such physical factors as lighting, acoustics, and the use of color have psychological implications and so should be planned carefully to provide an atmosphere that is conducive to learning.

Evaluation of facilities may take two forms: evaluation *for* facilities and evaluation *of* facilities. Evaluation *for* facilities includes a definition of the nature and extent of the educational program to be offered and the development of long-range plans to house the program; it might include labor surveys, follow-up studies, and review of needs by an advisory council. Evaluation *of* school facilities involves the congruence of a particular building, site, and type of equipment with the educational program that is operated in the facility; it would thus compare the existing facility with the needs of the program being operated, taking into consideration such factors as instructional needs, safety, and aesthetics.

An examination of evaluation instruments for vocational education developed by state departments of education, the American Vocational Association, accrediting agencies, and others reveals that facilities evaluation is included in the evaluation criteria. The following sources include extensive treatment of facilities evaluation:

Lane Ash, *National Study for Accreditation of Vocational-Technical Education* (Washington, D.C.: American Vocational Association, 1972).

Milton E. Larson and Duane L. Blake, *Planning Facilities and Equipment for Comprehensive Vocational Education Programs for the Future*, Final Report (Fort Collins: Colorado State University).

Richard F. Meckley et al., *A General Guide for Planning Facilities for Vocational-Technical Education*, Final Report (Columbus: The Center for Vocational and Technical Education, The Ohio State University, 1969).

Harris W. Reynolds et al., *Evaluative Criteria for Vocational-Technical Programs* (Harrisburg: Bureau of Curriculum Planning and School Evaluation, Pennsylvania State Department of Education, 1967).

Research Series No. 45, "A System for State Evaluation of Vocational Education," Interim Report (Columbus: The Center for Vocational and Technical Education, The Ohio State University).

Evaluating Through Needs Assessment

Needs assessment as a process in curriculum development was discussed in Chapter 7. A need was defined as the *discrepancy* that exists between what is desired and what exists. Discrepancies may be identified between the actual and the desired or between two groups in terms of a given variable (for example, home economics students versus business education students on a variable such as economic understanding).

Once educational needs have been specified in terms of discrepancies, then measurable objectives can be generated by stating goals or objectives as the reduction of needs over time. Needs assessments may also be used to study the effect of interventions that are planned to reduce such needs, because the needs assessment describes the state of affairs that exists initially. In other words, a needs assessment presents a diagnosis—identification of the needs and their interrelationships. The most effective assessment is therefore one that is detailed enough to suggest a prescription.

To use needs assessment effectively, vocational educators need to be familiar with measurement and the collection and interpretation of data.

Needs assessment as formative evaluation

In some situations, the main difference between a formative and a summative evaluation is the purpose for which it will be used. The same is true of the needs assessment. During the formative stages of curriculum development, data from standardized tests, enrollment and attendance statistics, inventories of equipment, instructional materials, and library resources provide *validated* facts about the current conditions of the school.

Carefully constructed instruments (questionnaires, opinionnaires, interview schedules) are tools through which people (teachers, administrators, students, parents, community representatives) have a direct input into the curriculum construction process. The Appendix contains an example of an instrument that may be used to obtain *felt or perceived* needs. Because the instrument is concerned with obtaining data about a specific curriculum, it should be constructed to reflect the objectives, facilities, and instructional program of the particular school involved.

Needs assessment instruments do not need to be overly sophisticated, but they do need to be properly constructed to obtain the desired data. Suppose, for example, you want several graduates to rate the assistance they received at school in various activities. The specific objectives or competencies may be identified as a basis for student rating, as in the following example:

| | Amount of help from school | | |
Competency	Great deal	Somewhat helpful	Little/no help
1. Getting a job			
2. Preparing for further education			
3. Understanding my abilities and interests			
4. Using my money wisely			

Data gained from such an instrument reflect the felt needs of students and provide valuable input into the instructional planning and evaluation process.

Needs assessment as summative evaluation

To what extent do the people involved feel that the curriculum has been effective in realizing its objectives? Has a program designed, for example, to reduce absenteeism and the school drop out rate been successful? Is the achievement of students enrolled in an individualized instruction program equal to or superior to that of students enrolled in traditional programs? These are typical of the questions that might be raised at the end of a trial period for a revised curriculum or pilot program. The same or similar instruments that were used in formative evaluation now become instruments for summative evaluation.

MEASUREMENT AND DATA COLLECTION

This section of the chapter focuses on some of the more common instruments used in evaluation, including standardized tests, criterion-referenced measures, performance (work-sample) tests, rating scales, and inquiry forms. Informal evaluation procedures are also covered.

Standardized Tests

Standardized tests are usually classified as norm-referenced, which means that an individual's performance is examined in relation to the performance of other persons. The test manual should explain the characteristics of the population used to establish the norm.

Before selecting a test, consider the following steps:

1 Determine the purpose for testing

Because tests may be given for any number of reasons, the purpose for testing must be held clearly in mind so that an appropriate instrument may be selected.

2 Identify suitable tests

Several tests may appear to be appropriate for the purpose identified. One of the most useful sources of assistance in locating and selecting suitable tests is the *Mental Measurement Yearbook*, edited by Oscar K. Buros (24). Available tests are listed and described, including such factors as cost, coverage, source, and a critical review.

3 Evaluate the test

Before the final decision is made on a test, it should be carefully evaluated in terms of such factors as reliability, validity, economy, ease of administration, adequacy of the manual, relevance of norms, and appropriateness of content for students. One way to become familiar with a test is to take it yourself and then administer it to a few students. Specimen sets are available from publishers at a nominal cost.

Standardized tests possess several limitations that should be kept in mind:

1. Although a test may be standardized with regard to administration and scoring, it may be inappropriate for certain groups of individuals. Items may not be relevant or of the proper difficulty.

2. In an effort to develop a test that is brief, the test developer may sacrifice depth and breadth in sampling and may establish unrealistic time limits.

3. With certain students, group tests may not be the best measure of ability. Misread or misunderstood directions may result in incorrect responses to questions that these students may, in some other test format, answer correctly.

4. The format of the test limits the type of items used. For example, machine-scored tests are generally multiple choice, a format that does not adequately sample all behaviors.

Criterion-Referenced Measures

Recently there has been an increased emphasis on the use of criterion-referenced tests, which relate test performance to absolute standards that are usually stated in terms of behavioral objectives. These tests are especially valuable for assessing student mastery of specified objectives.

Otto (25) presents some contrasts between standardized achievement (norm-referenced) tests and criterion-referenced tests (absolute standards):

1. *Standardized tests have a low degree of overlap with the objectives of instruction at any given time and place. The overlap for criterion-referenced measures is absolute, for the objectives of instruction are the referents.*

2. *Norm-referenced tests are not very useful as aids in planning instruction because of the low overlap just mentioned. Criterion-referenced measures can be used directly to assess the strengths and weaknesses of individuals with regard to instructional objectives.*

3. *Because of their nonspecificity, norm-referenced tests often require skills or aptitudes that may be influenced only to a limited extent by experiences in the classroom. This cannot be so for criterion-referenced measures because the referent for each test is also the referent for instruction.*

4. *Standardized tests do not indicate the extent to which individuals or groups of students have mastered the spectrum of instructional objectives. There is no such problem with criterion-referenced measures because they focus on the spectrum of instructional objectives in a given situation.*

The reader is cautioned that the above comparisons are not to be interpreted as implying that norm-referenced tests are of no value and that criterion-referenced tests are the solution to all testing problems. It is not usually a matter of choosing between the two types of tests. Instead, the two types of measurement should complement each other, with the appropriate type chosen according to the testing purpose.

Criterion-referenced testing has limitations. The most obvious relates to the appropriate selection of objectives reflecting goals in the three learning domains: affective, cognitive, and psychomotor. Too frequently, the hard-to-measure qualities are slighted. Objectives that focus on initial mastery may take precedence over those that focus on retention of skill and application to a new situation.

Specifying the universe of tasks to be dealt with is of extreme importance. In no type of testing situation will a good test compensate for poor objectives. Of special importance to vocational education is the task of determining proficiency standards. Should perfect, near-perfect, or less demanding performance be required? Should the same standards apply to all situations? to all students?

At the present time the number of criterion-referenced tests on the market within the field of vocational education is somewhat limited. Consequently, teachers are confronted with the task of devising their own criterion-referenced instruments.

Performance Tests

One of the more common types of evaluation in vocational education is the performance test, in which the student is asked to demonstrate a given activity. The product, then, is evaluated according to a predetermined standard. This *work-sample* test requires the student to perform a segment of an operation using tools, materials, and methods that are characteristic of the total task. In most instances, these tests might best be classified as simulated-condition examinations that are based on essential job activities, presented in such a manner as to approximate the real work situation.

Consideration must be given to whether the product of the activity, the process, or both are to be observed and measured. In some cases, the obvious procedure is to evaluate the activity in process. For example, the techniques employed by a typist, such as position, touch, and evenness of stroke, provide clues that assist the teacher in diagnosing difficulties and in prescribing improved work methods. In other types of activities, in which the product is all-important, the scoring or evaluating should focus on the output. When possible, the product should be measured against an objective standard, such as a micrometer, ruler, gauge, or pattern. Not all products can be measured objectively. Sometimes more subjective measures such as checklists or rating scales are more appropriate.

Rating Scales

Earlier in the chapter we noted that it is not always possible to use an objective means of evaluating a student's performance. In many cases, a number of separate tasks must be accomplished producing the finished product, so a number of variables must be considered in evaluating the student's performance. One technique that has proved useful under these conditions is the rating scale. Figure 10.5 presents a sample rating scale for evaluating student performance in woodworking.

The use of such a rating system does not guarantee reliability in judging individual differences in students' performance. Unreliability in such judgments may be the result of a number of factors. For example, evaluating a task on which students show only small individual differences makes it difficult to establish reliability. In addition, inadequate instructions to the rater, lack of training in using these particular rating instruments, and poorly designed instruments may also cause unreliability.

Rating scales constitute a form of evaluation that relies heavily on subjective judgment of amount, degree, or quality. Such rating devices are used on the assumption that better judgment can be obtained on the overall product by focusing attention on one aspect at a time. They are also based on the assumption that the general value of the product can be approximated by a summation of the values of the parts.

The rating scale has proved useful in evaluating teacher performance. Since subjective evaluation may be biased by a number of different types of error, a carefully developed rating scale usually results in higher reliability than subjective evaluations made without the use of such a scale. Such instruments are now in general use in many colleges. Their use by students allows instructors to gain valuable insights into their teaching effectiveness as perceived by students—the chief beneficiaries of instruction. Likewise, they provide evidence of teacher effectiveness to the school administration. Such

1. *Evidence of excessive glue under finish/damage from glue*

1	2	3	4	5	6	7
Bubbles of glue under finish		Considerable discoloration		Slight discoloration		No evidence of glue

2. *Evidence of clamp damage*

1	2	3	4	5	6	7
Splitting		Deep impressions		Marred surface		No evidence of clamps

3. *Evidence of inconsistent clamping pressure in assembly (squareness)*

1	2	3	4	5	6	7
Parts do not fit		Considerable warp		Some distortion		All parts square

4. *Evidence of lamination problems*

1	2	3	4	5	6	7
Splitting/ open joint		Buckling/ wide joint		Slight offset		Flat/tight joint

5. *Evidence of the improper use of fasteners (screws)*

1	2	3	4	5	6	7
Not holding/ head-stripped		Loose/head damage		Poor seating		Secure/no head damage

6. *Evidence of the improper use of fasteners (finish nails)*

1	2	3	4	5	6	7
Bent nail/ surface damage		Nail showing		Under- or over-filled		Fill blends with surface

Figure 10.5 Evaluation form for a woodworking project. Source: *Handbook on Formative and Summative Evaluation of Student Learning* by Benjamin S. Bloom, J. Thomas Hastings, George F. Madaus. ©1971 by McGraw-Hill, Inc. Used with permission of McGraw-Hill Book Company.

evidence may be used to document promotion, raises in salary, or the reverse, as the case may be. The effectiveness of such instruments is further conditioned by their use, in good faith, by students, teachers, and administrators.

Inquiry Forms

When data are collected from respondents in a written form, the instruments are referred to as inquiry forms. Examples include schedules, questionnaires, and opinionnaires. Although often misused, the questionnaire can be a useful data-gathering instrument to the vocational educator if it is properly constructed and administered. Through its use, information can be obtained from varied and scattered sources. The typical questionnaire contains three types of items: (a) identifying information, (b) factual census-type data, and (c) subject matter items. The subject matter may be geared to solicit opinions, information, advice, or explanations.

The inquiry form is especially useful in conducting needs assessment. A well-constructed instrument can be used to collect data from a large number of students, teachers, parents, and business or community leaders. The ratio of returns to the number of questionnaires sent out is important, as is the representative nature of the replies. Thus the sample selected for the survey may be representative, but the results may be biased if only a small fraction return the form.

Informal Procedures

In the process of evaluation, situations arise that call for data that are not readily available from existing school records or examinations. Informal procedures provide an appropriate technique in such cases. Examples of informal procedures include the following: 1. *Informal observation*—an effective technique used by skillful teachers and supervisors for gathering information about students and other school personnel; purposeful observation can provide real insight into the performance of the student or teacher. 2. *Anecdotal records*—in their simplest form, a chronological collection of work samples and observation of happenings; these help the teacher keep in mind the developing characteristics of students. 3. *Informal tests*—teacher-made nonstandardized tests and evaluations that accompany instructional materials; this is a widely used technique that provides a quick check of student progress. 4. *Checklists*—generally in two categories: those completed by the student (such as questionnaires relating to work habits, inventories, and attitudes), and those completed by the teacher (such as assessments of the welding techniques used by a student).

MEASURING COGNITIVE, AFFECTIVE, AND PSYCHOMOTOR OUTCOMES

Because the goals of education are focused on the growth and development of the total individual, vocational educators must be concerned with cognitive, affective, and psychomotor behaviors. They must develop a thorough comprehension of students as thinking, feeling, moving beings. Without such com-

prehension, educators will continue to experience difficulty in selecting relevant learning experiences in the three learning domains.

Behavior may be conceptualized as falling into only one of the three
learning domains, even though, in reality, an individual's behavior is usually
observed as a combination of all three. When studying ways to bring about
desirable behavior change, educators must isolate behavior into component
parts; writing relevant behavioral objectives, educators in every curriculum
focus on the primary concern and categorize objectives into these three classifications.

Cognitive Domain

Historically our educational institutions have placed high priority on cognitive
outcomes. This emphasis may be attributed, in part, to the fact that our system
of education, as Bloom et al. (26) have stated, "is geared to producing people
who can deal with words, concepts, and mathematical or scientific symbols
so necessary for success in our technical society." Extensive research and development have produced the cognitive instructional strategies that are widely
used in our schools. However, the pedagogic techniques used in cognitive
development are not always appropriate to affective development.

Bloom et al. (27) present Baldwin's modification of the original cognitive
taxonomy, which they have found to be successful in working with industrial
arts teachers. The modified system contains four levels—knowledge, understanding, application of knowledge, and application of understanding. *Evaluation of knowledge* requires assessing the student's recall of specific information or responses previously practiced in learning experiences. At the
understanding level, behaviors such as interpretation, translation, summari-
zation, analysis, and detection of similarities and differences, which demonstrate understanding, as well as recall of knowledge are evaluated.
Application of knowledge calls for evaluating the student's ability to apply
previously learned knowledge to the solution of a known problem.

The most complex of the four levels is *application of understanding*. At
least one element of the problem, either in the condition or in the solution
required, must be new to the student; that is, it is expected that the student has
not experienced this problem before.

It is evident from the brief description of measurement of the cognitive
levels that evaluation strategies for the upper levels are more complex and
sophisticated. It is logical to assume that more formative evaluation is also
needed so that the student gains insight into the processes he or she uses or
misuses in the effort to realize educational objectives.

Affective Domain

There is general agreement that it is more difficult to measure objectively the
affective domain. In fact, how to evaluate affective objectives with validity,

reliability, and objectivity may well be the number one research problem presented by the affective domain. Although an individual teacher may successfully evaluate changes in student behavior at the lower level of the taxonomy—receiving and responding—it becomes increasingly difficult to measure changes on the more complex levels. For instance, the teacher will probably not be able to maintain the same standards over a sufficient period of time to observe measurable changes in the student's more complex affective behaviors. This difficulty suggests that evaluation plans for measuring affective behavior should cover several years and should involve the cooperative efforts of several teachers. Such an approach would permit the collection of longitudinal data necessary to appraise the more complex behaviors, such as valuing, conceptualization, and organization.

Another problem related to the determination of affective objectives is that it is not generally considered appropriate to assign a grade for attitudes, values, interests, and appreciations. Affective behaviors do not lend themselves as readily to paper-and-pencil measurement as do cognitive behaviors. There is also a greater possibility of "faking" desired responses, especially if the student believes that he or she is to be graded on them.

Formative evaluation is probably more appropriate than summative evaluation for assessing affective behavior. The diagnostic tools can provide feedback for students, indicating their progress toward predetermined goals. Both group and individual affective data are valuable. Group data, which make it possible for the individual to respond anonymously, provide evidence needed for curriculum decisions, whereas individual data are necessary for self-evaluation and guidance. Some of the more common tools used to measure affective behavior are the interview, open-ended questionnaire, closed-item questionnaire, semantic differential, and projective techniques.

Psychomotor Domain

In the psychomotor domain learning objectives emphasize muscular or motor skills, manipulation of materials and objects, or neuromuscular coordination. The psychomotor taxonomy of behaviors provides a framework for physical education, special education, fine arts, and vocational-technical education programs. In a sense, the psychomotor domain lends itself readily to the development and measurement of educational objectives because such behaviors are observable and so most of them can be objectively measured.

Research and study in the psychomotor domain has lagged behind that in the affective and cognitive domains. Psychologists have focused their research on motor behavior for which no specific training has been provided and which may thus be considered aptitude rather than achievement. Few, if any, of these tests are of value for measuring specific motor skills taught through vocational education programs.

The specification of educational objectives and, in turn, desired student behavior provides a framework for developing evaluation measures. Preparation of tables, in which the content or skill is listed on one axis and the taxonomical level on the other axis, helps the teacher to prepare or select measurement instruments that include the essential content in the desired proportion of its importance. Figure 10.6 provides an example.

An early model for classifying behaviors in the psychomotor domain was organized by Ragsdale (28), who categorized such behaviors as *object-motor activities* (manipulating objects), *language-motor activities* (recording, receiving, and communicating ideas), and *feeling-motor activities* (communication of attitudes, feelings, and emotions through the medium of movement).

Simpson's model (29) contains seven hierarchical classification levels, each containing several subcategories. Simpson's model is useful when analyzing one particular movement skill that a student is attempting to master. The learner goes through the phase of interpreting the stimulus (*perception*); he or she then prepares for active response (*set*); because the skilled movement is new to him or her, the learner must first initiate what he or she perceives the task or movement to be. After some imitation (*guided response*), the learner practices the movement through trial-and-error learning. When the learner has acquired confidence in his or her performance of the movement, he or she is at

Content/skills	Mechanism	Complex overt response	Adaptation	Origination	Total test items
1.					
2.					
3.					
4.					
5.					
Total test items					

Figure 10.6 Matrix for developing test items in the psychomotor domain. Note that this matrix is based on Levels 4–7 of Simpson's taxonomy because these are the levels that are appropriate for vocational education evaluation. Levels 1–2, perception and set, are not readily observable behavior. Level 3, guided movement, may be classified as formative evaluation in the early stages of certain skills.

the *mechanism* level; in other words, the movement pattern becomes habitual, progressing into a smooth *complex overt response*. When the learner has mastered the skilled movement, he or she is able to modify it (*adaptation*) and then to create movement patterns based on the acquired skilled movement (*origination*).

Harrow (30) provides a model complete with classification levels, subcategories, and divisions for classifying movement unique to the psychomotor domain. Level 1 is *reflex movements* (unconscious); Level 2 is categorized as *basic-fundamental movements* (inherent motor patterns based on reflexes); Level 3 lists *perceptual abilities* (cognitive-psychomotor; that is, data used by the brain centers for making response decisions); Level 4 comprises *physical abilities* (foundational to skill development and including strength, agility, endurance, etc.); Level 5 defines *skilled movements* (movements that are considered reasonably complex and that require learning—divided into beginning, intermediate, advanced, and highly skilled levels); Level 6 is *nondiscursive communication* (style of movement that communicates feelings about one's objective self to the perceptive observer). Table 10.2 summarizes these three models for classifying behaviors in the psychomotor domain.

Many of the psychomotor tasks in vocational education result in products that can be evaluated as evidence of degree of mastery of the psychomotor skill. Figure 10.5, an evaluation form for a woodworking project, is one such example. The evaluation of a typed letter would represent a means of assessing a student's mastery of the keyboard. Psychomotor tests designed to assess student performance of a specific skill may be more commonly known as work-sample or performance tests, a subject that was discussed earlier in the chapter. In objective measurement of the student's performance, the teacher may use an educational standard or an employment standard to which he or she compares the object or product being judged.

There are problems unique to psychomotor testing. In the majority of cognitive tests, the instructions are written and are the same for all students. In many situations involving psychomotor testing, however, the directions are given orally on an individual or small-group basis, which increases the chance of variation and so may produce differing results in student performance. Individual and small-group evaluation makes it more difficult to control environmental factors. It is also important that materials, tools, and equipment be comparable for all students.

A learner's intention to use a newly acquired skill makes the acquisition of that skill more personally important. A student learns to type to facilitate work as a teacher aide or in the school office; a student may learn to work with engines to maintain his or her automobile. Learners convert opportunities into learning when they recognize the personal values of the particular skill. Frequently, the skill (typing, engine repair, etc.) also involves income-producing aspects, which further enhance the learning potential.

If the primary concern of the vocational educator is to bring about manipulative or movement behavior change in the learner, the educational goal is

Table 10.2 Three Models for Classifying Psychomotor Behaviors

Ragsdale model	Simpson model	Harrow model
1 object-motor (manipulating or acting with direct reference to an object)	1 perception (interpreting) 2 set (preparing)	1 reflex movements (segmental reflexes, intersegmental reflexes, suprasegmental reflexes)
2 language-motor (movements of speech, sight, handwriting)	3 guided response (learning) 4 mechanism (automatizing)	2 basic-fundamental movements (locomotor movements, nonlocomotor movements, manipulative movements)
3 feeling-motor (movements communicating feelings and attitudes)	5 complex overt response (performing) 6 adaptation (modifying) 7 origination (creating)	3 perceptual abilities (kinesthetic discrimination, visual discrimination, auditory discrimination, tactile discrimination, coordinated abilities)
		4 physical abilities (endurance, strength, flexibility, agility)
		5 skilled movements (simple adaptive skill, compound adaptive skill, complex adaptive skill)
		6 nondiscursive communication (expressive movement, interpretive movement)

in the psychomotor domain, and the teacher can prepare a relevant evaluation of the stated goal. It should be recognized, however, that many educational goals will have cognitive, psychomotor, and affective aspects; in such cases, each aspect of the stated educational goal must be evaluated.

Throughout this chapter we have emphasized the importance of the role of judgment as a factor in evaluation and decision making. The main emphasis of the "professional judgment" approach to evaluation is that of application of professional expertise to yield judgments about quality or effectiveness of programs. In the discussion of accreditation that follows, self-study and the maintenance of defined standards are formalized.

EVALUATION FOR ACCREDITATION

The accreditation movement among school administrators, which has become the most formalized of the "professional judgment" approaches to evaluation, arose during the 1920s and 1930s in the United States. In accreditation, standards for schools, colleges, and universities are generally arrived at through the collective judgments of persons possessing some expertise in the field of education. Institutions are asked to undergo an extensive self-study, based on a set of guidelines (evaluative criteria) provided by the accrediting agency. (The evaluative criteria are published by the National Study of School Evaluation, 2201 Wilson Boulevard, Arlington, Va. 22201.) There are usually two sections of evaluative criteria, General and Subject Field, as follows:

General criteria

Section   1 Manual
           2 School and Community
           3 Philosophy and Objectives
           4 Curriculum
           5 Student Activities Program
           6 Educational Media Services—Library and Audiovisual
           7 Guidance Services
           8 School Facilities
           9 School Staff and Administration
           10 Individual Staff Member
           11 Summary of Self-Evaluation

Subject-field criteria

Section   4-1   Agriculture
           4-2   Art (including Crafts)
           4-3   Business Education
           4-4   Distributive Education
           4-5   Driver and Traffic Safety
           4-6   English
           4-7   Foreign Languages
           4-8   Health Education
           4-9   Home Economics
           4-10 Industrial Arts
           4-11 Mathematics
           4-12 Music
           4-13 Physical Education
           4-14 Religion
           4-15 Science
           4-16 Social Studies
           4-17 Special Education
           4-18 Trade, Technical, and Industrial Education

Experts conduct a site visit at regular intervals. Regional associations, such as the Southern Association of Colleges and Schools, reevaluate school programs once every ten years. (Separate commissions, within the association, are maintained for elementary schools, secondary schools, post–high school two-year vocational-technical schools, and colleges.) Using a set of criteria developed by the accrediting agency, the visiting team observes the operation of the institution, meets with officials, and talks with teachers, students, and others connected with the institution's operation. The visiting team deliberates on the quality of the program and writes a final report that is sent to the accrediting agency. Throughout its visit and in writing its recommendations, the visiting team takes a position of helpfulness. The agency then meets, deliberates, and takes any action that seems advisable. If deficiencies are found in the program, certification is withheld until the substandard conditions are corrected. Membership in the accreditation organization is entirely voluntary on the part of the schools, but schools do feel considerable pressure to join. (Both regional and state accrediting agencies are private organizations, and a modest fee is charged for membership services.)

The purpose of an accreditation agency is to stimulate the school to achieve and maintain a high level of professional competence. Colleges and state departments of education tend to place a premium on membership by high schools. Many colleges place restrictions on the admission of students from unaccredited high schools. Colleges, in turn, aspire to membership in state, regional, and specialized (for example, the National Council for the Accreditation of Teachers) accrediting associations as a symbol of professional excellence.

Accreditation is also available to private, proprietary schools through national, regional, and sometimes state organizations. For example, the national Association of Independent Schools of Business has done much to upgrade the quality of work done in the private schools of business.

Because of the leniency of laws in many states there are, unfortunately, flagrant violations by some organizations that establish schools for various purposes without adequate faculty, buildings, or facilities. Many of these schools advertise themselves as "universities" and offer graduate "degrees," sometimes through accelerated or correspondence-type courses or on the payment of a fee. Wherever such schools are found, it is the responsibility of the legislature and the state education department to investigate and take corrective action.

NATIONAL STUDY TEAMS

The National Institute of Education, charged by Congress with responsibility for basic research in education, is now involved in a four-year study of the impact of vocational education. Its findings are scheduled to be delivered to Congress and the president prior to hearings on the reauthorization of the Vocational Education Act in 1982. Likewise, the American Vocational Association appointed a series of planning and legislative task forces to prepare recommendations for the 1982 vocational education reauthorization legislation.

Evaluating the outcomes of vocational education is a key issue in the 1982 vocational legislation. It is essential to identify vocational education outcomes beyond program quality indicators. Outcomes of vocational education must show that significant contributions have been made toward increasing the productivity of the workforce (31).

SUMMARY

Evaluation in vocational education is a systematic process of obtaining information for judging the effectiveness of programs in relation to acceptable criteria or objectives. An effective approach is based on principles that reflect a clear sense of direction, flexibility to change, and a desire to improve and upgrade all persons, programs, and processes involved. The benefits of evaluation may be categorized in terms of individual student growth, program operations, society and the economy, credibility, costs, time and installation considerations, organizational change, personnel needs, and equipment requirements.

A systems approach to evaluation involves (a) stating what is to be evaluated; (b) establishing quantifiable criteria and data needed for making decisions; (c) collecting the data; (d) analyzing the data in terms of the criteria; and (e) evaluating the extent of goal attainment and providing information for decision makers. Such a systematic approach is employed in the Context-Input-Process-Product Evaluation Model (CIPP) and the Phi Delta Kappa Evaluation Model.

Program evaluation requires the identification of program goals and a systematic, critical look to determine to what degree the goals are being met. Cooperative judgments are involved at many different points during the completion of an evaluation study. Among the major elements to be evaluated are the curriculum, the progress of individual students, vocational personnel, the instructional process, and facilities. Evaluation of these determinants involves both formative (process) and summative (product) forms of evaluation. Summative evaluation is concerned with judging the effectiveness of the curriculum, grading students, or assessing the effectiveness of personnel at key terminal points. The basic objective of formative evaluation is interim feedback to the student. Competency-based approaches are increasingly being applied to program evaluation; these call for the performance of predetermined competencies.

Measurement and data collection represent key steps in the evaluation process. Formal measures used in vocational education include standardized tests, criterion-referenced measures, performance tests, rating scales, and inquiry forms. Informal measures used most frequently include observation, anecdotal records, informal teacher-made tests, and checklists. The purpose of most classroom measurement devices is to evaluate the extent to which a student has attained the objectives of a course. Classroom tests, however, may be developed to motivate learning, determine class progress, isolate individual learning difficulties, provide guidance data, aid in supervision, serve in re-search studies, and certify student employability. Needs assessment is consid-ered as a tool to establish collective involvement of those affected by the school program toward determining program needs. The needs assessment process may be viewed as both formative and summative in its purposes. As a formative evaluation technique, data are gathered from key school publics that provide input into the formation of the curriculum, facilities, and personnel. As a sum-mative evaluation tool, data are collected at the end of a given period of time to determine how well the goals of a program have been achieved.

Behavior may be conceptualized as falling into one of three learning domains—cognitive, affective, or psychomotor—even though, in reality, an individual's behavior is usually observed as a combination of all three. Educators are more proficient in measuring cognitive behavior because our educational institutions place high priority on training persons to work with words, concepts, and symbols that are essential to success in our society. It is more difficult to assess affective behavior than cognitive or psychomotor be-havior. Few instruments that are valid, reliable, and objective are available, and it is difficult to measure affective outcomes within a short period of time. Cooperative evaluation plans covering several years and involving the joint efforts of many people are needed. Commonly used instruments for measuring affective outcomes include interviews, questionnaires, semantic differential, and projective techniques. Many psychomotor tasks in vocational education result in products that can be evaluated as evidence of a degree of mastery of psychomotor skill. Performance tests, including work samples, provide a rela-tively objective measurement tool for appraising the student's output in rela-tion to a standard. Such tests are used both as formative and as summative evaluation devices.

This chapter also examines the role of accrediting agencies in relation to the evaluation process. National, regional, state, and local agencies are viewed as primarily consultative, providing judgmental and other assistance needed by vocational educators to maintain improved programs.

It has been said that teachers and administrators do not want to be evaluated or to expose their programs to public scrutiny except in a most favorable light. The school administrator's preoccupation with avoidance of conflict has been preempted by a barrage of value conflicts, which show that the school is no longer "one happy family." The threat of awakened minorities, the organizing of teachers, and voter disenchantment with rising taxes, all have eroded public confidence in the school system. People now want proof of good education; and it is here that evaluation must play an increasingly important role.

It would be naive to suggest that adequate evaluation models exist. The efficient compliance with a master plan (attractive in the face of disunity) argues for a systems analysis type of evaluation. But such highly centralized evaluation plans do not always coincide with the talents of the people who must deal with them. Some contend that the techniques of systems analysis would make our schools more impersonal and inflexible than they are now. There is no one alternative. But grandiose evaluation schemes cannot substitute for negotiation, compromise, personal influence, and other manifestations of political rationality.

Various techniques exist for evaluating instruction, cutting costs, and determining public opinion. Evaluation can help one group to communicate with another, and it can help the administrator to justify his or her program. Under the separation of powers within the school system, teachers can possess considerable autonomy in how they operate. At the same time, the administrator is justified in seeking some evidence of good work—and so is the public from the administrator. Such evidence should be gathered in modest proportions.

ACTIVITIES

For review

1. Compare a minimum of three definitions of evaluation, noting their differences and similarities. With which definition do you most nearly agree? Why?

2. Summarize at least four principles that should underlie an effective evaluation program.

3. What are two criteria that should be considered in selecting an evaluation model?

4. Differentiate between formative and summative evaluation and give an example of each.

5. What *informal* evaluation tool would a teacher use to note changes in a student's attitude?

6. How may a needs assessment be employed as a formative-type evaluation? As a summative-type evaluation?

7. What is a standardized test? What points should be considered in selecting such a test for use with students?

8. What advantages does the criterion-referenced vocational test have over the standardized test?

9. What is a work-sample and how is it used in vocational classes?

10. What types of instruments may be used for informal evaluation purposes?

11. Explain how accreditation is used in schools, colleges, or universities.

12. Briefly describe Bloom's cognitive taxonomy.

13. Identify some of the problems associated with measurement of the affective domain.

14. Describe at least one problem that is unique to psychomotor testing.

For discussion

1. Justify the inclusion of evaluation as a component of curriculum construction.
2. Explain the relationship of evaluation to decision making as illustrated in the CIPP model.
3. Justify the use of value judgment in evaluation.
4. Why should plans for evaluation be initiated in the early stages of vocational program planning?
5. What reasons can you cite both for and against the evaluation of teachers by their students?
6. Student accomplishment is an important measure of the performance of a teacher. What factors must be kept in mind when evaluating a teacher on the basis of student performance?
7. Explain how a rating scale might be used in evaluating vocational student performance.
8. The role of the department head is crucial to evaluation of teaching. Explain.
9. Cite a classroom situation for which teacher-made tests should be constructed even though published tests are available for the text being used in the course.
10. What caution should teachers observe in comparing classroom scores with national norms?
11. What are some of the tangible and intangible benefits to be derived from the evaluation of vocational programs?
12. To what extent may classroom examinations be regarded as *vocational* tests?
13. What are the chief strengths and weaknesses of accreditation-type evaluations?
14. Evaluate these statements. Do you agree or disagree with each of them? Give reasons for your answers.
    (a) "Teachers and administrators do not want to be evaluated or to expose their programs to public scrutiny except in a most favorable light."
    (b) "The techniques associated with a systems approach tend to dehumanize education."
    (c) "It is naive to think that adequate evaluation models exist."
    (d) "When a teacher tests, he or she is not teaching."

For exploration

1. What are the predominant issues facing vocational educators today? How are they related to evaluation?

2. Using the matrix in Figure 10.6, develop a test measuring psychomotor skill development for a short segment (one day to one week) for a vocational course taught in your school's curriculum.

3. Both state department of education personnel and accrediting organization personnel are concerned with standards. In what respect are such standards alike? In what respects are they different?

4. Read at least three magazine articles dealing with construction or use of performance tests. Prepare separate brief reports of the contents of each article, including a synopsis and the author's summary and conclusions. Give your criticisms of each article.

5. Analyze and comment critically on two selected teacher-made objective examinations, preferably tests obtained from classroom teachers.

6. Using the discussion in the chapter and the sample instrument in the Appendix, develop a needs assessment instrument for your vocational program. Include items related to philosophy and objectives, equipment and facilities, teachers, course offerings, instructional materials, methods, committees and organizations, and community employment needs.

7. Administer a needs assessment instrument to a sample of students, faculty, administrators, parents, and community representatives, and prepare a summary of the results. Emphasize the changes in the program recommended by the respondents.

8. Using the Checklist for Evaluating Classroom Organization, Figure 10.3, evaluate (a) a vocational class that you teach, or (b) a class taught by someone else.

9. Select one course that you teach and prepare a master plan for student evaluation to include the following:
   (a) objectives of the plan
   (b) type of evaluation to be used (diagnostic, formative, summative)
   (c) examples (standardized test, checklist, etc.)
   (d) time schedule

REFERENCES

1. Benjamin S. Bloom, J. Thomas Hastings, George F. Madaus, *Handbook on Formative and Summative Evaluation of Student Learning* (New York: McGraw-Hill Book Company, 1971), p. 8. (Reproduced with permission.)

2. P. A. Taylor and T. O. Maguire, "A Theoretical Evaluation Model," *Manitoba Journal of Educational Research,* Vol. 1, 1966, pp. 12–17; also in *Curriculum Evaluation,* David A. Payne, ed. (Lexington, Mass.: D. C. Heath and Company, 1974), p. 11.

3. Margaret Ammons, "Evaluation: What Is It? Who Does It? When Should It

Be Done?" in *Assessment Problems in Reading*, Walter H. MacGinite, ed. (Newark, Del.: International Reading Association, 1973), p. 69.

4. Wilbur Harris, "The Nature and Function of Educational Evaluation," *Peabody Journal of Education*, Sept. 1968; quoted in N. L. McCaslin, "Program Evaluation: Problems, Prerequisites, Characteristics, and Implementation," in *Improving Administrative Programs of State Vocational Education Agencies* (Columbus: Center for Vocational and Technical Education, 1974), p. 91.

5. Egon Guba and Daniel L. Stufflebeam, *Evaluation: The Process of Stimulating, Aiding, and Abetting Insightful Action*, address to the Second National Symposium for Professors of Educational Research (Columbus: Evaluation Center, The Ohio State University, 1968).

6. Ralph W. Tyler, *Basic Principles of Curriculum and Instruction* (Chicago: University of Chicago Press, 1949), p. 105.

7. Phi Delta Kappa National Study Committee on Evaluation, Daniel Stufflebeam, chairman, *Educational Evaluation and Decision Making* (Itasca, Ill.: F. E. Peacock Publishers, Inc., 1971), p. 40. (Reproduced with permission.)

8. J. Chester Swanson, "Criteria for Effective Vocational Education," in *Contemporary Concepts in Vocational Education*, Gordon F. Law, ed. (Washington, D.C.: American Vocational Association, 1971), pp. 23–24. (Reproduced with permission.)

9. William L. Hull and Randall L. Wells, *Innovations Evaluation Guide* (Columbus: The Center for Vocational and Technical Education, The Ohio State University, 1972).

10. Selma J. Mushkin and William Pollak, "Analysis in a PPB Setting," in *Economic Factors Affecting the Financing of Education*, R. L. Johns, I. J. Gaffman, Kern Alexander, and D. H. Stollar, eds. (Gainesville, Fla.: National Educational Finance Project, 1970), p. 329.

11. N. L. McCaslin, "Program Evaluation: Problems, Prerequisites, Characteristics, and Implementation," in *Improving Administrative Activities of State Vocational Education Agencies*, 6th Annual National Leadership Development Seminar for State Directors of Vocational Education, Daniel E. Koble, Jr., and Robert U. Coker, eds. (Columbus: The Center for Vocational and Technical Education, The Ohio State University, 1974), pp. 94–96.

12. Robert A. Burnham, "Systems Evaluation and Goal Disagreement," in *School Evaluation, The Politics and Process*, Ernest R. House, ed. (Berkeley, Ca.: McCutchan Publishing Corporation, 1973), p. 245.

13. Phi Delta Kappa National Study Committee on Evaluation, *Educational Evaluation and Decision Making*, pp. 27–30. (Reproduced with permission.)

14. Daniel L. Stufflebeam, "Toward a Science of Educational Evaluation," in *Evaluation of Education* (Englewood Cliffs, N.J.: Educational Technology Publications, 1973), p. 22.

15. Ibid., p. 25.

16. Ibid.

17. J. Galen Saylor and William M. Alexander, *Planning Curriculum for Schools* (New York: Holt, Rinehart and Winston, Inc., 1974), pp. 302-3.

18. Phi Delta Kappa National Study Committee on Evaluation, *Educational Evaluation and Decision Making*, p. 156. (Reproduced with permission.)

19. Benjamin S. Bloom et al., *Handbook on Formative and Summative Evaluation*, p. 91. (Reproduced with permission.)

20. Dale L. Bolton, *Teacher Evaluation* (Washington, D.C.: National Center for Educational Communication, 1971); quoted in J. Marvin Robertson, *Personnel Evaluation* (Columbus: The Center for Vocational and Technical Education, The Ohio State University, 1973), p. 3.

21. Ibid., p. 5.

22. Ibid., p. 2.

23. Dwight Beecher, *The Teaching Evaluation Record* (Educators Publishing Company, 1972).

24. Oscar K. Buros, ed., *The Eighth Mental Measurement Yearbook*, Vol. I and II (Highland Park, N.J.: Gryphon Press, 1978).

25. Wayne Otto, "Evaluating Instruments for Assessing Needs and Growth in Reading," in *Assessment Problems in Reading*, Walter H. MacGinitie, ed. (Newark, Del.: International Reading Association, 1973). (Reprinted with permission of Wayne Otto and International Reading Association.)

26. Bloom et al., *Handbook on Formative and Summative Evaluation*, p. 225.

27. Ibid., p. 864.

28. C. E. Ragsdale, "How Children Learn Motor Types of Activities," in *Learning and Instruction*, Forty-ninth Yearbook of the National Society for the Study of Education (Chicago: University of Chicago Press, 1950), pp. 69-91.

29. Elizabeth J. Simpson, "The Classification of Educational Objectives: Psychomotor Domain," University of Illinois Research Project No. OE 5, 1966, pp. 85-104.

30. Anita J. Harrow, *A Taxonomy of the Psychomotor Domain* (New York: David McKay Company, 1972), pp. 96-97.

31. Charles O. Hopkins, "Is the Proof in Our Planning and Evaluation?" *Vocational Education*, Vol. 54, No. 8, Nov./Dec. 1979, p. 62.

APPENDIX A

∎

Sample Needs Assessment Instrument

The format and content of a needs assessment instrument should be adapted to the educational, social, and business-industrial needs of each community. Input from educators, students, parents, and lay people is solicited during the formative stages of program revision.

The following instrument is a sample modification of a needs assessment originally developed by Marilyn G. Butler of South Gwinnett High School, Snellville, Georgia.

Part 1 provides an overall evaluation of the current business education program. Part 2 includes a detailed assessment of actual and ideal program priorities. The instrument could be adapted for use with any vocational program.

SAMPLE NEEDS ASSESSMENT FOR BUSINESS EDUCATION PROGRAMS

Part 1

Directions

Please evaluate the business education program at _____
in each of the ten areas described below. Under each heading are two descriptive paragraphs headed "Inferior" and "Superior," and five blanks labeled "Inferior," "Below average," "Average," "Above average," and "Superior."

Read each of the paragraphs. If the paragraph labeled "Inferior" describes current actual practices relating to business education, place an X in the first blank
("Inferior"). If the department meets all the criteria listed under the "Superior"
heading, place an X in the last blank ("Superior"). If the department meets
some, but not all, of the "Superior" statements, place an X in the most appropriate middle blank. Please list your recommendations for helping the department achieve a "Superior" rating.

A Instructional materials

INFERIOR. Little supplementary material is available. Textbooks and other
teaching materials are out of date and in poor condition. There is no centralized
instructional materials center.

SUPERIOR. Teachers regularly use such supplementary materials as books,
magazines, newspapers, transparencies, filmstrips, films, tapes, and sound-
slides. A multimedia center for the department provides a check-out and
check-in system. Materials and equipment are up to date, maintained in good
operating condition, and in frequent use. Money is allocated for rental of films.

Inferior	Below average	Average	Above average	Superior
_____	_____	_____	_____	_____

Action needed to close the gap:

B Library resources

INFERIOR.   Library is poorly stocked—no subscriptions to business periodicals;
no references for economics, business law, or secretarial science. There are few
audiovisual aids and very little encouragement to students and staff to use
facilities.

SUPERIOR.   Library has comprehensive, extensive collections, including
periodicals; national, state, and local newspapers; economics and law books;
secretarial handbooks; file of pamphlets for use in business classes. Library is
open before and after school as well as during school hours. Qualified librar-
ians assist and encourage student and staff use. Audiovisual section has sufficient number of projectors of various types, recorders, record players, and
cassette tape players, overhead projectors, and opaque projectors.

Inferior	Below average	Average	Above average	Superior
_____	_____	_____	_____	_____

Action needed to close the gap:

C Physical facilities and equipment

INFERIOR. Classrooms are too small, with insufficient electrical outlets for multipurpose requirements. Environmental conditions of the classrooms are not conducive to concentration and efficient work.

SUPERIOR. There are at least two multipurpose classrooms with sufficient electrical outlets for machines; two typewriting classrooms with provisions for electrical typewriters; one general purpose classroom furnished with tables suitable for accounting instruction. Environmental conditions in all classrooms are conducive to businesslike work.

Inferior	Below average	Average	Above average	Superior
_____	_____	_____	_____	_____

Action needed to close the gap:

D Staff

INFERIOR. Fewer than 10 percent of the staff members possess master's degrees. Staff does not keep abreast of current trends and methods; shows little interest in teaching as a profession; little enthusiasm. Staff members do not possess practical work experience.

SUPERIOR. At least 60 percent of the staff members possess master's degrees. All staff members are engaged in staff development activities for improving skills and keeping up to date with research and developments in business education. They are enthusiastic, active participants in professional organizations and growth activities, including work experience.

Inferior	Below average	Average	Above average	Superior
_____	_____	_____	_____	_____

Action needed to close the gap:

E Course offerings

INFERIOR. The business education program offers basic instruction in typewriting, shorthand, accounting, business English, and business mathematics. No advanced classes are offered, and there are no courses in consumer economics or business organization and management, and no cooperative work-study program.

SUPERIOR.   A variety of courses are offered in the program. Courses are offered for vocational, job-entry skill development as well as for personal use. In addition to basic skill and career exploration courses, advanced classes and a cooperative vocational office training work-study program are provided.

| | Below | | Above | |
Inferior	average	Average	average	Superior
_____	_____	_____	_____	_____

Action needed to close the gap:

F   Instructional methods

INFERIOR.   Instruction is based on the lecture method, with all students working at the same speed.

SUPERIOR.   A variety of instructional strategies are used, fitting the method to the particular group and/or topic. There is recognition that students learn optimally at different rates and through different modes and provision is made for individualized instruction wherever possible. Students are involved in determining goals and self-evaluation. Instruction is well planned and provides immediate feedback to students concerning progress.

| | Below | | Above | |
Inferior	average	Average	average	Superior
_____	_____	_____	_____	_____

Action needed to close the gap:

G   Community employment needs

INFERIOR.   Students are given little or no employment information about job opportunities in the area and no preparation for job interviews. Course offerings are not adapted to changing job requirements or varying needs of the students in achieving job success.

SUPERIOR.   Job and career information is integrated into the classes wherever appropriate. A career information center is provided by the counseling department. Instruction in interview and job application techniques is given. As job requirements and employment needs change, attention is given to the feasibility of adaptation of course offerings and instruction.

| | Below | | Above | |
Inferior	average	Average	average	Superior
_____	_____	_____	_____	_____

Action needed to close the gap:

H Equipment used in business and industry

INFERIOR. Equipment in the business education program is obsolete. Type-writers, transcribing machines, calculators, and data processing equipment are out of date. No provisions are made for replacement on a regular basis.

SUPERIOR. Equipment is replaced on a regular basis (every 3–5 years). Demonstration of equipment by office suppliers and field trips to companies enable students to learn about modern equipment that cannot be purchased by the school. Equipment used for instruction is representative of that used in the employment community.

Inferior	Below average	Average	Above average	Superior
_____	_____	_____	_____	_____

Action needed to close the gap:

I Advisory committee

INFERIOR. An advisory committee does not exist, or it functions in name only. No opportunities are provided for the committee to make suggestions to the school or to be involved in curriculum planning and evaluation.

SUPERIOR. An advisory committee is actively involved in a consultative role, advising the business education teachers about office-job requirements, job opportunities for graduates, and appraisal of the effectiveness of the job preparation of students.

Inferior	Below average	Average	Above average	Superior
_____	_____	_____	_____	_____

Action needed to close the gap:

J Youth organizations

INFERIOR. A youth organization exists (Future Business Leaders of America, Office Education Association, Pi Omega Pi, etc.), but there is little student interest and little encouragement of student participation.

SUPERIOR. Students actively participate in the business youth organization. They are provided opportunities to deal with actual problems. Membership is voluntary, and activities are conducted during school and after school. The club is highly visible to the community.

Inferior	Below average	Average	Above average	Superior
_____	_____	_____	_____	_____

Action needed to close the gap:

Part 2

Directions

Read each of the following statements describing a specific practice or principle relating to business education. Under the column headed "Actual," place an X in the appropriate blank to indicate your agreement or disagreement with this practice or principle as it is presently carried out in the school. Under the column headed "Ideal," place an X in the appropriate blank to indicate a recommended view of the principle or practice.

Actual			Philosophy and objectives	Ideal		
Yes	No	No opinion		Yes	No	No opinion
___	___	_____	**1** The basic purpose of business education is job preparation.	___	___	_____
___	___	_____	**2** Business education has two objectives: personal use and job preparation.	___	___	_____
___	___	_____	**3** A major objective of business education is to prepare students to be intelligent consumers.	___	___	_____
___	___	_____	**4** Business students try to specialize in one field, such as clerical, secretarial, management, or data processing.	___	___	_____
___	___	_____	**5** Business education objectives are developed by the faculty.	___	___	_____

Actual			Equipment and facilities	Ideal		
Yes	No	No opinion		Yes	No	No opinion
___	___	___	**6** Electric typewriters are provided in all typewriting classes.	___	___	___
___	___	___	**7** An office training classroom is set up like a modern business office.	___	___	___
___	___	___	**8** A variety of name-brand business machines are provided.	___	___	___
___	___	___	**9** The business program uses modern equipment similar to that in an up-to-date business office.	___	___	___
___	___	___	**10** All business education rooms are adjoining.	___	___	___
___	___	___	**11** The business education department is air conditioned.	___	___	___
___	___	___	**12** The business education department operates a center containing audiovisual materials and equipment and other resources.	___	___	___
___	___	___	**13** Each business education lab is equipped with adequate storage space, filing cabinets, and counter space.	___	___	___
___	___	___	**14** Selection of equipment is made by business education teachers.	___	___	___
___	___	___	**15** Instruction is offered in the use of the full-key adding machine.	___	___	___
___	___	___	**16** Instruction is offered in the use of the electronic calculator.	___	___	___

			Equipment and facilities (continued)			
Actual				**Ideal**		
Yes	No	No opinion		Yes	No	No opinion

			17 Instruction is offered in the use of the IBM Selectric typewriter.			
—	—	————		—	—	————
			18 Instruction is offered in the use of transcribing equipment.			
—	—	————		—	—	————
			19 Instruction is offered in the use of key-punch equipment.			
—	—	————		—	—	————
			20 Instruction is offered in the use of unit record equipment.			
—	—	————		—	—	————
			21 Instruction is offered in the use of computer terminals.			
—	—	————		—	—	————

Business teachers

			22 Business education teachers have a baccalaureate degree.			
—	—	————		—	—	————
			23 Business teachers are employed on a 12-month contract.			
—	—	————		—	—	————
			24 Business teachers are highly proficient in the skills they teach.			
—	—	————		—	—	————
			25 Business teachers are broadly trained in the field.			
—	—	————		—	—	————
			26 Business teachers are required to update methods through in-service or college courses.			
—	—	————		—	—	————
			27 Business teachers are required to have one year of work experience.			
—	—	————		—	—	————

**Business teachers
(continued)**

Actual				Ideal		
Yes	No	No opinion		Yes	No	No opinion

28 Business teachers acquire practical work experience by working in an office for three months every five years.

___ ___ _____   ___ ___ _____

29 Business teachers are specialists in the use of audiovisual equipment.

___ ___ _____   ___ ___ _____

30 Business teachers are trained in specialized areas such as data processing, accounting, and shorthand.

___ ___ _____   ___ ___ _____

31 Business teachers make frequent surveys of business education programs in other schools for comparison and suggestions.

___ ___ _____   ___ ___ _____

Course offerings

32 Typewriting is offered at the eighth-grade level.

___ ___ _____   ___ ___ _____

33 Typewriting is required of all high school students.

___ ___ _____   ___ ___ _____

34 Consumer education courses are offered by the business program.

___ ___ _____   ___ ___ _____

35 Shorthand is offered even though there is widespread use of transcribing equipment in business.

___ ___ _____   ___ ___ _____

36 A course in data processing is offered to high school students.

___ ___ _____   ___ ___ _____

	Actual		Course offerings (continued)		Ideal	
Yes	No	No opinion		Yes	No	No opinion
—	—	————	**37** Instruction in the use of modern duplicating equipment is required of all vocationally-oriented students.	—	—	————
—	—	————	**38** Quarter hours of credit are given according to the percentage of work completed rather than on a pass-fail basis.	—	—	————
—	—	————	**39** The business math course is limited to students interested in a business career.	—	—	————
—	—	————	**40** An introductory course exploring business careers is offered at the ninth-grade level.	—	—	————
—	—	————	**41** A suggested program of study is available for students who are interested in pursuing a business career.	—	—	————
—	—	————	**42** A work-study program is provided for vocationally-oriented students.	—	—	————
—	—	————	**43** Business education courses are provided in one-hour periods.	—	—	————
—	—	————	**44** Business education courses are taught on a flexible schedule.	—	—	————
—	—	————	**45** Advanced business education skill courses are taught in a block (two or more periods).	—	—	————

	Actual		Instructional methods and materials		Ideal	
Yes	No	No opinion		Yes	No	No opinion
___	___	_____	**46** Students are allowed to work at their own rate.	___	___	_____
___	___	_____	**47** Students are able to contract for grades according to the amount of work completed.	___	___	_____
___	___	_____	**48** Evaluation in advanced skills courses is based on accepted business practices.	___	___	_____
___	___	_____	**49** Students are able to choose units of work according to vocational interests.	___	___	_____
___	___	_____	**50** Instruction includes a variety of resources including community personnel as speakers, field trips, etc.	___	___	_____
___	___	_____	**51** Instruction in office skills includes simulated job activities.	___	___	_____
___	___	_____	**52** Students are allowed to evaluate teachers.	___	___	_____
___	___	_____	**53** Students are involved in cooperative evaluation of their work.	___	___	_____

Community employment needs

	Actual				Ideal	
___	___	_____	**54** Students are given information about job opportunities in the employment community.	___	___	_____
___	___	_____	**55** Periodic follow-up studies are conducted to determine the relationship between course offerings and occupational roles.	___	___	_____

	Actual		**Community employment needs (continued)**	**Ideal**	
Yes	No	No opinion		Yes	No	No opinion

56 Counseling and placement services are provided.

57 Frequent surveys are made to determine the type of office machines used in the business community.

Committees and organizations

58 An advisory committee is used in a consultative role.

59 Former students serve on advisory committees.

60 People in business are included on the advisory committee.

61 Each school committee involved in the administration of business education includes student representatives.

62 Business education club activities are held after school hours.

63 Membership in the business club is voluntary.

APPENDIX B

■

List of Vocational Education Programs

This appendix is to be used to assist individuals who are interested in placing the vocational programs contained in this classification in their traditional areas. This is not meant to be a separate classification, but it is a subset of the entire classification and is only included to provide additional assistance.

It should be noted that in addition to vocational programs there are vocational student organizations that serve as an integral part of the total instructional program. These organizations significantly help secondary, postsecondary, and college students develop vocational/career competencies and leadership skills. Vocational student organizations recognized by the U.S. Department of Education are:

Future Farmers of America (FFA)
National Postsecondary Agriculture Student Organization (NPASO)
Future Business Leaders of America (FBLA)
Office Education Association (OEA)
Distributive Education Clubs of America (DECA)
Health Occupation Students of America (HOSA)
Future Homemakers of America (FHA & HERO) Chapters
American Industrial Arts Student Associations (AIASA)
Vocational Industrial Clubs of America (VICA)

Source: *A Classification of Instructional Programs*, National Center for Educational Statistics 81-323, U.S. Department of Education (Washington, D.C.: U.S. Government Printing Office, February 1981), pp. 181–191. As this book is going to press, this new classification system is being adopted. A gradual changeover is expected. The new system should be widely used during the mid 1980s.

Agriculture/Agribusiness

(From Agribusiness and Agricultural Production, Category 01 of the Classification)

01.01 *Agricultural Business and Management*
    01.0101 Agricultural Business and Management, General
    01.0104 Farm and Ranch Management

01.02 *Agricultural Mechanics*
    01.0201 Agricultural Mechanics, General
    01.0202 Agricultural Electrification, Power, and Controls
    01.0203 Agricultural Mechanics, Construction, and Maintenance Skills
    01.0204 Agricultural Power Machinery
    01.0205 Agricultural Structures, Equipment, and Facilities
    01.0206 Soil and Water Mechanical Practices
    01.0299 Agricultural Mechanics, Other

01.03 *Agricultural Production*
    01.0301 Agricultural Production, General
    01.0302 Animal Production
    01.0303 Aquaculture
    01.0304 Crop Production
    01.0305 Game Farm Management
    01.0399 Agricultural Production, Other

01.04 *Products and Processing*
    01.0401 Agricultural Products and Processing, General
    01.0402 Food Products

    01.0403 Nonfood Products
    01.0499 Agricultural Products and Processing, Other

01.05 *Agricultural Services and Supplies*
    01.0501 Agricultural Services and Supplies, General
    01.0502 Agricultural Services
    01.0503 Agricultural Supplies Marketing
    01.0504 Animal Grooming
    01.0505 Animal Training
    01.0506 Horseshoeing
    01.0599 Agricultural Services and Supplies, Other

01.06 *Horticulture*
    01.0601 Horticulture, General
    01.0602 Arboriculture
    01.0603 Floriculture
    01.0604 Greenhouse Operation and Management
    01.0605 Landscaping
    01.0606 Nursery Operation and Management
    01.0607 Turf Management
    01.0699 Horticulture, Other

01.99 *Agribusiness and Agricultural Production, Other*
    01.9999 Agribusiness and Agricultural Production, Other

(From Renewable Natural Resources, Category 03 of the Classification)

03.01 *Renewable Natural Resources, General*
    03.0101 Renewable Natural Resources, General

03.02 *Conservation and Regulation*
    03.0201 Conservation and Regulation, General
    03.0202 Conservation
    03.0203 Resources Protection and Regulation
    03.0299 Conservation and Regulation, Other

03.03 *Fishing and Fisheries*
    03.0301 Fishing and Fisheries, General
    03.0302 Fisheries
    03.0399 Fishing and Fisheries, Other

03.04 *Forestry Production and Processing*
    03.0401 Forestry Production and Processing, General
    03.0402 Forest Production
    03.0403 Forest Products Utilization
    03.0405 Logging
    03.0406 Pulp and Paper Production
    03.0499 Forestry Production and Processing, Other

03.06 *Wildlife Management*
    03.0601 Wildlife Management

03.99 *Renewable Natural Resources, Other*
    03.9999 Renewable Natural Resources, Other

(From Parks and Recreation, Category 31 of the Classification)

31.02 *Outdoor Recreation*
    31.0201 Outdoor Recreation

Business and Office

(From Business and Management, Category 06 of the Classification)

06.04 *Business Administration and Management*
    06.0401 Business Administration and Management, General
    06.0404 Systems Efficiency Analysis

Business and Office (continued)

(From Business and Office, Category 07 of the Classification)

07.01   **Accounting, Bookkeeping, and Related Programs,**
        General
        07.0101   Accounting
        07.0102   Accounting and Computing
        07.0103   Bookkeeping
        07.0104   Machine Billing, Bookkeeping, and
                  Computing
        07.0199   Accounting, Bookkeeping, and Related
                  Programs, Other

07.02   **Banking and Related Financial Programs**
        07.0201   Banking and Related Financial
                  Programs, General
        07.0202   Credit Collection Clerk
        07.0203   Insurance Clerk
        07.0204   Loan Clerk
        07.0205   Teller
        07.0206   Transit Clerk
        07.0299   Banking and Related Financial
                  Programs, Other

07.03   **Business Data Processing and Related Programs**
        07.0301   Business Data Processing and Related
                  Programs, General
        07.0302   Business Computer and Console
                  Operation
        07.0303   Business Data Entry Equipment
                  Operation
        07.0304   Business Data Peripheral Equipment
                  Operation
        07.0305   Business Data Programming
        07.0306   Business Systems Analysis
        07.0399   Business Data Processing and Related
                  Programs, Other

07.04   **Office Supervision and Management**
        07.0401   Office Supervision and Management

07.05   **Personnel and Training Programs**
        07.0501   Personnel and Training Programs,
                  General
        07.0502   Educational Assisting and Training
        07.0503   Personnel Assisting
        07.0599   Personnel and Training Programs, Other

07.06   **Secretarial and Related Programs**
        07.0601   Secretarial and Related Programs,
                  General
        07.0602   Court Reporting
        07.0603   Executive Secretarial
        07.0604   Legal Secretarial
        07.0605   Medical Secretarial
        07.0606   Secretarial
        07.0607   Stenographic
        07.0608   Word Processing
        07.0699   Secretarial and Related Programs, Other

07.07   **Typing, General Office, and Related Programs**
        07.0701   Typing, General Office, and Related
                  Programs, General
        07.0702   Clerk-Typist
        07.0703   Correspondence Clerk
        07.0704   Duplicating Machine Operation
        07.0705   General Office Clerk
        07.0706   Mail and Order Clerk
        07.0707   Receptionist and Communication
                  Systems Operation
        07.0708   Shipping, Receiving, and Stock Clerk
        07.0709   Traffic, Rate, and Transportation Clerk
        07.0710   Typing
        07.0799   Typing, General Office, and Related
                  Programs, Other

07.99   **Business and Office, Other**
        07.9999   Business and Office, Other

Marketing and Distribution

(From Business and Management, Category 06 of the Classification)

06.17   **Real Estate**
        06.1701   Real Estate, General
        06.1702   Commercial Property

        06.1703   Property Management
        06.1707   Residential Property
        06.1799   Real Estate, Other

(From Marketing and Distribution, Category 08 of the Classification)

08.01   **Apparel and Accessories Marketing**
        08.0101   Apparel and Accessories Marketing,
                  General
        08.0102   Fashion Merchandising
        08.0104   Footwear Marketing
        08.0105   Jewelry Marketing
        08.0199   Apparel and Accessories Marketing,
                  Other

08.02   **Business and Personal Services Marketing**
        08.0201   Business and Personal Services
                  Marketing, General
        08.0202   Display
        08.0203   Marketing of Business or Personal
                  Services
        08.0299   Business and Personal Services
                  Marketing, Other

08.03   **Entrepreneurship**
        08.0301   Entrepreneurship, General

Marketing and Distribution (continued)

(From Business and Management, Category 06 of the Classification)

06.18 **Small Business Management and Ownership**
  06.1801 Small Business Management
  06.1802 Small Business Ownership
  06.1899 Small Business Management and
           Ownership, Other

08.04 **Financial Services Marketing**
  08.0401 Financial Services Marketing, General
  08.0402 Banking Marketing
  08.0403 Credit Marketing
  08.0404 Credit Union Marketing
  08.0405 Savings and Loan Marketing
  08.0406 Securities and Commodities Marketing
  08.0499 Financial Services Marketing, Other

08.05 **Floristry, Farm and Garden Supplies Marketing**
  08.0501 Floristry, Farm and Garden Supplies
           Marketing, General
  08.0502 Farm and Garden Supplies Marketing
  08.0503 Floristry

  08.0599 Floristry, Farm and Garden Supplies
           Marketing, Other

08.06 **Food Marketing**
  08.0601 Food Marketing, General
  08.0602 Convenience Store Marketing
  08.0603 Speciality Foods Marketing
  08.0604 Supermarket Marketing
  08.0605 Wholesale Food Marketing
  08.0699 Food Marketing, Other

08.07 **General Marketing**
  08.0701 Auctioneering
  08.0702 Industrial Sales
  08.0703 International Marketing
  08.0704 Purchasing
  08.0705 Retailing
  08.0706 Sales
  08.0707 Wholesaling
  08.0799 General Marketing, Other

(From Business and Management, Category 06 of the Classification)

06.14 **Marketing Management and Research**
  06.1401 Marketing Management
  06.1402 Marketing Research
  06.1499 Marketing Management and Research,
           Other

08.08 **Home and Office Products Marketing**
  08.0801 Home and Office Products Marketing,
           General
  08.0802 Appliance Marketing
  08.0803 Building Materials Marketing
  08.0804 Floor Coverings, Draperies, and
           Upholstery Marketing
  08.0805 Furniture Marketing
  08.0806 Hardware Marketing

  08.0807 Office Products and Equipment
           Marketing
  08.0808 Specialty Home Furnishings Marketing
  08.0899 Home and Office Products Marketing,
           Other

08.09 **Hospitality and Recreation Marketing**
  08.0901 Hospitality and Recreation Marketing,
           General
  08.0902 Marketing of Hotel/Motel Services
  08.0903 Marketing of Recreational Services
  08.0904 Recreational Products Marketing
  08.0905 Waiter/Waitress and Related Services
  08.0999 Hospitality and Recreation Marketing,
           Other

(From Business and Management, Category 06 of the Classification)

06.07 **Institutional Management**
  06.0701 Hotel/Motel Management
  06.0702 Recreational Enterprises Management
  06.0703 Resort Management
  06.0704 Restaurant Management
  06.0705 Transportation Management
  06.0799 Institutional Management, Other

08.10 **Insurance Marketing**
  08.1001 Insurance Marketing, General
  08.1002 Accident and Health Insurance
           Marketing
  08.1003 Life Insurance Marketing
  08.1004 Property and Casualty Insurance
           Marketing
  08.1099 Insurance Marketing, Other

08.11 **Transportation and Travel Marketing**
  08.1101 Transportation and Travel Marketing,
           General

  08.1102 Freight Transportation Marketing
  08.1103 Passenger Transportation Marketing
  08.1104 Tourism
  08.1105 Travel Services Marketing
  08.1106 Warehouse Services Marketing
  08.1199 Transportation and Travel Marketing,
           Other

08.12 **Vehicles and Petroleum Marketing**
  08.1201 Vehicles and Petroleum Marketing,
           General
  08.1202 Agricultural Implements and Machinery
           Marketing
  08.1203 Automotive Vehicles and Accessories
           Marketing
  08.1204 Petroleum Wholesaling
  08.1205 Recreational Vehicles and Accessories
           Marketing
  08.1206 Service Station Retailing

Marketing and Distribution *(continued)*

(From Business and Management, Category 06 of the Classification [continued])

08.1207   Vehicle Rental and Leasing
08.1299   Vehicles and Petroleum Marketing,
          Other

08.99   Marketing and Distribution, Other
08.9999   Marketing and Distribution, Other

(From Communications, Category 09 of the Classification)

09.02   Advertising
09.0201   Advertising

Health Occupations

(From Allied Health, Category 17 of the Classification)

17.01   Dental Services
17.0101   Dental Assisting
17.0102   Dental Hygiene
17.0103   Dental Laboratory Technology
17.0199   Dental Services, Other

17.02   Diagnostic and Treatment Services
17.0201   Cardiopulmonary Technology
17.0202   Dialysis Technology
17.0203   Electrocardiograph Technology
17.0204   Electroencephalograph Technology
17.0205   Emergency Medical Technology-
          Ambulance
17.0206   Emergency Medical Technology-
          Paramedic
17.0207   Medical Radiation Dosimetry
17.0208   Nuclear Medical Technology
17.0209   Radiograph Medical Technology
17.0210   Respiratory Therapy Technology
17.0211   Surgical Technology
17.0212   Ultrasound Technology
17.0299   Diagnostic and Treatment Services,
          Other

17.03   Medical Laboratory Technologies
17.0301   Blood Bank Technology
17.0302   Chemistry Technology
17.0303   Clinical Animal Technology
17.0304   Clinical Laboratory Aide
17.0305   Clinical Laboratory Assisting
17.0306   Cytotechnology
17.0307   Hematology Technology
17.0308   Histologic Technology
17.0309   Medical Laboratory Technology
17.0310   Medical Technology
17.0311   Microbiology Technology
17.0399   Medical Laboratory Technologies, Other

17.04   Mental Health/Human Services
17.0401   Alcohol/Drug Abuse Specialty
17.0402   Community Health Work
17.0403   Genetic Counseling
17.0404   Home Health Aide
17.0405   Mental Health/Human Services
          Assisting

17.0406   Mental Health/Human Services
          Technology
17.0407   Rehabilitation Counseling
17.0408   Therapeutic Child Care Work
17.0499   Mental Health/Human Services, Other

17.05   Miscellaneous Allied Health Services
17.0501   Animal Technology
17.0502   Central Supply Technology
17.0503   Medical Assisting
17.0504   Medical Illustrating
17.0505   Medical Office Management
17.0506   Medical Records Technology
17.0507   Pharmacy Assisting
17.0508   Physician Assisting-Primary Care
17.0509   Physician Assisting-Specialty
17.0510   Podiatric Assisting
17.0511   Veterinarian Aide
17.0512   Veterinarian Assisting
17.0513   Ward Clerk
17.0599   Miscellaneous Allied Health Services,
          Other

17.06   Nursing-Related Services
17.0601   Geriatric Aide
17.0602   Nursing Assisting
17.0603   Obstetrical Technology
17.0604   Pediatric Aide
17.0605   Practical Nursing
17.0606   Ward Service Management
17.0699   Nursing-Related Services, Other

17.07   Ophthalmic Services
17.0701   Ophthalmic Dispensing
17.0702   Ophthalmic Laboratory Technology
17.0703   Ophthalmic Medical Assisting
17.0704   Optometric Assisting
17.0705   Optometric Technology
17.0706   Orthoptics
17.0799   Ophthalmic Services, Other

17.08   Rehabilitation Services
17.0801   Art Therapy
17.0802   Corrective Therapy
17.0803   Dance Therapy

Health Occupations (continued)

(From Allied Health, Category 17 of the Classification [continued])

17.0804	Exercise Physiology
17.0805	Manual Arts Therapy
17.0806	Music Therapy
17.0807	Occupational Therapy
17.0808	Occupational Therapy Assisting
17.0809	Occupational Therapy Aide
17.0810	Orthotic/Prosthetic Assisting
17.0811	Orthotics/Prosthetics
17.0812	Orthopedic Assisting
17.0813	Physical Therapy
17.0814	Physical Therapy Aide
17.0815	Physical Therapy Assisting

17.0816	Recreational Therapy
17.0817	Recreational Therapy Technology
17.0818	Respiratory Therapy
17.0819	Respiratory Therapy Assisting
17.0820	Speech/Hearing Therapy Aide
17.0821	Speech-Language Pathology/Audiology
17.0899	Rehabilitation Services, Other

17.99   Allied Health, Other
17.9999   Allied Health, Other

(From Health Sciences, Category 18 of the Classification)

18.11   Nursing
18.1101   Nursing, General

Home Economics

(From Architecture and Environmental Design, Category 04 of the Classification)

04.05   Interior Design
04.0501   Interior Design

(From Vocational Home Economics, Category 20 of the Classification)

20.01   Consumer and Homemaking Home Economics
20.0101   Comprehensive Consumer and Home-making Home Economics
20.0102   Child Development, Care, and Guidance
20.0103   Clothing and Textiles
20.0104   Consumer Education
20.0105   Exploratory Homemaking
20.0106   Family/Individual Health
20.0107   Family Living and Parenthood
20.0108   Food and Nutrition
20.0109   Home Management
20.0110   Housing, Home Furnishing and Equipment
20.0199   Consumer and Homemaking Home Economics, Other

20.02   Child Care and Guidance Management and Services
20.0201   Child Care and Guidance Management and Services, General
20.0202   Child Care Aide/Assisting
20.0203   Child Care Management
20.0204   Foster Care/Family Care
20.0205   Teacher Aide
20.0299   Child Care and Guidance Management and Services, Other

20.03   Clothing, Apparel, and Textiles Management, Production, and Services
20.0301   Clothing, Apparel, and Textiles Management, Production, and Services, General

20.0302   Clothing Maintenance Aide
20.0303   Commercial Garment and Apparel Construction
20.0304   Custom Apparel/Garment Seamstress
20.0305   Custom Tailoring and Alteration
20.0306   Fashion/Fabric Coordination
20.0307   Textiles Testing
20.0308   Wedding/Specialty Consulting
20.0399   Clothing, Apparel, and Textiles Management, Production, and Services, Other

20.04   Food Production, Management, and Services
20.0401   Food Production, Management, and Services, General
20.0402   Baking
20.0403   Chef/Cook
20.0404   Dietetic Aide/Assisting
20.0405   Food Catering
20.0406   Food Service
20.0407   Food Testing
20.0408   School Food Service
20.0499   Food Production, Management, and Services, Other

20.05   Home Furnishings and Equipment Management, Production, and Services
20.0501   Home Furnishings and Equipment Management, Production, and Services, General

Home Economics (continued)

(From Vocational Home Economics, Category 20 of the Classification [continued])

20.0502 Custom Drapery and Window Treatment Design/Making
20.0503 Custom Slipcovering and Upholstering
20.0504 Floral Design
20.0505 Home Decorating
20.0506 Home Furnishings Aide
20.0507 Home-Service Assisting
20.0599 Home Furnishings and Equipment Management, Production, and Services, Other

20.06   Institutional, Home Management, and Supporting Services
20.0601 Institutional, Home Management, and Supporting Services, General

20.0602 Companion to the Aged
20.0603 Consumer Aide/Assisting
20.0604 Custodial Services
20.0605 Executive Housekeeping
20.0606 Homemaker's Aide
20.0607 Therapeutic Recreation Aide
20.0699 Institutional, Home Management, and Supporting Services, Other

20.99   Vocational Home Economics, Other
20.9999 Vocational Home Economics, Other

Industrial Arts

(From Industrial Arts, Category 21 of the Classification)

21.01   Industrial Arts
21.0101 Industrial Arts, General
21.0102 Construction
21.0103 Drafting and Design
21.0104 Electricity/Electronics

21.0105 Energy, Power, and Transportation
21.0106 Graphic Arts
21.0107 Manufacturing/Materials Processing
21.0199 Industrial Arts, Other

Technical Education

(From Agricultural Sciences, Category 02 of the Classification)

02.03   Food Sciences
02.0306 Food Technology

(From Renewable Natural Resources, Category 03 of the Classification)

03.04   Forestry Production and Processing
03.0404 Forest Products Processing Technology

(From Consumer, Personal, and Miscellaneous Services, Category 12 of the Classification)

12.03   Funeral Services
12.0301 Funeral Services

(From Communication Technologies, Category 10 of the Classification)

10.01   Communication Technologies
10.0101 Educational Media Technology
10.0102 Motion Picture Technology
10.0103 Photographic Technology
10.0104 Radio and Television Production and Broadcasting Technology
10.0199 Communication Technologies, Other

Technical Education (continued)

(From Computer and Information Sciences, Category 11 of the Classification)

11.02   *Computer Programming*
         11.0201   Computer Programming

11.03   *Data Processing*
         11.0301   Data Processing

11.04   *Systems Analysis*
         11.0401   Systems Analysis

(From Engineering and Engineering-Related Technologies, Category 15 of the Classification)

15.01   *Architectural Technologies*
         15.0101   Architectural Design and Construction
                   Technology
         15.0102   Architectural Interior Design
                   Technology
         15.0199   Architectural Technologies, Other

15.02   *Civil Technologies*
         15.0201   Civil Technology
         15.0202   Drafting and Design Technology
         15.0203   Surveying and Mapping Technology
         15.0204   Urban Planning Technology
         15.0299   Civil Technologies, Other

15.03   *Electrical and Electronic Technologies*
         15.0301   Computer Technology
         15.0302   Electrical Technology
         15.0303   Electronic Technology
         15.0304   Laser Electro-Optic Technology
         15.0399   Electrical and Electronic Technologies,
                   Other

15.04   *Electromechanical Instrumentation and
         Maintenance Technologies*
         15.0401   Biomedical Equipment Technology
         15.0402   Computer Servicing Technology
         15.0403   Electromechanical Technology
         15.0404   Instrumentation Technology
         15.0499   Electromechanical Instrumentation and
                   Maintenance Technologies, Other

15.05   *Environmental Control Technologies*
         15.0501   Air Conditioning, Heating, and
                   Refrigeration Technology
         15.0502   Air Pollution Control Technology
         15.0503   Energy Conservation and Use
                   Technology
         15.0504   Sanitation Technology
         15.0505   Solar Heating and Cooling Technology
         15.0506   Water and Wastewater Technology
         15.0599   Environmental Control Technologies,
                   Other

15.06   *Industrial Production Technologies*
         15.0601   Chemical Manufacturing Technology
         15.0602   Food Processing Technology
         15.0603   Industrial Technology
         15.0604   Manufacturing Technology
         15.0605   Marine Products Technology
         15.0606   Optical Technology
         15.0607   Plastic Technology
         15.0608   Safety Technology
         15.0609   Textile Technology
         15.0610   Welding Technology
         15.0699   Industrial Production Technologies,
                   Other

15.07   *Quality Control and Safety Technologies*
         15.0701   Occupational Safety and Health
                   Technology
         15.0702   Quality Control Technology
         15.0799   Quality Control and Safety
                   Technologies, Other

15.08   *Mechanical and Related Technologies*
         15.0801   Aeronautical Technology
         15.0802   Agricultural Equipment Technology
         15.0803   Automotive Technology
         15.0804   Marine Propulsion Technology
         15.0805   Mechanical Design Technology
         15.0899   Mechanical and Related Technologies,
                   Other

15.09   *Mining and Petroleum Technologies*
         15.0901   Coal Mining Technology
         15.0902   Mining (Excluding Coal) Technology
         15.0903   Petroleum Technology
         15.0999   Mining and Petroleum Technologies,
                   Other

15.99   *Engineering and Engineering-Related Technologies,
         Other*
         15.9999   Engineering and Engineering-Related
                   Technologies, Other

(From Law, Category 22 of the Classification)

22.01   *Law*
         22.0103   Legal Assisting

(From Library and Archival Sciences, Category 25 of the Classification)

25.03   *Library Assisting*
         25.0301   Library Assisting

Technical Education (continued)

(From Military Technologies, Category 29 of the Classification)

29.01 *Military Technologies*
29.0101 Military Technologies
29.0199 Military Technologies, Other

(From Science Technologies, Category 41 of the Classification)

41.01 *Biological Technologies*
41.0101 Biological Laboratory Technology
41.0102 Oceanographic (Biological) Technology
41.0199 Biological Technologies, Other

41.02 *Nuclear Technologies*
41.0201 Nuclear Materials Handling Technology
41.0202 Nuclear Power Plant Operation
        Technology
41.0203 Nuclear Power Plant Radiation Control
        Technology
41.0204 Radiologic (Physical) Technology
41.0299 Nuclear Technologies, Other

41.03 *Physical Science Technologies*
41.0301 Chemical Technology
41.0302 Geological Technology
41.0303 Metallurgical Technology
41.0304 Meteorological Technology
41.0305 Oceanographic (Physical) Technology
41.0399 Physical Science Technologies, Other

41.99 *Science Technologies, Other*
41.9999 Science Technologies, Other

(From Protective Services, Category 43 of the Classification)

43.01 *Criminal Justice*
43.0105 Criminal Justice Technology

43.02 *Fire Protection*
43.0201 Fire Control and Safety Technology

(From Transportation and Material Moving, Category 49 of the Classification)

49.01 *Air Transportation*
49.0101 Air Transportation, General
49.0102 Airplane Piloting and Navigation
49.0103 Aviation Computer Technology
49.0105 Air Traffic Control

49.03 *Water Transportation*
49.0303 Commercial Fishing Operation
49.0304 Deep Water Diving and Life Support
        Systems
49.0305 Marina Operations

(From Visual and Performing Arts, Category 50 of the Classification)

50.08 *Graphic Arts Technology*
50.0801 Graphic Arts Technology

Trade and Industrial

(From Consumer, Personal, and Miscellaneous Services, Category 12 of the Classification)

12.01 *Drycleaning and Laundering Services*
12.0101 Drycleaning and Laundering Services,
        General
12.0102 Drycleaning
12.0103 Laundering
12.0199 Drycleaning and Laundering Services,
        Other

12.04 *Personal Services*
12.0401 Personal Services, General
12.0402 Barbering
12.0403 Cosmetology
12.0404 Electrolysis
12.0405 Massage
12.0499 Personal Services, Other

(From Protective Services, Category 43 of the Classification)

43.01 *Criminal Justice*
43.0107 Law Enforcement
43.0109 Security Services

43.02 *Fire Protection*
43.0203 Firefighting

Trade and Industrial (continued)

(From Construction Trades, Category 46 of the Classification)

46.01   Brickmasonry, Stonemasonry, and Tile Setting
46.0101   Brickmasonry, Stonemasonry, and Tile Setting, General
46.0102   Brick, Block, and Stonemasonry
46.0103   Tile Setting
46.0199   Brickmasonry, Stonemasonry, and Tile Setting, Other

46.02   Carpentry
46.0201   Carpentry

46.03   Electrical and Power Transmission Installation
46.0301   Electrical and Power Transmission Installation, General
46.0302   Electrician
46.0303   Lineworker
46.0399   Electrical and Power Transmission Installation, Other

46.04   Miscellaneous Construction Trades
46.0401   Building Maintenance
46.0402   Concrete Placing and Finishing

46.0403   Construction Inspection
46.0404   Drywall Installation
46.0405   Floor Covering Installation
46.0406   Glazing
46.0407   Insulation Installation
46.0408   Painting and Decorating
46.0409   Plastering
46.0410   Roofing
46.0411   Terrazzo Installation
46.0499   Miscellaneous Construction Trades, Other

46.05   Plumbing, Pipefitting, and Steamfitting
46.0501   Plumbing, Pipefitting, and Steamfitting, General
46.0502   Pipefitting and Steamfitting
46.0503   Plumbing
46.0599   Plumbing, Pipefitting, and Steamfitting, Other

46.99   Construction Trades, Other
46.9999   Construction Trades, Other

(From Mechanics and Repairers, Category 47 of the Classification)

47.01   Electrical and Electronics Equipment Repair
47.0101   Electrical and Electronics Equipment Repair, General
47.0102   Business Machine Repair
47.0103   Communications Electronics
47.0104   Computer Electronics
47.0105   Industrial Electronics
47.0106   Major Appliance Repair
47.0107   Motor Repair
47.0108   Small Appliance Repair
47.0109   Vending and Recreational Machine Repair
47.0199   Electrical and Electronics Equipment Repair, Other

47.02   Heating, Air Conditioning, and Refrigeration Mechanics
47.0201   Heating, Air Conditioning, and Refrigeration Mechanics, General
47.0202   Cooling and Refrigeration
47.0203   Heating and Air Conditioning
47.0299   Heating, Air Conditioning, and Refrigeration Mechanics, Other

47.03   Industrial Equipment Maintenance and Repair
47.0301   Industrial Equipment Maintenance and Repair, General
47.0302   Heavy Equipment Maintenance and Repair
47.0303   Industrial Machinery Maintenance and Repair
47.0304   Mine Equipment Maintenance and Repair
47.0305   Oil and Gas Drilling Equipment Operation and Maintenance
47.0399   Industrial Equipment Maintenance and Repair, Other

47.04   Miscellaneous Mechanics and Repairers
47.0401   Electromechanical, Hydraulic, and Pneumatic Instrument Repair
47.0402   Gunsmithing
47.0403   Locksmithing and Safe Repair
47.0404   Musical Instrument Repair
47.0405   Operation, Maintenance, and Repair of Audio-Visual Equipment
47.0406   Shoe and Boot Repair
47.0407   Sporting Goods Equipment Repair
47.0408   Watch Repair
47.0499   Miscellaneous Mechanics and Repairers, Other

47.05   Stationary Energy Sources
47.0501   Stationary Energy Sources, General
47.0502   Conventional Electric Power Generation
47.0503   Industrial Nuclear Energy
47.0504   Pumping Plants
47.0599   Stationary Energy Sources, Other

47.06   Vehicle and Mobile Equipment Mechanics and Repairers
47.0601   Vehicle and Mobile Equipment Mechanics and Repairers, General
47.0602   Aircraft Mechanics
47.0603   Automotive Body Repair
47.0604   Automotive Mechanics
47.0605   Diesel Engine Mechanics
47.0606   Small Engine Repair
47.0699   Vehicle and Mobile Equipment Mechanics and Repairers, Other

47.99   Mechanics and Repairers, Other
47.9999   Mechanics and Repairers, Other

Trade and Industrial (continued)

(From Precision Production, Category 48 of the Classification)

48.01   **Drafting**
    48.0101 Drafting, General
    48.0102 Architectural Drafting
    48.0103 Civil/Structural Drafting
    48.0104 Electrical/Electronics Drafting
    48.0105 Mechanical Drafting
    48.0199 Drafting, Other

48.02   **Graphic and Printing Communications**
    48.0201 Graphic and Printing Communications,
        General
    48.0202 Bookbinding
    48.0203 Commercial Art
    48.0204 Commercial Photography
    48.0205 Composition, Make-up, and Typesetting
    48.0206 Lithography, Photography, and
        Platemaking
    48.0207 Photographic Laboratory and Darkroom
    48.0208 Printing Press Operations
    48.0209 Silk Screen Making and Printing
    48.0299 Graphic and Printing Communications,
        Other

48.03   **Leatherworking and Upholstering**
    48.0301 Leatherworking and Upholstering,
        General
    48.0302 Saddlemaking and Repair
    48.0303 Upholstering
    48.0399 Leatherworking and Upholstering,
        Other

48.04   **Precision Food Production**
    48.0401 Precision Food Production, General
    48.0402 Meatcutting
    48.0403 Slaughtering and Butchering
    48.0499 Precision Food Production, Other

48.05   **Precision Metal Work**
    48.0501 Precision Metal Work, General
    48.0502 Foundry Work
    48.0503 Machine Tool Operation/Machine Shop
    48.0504 Metal Fabrication
    48.0505 Metal Patternmaking
    48.0506 Sheet Metal
    48.0507 Tool and Die Making
    48.0508 Welding, Brazing, and Soldering
    48.0599 Precision Metal Work, Other

48.06   **Precision Work, Assorted Materials**
    48.0601 Industrial Ceramics Manufacturing
    48.0602 Jewelry Design, Fabrication, and Repair
    48.0603 Optical Goods Work
    48.0604 Plastics
    48.0699 Precision Work, Assorted Materials,
        Other

48.07   **Woodworking**
    48.0701 Woodworking, General
    48.0702 Furniture Making
    48.0703 Millwork and Cabinet Making
    48.0799 Woodworking, Other

48.99   **Precision Production, Other**
    48.9999 Precision Production, Other

(From Transportation and Material Moving, Category 49 of the Classification)

49.01   **Air Transportation**
    49.0106 Flight Attendants

49.02   **Vehicle and Equipment Operation**
    49.0201 Vehicle and Equipment Operation,
        General
    49.0202 Construction Equipment Operation
    49.0203 Material Handling
    49.0204 Mining Equipment Operation
    49.0205 Truck and Bus Driving
    49.0299 Vehicle and Equipment Operation,
        Other

49.03   **Water Transportation**
    49.0301 Water Transportation, General
    49.0302 Barge and Boat Operation
    49.0306 Marine Maintenance
    49.0307 Merchant Marine Officers
    49.0308 Sailors and Deckhands
    49.0399 Water Transportation, Other

49.99   **Transportation and Material Moving, Other**
    49.9999 Transportation and Material Moving,
        Other

Index

Evaluation (continued)
    principles of, 277–279
    program, 288–300
    scope of, 276–277
    steps in, 285, 288
    systems, 282, 283–285
    systems approach to, 313
    in vocational-technical education, 275–319
Evans, Rupert N., 71, 72, 110, 224

Facilities
    evaluating, 298–299
    in needs assessment, 323–325, 327–328
Faculty, public relations contacts with, 269
Fair Labor Standards Act, 17
Fanslow, Alyce M., 220
Far West High School (Oakland, California),
    100–101
Farmer, Geraldine M., 226
Federal Board of Vocational Education,
    32, 33, 188
Federal Council on Educational Research, 46
Federal legislation
    history of, 29–46, 50–53
    philosophical effects of, 66–68
Feedback, in evaluation, 283–284
Felt needs, 187, 214
Fess-Kenyon Act, 35, 49
Finch, Alton V., 139
Fine arts and humanities occupations,
    cluster, 115
Fitzpatrick, John C., 56
Flat grants, in state funding, 163
Ford Foundation, 229
Formative evaluation, 289–290, 292–293
    needs assessment as, 299–300
Formative-summative evaluation, 289–290
Four-year programs, in career education,
    118–119
Fraser, John M., 4, 7–8, 22
Fund for the Advancement of Education, 229
Funding, of vocational education, 73–74,
    163–165
Future Business Leaders of America, 143, 195
Future Data Processors, 143, 195
Future Farmers of America, 143, 191
Future Homemakers of America, 143, 207
Future Secretaries of America, 143, 195

General education, vocational education
    vs., 63
General Education Provisions Act, 46
General welfare, vocational education and,
    70–73
George-Barden Act, 34–35, 38, 39, 49, 50, 196
    industrial education and, 208
    nursing education and, 199
George-Deen Act, 34, 35, 49, 196
George-Ellzey Act, 34, 35, 49, 56
George-Reed Act, 33–34, 35, 49, 56
GI Bill of Rights. See Servicemen's
    Readjustment Act
Ginzberg, Eli, 8, 125, 126, 136
Girtman, Carolyn J., 205
Glennan, Thomas, 234

Goldhammer, Keith, 3, 99
Goods producing industries, 20–21
Graduate programs, in career education,
    120–121
Growth
    employment needs, 18
    within industries, 18–19
Guba, Egon, 277
Guidance personnel, public relations
    contacts with, 269–270
Guilford-Zimmerman Aptitude Survey, 125
Gunby, Phil, 201
Gysbers, Norman E., 138

Haas, Kenneth B., 219
Haddad, John, 202–203
Halchin, Lilla C., 204
Hansen, Lorraine S., 129
Harris, Wilbur, 277
Harrow, Anita J., 309
Harrow model, 310
Harvard University, origin, 118
Hastings, J. Thomas, 276, 292, 304, 306
Hatch Act, 30, 49
Hatcher, Hazel M., 204
Hawaii Career Development Continuum, 112
Hawaii model, for career education,
    102–103, 105
Health Amendments Act, 199
Health, Education, and Welfare, Department
    of, 143, 144
Health occupations
    cluster, 115
    education, 199–203
    job titles, 200
    program classifications, 199–200
Health Occupations Student Association,
    203, 212
Health Professions Educational Assistance
    Act, 51
Health Professions Educational Assistance
    Amendments, 51
Hendrick, I., 4
HERO, 207
Herr, Edwin L., 84, 94
Herzberg, Fred, 6, 7, 22
High school, career guidance in, 129–130
Higher education, career education through,
    117–121
Higher Education Act, 42, 46, 52
Higher Education Facilities Act, 46, 51
Hill, Alberta D., 204, 206
Hill, E. Joy, 201
Home-community-based model, for career
    education, 101–102
Home Economics Division of the American
    Vocational Association, 205–207
Home economics education, 32–35, 203–207
    instructional areas, 203
    objectives, 205
    publications in, 205
    social changes affecting, 204–205
Home Economics Education Association, 205